**Children
in Cooperation
and Competition**

Children
in Cooperation
and Competition

Toward a Developmental
Social Psychology

Emmy A. Pepitone
Bryn Mawr College

LexingtonBooks
D.C. Heath and Company
Lexington, Massachusetts
Toronto

Library of Congress Cataloging in Publication Data

Main entry under title:
    Children in cooperation and competition.

    1. Cooperativeness in children. 2. Competition (Psychology) in children.
I. Pepitone, Emmy Angelica Berger, 1924-
BF723.C69C48   155.4'18   79-3909
ISBN 0-669-02842-8

Copyright © 1980 by D.C. Heath and Company

Published simultaneously in Canada.

Printed in the United States of America.

International Standard Book Number: 0-669-02842-8

Library of Congress Catalog Card Number: 79-3909

Contents

List of Figures

List of Tables

Preface and Acknowledgments

The research described in this book may be said to have had its official inception a decade ago, when I received two successive grants from the U.S. Department of Health, Education and Welfare for the study of "the effects of instructional practices on student learning, emotional growth, and interpersonal relations." To pinpoint beginnings, however, is in many ways arbitrary. It would be more correct to relate this research to the several years of my association with faculty and students at the Research Center for Group Dynamics of the University of Michigan, where I was a member of the group-productivity program directed by J.R.P. French, Jr. In the early 1950s enthusiasm there for small-group research based on Lewinian situational models was strong, as was confidence in the researcher's omnipotence to create just about any kind of controlled laboratory situation deemed necessary for social-hypothesis testing. My own work, for instance, dealt with performance as a function of member responsibility to the group—a rather complex variable to attempt to create in the laboratory while controlling for the many factors generally inextricably associated with it. The solution was to tell one of two pairs of coworkers that the other, in a different room, was carrying out work that was either more or less important for the success of the group than their own work, when, in fact, for purposes of control, both dyads were assigned exactly the same task.

Later, when I joined the Department of Education and Child Development at Bryn Mawr College, teaching graduate students many of whom were simultaneously employed in various clinical professions, I defined part of my teaching role to supplement their emphasis on children's personal dynamics with understandings derived from the study of group dynamics. It became clear that the various theories that dealt with situational social influence needed to be elucidated by observation of children's behavior in group settings. Local elementary schools were relatively easily accessible to us because of longstanding professional relationships between the Child Study Institute—part of our department—and the area's school district. It seemed likely that demonstrating the effects of situational social variables on school children could be accomplished most easily and dramatically by watching children doing something by themselves, as opposed to carrying out the same activity in group settings. Social psychologists will recognize this approach as that associated with F.H. Allport during the early twenties. Child psychologists may remember the flood of comparable research with very young children somewhat later, during the early days of the child-study movement.

In my view, Allport raised issues that are still very much with us, and studies of children in the 1930s constitute some of the best descriptive accounts of interaction among children. The inconclusiveness of this work can be ascribed to a large degree to the unsystematic, idiosyncratic collection of data, based on different tasks and methodologies, which made results uncomparable. Regarding uniformity of methodology in the area of group performance and productivity, the recent state of affairs has not changed appreciably. Here, then, was an opportunity to utilize the periods devoted to systematic observation of children's interactions toward also developing of a task that could be used in a variety of situations and with children of different ages. The outcome was the methodology described in chapter 3 and used in the majority of the studies reported in this book. The students who participated in creating the methodology—primarily Beth Hannah, Jane Crawford, and Nancy Torop—recognizing my involvement and perhaps obsessional insistence on a uniform task, dubbed the round tabletop on which the children work the Pepitone board. Now it is simply referred to as the Pep board.

During our classroom observation and subsequent exploration of the interaction of small groups of children outside the regular classroom, we noticed their frequent rivalries. This included such behaviors as trying to be the first to answer the teacher's question, covering up their own work so their neighbors could not see it, and many subtle ways of stealing surreptitious glances at the work of others. Several graduate students began to focus on the dynamics that might evoke such competition, of added relevance at that time in the light of high school students' objections to alleged excessive pressures of existing grading and testing practices. Other noticed how relatively infrequently children helped one another when collaborating. The direction of these empirical questions was much to my liking, as it pointed toward already existing important theoretical formulations in the area of competition and cooperation as well as in social comparison theory, both of long-standing interest to me.

Gradually, individual research projects began to emerge. Beth Hannah's inquiry into the role of task similarity in children's social comparisons culminated in the first of several doctoral dissertations in the area of competition and cooperation that serve as the basis for the various chapters in this book. This first study required an inordinate amount of care and attention to minute details involved in creation and measurement of the desired variables. In chapter 4 we tried to convey a sense of the effort and planning devoted to this aspect of the research process, which is generally not made explicit in discussion of research.

The various separate investigations assumed programmatic features by the similar-problem focus of several researchers, by their uniform theoretical approach, and by use of a fairly common methodology. Continuity of the research was brought about also by the persons involved in the research process. I directed each of the theses and dissertations. Typically, the observers or coders of one study became the experimenters in their own project. For example, Jane Crawford, Hannah's main assistant, in her simultaneous research toward fulfillment of a master's degree, used the methodology they had just developed, following implications of social-reality theory by varying presence or absence of a model while several children worked on identical tasks in a group setting (chapter 4). Subsequently, she became an observer both in Christa Vanderbilt's research on helping behaviors of kindergartners and in my research on role-related cooperation (both in chapter 5).

During pilot work for my scarcity studies (chapter 8), I was assisted by Helen Solomons. She spent whatever free moments we had watching newly sex-integrated classes in the gymnasium. Her own doctoral dissertation on sex-role-mediated achievement behaviors in sex-integrated team games was the outcome (chapter 9). Her work helped my theoretical formulations about competitive counteractions (chapter 2). My own research into role-related cooperation had created only rather general task and group roles; Nina Korsh continued this line of inquiry by particularizing and increasing role requirements in her doctoral research on collaboration in the open classroom (chapter 10).

A different model of collaboration between researchers emerged in the work of Helen Loeb and Eleanor Murdoch in that they carried out parallel studies involving the total population from two elementary schools located in two socioeconomically different school districts (chapter 6). Their data on interpersonal behaviors and performance of children at different ages in competitive and cooperative conditions were also instrumental in shaping my final distinctions within competitive conditions and among different types of cooperative tasks. Children's use of social comparisons, as it emerged from this work, came to Vivian Seltzer's attention in connection with her interest in adolescent reference groups. It helped to focus her doctoral research on comparisons of adolescents, as reported in chapter 7. Judy Coché combined her interests in family dynamics with our methodology by using the Pep board as a family task; her doctoral study (chapter 11) is in some sense a summation of many variables studied earlier in the face-to-face children's groups.

The interdependencies among all of the studies should be evident from the above. Nevertheless, I should like to express formally my acknowledgment to all of the contributors. As a group, they illustrate the finding that emerged in several of their studies—that similarity and difference can be potentially unifying or divisive. In our case, both led to harmonious and productive outcomes. From diverse backgrounds, we were united by a common interest in the study of children and a desire to help in their growth. We found ourselves in agreement that theory and practice can and should be mutually enhancing and that a multidisciplinary approach is essential. Further, we believe that children must be understood in terms of their family context and within their larger social worlds. Within these commonalities, each contributor brought her particular expertise to our endeavor. Their creative efforts speak for themselves. I am particularly gratified because our common endeavors have allowed each person to pursue her own interests while simultaneously profiting from and giving to the others. This, to me, is what collaborative research is all about. Certainly, intellectual exchange with each collaborator has brought out the best in me; the final product represents us all. Collaboration has been a pleasure and a privilege.

The fact that this particular group of women came to the Department of Education and Child Development at Bryn Mawr College is no accident; these attitudes characterize the department as well. I wish to express my gratitude to each of my colleagues and good friends for their intellectual stimulation, constant support, and friendship. My special thanks go also to our secretaries, who indeed were indispensable.

Finally, my family—my family of origin, my husband, and my children—must be acknowledged. The greatest tribute I can pay to them all is that I feel no need to apologize for time taken from them, for they were steadfastly with me and behind me, and quite often ahead of me. A special word is necessary to and about my husband, Dr. Albert Pepitone, whose intimate knowledge of social psychology, broad perspectives, and highest standards provided guidance that helped my work come to fruition.

In spite of, and because of, all these supports I happily claim responsibility for the final outcome.

Introduction

This book consists of a series of interrelated investigations of children's social behaviors and performance in controlled competitive and cooperative situations. The developmental span ranges from toddlers through high school seniors, although the bulk of the research focuses on elementary school children. The principal methodology employed studied three children at a time for about an hour during their school day. They were taken to a spare classroom, presented with a large box of colored blocks, and asked to make a flat picture on a round table top. In some of the conditions, they were asked to work together; in others, to work by and for themselves; and sometimes explicitly to work against each other. Their behavior and performance were noted and recorded by observer teams according to a prearranged schedule.

Variations of this basic procedure were introduced to study the effects of some specific variables. For example, in some conditions, winning was made more important (degree of competitive motivation was varied); in others, different children were asked to carry out different kinds of activities that furthered the accomplishment of the common task (role differentiations were created); in still others, demands for the type of picture to be made differed (degree of the structuredness of the task was varied); or different amounts of needed materials were made available (degree of scarcity was varied).

Additionally we report on research that studied children's interactions in controlled school settings. High school seniors were asked to discuss with each other in small groups questions pertaining to achievement and other personal values. Observers focused on who compared himself to whom, and why. Teams of fifth-grade boys and girls were composed to vary systematically in game-related skills and their interaction observed during interteam competition. Here, observation concentrated on who threw the ball to whom, and how. In another study, groups of third graders were exposed to a standard human-relations training program and to additional interventions intended to help them to work together better. In this case, observers looked for subsequent positive and negative interactions. In yet another study, four-person families were examined as members worked on a common task in the laboratory.

The significance of our work and our interest in children's behavior and performance can be explained on different levels. On the most pragmatic level, we might simply say "because it is there." Children interact with each other in these different modes at home and at school. Research already exists that inquires into such relationships; our research was designed to add to such knowledge.

On a philosophic level, the behaviors under study may be said to involve universal human relationships. Whether individuals are to struggle in solitary fashion or to combine their strengths, whether primarily to pursue personal satisfactions, and, if so, at the expense of another's gain, whether to subjugate personal needs to the common good—these have been considered profound ethical questions of individual morality. From the broadest perspective, the very first philosophic attempts to account for the existence of separate natural objects in unity as well as diversity may be seen as having a parallel in accounts of the human condition. That is, the pre-Socratics' problem of the One and the Many in nature may be likened to moral and psychological issues derivable from the fact that each person is separate and unique, yet each must depend on many others.

From the psychological point of view, relatedness of one human being to another is the basic fact of existence. Even today, as we race toward the twenty-first century, there is still no other way for a fetus to grow but imbedded in another human being. And once the new person is expelled from the womb, another human being continues to be needed for the infant's survival. Psychoanalysts at the beginning of this century pointed to developmental implications of what Otto Rank referred to as the birth trauma. Today developmentalists and psychoanalysts alike describe the infant's and mother's emotional relatedness and explain that this symbiotic relationship gives the growing human being the needed courage to begin to separate and venture out on her own.

As young children move away from the complete oneness with their mother, they begin to perceive, and accept, themselves as separate persons. Nevertheless the longing to restore the lost closeness continues to exist. Needs for others conflict with the equally intense needs of growing children to distinguish themselves from others and to achieve separate self-hood. These psychodynamic problems of separation and return resurface throughout life, perhaps because we all have been "untimely ripped" from the womb in this highly mechanized society.

The preindustrial pace of life allowed for gradual growth both into separate individuals and into satisfying relationships with others. It is easy to romanticize these aspects of the past; social distance between members of a family may have actually been greater then than at present. Our point here is simply that we seem to hasten the development of children, and, for those who find this pace too stressful, we may arrest it altogether. Although we have more leisure time, there is little opportunity to savor it leisurely. For children, Raggedy Ann and Andy have given way first to seductive Barbie dolls and now to computerized space men. Being alone in impersonal society may be painful, being with others but unable to relate perhaps more painful still.

Thus we return to the societal level of analysis, the most directly relevant here, because we are dealing with the larger social forces that determine children's relatedness. America is considered the bastion of individualism, and so it was when the pioneer spirit, self-assertion, and individual inventiveness were the routes to fame and fortune. Some of the historically important cardinal values are summarized most succinctly in the Horatio Alger model, the definition of the self-made man, built on achievement strivings, individual effort, free enterprise, and the ultimate dessert: upward social mobility.

To stand alone today in the United States or to climb alone is not as easy or as advantageous or desirable as it was in the late nineteenth century. Many other countries are just moving into phases where individual initiative is needed to produce the significant material changes already accomplished in the United States. Here research has shown that in the 1970s, Greek and Japanese boys chose the more self-maximizing alternatives than did comparable American boys.

The image of people in the United States as individualistic and competitive has come to be accepted not only around the globe but has become the self-image of Americans themselves. This myth could be quickly dispelled by a count of the daily round of interdependent activities in which average Americans must engage at home and at work. Postindustrial society could not survive were it not for large-scale cooperative enterprises on the societal level and interpersonal helping, sharing, and collaborating on an intimate personal level as well. Throughout history, people have come together to share their joys and their sorrows and to accomplish feats that any one of them could not achieve alone. This may include coming together to beget a family, stalk an animal, surround an enemy, build pyramids or temples, cart boulders to Stonehenge perhaps to measure time, or send rockets to the moon. People have also come together to take measure of each other and of themselves in physical combat, in games, and in intellectual and artistic contests as well. Today we still come together in much the same ways; now the purpose may be to develop cures for cancer, to transplant organs, or to build atomic plants and bombers. The struggle between the wish to be with people, the need to depend on others on the one hand, and the desire to accomplish uniquely, independently, on the other, continues from childhood well into maturity.

From the sociocultural point of view, different values are attached by different societies at different times and in different places to different modes of interpersonal interaction. Most cultures ask their people to pursue personal goals yet also to be concerned with the good of their fellow humans. However, different societies, and often different groups within the same society, establish a different fulcrum for the balance between these coexisting yet divergent and potentially conflict-ridden directions of relating to others. Particular socialization practices at home and in school are seen as powerful mechanisms by which normative societal values are passed on concerning the nature and degree of approved individual or other orientation.

A recognition that specific forms of interpersonal relationships are shaped by larger normative social forces has directed interest to the social institutions in which these relationships are perpetuated and enforced. Educational institutions have increasingly come to be recognized as salient in this regard. Certainly the influence of society upon education is today accepted as axiomatic; education is rarely still considered as an inculcation of the young with eternal verities regardless of place, time, or the particular values of the society in which education occurs. Today's new historiography of education demonstrates increasingly that societal and cultural values are interlaced throughout the web of the educational process. What has only recently been recognized as an unconscious, unintentional transmission of values in the teaching process is still more recently seen by some as a deliberate process aimed at preserving the status quo in the schools.

Yet it must be remembered that the American public school system is more like a giant repository of all kinds of values, past and present, some entirely relevant today, some fitting, and some conflicting; ossified, like sedimentary rock, to give it its present complex, slow-changing structure. It must also be realized that this system had been completed in its contemporary form by the end of the nineteenth century and thus in all probability carries some of the dominant features of that era. There can be no question but that these features are clearly individual achievement-oriented values. It is ironic that the public school, which was conceived at the beginning of the nineteenth century as "the great leveling institution of the age," by the end of the century had turned into an obstacle race; all students were theoretically given the opportunity to gather at the start, but only a few could be the winners.

Mass education makes the subdivision of pupils inevitable, and historic precedent led to a subdivision into classes. Thus achievement became defined as progress through the grades, a movement upward toward higher and better rewards. Following the Horatio Alger model, operations were created that provided a fixed path to social mobility, a path liberally sprinkled with awards for superior effort and accomplishment along the way. The free enterprise system was extolled in nineteenth-century textbooks, and its inherent incentive value was paralleled by the grading system. All agree that this meritocracy extends into today's schools. On the preschool level, achievement orientations are primed with stars, stickers, and other symbols of scholarly success. The elementary years extend the symbols to include badges, certificates, and report cards. Formal arenas for besting are provided in form of spelling bees and other pupil contests. There is evidence that elementary school children, and especially boys, find pleasure and fun in competition. This is particularly true for sports contests, where the concept of fair play is much emphasized. Of course, the strengthening of the moral fiber as well as muscle in competition has been recognized since contests were invented.

By junior high school at the latest, competition has stopped being fun and games. The pace is now stepped up to include marking on the curve, honor rolls, and the ever-present goading on of grades as the key to college admission. The system reaches its apex in the senior years with specification of class rank, merit scholarships, a plethora of awards for achievement in a variety of subjects, and the constant shadow of college board scores cast over the high achievers.

The system continues. High achievers are considered, and ironically consider themselves, even more fortunate after overcoming the hurdle of standardized examinations for graduate schools with hardly a respite for yet other hurdles to come. Competition becomes more painful as the stakes become higher; the fun and games of early childhood often turn into deadly contests. By definition, where rewards are limited, some must be losers.

Throughout American educational history, there have been periodic endeavors to weaken competitive emphases in schools; we note some of these efforts in chapter 1. The 1930s provided a dramatic example of a clash between these two approaches. The concern in the 1960s with humanizing education introduced value-clarification programs and human-relations training into schools, and various more-structured cooperative learning plans in the 1970s.

Our intention here is not to argue in favor of one or the other form of interpersonal relating. On the contrary, our value premise is that society needs both individual initiative and collaborative effort. Children must interact in both of these modes today and in the future. We do not believe, as is fashionable to argue, that we cannot prepare our children for an uncertain future. As long as there are humans, there will have to be concern with human relationships, and basic requirements for relating to others are not likely to change drastically.

Competition, as we demonstrate throughout this volume, is not a solitary activity; rather it is just as social as cooperation in that it pits one individual against another. One consequence of competition may be glorious success, sometimes at the expense of another. However, success may bring attendant disapproval or rejection, even harder to endure than an actual loss. Cooperation is no panacea because it is equally open to strife and potentially hurtful social interactions if agreement among collaborators cannot be reached. Our research and theory emphasizes the numerous interpersonal skills required in cooperation. We tend to forget that cooperation needs to be learned also; in fact, to work together is perhaps a harder task in a society where such learnings are less emphasized.

Competition and cooperation are usually contrasted as opposites, and they are such in the sense we have described so far. However, our research was based on the assumption that each requires very different modes of interaction. Each involves very different behaviors, which need to be studied separately. This task is difficult since, especially in competition, the battleground is often internal and surfaces only in subtle, insignificant-appearing cues, as we learned from our own research. The uniform point of view and methodology common to a number of our studies permits the emergence of behavior patterns that suggest further investigation in competitive and cooperative situations.

The most seminal theories and important research on competition and cooperation have their origin in the field of social psychology. In our opinion, this discipline also offers concepts and theories that can aid our understanding of children's behaviors in competition and cooperation. As a social psychologist, this is my major orientation. However, it is also clear that children's social behaviors cannot be understood fully without taking their particular development into account. We therefore drew upon relevant developmental theories. In the process, we perceived some novel directions that, along with similar research across the two disciplines, may lead toward a developmental social psychology.

We have also pointed to the school environment as a highly relevant arena for both independence and interdependence training and hence also for study of these relationships. Interdisciplinary study has already begun to bring social psychological theories to bear on educational settings in what some refer to as a social psychology of education. Thus the three most directly concerned disciplines here are social psychology, developmental psychology, and education. Readers may not be equally familiar with each of these areas, so we have presented various overviews of conceptualizations within each of these disciplines, where these are needed. The hope is that they will further cross-fertilization between these areas and advance pursuit within any one of them.

Part I introduces readers to research and theory on competition and cooperation derived primarily from the field of social psychology. We concentrate on studies that involve children and draw upon whatever additional research is available from the related fields of child development, developmental psychology, education, and anthropology. Part II examines our programmatic research on interpersonal behaviors of children, concentrating on individual differences because of age, sex, and socioeconomic background. Part III addresses particular issues relative to children's competition and cooperation in peer group or family settings. The contributors bring their rich academic and professional backgrounds to their research and examine the implications of their findings for classrooms, for growth and development of children, and for family interaction.

Part I
Background

Major Trends in Research on Competition and Cooperation, 1897-1980

In this chapter, our primary concern is with an interpretation of major trends in nearly a century of research in the area of competition and cooperation. Our focus is on research that involved children. However, in order to assay main theoretical and methodological directions, it was sometimes necessary to examine studies that employed older persons (usually college students, the traditional subjects of laboratory research in psychology). Our purposes were threefold.

First, our principal aim was to describe research in competition and cooperation within the larger context of social psychology. Experimental social psychology had its beginnings in research on interpersonal rivalry, so that the field during its first thirty years may be said to have been almost synonymous with research on competition. As social psychology developed as a complex area within the behavioral sciences, research on competition and cooperation continued to be largely a function of social psychological theories and methodologies that were perceived as relevant to this field. As assumptions and directions of inquiry changed in social psychology—often themselves reflecting changes within the larger domain of psychology—so did research in the subarea of interest to us here. These relationships made it obvious that understanding the large body of accumulated research literature in cooperation and competition necessitates understanding its wider social psychological frame of reference. Considering the changing face of social psychology itself, a historical approach to research in competition and cooperation seemed most suitable, placed within the changing social psychological setting.

The research is examined by decades. This may seem to be an arbitrary division, and indeed it is because the same type of research is frequently continued smoothly from one decade into the next; certainly there is no abrupt break at the end of any one decade. Considering that our own research has extended over a decade, we are also all too aware of lags between the time in which research is executed and eventual publication. Nevertheless we did not have to strain to place various theoretical formulations or changes in methodology into rigid time slots; the material seemed to lend itself rather easily to various groupings. Our consideration of decades is treated loosely in the sense that the color of the 1920s, say, may be said to differ from that of the 1930s.

We concentrate on select studies representative of a period, examining each in considerable depth. This particular format thus differs from a conventional research review. We found that in the area of research under consideration—perhaps more than is the case in other areas—the particular methodology employed is crucial in interpretation of data, and knowledge of specific findings is essential for understanding the evolution of particular theoretical formulations. Often trends that could be discerned lay in crucially different methodologies and metatheoretical assumptions on which they were based and thus became the focus of our interest.

We also noted apparent relationships between dominant sociopolitical events and certain trends in behavioral science disciplines. This reflection led to our second purpose: to show some parallels between the sociocultural *Zeitgeist*, especially in the United States, and the research with which we are concerned. The questions raised and answers provided often seem affected by, and to some degree affected, societal values. No hard and fast relationships are implied, nor do we aspire to a systematic, in-depth sociocultural analysis of given historical periods. We merely wish to remind readers of some events in American society that seem to be reflected in the research of corresponding periods.

We emphasize in particular the societal context as it is mirrored in educational institutions. The introduction pointed to some of the reasons for the strong association of schools with questions pertaining to competitive or cooperative social interaction. In fact with few exceptions, classrooms are the exclusive source of field research available on children's competition and cooperation. In examining this research, it became apparent that the ebb and flow of values attached to individualistic and collectivist relations in the larger society during different epochs was reflected in, and occasionally itself reflected, some features of the structure and functioning of schools.

One last intention in this review was to provide a framework within which present and future work may be placed. Some of the studies in competition and cooperation were landmark ones in social psychology and deserve the closest study. Some of the early investigations and interpretations appear simplistic; others had a fresh grasp on fundamental issues and asked important questions that were often not pursued further. We found a positive methodological feature of the early research in its close examination of children's social behaviors. Our own research is in line with this approach and with what we sense may turn out to be a renewed trend in the investigation of children's social relations. Also consonant with our interdisciplinary approach to the study of children's cooperation and competition is recent research in the related fields of developmental psychology, anthropology and education. This research is examined in depth in consideration of the 1970s, particularly because it appears to continue with even greater vigor into the 1980s.

Beginnings and into the Twenties

Experimental research that dealt for the first time with questions of interpersonal competition did not originate in response to pressing societal concerns. Credit is generally given to an American, Triplett (1897), for being the first to inquire into factors associated with competitive performance. For his study of "dynamogenic stimulation" at Indiana University, Triplett obtained the official bicycle race records of the League of American Wheelmen, a society with more than two thousand members. Actually, precedence must be conceded to a Britisher, E.B. Turner, "a racing man himself," as Triplett acknowledged, who in 1889 had completed a three-year study of the physiology of pacing and waiting races. Results from both of these studies confirmed what apparently every serious racer—be it foot racer, wheel racer, or ice skater—knew even then: unpaced races against time only are slower than paced races against time, and they in turn are slower than performance in paced competition. Typical results of such a race are depicted in figure 1-1. The question was how to explain them.

Triplett gave over a half-dozen theories to account for the faster times of paced competition races: the suction theory ("the vacuum left behind the pacing machine draws the rider following it, along with it"); the shelter theory (the pacemaker or leading competitor serves as a shelter from the wind); the encouragement theory (the presence of a friend helps; "it is still as true as in Virgil's time that the winners 'can, because they think they can' "); hypnotic suggestions (the revolving wheel of the pacing machine produces "a sort of hypnosis" and increases physical endurance); a mixture of various brain worry theories (the leading man "is in a fidget the whole time whether he is going fast enough to exhaust his adversary . . . he is full of worry as to when that adversary means to commence his spurt . . . His nervous system is generally strung up; the impulse-giving power of the brain and the contractile power of the muscles" are dulled. "The follower, by contrast, rides automatically . . . his brain having inaugurated the movement leaves it to the spinal cord to continue. When he comes to the final spurt, his brain, assuming control again, imparts to the muscles a winning stimulus, while the continued brain work of the leader has brought great fatigue").

Triplett's last, and preferred, causal analysis of dynamogenic factors holds "that the bodily presence of another rider is a stimulus to the racer in arousing the competitive instinct; that another thus can be the means of releasing or freeing nervous energy for him that he cannot of himself release; and further, that the sight of movement in that other by perhaps sugesting a higher rate of speed, is also an inspiration to greater effort."

To test his favorite theory, Triplett designed an apparatus that required one subject alone, or two subjects side by side, to wind fishing reels that were clamped to a table. According to Triplett, it was a well-controlled ex-

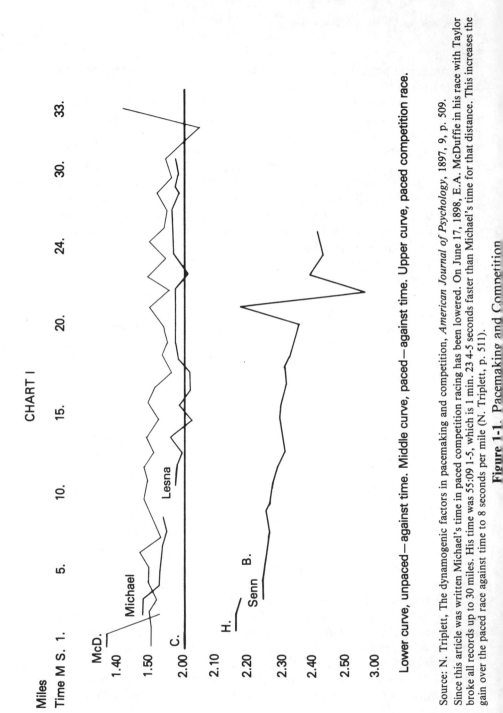

CHART I

Source: N. Triplett, The dynamogenic factors in pacemaking and competition, *American Journal of Psychology*, 1897, 9, p. 509. Since this article was written Michael's time in paced competition racing has been lowered. On June 17, 1898, E.A. McDuffie in his race with Taylor broke all records up to 30 miles. His time was 55:09 1-5, which is 1 min. 23 4-5 seconds faster than Michael's time for that distance. This increases the gain over the paced race against time to 8 seconds per mile (N. Triplett, p. 511).

Figure 1-1. Pacemaking and Competition

periment. There was no wind, no suction, and the average time for one trial—forty seconds—was too short to create either automatic movements or brain fatigue. During his work, over 250 subjects were tested, among them 40 children aged 9 to 13. He found that 20 of the 40 excelled their solitary records when working together, 10 were adversely affected when working simultaneously with another child, and 10 remained unaffected. His analysis claimed support for the dynamogenic factors, although he ascribed a large role to individual differences. For instance, young, nervous children or those with an intense desire to win were said to be over-stimulated so that proper functioning of motor centers was inhibited. Thus it is correct to state that the first laboratory research on competition was carried out by a Midwesterner, and included children among the subjects.

A few years later, a study from Würzburg, Germany, reported an investigation of the same solitary versus group conditions (Mayer 1903). In the light of later explicit concerns of the effects of competition on children's learning, it is of special interest that this early research studied school children's class work, which included reasoning, memory and imagination, as well as arithmetic and composition. The study of elementary school children may have received its impetus from the thriving German public school system, which had attained high standards of excellence by the turn of the century. Compulsory attendance, however, often meant classrooms of up to eighty or more children. Thus Mayer's reported results may have been highly relevant to school personnel, showing as they did that speed was generally increased under group conditions, but quality frequently decreased.

The first systematic attempt to study the influence of the group on individual behavior was begun by Moede in 1913 and carried out over a period of several years (Moede 1914, 1920) at the Leipzig laboratory, the first of its kind, which was founded by Wundt in 1879. Research there during the early period consisted almost exclusively of mental chronometry, the measurement of individual sensations and perceptions via reaction time and other psychophysical threshold determination. Moede introduced the social dimension into what had thus far been exclusively individual studies. Essentially he repeated much of this psychophysical research, adding conditions in which Leipzig University students performed the same judgments alone and in groups.

Moede's work thus constituted a bridge from the tradition of early laboratory research that was exclusively concerned with individual responses to social psychological research concerned with individual responses as influenced by others. Apparently Moede was unable to emerge with meaningful generalizations from under the massive data he had accumulated, and his work is practically unknown today. Nevertheless, his effect was considerable, though indirect; his work was known to one of

Wundt's most outstanding students, Hugo Münsterberg, whose originality had so impressed William James on his visit to Germany that he arranged a permanent professorship for Münsterberg at Harvard. It was Münsterberg who, according to G.W. Allport (1954), encouraged his brother, F.H. Allport, to take up where Moede left off.

F.H. Allport's textbook, *Social Psychology*, appeared sixteen years after the first texts with such titles (E.A. Ross 1908; McDougal 1908). Allport was quite clear that, as distinguished from general psychology, which dealt with the "interplay of stimulation and reaction between the individual and his environment," social psychology dealt with "stimuli and reactions arising between an individual and his fellow" (p. 3). Furthermore basing his argument on the recently published *Psychology from the Standpoint of a Behaviorist* (Watson 1919), he set out to discuss "social behavior . . . both as affording stimulation to others and as reaction to such stimulation from others."

Within this behavioristic framework, Allport made the important distinction between two types of social stimuli: face-to-face groups and coacting persons. He believed that since the former involve interpersonal interactions they "do not lend themselves to experimental control as readily as do coacting groups." His research thus dealt only with the latter, defined as "individuals working side by side and receiving stimulation from the sights and sounds of others doing the same thing." He referred to these social factors as social facilitation, which he distinguished from rivalry: "an emotional reinforcement of movement accompanied by a conscious desire to win" (p. 262). Both of these factors had been included earlier in Triplett's list of dynamogenic factors.

Allport distinguished further between social increments and decrements of average quantity of work done in the group compared with average work done alone. Corresponding gains and losses in the quality of work he referred to, respectively, as "social supervaluents" and "subvaluents." Allport's own research extended the study of influences of coacting groups to more complex mental activities, including free associations, discursive reasoning, and argumentative reasoning. As in previous research, tasks demanding the exercise of simpler cognitive activities were found to be facilitated by coacting groups. The more complex reasoning tasks tended to show social subvaluents, findings generally confirmed by later research.

Allport also corroborated Mayer's original findings of greater uniformity of psychophysical responses in group settings, including judgments of pleasantness and unpleasantness of odors, of weights, and in sensory modalities as well. He marveled at this "basic tendency to temper one's opinions and conduct by reference to the opinions and conduct of others." Anticipating some of the later findings in the area of social influence, he speculated that "we are seldom conscious of it, yet we are seldom, if ever, without it . . . . To think and to judge with others is to submit one's self unconsciously to their standards. We may call this the attitude of social conformity.''

In discussing the individual differences in degree of conformity, Allport stated that children are more susceptible to social facilitation than are adults. Although the actual term was coined considerably later, Allport also discovered social comparison. Individual introspective reports told of attempts to judge one's own progress from facilitative stimuli emitted by others, consisting of tapping of others' pencils, shuffling of feet, peripheral vision of others' speed, or cessation of their activity altogether.

As far as his theoretical analysis of competition was concerned, Allport used the term interchangeably with *rivalry* or the drive to excell others. Enlarging on Triplett's formulation, he commented that social facilitation, like any other coacting situation, always involves rivalry as well.

Allport's research served as a model for subsequent coaction research; the robustness of his results has stood over half a century. One logical outgrowth of his study was to attempt to control the ''sights and sounds of others doing the same thing'' by asking subjects to be merely present without engaging in work. Travis (1925) and Dashiell in 1930 (1935) thus each compared such audience conditions with various alone and/or coacting conditions. Again stronger effects of social facilitation and competition were found in that subjects in the alone conditions had the poorest performance, audience conditions clearly were sufficient to stimulate subjects to greater work, and the combination of audience and competitive instructions showed the strongest effects.

The total dedication and dispassionate analyses in this early research on competition are striking. Suggestions for applications to the larger social scene are striking in their absence. Also missing are considerations of other forms of social interaction; cooperation is never mentioned. Yet loud strains of such concerns could be heard at other institutions, notably Teachers College at Columbia University in New York.

At the center of the small but influential group of educator-philosophers stood John Dewey, social prophet and critic, filled with the sense of a rapidly changing America, attempting to recreate for children the lost meaningful family existence of an earlier America as he saw it. This was to be accomplished by fashioning a cooperative school community, he believed. Today Dewey's views have come under attack by revisionist historians of American education (such as Violas 1978), who consider his message an attempt to socialize children for the sweatshops and factories of industrial society. Dewey's attitude is best expressed by himself (Dewey 1966):

> A society is a number of people held together because they are working along common lines, in a common spirit and with reference to common aims. The common needs and aims demand a growing interchange of

thought and growing unity of sympathetic feeling. The radical reason that the present school cannot organize itself as a natural social unit is because just this element of common and productive activity is absent . . . . There is no obvious social motive for the acquirement of mere learning, there is no clear social gain in success thereat. Indeed, almost the only measure for success is a competitive one, in the bad sense of that term—a comparison of results in the recitation or in the examination to see which child has succeeded in getting ahead of others in storing up, in accumulating, the maximum of information. So thoroughly is this the prevalent atmosphere that, for one child to help another in this task has become a school crime . . . . Mutual assistance, instead of being the most natural form of co-operation and association, becomes a clandestine effort to relieve one's neighbor of his proper duties.

During this time, radiating from New York, heavily supported by the Child Development Institute at Teachers College and the newly founded Bureau of Educational Experiments (later Bank Street College of Education), the child development movement was in full swing. It combined research into child development—largely through observing children's behaviors—with experimental schools, parent education classes, and a plethora of child welfare agencies. A pivotal figure in these activities was Lawrence Frank, an indefatigable fund raiser for child study institutes across the city and ranging as far as Minnesota and California. He was equally interested in fostering scientific research about child growth and development, as well as practical matters concerned with children's health and general well-being. Other well-known personalities involved in childhood education and research were Lucy Sprague Mitchell, Barbara Biber, Lois Murphy and Gardner Murphy, and Carolyn Zachry, among others. Research and application were seen as mutually supportive, and the connection between knowledge of child development and its use in educational settings considered almost axiomatic.

Although Dewey was not actively involved, he supported the movements both in child development and in education, being a close friend of many whose professional careers were in those fields. Through his writing and lively personal exchanges, his views on the education of children found their way into elementary schools as well as Teachers College lecture halls.

The foremost interpreter and implementer of Dewey's social views on education was his former student and later colleague at Columbia University, William Heard Kilpatrick. His most significant contribution, which may be considered almost an operationalization of Dewey's views of cooperation in particular and education in general, is his introduction of the project method into school settings. Presented first in an essay in the *Teachers College Record* (1918) and detailed in his *Foundations of Method* (1925), it took the educational establishment by storm. Its methodology was characterized by Kilpatrick as "wholehearted, purposeful activity proceeding in a social environment." It synthesized some of the most important thought on pedagogy current at that time: focus on a child's purposeful activities derived from explications of the law of effect by Thorndike, then a powerful force also at Columbia; and on emphasis on the social environment built on Dewey's insistence that a child's experience must include from early on interaction with others to develop the moral character needed for living in the kind of community Dewey felt would be necessary for survival in the future.

Teachers in schools that embraced the child-centered progressivism of the era readily accepted this methodology. Projects of the newly created Lincoln School of Teachers College (1917) became models to be emulated across the country. Best known perhaps is the sixth-grade project on boats. Studies that included the history of construction and transportation led in turn to the study of geography, oceanography, art, literature, and so on, with each pupil pursuing his or her own interest and weaving it into the total group activity.

Another member of the Teachers College faculty became a celebrated actor in the history of competition and cooperation: Harold C. Rugg, who became director of research for the Lincoln School and participated in its effort to create textbooks to accompany the breadth of its activity projects. In his social studies textbooks, he marshalled evidence from diverse social sciences to paint a panoramic history of the changes that were sweeping across America, singling out for criticism the materialism and commercialism he saw in industrial society in general and the American business elite in particular.

This triumvirate of progressivists and their likeminded colleagues blended gradually with other voices raised against laissez-faire individualism in Depression America. They were both affected by and affected the events of the 1930s. Perhaps a social upheaval of great magnitude was needed to move the research reviewed here out of the shelter of the laboratory and closer toward the social issues of the day.

The Thirties

The form of this chapter was dictated by the tenets that competition and cooperation represent different ways in which people relate to each other and that different values are attached to these ways at different times and by different groups of people. The decade of the 1930s demonstrates these fervently held social attitudes and also serves as the context of research during this period.

The thesis advocating cooperative learning structures in the schools was followed by its antithesis. It took the form of an organized battle launched by a combination of various business sectors to preserve treasured values of freedom and independence for the youth of America. This episode demonstrates more than any national opinion survey or controlled laboratory study the deep-seated value structure of American individualism. It is a rare example of socioeconomic organizations actively and openly attempting to change the values and activities of another social institution, the public schools. Particularly relevant is the fact that these values centered on the place of competition in American society.

This period has been fully documented by S. Alexander Rippa, whose original interest developed into a doctoral dissertation written under direction of the noted historian Bernard Bailyn. This work culminated in a number of detailed accounts in several publications (Rippa 1958, 1959, 1962, 1964, 1976). His writings provide a sense of the gradual banding together of individual business organizations as well as influential industrial interests, such as du Pont, General Motors, and United Steel. In the midst of Depression America, a political groundswell in the business sector combined to form the Liberty League in 1934. Its leaders decided by uniting with other organizations, such as the National Association of Manufacturers (NAM) to, "sell free enterprise to people . . . to force the minds of public opinion back into the mold of Americanism" (Rippa 1976, p. 288).

The propaganda campaign that ensued utilized every possible source of media: highway billboards, a radio series ("The American Family Robinson"), and newspapers, including one weekly aimed expressly at youth. The message was always the same: to defend the American way of life. That lifestyle meant freedom to pursue personal interests unhampered by controls or outside interference. Every conceivable symbol that stood for individual achievement was glorified; by contrast, anything even vaguely associated with any kind of group activity was tainted as un-American.

It was inevitable that the searchlight turned to the schools. Since the influx of immigrants in the early 1900s, the schools had come to be seen as the bastions of flag-waving Americanism. They were the place where children were supposedly being socialized toward love of country and its glorious past and where they were motivated toward achievement and high individual aspirations to ensure America's future. But business wanted to find out what the schools were teaching, so informal inspections of textbooks were carried out by individual organizations, such as the American Legion and the New York State Economic Council. To their horror, they found that the best of the schools, Teachers College Lincoln School at the forefront, used social science textbooks that criticized the American system. Teachers College, and Rugg's textbooks in particular, seemed to flirt with, even extol, foreign ideas, including Russian collectivism.

Denouncements of these and other textbooks by business found their way into the press, with such headings as "Sovietizing Our Children" and "Treason in the Textbooks." The *Nation's Business* claimed that high school students were being indoctrinated to think competition evil. In the ensuing furor, some communities had public book burnings, and the Daughters of the American Revolution issued a resolution that all public school textbooks should be reviewed to eliminate un-American content.

By the end of the decade, the NAM had become the self-appointed stimulator "of a fuller understanding of private enterprise among educators." This included commissioning R.W. Robey, assistant professor of banking at Columbia University, "to abstract textbooks in the field of history, civics, sociology and economics in general in the public school system of the country to determine the extent of attempted un-American indoctrination." According to Rippa (1976, pp. 294-296), Robey and his staff of three other academics "prepared in a period of three months 563 abstracts of secondary school science books . . . totalling . . . more than 1,200 pages of single-spaced typescript." There was considerable backlash, primarily from educators who denounced the investigation as an attempt at indoctrination of American youth. But American entry into World War II replaced this issue with more dramatic headlines.

The social climate of the 1930s revolved around issues of individual freedom to compete and simultaneous fears of collectivist domination. It was during this period that two companion volumes sponsored by the Social Science Research Council (SSRC) appeared: May and Doob's *Competition and Cooperation* (1937) and Margaret Mead's *Cooperation and Competition among Primitive Peoples* (1936).

The SSRC had been founded in 1924, composed of seven major behavioral science organizations. The Sub-Committee on Competitive and Cooperative Habits was formed in 1934, chaired by Mark May, head of the Institute of Human Behavior at Yale, and including also Gordon Allport and Gardner Murphy. Its mandate called for "critical analysis of the state of knowledge, an outline of the existing frontiers, and a listing of immediately feasible small research problems to fill in the gaps and advance the frontiers." The May and Doob volume was the outcome. Its introduction places the research squarely into its contemporary context:

> The concepts of competition and cooperation . . . occupy a prominent place in historic and current social theory. Contemporary thinkers refer to America as an essentially competitive system, and the more liberal or radical of them praise Soviet Russia as a great cooperative commonwealth . . . . Leaders of thought at the present time nearly all agree that in the Western World competition has produced a rich technological culture which now, because of radically altered conditions, can be enjoyed by men only if they learn to displace the no longer productive competitive practices with new, as yet only partially discovered, cooperative ways of living. Formerly nearly all the virtues of society were attributed to individualistic competition, but now the reverse judgment prevails. As the older practices suitable to newly formed industrial societies possessed of

high social mobility, become less productive, they are more and more frequently declared anachronistic. The very term "competition" has become
dyslogistic, and "cooperation" has become freighted with eulogy.
[Pp. 2-3.]

The major body of the work is taken up with theory and research
relating to competition and cooperation. After claiming that a framework
of guiding concepts was essential to reduce the existing haphazardly accumulated research in the field, May and Doob outlined such a scheme.
Their basic postulates, twenty-four in all, helped to organize already existing research and made definitional distinctions maintained in subsequent
work. For example, postulate 5 states that "individuals compete with one
another when they are striving to achieve the same goal that is scarce and
when they are prevented by the rules of the situation from achieving this
goal in equal amounts." According to postulate 6, "individuals cooperate
with each other when they are striving to achieve the same or complementary goals that can be shared and when they are required by the rules of the
situation to achieve this goal in nearly equal amounts." The authors also
hold that cooperation and competition do not constitute polar opposites, a
proposition that went unheeded in research during later decades. Following
the emphasis on learning theory, they proposed that "human beings of
original nature strive for goals, but striving with others (cooperation) or
against others (competition) are learned forms of behavior."

Marshaling support for this proposition, May and Doob turned to
already existing research on preschool children. At this point, their review
intersects with the history of early childhood research of the 1930s. They
repeat Bühler's (1930) observations of the 6 month old "who strives for the
object he wants and not *against other* children." Two and 3 year olds are
said to behave only in relation to materials since they have not yet
discovered the other as competitor, a finding corroborated also by Leuba
(1933). Parten (1933) described how children under the age of 3 seldom
engaged in organized play, and Shirley (1933) underscored how babies
engage in simple cooperative play with adults and, by their second year,
cooperate with adults while being dressed. For competition, Greenberg
(1932) posited a sequence: at ages 2 and 3, it is not observable; ages 3 and 4
discover others as potential competitors, with clear ideas of excelling; 4 to 6
year olds manifest a desire to excel; and 6 and 7 year olds regard others as
obstacles to be removed. Here, certainly, are the clear beginnings of
developmental social psychology, but they were not pursued for several
decades.

May and Doob concluded that "neither striving with others, or against
others for desired goals . . . can be said to be the more genetically basic, fundamental or premordial" (p. 25). However, they cautioned against methodological shortcomings: "when one experiment in the existing literature is

compared with another, practically never do we find that the variables involved are controlled in precisely the same fashion or even that they are controlled
at all. . . . Age, sex, socio-economic status . . . number of subjects . . .
nature of tasks to be performed . . . instructions . . . these are some of the
variables which prevent our generalizations from being either very precise
. . . making them mere crude approximations of the truth, if there be truth"
(p. 25).

May and Doob also reviewed the early social psychological research in the
area of "alone and together" experiments, with some cross-cultural material
added from Russia (Elkin 1926) along the same lines. However, the authors
were singularly unimpressed by the findings: "no one should collapse with
awe when it is determined that more words were scanned less well in the latter
situation than in the former. High school orators knew long before social
psychology tried to be experimental that a speech recited perfectly in the
privacy of the bedroom might suffer a number of changes when it was
delivered before an audience" (p. 31). Their methodological critique is well
taken; they claimed that the investigator's apparent surprise that "together
conditions" affect problem-solving behavior "doubtless resulted from the
crude S-R formula then in vogue." Again they pointed to the loose
methodology ("the social variables are all mixed up") and ended their review
of this laboratory research with the recommendation that "future
research . . . be along the line of defining more specifically and
psychologically the influence of 'others' when they are variously and experimentally controlled as competitors, cooperators, on-lookers, 'rooters,'
'by-standers,' etc., or when they are physically present or psychologically apparent, or when they have certain predetermined attitudinal relations to the
subjects of the experiments" (p. 34).

Of particular interest is May and Doob's scrutiny of the American school
system as to its respective emphases on cooperation and competition. They
started from a broad sociocultural perspective, cautioning readers to
remember that

> the purpose of education is to transmit a culture from generation to generation,
> perpetuating some parts of it and modifying others. If the culture is basically
> competitive, therefore, and if those adults who control the schools—and in-
> cidentally pay the bills—are themselves convinced both intellectually and emo-
> tionally that the competitive aspects of the culture should be perpetuated, it
> follows inevitably that the schools will be honeycombed with competitive situa-
> tions and that competition will be an approved and rewarded form of
> behavior. . . . It is generally agreed that the Western European and North
> American culture (with the exception of certain minority groups) are basically
> more competitive than cooperative. There are, however, in those cultures an
> apparently increasing number of individuals who, for various reasons, have
> developed levels of aspirations that seem to be best reached by cooperative
> rather than by competitive behavior. They are . . . presumably the

organizers and promoters of all kinds of cooperative clubs, associations, committees and activities. They are also the ones who idealize cooperation and deprecate the evils of competitively minded members . . . admit that all of this is true in theory, but insist that, after all, competition works best in practice. The state of affairs in American culture then is that, *while paying respectful homage to cooperative ideals, we go right on with our competitive system* and justify it on the grounds that "human nature" is basically and fundamentally competitive and always will be so. . . . In the public school . . . we thus find this curious paradox: The basic structure of the system is competitive: but the ideals of cooperation are emphasized. . . . The set-up of the school is such that a large portion of the daily activities of the pupils is more competitive than cooperative. At the same time all of the human virtues and attitudes that are favorable to cooperation are stressed! [Pp. 81-82]

Readers were referred to sample studies demonstrating that individual remuneration stimulates greater efficiency of work than group remuneration in children of all ages. The authors were exceedingly critical of this work, insisting that it merely demonstrates the relative strength of certain incentives in specific cultural circumstances. It does not, and should not, claim that their absolute strength under all circumstances has been proven:

To be sure, it is useful to know that American children can be bribed with toys and money to perform in a particular fashion, if anyone cares to bribe them to do so. But the net result of work of this kind is not an insight into so-called "human nature," rather a knowledge of how certain human beings from a certain culture can be motivated to perform particular tasks. [P. 40]

On the question of social interactions and performance in American public schools, they concluded:

In the American public schools, children work more efficiently in competitive than in cooperative situations. This proposition is quite consistent with our theory. The evidence shows that American public schools stress and approve individual achievement and hence children may be said to possess the knowledge that their levels of aspiration can be achieved competitively. They are strongly motivated to be the best in the class or at the top of the list, or to be the one who is chosen for this or that. We wish to emphasize just as strongly as we possibly can that this proposition refers to the American public schools and that it says nothing about the relative strengths of competition and cooperation in other cultures. . . . It happens that investigators have attempted very glibly to solve the problem by experimenting with children in the American culture. Their work, as they have left it, is one of the clearest examples of the insidiousness of a short-sighted methodological approach that the literature most unfortunately possesses. All that their efforts demonstrate is the proposition as we have formulated it above; absolutely no broader inference is permissible. [P. 38]

This strong relativistic cultural orientation is carried over into an anthropological chapter that attempts to integrate the detailed descriptions of the thirteen primitive cultures studied by Mead and her associates (1937).

The Forties

Of major importance in this decade are two somewhat different events, both causally connected with World War II: the upsurge of innovative behavioral science methodologies and the emergence of group dynamics stimulated by Kurt Lewin. At the end of the decade, they merged to generate a theoretical formulation and a piece of pivotal research in the area of cooperation and competition.

In the pre-World War II period, the social sciences were in their infancy as far as methodological sophistication was concerned. In response to the need for classification and selection of soldiers in World War I, dramatic developments in the methodology of intelligence testing had occurred. During the subsequent decade, measurement of personality traits and social attitudes began to follow suit, but slowly. The demands of World War II accelerated new approaches and accomplishments in all branches of scientific endeavor.

The suddenness of the attack on Pearl Harbor and the later American involvement in diverse theaters of war required that large masses of people be immediately readied and assigned to different service branches and governmental agencies. One of the wartime agencies set up by the president and Congress to meet a variety of needs created by the war was the Office of Strategic Services (OSS). Its psychological staff was charged with developing procedures that would permit an assessment of recruits' capabilities to carry out their assignments. This assignment turned out to be a test of the staff's ingenuity. It required construction of screening devices in the face of several unknowns; recruits were to be sent to parts of the world unfamiliar to most of them, including the psychologists who were to predict the recruits' performance in those places. Nor was it clear how civilian skills used in previous employments would be generalizable to new jobs with which the staff was also not acquainted. Staff had to decide, for example, what capabilities would be required of a demolitions instructor, a resistance leader, and a paratrooper.

Some of the methodology employed the usual assessment methods: personal interviews, questionnaires, sociometric tests, projective tests, and other personal inventories. But it became evident to OSS personnel that most of the assignments were likely to involve skills for which no conventional measurement devices existed: how to get along with others, to assume leadership functions, and to engage in and to organize others to engage in collaborative activities. Thus evolved what is generally considered the methodology that put social psychology over the threshold of adolescence into maturity: observation of social interactions under deliberately created and controlled conditions. Obviously recruits could not be studied in the field situations in which they were to function, and conventional laboratory conditions—measurement of reaction time on pursuit rotors, discrimination measures of various sense modalities, galvanic skin responses, or recall of various stimulus words—were of no help. The creative solution that emerged entailed a combination of simulated field situations, which simultaneously permitted control over many of the confounding variables that generally appear in actual field situations. Thus, for instance, to determine leadership skills, candidates were asked to organize and lead men across a stretch of road described as having been mined; or a small brook was said to be a stream and candidates were given wooden logs and other materials to use to build a bridge over it. In another, a single candidate was faced with "assistants" who refused to help or contribute their share toward carying out the common work assignment. The methodology is described in detail in the resulting postwar volume, *Assessment of Men* (U.S. OSS Staff 1948).

One of the advisers to the OSS staff on the psychological warfare programs was Kurt Lewin, who played a key role in the development of American social psychology, including research and theory in competition and cooperation. Lewin had emigrated with his family to the United States in 1933 under the auspices of the Emergency Committee on Displaced Scholars and a two-year grant to teach at Cornell. Subsequently he was appointed professor of child psychology at the Iowa Child Welfare Station. Almost immediately upon his arrival, he was accorded an important part in the American psychological scene. Lewin is another example of momentous political events indirectly affecting the course of social psychology; this time the events were of international magnitude in the gathering storm of Hitler Germany, and they intersected with the personal life of one individual.

Lewin participated in several wartime committees, among them, and at the personal request of Margaret Mead, the Committee on Food Habits of the National Research Council, which was charged with advising governmental agencies how to alter the habits and tastes of Americans during a period of wartime shortage. In a narrow sense, this was a continuation of Lewin's study of the effects of social pressures on eating habits of children begun in the early days of his work at the Cornell nursery school. In a wider sense, it was a continuation of his work of the preceding decade when he and his students were reproducing segments of live environments in his own Berlin laboratory. It represented a continuation of the particular issue researched and also the underlying theoretical approach.

Understanding the Lewinian approach is the key to understanding the research. Lewinian theory is above all a method, a tool for approaching psychological events that needed to be explained. In contrast to the then-dominant American learning theory, which focused on historical antecedents of a person's behavior, Lewin emphasized the direct effect of present situations on a person's behavior. This principle of contemporaneity (Lewin 1943) is crucial. It requires that the psychologist consider the psychological field as it exists for a person at a moment in time. Such a conceptualization is uniquely suited to deal with an individual's important issues. Thus in discussing nursery children's eating problems, Lewin considered the forces that were moving the child toward and away from food: their respective likes and dislikes and the functions of increasing the attractiveness of special foods or of specific punishments for not eating.

Analyses like these led to the next question: which forces would have to be changed in the life space of the child to lead to a change in eating habits. Thus formulated, experiments could follow that actually manipulated the hypothesized forces and observed outcomes. When questions shifted later to inquiry about adult food habits, the transformation could easily be made by use of the same concepts, even though the particular force constellations of the adult life space were hypothesized to be different. In this manner, Lewin could investigate the question of why people eat what they do by following food from its various sources—the market, gardens, fields—step by step through a series of decisions until it reaches the table. This channel theory is fully discussed in Cartwright (1951, chap. 8). When it came to changing peoples' eating habits—be it getting college students to increase their consumption of whole wheat bread rather than white, adults to eat nutritious glandular meats that were in ample supply during wartime, or mothers to feed babies cod liver oil or orange juice—the first question always was to understand the forces that were operating in the life space. This included forces that would make a person want to eat the recommended foods, as well as those that resisted change: cod liver oil had unpleasant odors for some, the consistency of glandular foods was repulsive to others, and so forth. Once these forces were understood, questions could be asked of how these constellations might be changed. In the particular case of foods, it was found that discussion with other people and agreement to try new foods led to a greater change than providing intellectual information extolling the virtues of these foods. Eventually this approach led to the formulation of group decision as an important mechanism for reducing resistance to change in individual behavior (Lewin 1947; Cartwright and Zander 1953).

These examples emphasize several features characterizing Lewinian theory and research. One is that field theory permits the analysis of a variety of problems, from the behavior of small children under conditions of frustration (Barker, Dembo and Lewin 1941) and students' reactions to success and failure (Lewin et al. 1944), to organized and unorganized groups under conditions of fear (French 1944). In considering forces acting on the person in his life space, the person is always seen against an environmental background. This means that the stress is on interaction with the environment, on movement and action within it, and on potential change. Thus field theory is not only uniquely suited to a diagnosis of problems, but it furnishes action implications as well—hence the oft-quoted Lewinian maxim, "There is nothing so practical as a good theory." Conceptualization of a problem yields an implication for experimental research as well as for action. For Lewin, the two were mutually supportive. An equally important axiom for him was, "No action without research, no research without action."

Lewin increasingly emphasized the role of people in each other's life space. He began to move from a concern with individual dynamics to formulations that would fall into social psychology proper, concerned with group dynamics. This is illustrated by perhaps one of his most important works: the Lewin, Lippitt, and White (1939) studies of social climates in children's groups. This research was rooted in the sociopolitical climate of the period. Lewin was deeply troubled by and involved with the threat to democracy abroad and questions raised about the viability of democracy at home, and these issues eventually found their way into the Lewinian laboratory. The major experiment was done with 10- and 11-year-old boys who met in the natural setting of their scout club and carried out workshop activities, such as woodworking and mask making. As an experiment in social space, the children's activities were preselected and the leaders were carefully trained to behave in predetermined ways that would correspond to a conceptualization of autocratic and democratic leadership styles. The implication here is that leadership style, contrary to the then popular assumptions, is not an inborn personal quality but can be learned. Marrow (1969, p. 126) quoted Lewin on this finding:

> On the whole, I think that there is ample proof that the difference in behavior in autocratic and democratic situations is not a result of differences in individuals. There have been few experiences for me as impressive as seeing the expression on children's faces during the first day under an autocratic leader. The group that had been formerly friendly, open, cooperative, and full of life, became within a short half-hour a rather apathetic-looking gathering without initiative.

In 1945, Lewin's vision for the study of research and theory and its application in social action was realized. He established the Commission on Community Interrelations (CCI) in New York City and the Research Center for Group Dynamics (RCGD) in the Department of Economics and Social Sciences at the Massachusetts Institute of Technology (MIT) in Cambridge. CCI, under the leadership of Stuart Cook, dealt with intergroup relations of all kinds. Perhaps the theme that most united its various efforts was that of racial and religious prejudice, intolerance, and divisive social and cultural differences. To Lewin, "a minority problem was meaningless without its counterpart majority problem. . . . The negro problem is a problem of the whites, the jewish problem, of the christians" (ibid., p. 200).

The list of Lewin-inspired major action research projects of the 1940s is impressive. They included the National Training Laboratory Workshop, initiated in 1947, and a study of interracial housing (Deutsch and Collins 1951). The former is generally considered among the most ambitious and influential Lewinian action research projects. A key figure in the development of theory and methodology for both of these studies was Morton Deutsch. He had followed Lewin to MIT, becoming part of the small group of graduate students working with Lewin and his colleagues. Several of this group received their first teaching experiences in charge of sections of a large undergraduate course in social psychology, given by the RCGD for the department. Deutsch determined that he would make additional use of the students in his two sections as participants in a naturalistic study of the effects of differential grading practices. Thus was launched his seminal study, a doctoral dissertation on the effect of cooperation and competition upon group process (Deutsch 1949a, 1949b). The design and procedures closely resembled those of normal classroom proceedings. At the first meeting of the various sections, over fifty volunteers were obtained for some smaller sections that would give the instructor an opportunity to experiment with different methods of improving the course. Instead of meeting three times a week for one hour, these experimental sections were to meet once a week for three hours. Within the constraints of their course schedules, students were assigned randomly to ten five-person groups. Based on a preliminary performance test, the ten groups were categorized into five pairs, with the performance of the two groups within each pair matched. One group from each pair was then randomly assigned to the cooperative treatment, and the other groups were assigned to a competitive treatment.

The experimental treatment lasted five weeks. During this period, all groups, regardless of treatment, were asked each week to solve a puzzle, said to test their ability to think logically (as a group in the cooperative condition and as individuals in the competitive condition), and to analyze a human relations problem, which would be evaluated both by the quality of the discussion and insights, and the quantity of new ideas incorporated in the final recommendations for action on the given issue. All students were told that half of their course grade would depend on their performance on these two problems.

Up to this point, all groups were given identical instructions. The only difference was in the reward structures, following Deutsch's conceptualization of cooperative and competitive conditions. Students in competitive groups were told that their grade depended on their individual contributions, and in cooperative conditions, the evaluation would be based on group discussion and performance, each student within a given group receiving the same grade. In each competitive group, the highest individual contributor was to receive a rank of one, the next one a rank of two, and so forth. To raise motivation further, the contributor in the competitive condition with the highest average rank over the five-week period was promised an excuse from one term paper and an automatic honors grade. In cooperative conditions, all five students in the group that averaged highest over the five-week period would similarly be excused from writing a paper and all five would be given an honors grade.

Deutsch, as had May and Doob (1937) a decade earlier, concentrated on differences in goal structure: common in cooperation (May and Doob tended to refer to it as shared) and exclusive in competition (May and Doob claimed that individuals in that condition cannot achieve their goals "to the same degree"). Deutsch, utilizing Lewinian spatial and vector terms, defined the two conditions more exactly. In his view, competitive conditions are such that if one individual enters the goal region, the others are ipso facto excluded from entering the goal region, at least to some extent. In cooperation, by contrast, one member's entrance into the goal region automatically ensures the entrance of others into the goal region as well.

May and Doob, and Deutsch, were cognizant of the fact that both working conditions involve interdependencies. Members are made interdependent by the very nature of the goal structures. This is more easily comprehended in cooperative conditions. Where several persons work for a common goal, the contribution of any one member moves the others along and brings them closer to their goal as any one member moves closer. Each positive step is a positive step for all; each misstep is a misstep for all. They are, according to Deutsch, promotively interdependent (striving with each other, as May and Doob put it). The Horatio Alger hero, the definition of the self-made, self-reliant man, includes the notion of independence from others. In competition, according to Deutsch, such independence exists only in the sense that persons stride out alone, with no help from others. Individual fates are linked together since one person's step toward the goal has adverse effects on the other's goal attainment. They are, said Deutsch, contriently interdependent (striving against each other, said May and Doob).

These two contrasting models are pure in the sense that they rarely exist in this state in actual situations. Most occasions are highly complex, often involving a set of individuals with many goals, some of which may be contrient relations, while the same individuals may be promotively interdependent with respect to some other goals. Such is the case, for instance, in team sports, where striving to maintain or raise one's own standing affects the standing of another teammate, often adversely, yet may also contribute to the common score.

In the next chapter, we discuss certain theoretical limitations of Deutsch's emphasis on different goal interdependencies as the sole distinguishing feature between cooperative and competitive conditions. His unquestioned contribution is the clarity of distinction between competitive or cooperative conditions and the behaviors they elicit. In the literature of the 1930s, this distinction was often blurred. There were descriptions of children's competing or toddlers' cooperating, with consequent neglect of the behaviors that were actually taking place. The strength of Deutsch's orientation is that he went beyond definitions and concentrated in his research on the behavioral processes that emerged as a consequence of the cooperative or competitive working conditions in which a person was placed (Deutsch 1949b). He accomplished further rigor by extending his theoretical analysis by the use of such concepts as substitutability (in cooperation, one member's execution of an act may serve an equivalent function for any other member; this is not so in competition); positive and negative cathexes (holdovers from early psychoanalytic formulations since attraction as a concept in group dynamics theory was still being developed); and positive and negative inducibility (the concept of social influence was also only being developed).

With these concepts, Deutsch (1949a) generated some thirty-four hypotheses. He put them to experimental tests, using a methodology adapted from the leadership training workshops. It included four observers per group who recorded the types of member participations (who spoke to whom, for how long, and in what manner) and different member roles and work procedures. Upon completion of each session, the observers also rated various group process dimensions (member involvement, communication difficulties, attentiveness, acceptance and rejection, and so forth), as did the students, who also completed an extended questionnaire after the study ended.

On the whole, the Deutsch hypotheses were strongly supported. He found, for example, that there were no differences in student involvement in the two conditions, but cooperative groups displayed more coordinated effort, more division of labor, more acceptance of others' ideas and suggestions, more agreement in general, and more helpfulness and fewer communication difficulties. This superior group process was also reflected in various productivity measures. Students in competitive groups showed more obstructive and aggressive interaction, especially on the human relations problem. These results have stood the test of time remarkably well, and subsequent research has not added a great deal more information about the behavioral processes elicited in these very different working conditions.

Before Deutsch's dissertation was completed, Lewin died at the age of 57 (February 11, 1947). He had been able to put his visions into operation and to begin to chart a course for social psychology, but he did not bring it to fruition himself or witness the accomplishments of others who followed his path.

The Fifties

During this decade, there was some consolidation and further development of postwar advances in the major social psychological areas of attitude measurement and the small group. Without question, the sheer quantity of research reached a new high. Small-group experiments particularly were characterized by an ingenuity of design and the operationalization of group dynamics concepts. Laboratory techniques reached new heights of imagination and control by the use of paid participants—"stooges"—who posed as group members and, according to prearranged scripts, attempted systematically to exert influence on *actual* group members. Among the most active areas of research was that of face-to-face social influence. Festinger and his associates at the Research Center for Group Dynamics focused on the sources of normative pressures in small groups, and Asch at Swarthmore defined the conditions under which individual conformity occurred. The explosion of conformity studies occurred in a period when students, including almost 8 million World War II and Korean veterans, were being described by a University of Pennsylvania professor as "gloriously contented", that is, passive and accepting of others, including their influences (Jacobs 1957).

Internationally there was a mix of cold war freezes on the one hand and moves toward an interdependent world on the other. In the latter category was the creation of the United Nations Scientific and Cultural Organization (UNESCO), whose purpose was "to promote international cooperation in education, science and culture." At the same time, several investigations of intergroup conflict and the role of superordinate goals in the reduction of intergroup hostility were made. Among the most relevant for our purposes is Sherif's study of the creation of intergroup competition and its subsequent effects and restoration of friendly relations (Sherif et al. 1961).

The studies were carried out at three summer camps between 1949 and 1954. Control included the selection of the subjects (11- and 12-year-old boys from different schools and neighborhoods and stable white middle-class Protestant families), cabin assignments (at first best friends were allowed to form and then were deliberately split up and assigned to different cabins), selection of different activities (including four team activities—softball, football, soccer, and volley ball—among hiking, swimming, and other typical camp activities), and observation and recording of the boys' behaviors.

Each experiment was conducted over a period of approximately three weeks and consisted of several stages. First was the experimental formation of in-groups. The method of cabin assignment demonstrated that even though boys were separated from their original buddies, new and strong friendships could be formed within the experimentally determined in-groups. In the second stage, group formation, the children were divided into two large groups, who from then on did not meet until the next stage, approximately one week later. Boys in each of the two groups engaged in activities that were attractive to them and required interdependent interaction to increase their cohesiveness. During an outdoor hike, they divided labor in cooking the raw foods that had been supplied instead of eating already prepared meals. Gradually strong in-group feelings developed, with an accompanying status structure and unique ways of doing things (for instance, in one of the groups norms were created that banned swearing and boys prayed to defeat their opponents before each game). Thus two strong and cohesive in-groups were established. The fourth stage, intergroup conflict, was the major hypothesis-testing interest. It was assumed that

> when members of two groups come into contact with one another in a series of activities that embody goals which each urgently desires, but which can be attained by one group only at the expense of the other, competitive activity toward the goal changes, over time, into hostility between the groups and their members and . . . conflict between two groups tends to produce an increase in solidarity *within* the groups. [P. 239]

The experimental tests consisted of a set of tournaments between the two teams, with the usual prizes and trophies offered. As the tournament went on and tension mounted, the good sportsmanship turned to strong negative feelings for the other group.

The fourth stage was characterized by an intensification of frustration of one group by another. The experimenters arranged it so that one group engaged in activities that would frustrate the other (for instance, one group arrived first at the scene of a feast and ate the best foods, leaving the others soggy remains). Soon active conflict broke out; one group would raid the other, destroy their property, and otherwise insult and/or frustrate them. Extreme social distance or exclusivity among the two groups had been established.

The final stage, reduction of intergroup hostilities, was another important hypothesis-testing phase. Sherif's assumption was strongly supported that mere contact between two groups engaged in pleasant activities that require no interdependent contact will not change the intergroup feelings of hostility. The principal hypothesis here maintained that

> when conflicting groups come into contact under conditions embodying goals that are compelling for the groups involved, but cannot be achieved by a single group through its own efforts and resources, the group will tend to cooperate toward this *superordinate goal.* . . . Such cooperation . . . will have a *cumulative* effect toward reducing the social distance between them, changing hostile attitudes and stereotypes, and hence reducing the possibility of future conflicts between them. [P. 255].

Through a series of deliberate simulated experimental crises (reminiscent of the OSS problem situations), the camp was faced with situations such as the breakdown of the camp's water supply, with every boy needed to locate the source of trouble in the pipes; or an unavailability of camp funds for camp movies for the last night so that the boys had to collect money together. Another time the camp truck got stuck in the mud and had to be dug out. Such intergroup contacts in the striving for superordinate goals did reduce intergroup hostility, but, according to the experimenters, it took considerably longer to achieve harmony than they anticipated.

This study offered the most detailed account available of interpersonal behaviors that develop under cooperative and competitive conditions. It substantiates Deutsch's major findings of positive interpersonal behaviors characteristic of cooperative conditions and negative behaviors typically found in competitive conditions. Deutsch's was a study of interpersonal behaviors within given groups only, but Sherif dealt with intragroup as well as intergroup behaviors. Thus he extended Deutsch's research by describing the process by which intergroup relations are established and suggesting how undesirable relations may be changed. Intergroup hostilities are created by strengthening within-group interdependencies and facing the respective groups with contrient goals; prosocial behaviors are created by the establishment of interdependencies between groups through superordinate goals and common tasks.

Another original laboratory research along these lines was carried out by Mintz (1951). His study derived from an interest in explaining maladaptive social behaviors that are frequently observed in groups who panic. One example is a crowd leaving a theater. Under normal conditions, it takes a few minutes to empty it, but when a fire alarm is sounded, individuals often push their way to exits, exits become blocked, and those who want to escape most become the cause of their own undoing as well as that of others. In explaining this behavior, Mintz rejected interpretations proposed earlier in terms of the disorganizing character of emotions or other alterations in personality of individuals under panic. Instead he ascribed the cause to the particular characteristics of such situations: their unstable reward structure. Specifically he proposed that individuals who would normally behave cooperatively—wait their turn, permit others to pass, even hold doors open for each other—in situations of panic behave in accord with their own self-interests. Persons in panic compete for space at the exits and thus may prevent each other from obtaining any rewards at all. Panic thus turns a potentially cooperative situation that would benefit each individual into a competitive situation that may benefit none.

Mintz devised a simple test for his hypothesis. He studied twenty-six groups, each consisting of fifteen to twenty-one college students. They were given a ten-inch-high glass bottle with a narrow neck. Each subject in a given group was to hold a string with an attached cone located inside the bottle. The task was to remove these cones from the bottle; however, because of the narrow neck, only one cone at a time could be removed. Two cones pulled up at the same time blocked each other, and any additional cones created the proverbial bottleneck.

Two basic conditions were created. In a cooperative condition, the situation was presented as a study of ability to collaborate with others. In a reward-and-fine condition, subjects were told they would play a game, the object of which was for each person to pull the cone out before a certain time limit. A system of graded monetary rewards and fines was announced so that everyone could potentially win—just as in the cooperative situation—if the cone were pulled out in time. The amounts were trivial, ranging from ten cents to twenty-five cents. Rewards and fines were introduced simply to underscore the game feature of the procedures and to demonstrate that even under such minimally threatening experimental conditions, maladaptive characteristics of panic situations could be produced.

The results were as expected. In the rewards-and-fines condition, bottlenecks developed as members competed to remove their own cone before the others. In the cooperative condition, bottlenecks never occurred. Each group quickly worked out orderly sequences of escape. In spite of the time taken up by the arrangements that needed to be made among members, the average time was significantly shorter in the cooperative conditions.

One of the variations of this situation was a heightened threat condition in which water was slowly fed into the bottom of the bottle. The object was to remove the cones before they became wet. The results remained essentially unchanged; still no bottlenecks developed under conditions of cooperation.

Mintz's research was the first to demonstrate that personal motivations may transform a situation into a competitive one, even when a cooperative solution is possible that would result in greater individual gain as well, a generalization later confirmed in several studies, with different methodologies, and with adult subjects as well as with children.

Further research on competition and cooperation did not issue from the Research Center for Group Dynamics. Most of that research explored still other novel theoretical formulations in the field of group dynamics. An important area, under the leadership of Festinger, focused on different aspects of social influence processes in communication. This research eventuated in several important theories, including dissonance theory and social comparison theory.

The early research showed that members communicated with each other in order to establish unanimity, or at least agreement. According to Festinger, there is a dual value in such uniformity: it allows groups to function, and it strengthens attitudes or opinions held by individual members.

The earlier formulation (Festinger 1950) emphasized primarily issues related to the first relationship: pressures exerted in groups on individuals. Individual group members were seen to put pressure on others, especially deviants, to come to agree with the group so that the purposes of the group as a whole could be served. Had this type of conceptualization been pursued, social psychology might have moved in quite different directions, perhaps developing concepts needed to describe different member behaviors in their attempts to reach a common goal. If so, the field would have invited the study of cooperation.

It was the second function of groups, however, in the service of individuals, that was taken up with great vigor at the time. The later publication (Festinger 1954) presented a formal exposition of social comparison theory. The focus was on the uses that individuals make of others to attain their own unique ends. Far from being hedonistic, it depicts individuals in pursuit of understanding themselves, others, and the world. It asserts that when objective ways of obtaining correct information are not available and when no means of validating opinions, values, and so forth are available, other persons serve as standards of veridicality. The epistemological argument may not have a Platonic or Kantian sweep, but its simplicity is deceptive. Freud may have sensitized us to our emotional interdependence; social comparison theory depicts humans as being dependent on each other on the rational level as well.

The influence of this theory in social psychology has been enormous. In our view, by focusing on interpersonal dynamics, it has contributed greatly to moving social psychology away from an emphasis on the group and into concern with person-to-person relations, a steadily increasing orientation of the discipline today. Social comparison theory has generated a very large body of research, and it shows no signs of abating.

During the 1950s, social comparison theory was not utilized as a basis for research on competition and cooperation. What research there was in this field was carried out by social psychologists who generally lacked a field-theoretical orientation. Because of its obvious importance, Deutsch's basic design was replicated, with some variations on the major theoretical theme of different goal interdependencies.

The first of this type of study followed closely on the heels of the Deutsch (1949) study. Stendler, Damrin, and Haines's (1951) exploratory research is of particular interest because it attempted to replicate the essential features of Deutsch's research in an investigation with second-grade school children. The authors studied a group of eight children who remained after school to paint two murals over a period of four days. Children were used as their own controls. Rewards for painting were packages of stickers like those elementary teachers give for outstanding work. In the cooperative condition, children were promised that if their mural was good enough to hang in the classroom, each would be given a package of stickers. In the competitive condition, which followed, the child who had painted the best would receive the reward. The others would receive no reward.

The group process seemed somewhat chaotic. In the competitive condition, two children disqualified themselves at the outset, asserting their inadequacy at painting. Nevertheless interaction generally resembled that found with college students. In cooperative work, children tended to break up into subgroups that worked together with much chatty banter back and forth, full of good humor and praise for each other's work. When competing, children tended to work alone, and there were indications of more negative interpersonal behaviors and somewhat less friendly interaction. Although children were used as subjects, the effects of factors related to their development were not considered.

Two other studies using college students (Grossack 1954; Gottheil 1955) focused on the effects of goal structure on group cohesiveness, a concept that gave promise of turning into a key variable to be considered in the study of group process. As was expected, cooperative work conditions heightened perceived attractiveness of members, and competitive conditions did not.

Research from this period was beginning to demonstrate that features of the reward structure other than degree of exclusivity were crucial in determining behavior in cooperative and competitive situations. In another of the few investigations of children during the 1950s, Phillips and D'Amico (1956) found that if during competitive games rewards were fairly evenly distributed—each child was able to win one of the games—children's behavior was friendlier and the cohesiveness increased as compared to groups in which only a few children were consistently the winners. This suggestive study points to the likely operation of normative influences such as principles of justice, fairness or equity determining importantly children's reactions in competitive actions.

Another significant clarification of the Deutsch study came at the end of this decade. Hammond and Goldman (1961) pointed out that Deutsch's goal conditions had been somewhat confounded. Members in each cooperative group in his study were to receive identical grades, and each group was compared with the other four groups so that the group with the highest average could be given an honors grade. Hammond and Goldman pointed out that the cooperative condition was not pure since members in that condition were also competing against the other four groups. From Sherif's study alone, it can be inferred that motivation should be higher under those conditions.

Hammond and Goldman removed the confounding factor by refining Deutsch's conditions through the addition of two more experimental conditions. They reproduced Deutsch's conditions as closely as possible, designating them as individual competitive and group competitive, respectively. The additions consisted of one individual noncompetitive condition (individuals received credit for their own work without keeping any others from receiving credit also) and a group noncompetitive condition (equal credit was also given to each member within a group but without regard to the performance of other groups). Their results showed unambiguously that competition, regardless of whether individual or group, is detrimental to group process and that performance benefits by cooperative conditions whether it involves additional intergroup competition or not. Their results thus mean that superior performance in Deutsch's study was not attributable to intergroup competition but was a function of the cooperative goal structure. Further it was inferred that the degree of positive interaction found in Deutsch's cooperative groups was likely to be an underestimation because it was apparently being depressed by the competitive component. There were some minor discrepancies in the two sets of results, but most likely they were attributable to slight methodological differences.

One of the most significant contributions in the area of competition and cooperation in this decade was provided by Deutsch who over a period of five years, sponsored by ONR, had been extending his theory and conducting research into cooperative conditions (Deutsch 1951, 1957, 1958, 1962). His concern was primarily with factors that determine an individual's decision to cooperate with another. In his first set of studies, he had focused on behaviors that derived from two different goal structures (contrient and promotively interdependent); now he turned to a consideration of factors determining "the resultant effective valence of cooperation as a path to each potential cooperator's goal" (Deutsch, 1957, p. 3).

He singled out two sets of factors: the desirability of the path and the subjective estimate of the probability that the path will lead to the desired goal. The determinants of the desirability of the path included valence of activities in which one expects to engage, valence of potential cooperators, valence of being identified as a member of the cooperating group, and evaluation of the degree to which the path leads to the desired goal.

The experimental methodology involved the familiar simulated environmental designs. As Deutsch said in describing one of the experiments: "Taking a cue from current national and international preoccupations, we told the subject that he was a spy who must steal a document within a specified short period of time" (1957, p. 7). The document was hidden inside a nest of boxes with combination locks that could be opened either by the subject alone or with assistance from another person. The subject then had to choose between various cooperative paths or an individual path. The series of studies that employed this methodology in fact extended Allport's inquiry into effects of working alone or in a group setting. For instance, the results showed that an experience of failure is more likely to lower the subjective probability of success with respect to future action among individuals working cooperatively and that the more successful an individual's past group experience, the more favorable is his estimate of subsequent success by means of group action.

In his theoretical treatment, Deutsch developed the concepts of trust and suspicion as relevant in cooperation. The experimental situations devised to test a variety of hypotheses (establishing conditions under which mutual trust will occur) involved the use of two-person games. This methodology began to be increasingly emphasized in social psychology during the 1950s, partly as a result of the development of mathematical game-theory models. By the end of the decade, social psychology was moving steadily away from field theoretical analyses in the dynamics of interpersonal situations, leaning toward the more generally held reinforcement models of behavior theory. For example, Thibaut and Kelley (1959) wrote a book that reflected and contributed to this trend. Their conceptualization of human motivation in social interaction was essentially one of a calculus of gains and losses. Interacting persons were said to be motivated to maximize their gains and minimize their losses. The authors further assumed that much of behavior reflects a conflict between motives to compete against others or to cooperate with others. Thus a conflict model had come to be seen as an appropriate conceptualization for research and theories in cooperation and competition.

The Sixties

The Social Context of Education

Many social analysts consider this decade one of the most turbulent periods in American history, with major conflict centered around civil rights. Arguments reached deeply into beliefs, values, and life-styles and into questioning the social structure that perpetuated them. Schools were especially singled out as public institutions where children's inhumanity to children was fostered.

Attacks focused primarily on the school's presumed socialization of children toward competitive interrelations with others. So-called radical romantic critics of education (such as Goodman 1960, and Friedenberg 1963 in the United States, and Neill 1969 in Great Britain) were at the forefront of those condemning schools, calling them oppressive, high pressured, boring, regimented, cutthroat, and irrelevant. Educators who espoused these beliefs embraced, and in turn were embraced by, various youth groups. Clamour was strong for loosening or doing away altogether with existing educational structures, banishing grades, removing admissions requirements, introducing relevant courses into curricula, removing prior regulations to permit free choice, and allowing student participation in all such administrative and curricular decisions. Mass media kept these youth revolts in the public eye, treating it periodically to glimpses of sit-ins in front of high school principals' offices or to overnight campouts in college deans' or admissions' quarters.

These incidents were symptoms of wider conflicts. The polar conflict involves a society's normative prescriptions: whether to extol its citizens to distinguish themselves over others (and in order to do so, to depreciate others) or to live and work together peaceably. This conflict is most evident in the schools. In the 1930s, the introduction of cooperative learning procedures was strongly opposed by another segment of society in defense of a more individualistic style. In fact, the reactions of the 1930s to alleged progressivists' predilections for collective classroom practices never really died. Temporarily submerged during the war years, criticism reappeared and exploded in scathing condemnation of progressive education. In 1953 alone, bookstores offered this choice among current best-sellers: Lynd's *Quackery in the Public Schools*, Bestor's *Educational Wastelands*, Hutchins's *The Conflict in Education*, and a year later, Smith's *The Diminished Mind*.

The call in all of these books was for the cultivation of the ability to think through training in the basic academic disciplines. The Council for Basic Education was founded in 1956 "to advance the view that schools exist to provide the essential skills of language, numbers, and orderly thought, and to transmit in a reasoned pattern the intellectual, moral, and aesthetic heritage of civilized man" (Cremin 1961, p. 346). In 1957, the Russians' launching of the first satellite occasioned a shocked public outcry that demanded an end to coddling children in school and a return to rigorous schooling. Admiral Hyman Rickover expressed the general sentiments: "Our technological supremacy has been called into question, and we know we have to deal with a formidable competitor. . . . Parental objectives no longer coincide with those professed by the progressive educationists" (ibid. p. 347). His plea for a return to basics in education was widely supported (see Gardner 1961).

A sound basic education with academic breadth and rigor tends to be interpreted by many—laymen as well as educators—as demanding the impersonal, silent, stern, barren, memorizing-reciting procedures that have characterized most of the past history of education. In response to the challenge of the 1950s for excellence, admissions requirements were raised in schools and the amount of knowledge required of students increased. In attempts to enforce these standards, assessment methods were used including daily objective quizzes, standard achievement tests for entry into most colleges, and qualifying examinations for entry into graduate institutions.

With the rising expectations of the 1960s, for increased educational opportunities for all segments of society protests were inevitable from those most affected—the students—and those associated with the young—parents and educators. Once again, the pendulum began to swing away from competitive structures and to move toward an emphasis on individualized learning or cooperative learning structures. Open classrooms and integrated days of the British experimental elementary schools were quickly adapted to

American settings. Alternative high schools appeared to humanize schooling and provide opportunities for individuals in group settings. Peer teaching, cross-age learning, and value-clarification programs were introduced into the schools.

Yet in a society that prizes its individualistic ethos, cooperative learning programs cannot be integrated comfortably into the curricula of most public schools; they are, like minority group children, a foreign import. Furthermore proponents of cooperative learning structures, put on the defensive, demanded unconditional support. Others, espousing the ideology that humanistic values are not amenable to scientific scrutiny, rejected any attempts to evaluate their new projects. This type of anti-intellectual attitude prevented any demonstration of real or potential strengths; not having diagnosed specific weaknesses, supporters of cooperative learning programs lost the chance to improve them. After the humanistic flurry of the 1960s had peaked, some programs were left to die untested; others, found wanting, were abandoned altogether. Some, including many structural changes made in schools, survived.

Research in Contrasting Competitive and Cooperative Working Conditions

During the 1950s, studies in this area typically varied specified features of competitive or cooperative situations and determined consequent interpersonal behaviors. In the 1960s, the focus shifted toward juxtaposition of the two goal structures and an increased concern with contrasting performance in these respective conditions. Miller and Hamblin (1963) listed twenty-four studies in this field, fourteen of which showed that competition had resulted in greater productivity than had cooperative conditions; the remaining ten studies had found opposite results. The authors hypothesized that the two conditions were not unidimensional. They argued that differential performance results could be accounted for by postulating not only different goal interdependencies but differences in task interdependence as well. The role of task interdependence had been singled out somewhat earlier by Thomas (1957), an important theoretical advance, pursued further in other research during this period (Raven and Eachus 1963; Jones and Vroom 1964; Crombag 1966).

Minisystems in Social Psychology

The theoretical structures that had been developed in the 1950s were now being expanded into more precise theoretical formulations. In the process, however, the social psychological theories of the 1960s took a different direction from earlier ones, moving from concerns with dynamics of groups to a primary concern with individual dynamics.

It took at least a decade for a number of such minitheoretical systems to develop, and often longer to make their appearance in print. Heider's influential cognitive balance theory, published in 1946, found its variants about a decade later in cognitive consistency theories:—Osgood and Tannenbaum (1955), Abelson and Rosenberg (1958), and Festinger (1957)—all of which was brought together in comprehensive form in a volume edited by Feldman (1966). The interests of the 1950s in social influence processes continued in Brehm's *Theory of Psychological Reactance* (1966) and Jones's *Theory of Ingratiation* (1966). Although Heider's 1958 volume contained the basic outlines of attribution theory, it was left for Kelley (1967) to formalize and add experimental support. Theory and research on relative deprivation, with origins dating as far back as World War II (Stouffer et al. 1949), integrated by Adams (1965) and Pettigrew (1967), contributed importantly to the currently dominant equity theory. A final important example is Festinger's original statement of social comparison theory (1954), which stimulated over seventy studies to which a whole journal issue was devoted a little over a decade later (Latané 1966).

These were the major theoretical models that dominated the late 1960s and generated the research of the 1970s. None of these minitheories, which were primarily concerned with cognitive processes within individuals, spoke directly to interpersonal behaviors in competition and cooperation. The effects of this emphasis on personal dynamics were felt indirectly in this area in that problems were recast in terms of dyadic interpersonal relationships. Game-theoretical formulations and related methodologies came to be seen as the most appropriate tools for investigating cooperation and competition. Working within the game-theoretical context, two social psychologists—Madsen and McClintock, respectively,—dominated research on children's competition and cooperation during the late 1960s and into the 1970s.

Contriency and Means Control in Conflict

In his 1969 presidential address at the meetings of the Eastern Psychological Association, Deutsch (1969) asserted that he was "brash enough to claim that the games people play as subjects in the laboratory experiments may have some relevance for war and peace." Continuing his interest in conflict resolution, Deutsch, in collaboration with Krauss, brought a field-theoretical conception to the design of an important piece of simulated action research (Deutsch and Krauss 1960). The study continued inquiry into forces that would increase or decrease competition or cooperation.

The task consisted of a board game in the shape of a road map, reminiscent perhaps of the Lewinian mapping of a life space. Two players, role-playing truckers from two different companies, were to originate their trip from two different locations and to deliver their merchandise at two different destinations. There were alternate routes provided, and, taking these, the two player-truckers would not have had to meet at all; both could arrive at their own destinations. So far in their locomotion through space, there were no overlapping regions, and the two individual goals were not contrient. However, a one-lane road was provided, which constituted an alternate, more direct, and shorter route. The truckers' pay was to be determined inversely to the amount of time spent on the road. The player who took the direct route clearly had an advantage because the players were told to amass as much money as possible for themselves. Taking the shorter route was to the advantage of both. Even though the individual goals were different, the means constituted by the overlapping region were an area of potential conflict. The players could have made several rational solutions, which would have been to their mutual advantage: they could have alternated in taking the shortest road or they could have agreed to wait a few seconds at the gate and take turns being first across the road and still both be early. But since they were competing for pay, very little of this kind of collaboration occurred. The truckers hurried to beat each other, each sitting at his end and waiting for the other to retreat to allow the self to pass on the one-way road. In another condition, each player's power to block the other was increased. Both were given gates at their respective ends that could lock the other out; they were, to use another favorite Lewinian term, *gatekeepers* who had *means control* over each other's activity regions by erecting barriers to locomotion. When each was provided this additional powerful weapon, the conflict was escalated. The degree of cooperation decreased, with both players often sitting behind their respective gates, growling at each other. Eventually one would give in, erect the barrier to make sure the other player could not take the shorter route either, and then back up and take the longer route himself. Both players ended up losing points. Both the trucking game and Mintz's earlier bottleneck study are excellent demonstrations of situations in which competitive behavior is maladaptive yet persons persist in it.

One more important issue needs to be pointed out. The trucking game limited the range of behavior in which the players might engage. A choice had to be made. Alternatives included to beat the other by being speedier, to outwait or to outwit the other by invectives at the gate; or to develop some sort of rational division of labor as a result of the stalemate. The focus was on alternative player strategies. This limitation of behavior possibilities meant moving toward further purification of the two conditions and further delimiting choice strategies of the two players. This could be accomplished by employing game matrixes that reduced the behavior of each player to one of two possible choices. And thus we find, indeed, by the end of the decade, almost exclusive focus on choice behavior as a function of the matrix provided (for example, Deutsch and Lewicki 1970). By then naturalistic studies of interpersonal behaviors under competitive and cooperative conditions had slowed to a trickle.

Several other noteworthy trends in social psychology of the 1960s may help to explain further the direction in cooperation and competition research. Within the minisystems, specific concepts were splintered into yet more miniscule, more easily measurable operations. For example, cooperation as behavior has been split up to include a variety of prosocial individual behaviors, in particular helping or empathy or other altruistic acts. The complex concept of cohesiveness has been reduced to a simple accounting of "A's attraction for B." In fact, the large, live, interacting groups of the 1940s and 1950s also disappeared and were replaced by dyadic interactions in competing or cooperating groups.

Perhaps the tightening economy of the late 1960s, which made obtaining grants more difficult, affected research design. Maintenance of paid participants and observers became more difficult. The economy not only affected research design but the very nature of theory making as well. It may have also contributed to the trend toward substitution of individual concepts for group concepts (Steiner 1972; A. Pepitone 1976).

Employment of the game-theoretical research model fits well into these trends. It is based on the assumption that choices are motivated by the need of each player to maximize gains and minimize losses. Furthermore it usually involves only two subjects who must make simple choices, which are operationalized by a push of a button. Experiments can even be conducted by one researcher working alone.

In experimental games, one's own success or failure is dependent on one's own choice strategy as well as that of a partner. The experimenter can arrange the rules in various ways. One person's gain, for example, may constitute another person's loss. Such zero-sum games represent the most essential features of contrient competitive situations. The experimenter can also arrange the reward structure in such a way that both participants can make choices that bring gains to both or losses to both. Choices in such nonzero-sum games reflect the promotively interdependent relationships characteristic of cooperative conditions.

Wrightsman, O'Connor, and Baker (1972), disclaiming complete coverage, listed over a thousand items in their bibliography, which covers mixed-motive games up to 1970. Among the most frequently investigated topics were effects of reward values and effects of the strategy of the other player and coalition formations. Perhaps the most striking finding, which runs consistently through all of the studies, is that players do not behave quite as rationally as expected. They do not always wish to maximize their gains and minimize their losses. Sometimes they prefer to take a loss if it enables them to maximize the difference between themselves and their competitor. Subjects, especially males, tend to prefer overwhelmingly to make competitive choices even when the matrix favors cooperative choices very heavily. However, cooperation can be influenced through instructions or permission to communicate.

This type of research has been criticized for its artificiality. Communication between the two members is generally not allowed, and there are large differences in choice behavior, depending on whether the reward consists of play money or real currency (Gergen 1969). There has also been concern over the value of choice behavior as a major approach to understanding competitive behavior in everyday life. One may well question with Vinacke (1969) the utility of choice behavior as a means of understanding, especially, cooperative behaviors. Even more critical is the fact that cooperative acts are seen simply as attempts to coordinate individual acts, so that each player can obtain her own reward. In fact, this definition abandons the concept of a mutually shared goal or of group participation in the fashioning of a common product.

The validity of gaming methodologies depends to a large extent on the subject's understanding of the matrixes that present the distribution of reward structures for both players. Of course, this cognitive prerequisite makes such games unsuitable for children, especially the very young who have not reached the necessary stage of cognitive development. But the difficulty can be obviated by the use of various tasks presumed to depend on minimal cognitive understanding and requiring only simple mechanical operations within the reach of even preschoolers.

Research on Children's Competitive or
Cooperative Preferences

Beginning with the mid-1960s, and extending through the 1970s, Madsen and his associates developed a series of dyadic games that allow comparison of children's preferences for competitive or cooperative interaction, across ages and various cultures. The earliest and perhaps best-known task is the marble pull game, which simulates essentially a tug-of-war. A plastic cup that can be separated in the middle is placed on a small table. Each half of the cup is attached to a string and held by a child at each end of the table. If both children pull simultaneously, the holder splits apart, and a marble in it rolls off to the side of the table. In such a case, no one wins. If one child lets go of the string, the other may pull the marble holder over to her side and let the marble drop into a goal cup provided there. The giving up of one allows the other to win. The game is played for marbles, which are then exchanged for prizes. In the marble pull game, there is always a conflict of interest in that the children's goals are contrient. There is no possibility for an equitable outcome, short of taking turns at winning (considered a cooperative act).

The cooperation board game is a modification of the marble game. It is designed so that behavior that is instrumental to one child's goal attainment is not necessarily detrimental to the goal attainment of the other. Instead of the cup, there is a movable pointer, to which several strings are attached. Each child holds one string in each hand. There are target spots in front of each child as well as on one or both sides. One child alone can easily pull the pointer onto his target spot, but if both children pull simultaneously in the opposite direction, it is difficult to move the pointer to any target spot. Both children have to coordinate their pulls on one side and refrain from pulling strings on the other side. The cooperation board thus requires more prolonged and more coordinated collaboration, which may permit simultaneous individual gains to both children, not possible with the marble pull game.

One of the early developmental investigations, consisting of six separate experiments and using both of these methodological tools, was carried out by Nelson in a doctoral dissertation directed by Madsen (Nelson 1970). Exploring over an age range of 5 to 10 years, he found no age and sex differences in cooperation with the marble pull game. This result could not be interpreted unambiguously, however. Young children, while making self-maximizing responses, could have been as capable of turn taking as could older ones and/or motivated to maximize their own gains by competitive responses. Older children could have been more adept at turn taking but also more competitively oriented. Nelson's second experiment, which employed the cooperation board, showed clear developmental trends that have been supported in most of the other studies. Five year olds had unequal interaction patterns, with one tending to be submissive and allowing the more assertive child to pull the target toward her end. Six year olds were most competitive; they prevented each other from winning by pulling simultaneously in both directions. Children 8 to 10 years old were significantly more cooperative; by the fourth and last trial, all pairs collaborated to receive a marble each.

Nelson devised still a third game, the pull-block Game, reminiscent of Mintz's bottleneck game. Each child had a rope with four blocks on each, which had to be pulled through a common opening. Here, too, blocking time, recorded automatically, showed no age or sex differences. However, systematic differences were found as the reward structure was varied. Although kindergartners were not affected by reward contingencies, all of the other age groups had significantly greater blocking times with individual rewards as opposed to group rewards. And interestingly, with individual reward conditions, boys had longer blocking times than the counterpart girls, presumably reflecting their stronger competitive motivations. Following through with more fine-grained analyses, Nelson also demonstrated that prior experience with group rewards increased subsequent collaborative behavior of children. He concluded from this series that older children generally can and do cooperate more with each other if this behavior is not interfered with by a simultaneous presence of competitive choice possibilities.

A later series of studies by Madsen and Kagan (Madsen 1971; Kagan and Madsen 1971, 1972a, 1972b) using the cooperation board and several additional game tasks essentially corroborated Nelson's findings, with some minor presumably task-related differences, and extended them. They showed that when American children are given cooperative and competitive response alternatives, older children (ages 7 to 11) overwhelmingly opt for the latter. In several studies, older children persisted in their competitive strategies, even if they were obviously maladaptive (just as did adults in the trucking game).

Refinement in methodology allowed for the elimination of several possible alternative interpretations of these results. Employing a cooperation box, Kagan and Madsen (1972a) showed that 7 to 11 year olds were quite capable of collaborating when necessary and when no alternative to cooperation was provided. The box contained a lid with four spring latches requiring the simultaneous use of four hands. Being instructed that they could proceed any way they wanted, "almost all pairs worked together vigorously to open the box." This study, aside from supporting Nelson's conclusions, removed the alternative interpretation that American children's competitive choice prevalence is a function of their inability to cooperate. One may entertain some reservations about the type of cooperation displayed: since in the cooperative condition each child was promised a toy located inside the box. It can be argued that each child simply opened the box for his or her own gain. Required collaboration was minimal, demanding only simultaneous individual action.

Children's various motive structures were investigated further using a choice card methodology (Kagan and Madsen 1972b), later adapted by various researchers in the 1970s, including an elaboration by Kagan (1977). Children sit facing each other, with large domino-like cards between them on a table. Different numbers of marbles are placed on the cards. A child is asked to make a choice from the nearest marbles, leaving whatever marbles remain on the partner's side for that person. The distribution of marbles on different cards constitutes different absolute and relative choice possibilities, just as do the matrixes presented to adults in the laboratory. Here 8 to 10 year olds were significantly more rivalrous than 5 to 6 year olds. Just like American adult subjects, older children attempted to lower the outcomes of their peers, even if it meant sacrificing own absolute gain.

These series of developmental researches were undertaken in cross-cultural settings, primarily involving Mexican and Mexican-American children in comparison with Anglo-American children. Unfortunately these early studies are confounded because the Anglo-American children were almost always from urban Los Angeles, and the Mexican and Mexican-American children in several comparisons were from small rural villages. In general, the studies show urban Anglo-American children of all ages to be least cooperative and most competitive, with this cultural difference tending to increase with age. Yet another methodology, the circle board game (Kagan and Madsen 1971), was especially useful in highlighting these differences. The object of the game is for children to take turns in making moves from one side of the board to the opposite, the winner being the one who reaches the opposite side in the fewest moves. Children may assist each other or block each move. Interestingly Mexican-American children tried to avoid conflict by making sideward moves rather than blocking opponents as did the Anglo-American children or taking turns assisting others as did the Mexican children. Competing Anglo-American children complained that the game was too hard and that no one could possibly win, ignoring the possible cooperative solution of taking turns in assisting each other.

Continuing into the 1970s was another series of experimental cross-cultural studies, these carried out in Israel (Shapira and Madsen 1969, 1974; Shapira and Lomranz 1972). All three studies employed the cooperation board. Here too, as expected, kibbutz children of elementary school age were found more cooperative than Israeli children raised in urban nonkibbutz settings. This was so regardless of the form of reward contingency, although even kibbutz children were affected somewhat adversely by individual rewards as compared with their performance under group rewards. A comparable group of rural Arab children was found less competitively motivated than an urban Israeli sample but more competitive than the kibbutz sample (Shapira and Lomranz 1972). One of the later studies (Shapira and Madsen 1974) showed that even when there is no need to contribute to the group, kibbutz children do so.

This research presents a consistent picture of rural children collaborating more than urban children, and middle-class urban American children being most strongly motivated to compete. This pioneering series does precisely what May and Doob had recommended over thirty years ago: that research in this area be conducted with uniform methodologies, over a wider age range, and in a variety of sociocultural settings. To be sure, there are some problems related to each of these features in the Madsen research. One is American children's frequent association of competition with games. If so, then game-theoretical research may stimulate competitive motivations that are not representative of their strength in other situations.

Most difficulties with this research are those inherent in all game-theoretical research: the absence of extended social interaction. Particularly salient as applied to children is Vinacke's (1969) general criticism of gaming methodologies' contribution to an understanding of behavior in cooperative situations. Questions pertaining to the development of a variety of interpersonal skills needed in cooperative situations are of signal importance in the study of children. Yet they are not, and perhaps cannot be, handled by the use of even as original gaming methodologies as those devised by Madsen and his associates. The general weakness of game-theoretical methodologies is that, by design, they demand minimal interpersonal interaction.

Game-theoretical research calls for highly limited responses. The result is that the researchers themselves are too often left guessing; they have a number of alternative interpretation possibilities to cope with, principally around issues of motivational significance of the observed choices. This is particularly true with regard to the youngest preschool sample. Considering the dominant-submission patterns reported by Nelson, conclusions appear hardly justified that the children's behavior represented a preference for cooperative interaction, much less that cooperation was a more dominant pattern for them than it was for the older children. The latter, faced only with limited-choice possibilities not of their own making, may act in terms of their guesses about experimenter expectations. One wonders to what extent older children perceive the experimenter's charge as encouragement to be self-assertive and to maximize their own relative gain. To ascribe such perception to cultural differences is fraught with difficulties also. The research ignores the possibility of cohort differences in children's intelligence, abilities, personalities, and so forth. Comparisons with Mexican and Mexican-American children leave one with an exaggerated impression of Anglo-American children's competitiveness, somewhat unjustified in the light of McClintock's subsequent cross-cultural findings.

One study that appeared in the mid-1960s obviated several of the shortcomings of game research (Goldberg and Maccoby 1965). The investigation is interesting for a number of reasons, although at the time it was little noticed. It is one of the few studies in this period that continued to be concerned with effects of group participation and takes off explicitly from Mintz's findings that group reward stimulate highly efficient collaboration among members who would otherwise compete to achieve their individual goals. The specific hypothesis tested was that previous experience in groups with changing participants affords an opportunity for trying out different roles and hence will result in a superior collaborative effort toward a group goal than will stable group membership. Subjects were groups of four second graders.

Although their hypothesis could have been pursued within the game-theoretical framework, the authors devised an ingenious, simple, alternative methodology. The group task consisted of building a tower with three-inch colored cubes. Blocks distributed equally to each child were color coded. Group goals and individual goals were clearly separated, the former being to build the highest tower as a group, the latter being candy awarded to each child for each block she managed to place onto the tower. Thus individual contributions were rewarded, but the task required group effort. The structure needed to be continuously stabilized while it was being erected; any one member could jeopardize the fate of the other members and the group as a whole.

This procedure yielded a variety of behavioral measures. The results were exceedingly interesting, perhaps just because the hypothesis was not confirmed. The study design and controls allowed unambiguous interpretation of the findings that performance was significantly better under stable group membership. The authors concluded that a stable group composition over a period of time allows the development of individual member roles and superior coordination of effort.

Goldberg and Maccoby did not address developmental issues in this research. Similarly although the Madsen series was concerned with age trends, conceptualization of developmental issues was minimal. The lack of attention to this factor may be in part a reflection of the times, considering that the American psychological community had its first major expert introduction to the foremost developmental theorist only in 1963, with the publication of Flavell's *The Developmental Psychology of Jean Piaget*. It is noteworthy, too, that in this book's index there is no category entry referring to social behavior or social development. The only social reference cited is to socialized speech. Search under "egocentrism" is rewarded with a subheading that reads: "removed by social interaction."

Two important areas of inquiry into children's social development mushroomed in the 1960s, however. One, the area of prosocial behaviors, received its impetus from social psychological theory and research; the other, that of children's social cognitions, was based on Piaget and developed rapidly into one of the most researched areas in American developmental psychology. Both areas are highly relevant to the study of children's collaborative interactions.

The study of altruism, empathy, sympathy, identification, and other prosocial motives and behaviors has as long a tradition as there was speculation about man's inhumanity to man. For social psychology, 1964 marked the beginning of intensified scientific inquiry into prosocial behaviors. It was occasioned by the subsequently well-publicized Kitty Genovese case, the case of a New York woman who was brutally murdered in the presence of many onlookers who made no attempts to save her. The murder started a flood of studies testing a variety of hypotheses to explain such bystander inaction. The most influential was the program initiated by Latané and

Darley (1968, 1970), who posited an inverse relation between number of witnesses present and readiness to help. Research multiplied rapidly and almost immediately involved an examination of parallel hypotheses with children as subjects. In a comprehensive review several years later of the major investigations on children's prosocial behaviors (Bryan 1975), we found approximately seventy studies (excluding studies dealing with cooperation and those prior to 1966). Staub's (1978, 1979) two volumes on adult and children's prosocial behavior attest to the continuing interest in this area.

The social responsiveness of children has been explored primarily in two areas of inquiry: study of aiding or rescuing behaviors and sharing or giving behaviors. The former parallels directly the methodology devised by Latané and Rodin (1969) in their study *A Lady in Distress*. It was followed almost immediately by Staub's (1970a, 1970b, 1971) sequel, *A Child in Distress*. Here subject A, in room A, hears sounds of distress from an adjacent room, as if someone had fallen off a chair. The question is whether A will rescue B. What conditions maintain or change a child's nonresponsiveness: situational cues, reinforcement, models, normative expectations, exhortations and prohibitions, or something else?

Some of the research continued to study helping behaviors, which had been examined sporadically in previous decades, including sharing (perhaps crayons needed to color a picture), giving (the favorite technique involves distribution of M&Ms to another child not necessarily present), or aiding (such as picking up materials dropped by the experimenter). There was some indication of inter-relationships between the various measures (Midlarsky and Bryan 1967), but on the whole, correlations between the various forms of helping are not very high and, we judge, unlikely to be any higher with collaborative behaviors.

Of at least equal relevance to our inquiry into children's cooperation is the area of children's social cognitions, which also witnessed large growth in number of published studies beginning in the late 1960s. Contrary to work on prosocial behavior, this research had its basis almost exclusively in developmental psychology and to a large extent was derived from Piaget's work on children's understanding of the physical world. Research and theory in this area addressed itself to the development of children's abilities to understand the internal reactions of another—what he or she perceives, thinks, feels, intends, and so on. Most of the theories that generated this research were variations of Piaget's stage model and depended heavily on the notion of age-related ability to make inferences about the internal states of others. The methodology involved the use of pictures, filmstrips, stories, or other children as particular stimulus figures, often in the context of social episodes, which then required of the subject various descriptions, interpretations, explanations, or understandable communications to another.

The social cognitions explored represent cognitive skills that appear essential to any interdependent collaborative interaction. Therefore this body of data seems exceedingly relevant to the study of children's interpersonal behaviors. Unfortunately the very extensive review by Shantz (1975), anticipating such hopes, is discouraging: "One might well expect that there would be a good deal of information relating the child's understanding of other people to his actual social behavior, but there is not. . . . In fact, the relation between social cognition and interpersonal behavior may be one of the largest unexplored areas in developmental psychology today" (p. 303). On the other hand Shantz concluded by placing her hopes in social psychology: "The use of adult social psychological theories might make an important contribution to the process of formulating questions about interpersonal understanding of the child" (p. 315). Clearly combined developmental and social psychological attack seemed indicated.

The Seventies

The decade was characterized by multidisciplinary and interdisciplinary focus on the child in the fields of education, anthropology, social psychology, and developmental psychology. The theories and methodologies used may forecast some possible trends of the next decades, and they constitute a bridge to research in which many of us may be active participants.

It would be no misnomer to call the 1970s the decade of the child. There appeared to be a confluence among different academic disciplines and various child-oriented professions, uniting in a common focus on children. There was a sense of freedom to transcend confining boundaries, reminiscent of the many child-welfare activities generated by the child study movement of the 1920s and 1930s. Such parallels were apparent in the emphasis on the rights of children, ranging from those with physical and psychological problems to the intellectually gifted. Consequent new state or federally mandated and financed programs were created for special education, child abuse, and day care. As had child psychoanalysts of the 1930s, so social psychiatry of the 1970s called attention to the needs of children. A five-volume series by Robert Coles (1977), for example, described the needs of children from all parts of the country and all walks of life. Relevant here too is the work of Kenneth Keniston, known for his studies of youth of the 1960s. A decade later, he became chairman of the Carnegie Council for Child Development and editor of its authoritative volume *All Our Children: The American Family under Pressure* (1977).

Keniston's title is entirely fitting; it signifies that the child was no longer considered in isolation or merely in its wider social context but in terms of the family system. Children's roles as transmitters of generational values and carriers of family dynamics were emphasized by as diverse family therapists as Minuchin (1974) and Boszormenyi-Nagy and Spark (1973). From their own distinct vantage points, anthropologists singled out children and their function as culture carriers (Whiting and Whiting 1975; Graves and Graves 1976).

Historians of education by no means stood outside the generational emphasis. Scholarly interest in the child in the family context was apparent in the work of Lawrence Cremin, professor of history of education and president of Teachers College at Columbia University. In the first of a projected three-volume history of American education (Cremin 1970), one section was devoted to a detailed description of children's education as received within households of colonial times. At the close of the decade, educators at Teachers College, with a long tradition of relating education to society, stood once again at the forefront of systematic historical research into the family as educator (Leichter 1979). Interestingly little attention was paid to the family as creator of various competitive and cooperative conditions in the life space of children. In this regard, the emphasis in the 1970s still was primarily on the school environment.

We return full circle through the family to the larger sociohistorical contexts of children's lives. Revisionist historians of education in particular began documenting diverse socializing functions of schools that may have fulfilled larger societal goals than merely serving cognitive instrumental functions (for example, Katz 1975; Karier 1975; Spring 1978).

As to educational institutions and activities of those involved in educating the young, the decade ended very differently from the way it had begun. Out of the plethora of creative, albeit haphazard, attempts of the 1960s to loosen traditional achievement-oriented structures in the classroom emerged the somewhat more systematic humanizing trends in the early 1970s. Many high schools and colleges had found at least some of the student demands of the 1960s reasonable. Many educational institutions had grown into less impersonal places, with widened course offerings that allowed for interdepartmental and other innovative combinations of learning content. Voices clamoring for deschooling had faded away.

At the end of the 1970s, the only consistent and incontrovertible fact was a constant fiscal crisis at all levels and in all types of educational institutions. Inflationary rates coupled with continuing low birthrates (in 1977 reaching the lowest point in American history) spell continuing entrenchment for educational institutions of the 1980s. Instructing a small number of pupils in one classroom—the essence of humanist education from Quintillian to Vittorino da Feltre and many contemporary teachers' dream—was obviously considered financially unsound. There was a drastic reduction in alternative schools, and many public and private schools were closed. For many schools that survived the financial crisis and continued to exist into the 1980s, entrenchment meant abolition of human relations programs and other so-called personal or cultural enrichment programs, more frequently being considered frills. Some cities included in this category even kindergarten and summer school instruction.

One of the positive contributions of the 1970s was a recognition that legislation pertaining to integration is insufficient in improving interpersonal relationships among diverse ethnic groups. Desegregation orders were being carried out more effectively during the 1970s, and continue to be so enforced into the 1980s. One of the few areas in which human relations were given their rightful priority in educational institutions at the end of the decade was in several pilot programs developed specifically in response to the perceived needs of newly desegregated schools. The projects were based on the common assumption that desegregation does not stop in the morning with the school bus at the schoolhouse door. Rather desegregation was seen as one of the first important steps in a long, complex process, which needs constant assessment and implementation. Here, then, was the potential for the development of a highly important, socially demanded area of action research. The diverse procedures were all based on creation of cooperative learning conditions in the classrooms. They are rooted in the contact theory of Allport (1954), who suggested that sheer contact alone, under certain conditions, may actually reinforce prejudice. He proceeded to spell out various factors—notably equal status contact or presence of common goals—whose presence might bring about positive interpersonal relations.

Cooperative Classroom Conditions and Ethnic Relations

We single out three major action programs developed on the assumption that integration must be carried out within a pattern of equal status interaction within the place where learning takes place. A persistent spokesperson for this point of view is Stuart Cook, now at the University of Colorado, who was the first director of the Commission on Community Interrelations (CCI) established by Lewin in the mid-1940s. One of the earliest and most dedicated proponents of action research, Cook is now implementing it in the classroom. Another important variation of this type of research is headed by DeVries, now at the Center for Creative Leadership at Greensboro, North Carolina, and Slavin, at the Center for Social Organization of Schools at Johns Hopkins University. Slavin's is clearly one of the largest, most ambitious classroom learning programs attempted. Based on Slavin's (1978) report, we counted for the period 1972-1978 over four thousand students who participated in classroom studies involving the two main procedures devised by the combined DeVries and Slavin research forces. The third of these programs, developed by Aronson at the University of California, has come to be known as the jigsaw approach to learning.

The three approaches are more similar to each other than they are different and share some common features of method and design. The large classroom is broken up into various small groups of four to six members. Each small group is deliberately composed of heterogeneous members, who represent the range of either differences in achievement scores or an equal mix of the various ethnic groups found in the classroom. In each program, members of the small groups are required to collaborate on learning tasks. Interestingly none of the three approaches utilizes a common interdependent reward structure; pupil evaluation is based in each case on individual student performance. The small groups are referred to as experimental groups and paired with control classrooms conducted by teachers lecturing in the traditional manner and students participating within the whole-class setting. Teachers generally are their own control by teaching one or more pairs consisting of both types of classrooms.

Group-dynamics theory points to three sources that serve as bases for a person's attraction to groups; attraction may reside in other group members, in the group's activities, or in the group goals (see, for instance, Cartwright and Zander 1968). Although not so described explicitly by any of the three research teams, in fact the three approaches differ in the particular source emphasized in their attempts to strengthen individual learning and mutual positive regard. That is, Cook et al. attempted to increase member interdependence by manipulation of member characteristics, Aronson by manipulation of the group's activities, and Slavin and DeVries by manipulations involving group and individual goals.

Cook's procedures are simplest, relying on small-group interaction processes to reveal characteristics of individual members to each others, which in turn are hypothesized to change their attitudes toward more positive liking. The major piece of classroom research (Weigel, Wiser, and Cook 1975) involved white, black, and Mexican-American seventh and tenth graders in newly desegregated high schools who found themselves in what Cook and his associates referred to as "involuntary cross-ethnic contact." In the six pairs of classrooms examined, students studied materials from a standard English course for one hour a day for one semester. In the small-group classrooms, cross-ethnic helping increased dramatically, as did cross-ethnic choices between white and Mexican-American students. Such trends were not found for black and white attraction toward each other, nor were favorable changes in beliefs established about other ethnic groups or in basic attitudes regarding integration.

The jigsaw approach (Aronson 1978; Aronson et al. 1975, 1977) relies most heavily on member interdependencies created by the structure of specific learning tasks. In essence, the approach structures interaction by giving each member within a small group one segment of the class lesson. Aronson describes the process as analogous to the assembly of a jigsaw puzzle. Each member is responsible for teaching his own part to the other members, but the student need not struggle alone with the learning part. Each student meets first with members of the other groups who have the same segment. These counterpart groups are homogeneous in learning content although not necessarily in learning skill. Children discuss the material with each other and organize it for later presentation to their respective jigsaw groups. Thus the learning process requires continuous collaborative interaction with others and demands responsible initiative and active participation of each child in a nonthreatening, almost cushioned environment. The model envisages the child as a contributor and active assimilator rather than a passive, teacher-dependent child or a child haunted by fear of failure or driven by needs to best others.

Evaluations of the effects of the process to date compared with traditional classes report significant increases in self-esteem, better attitudes toward school, and increased liking not only of members of their own work group but liking of other children in the jigsaw classroom as well (Blaney et al. 1977; Aronson, Bridgman, and Geffner 1978). Because of the known association between high self-esteem and better academic performance, Lucker et al. (1977) investigated the achievement of fifth- and sixth-grade students taught in jigsaw classrooms for two weeks. The achievement of Anglos remained unchanged, but Mexican-American students improved significantly even within this short period.

The origin of the third approach, the team game tournament (TGT) is detailed in DeVries and Slavin's (1978) joint review. They discussed its social context in the 1960s, singling out high school students' nonresponsiveness to academic subject matters, the increasingly widening range of skill levels in public schools, and the increased necessity for teaching basic skills in the face of student disinterest. Additional support for the methodology was found both in the group-dynamics literature on the effectiveness of intrateam cooperation and interteam competition as exemplified in the research of Sherif et al. (1961) and in reinforcement theory, which amply demonstrates the efficacy of reward contingencies.

The authors, oriented toward arousing each student's interest, attempted to motivate students by placing them sequentially in intrateam cooperative as well as interteam competitive conditions. In TGT, ideally, teams are equated in a given classroom so that each team contains a high achiever, two average achievers, and one low achiever. Members within given teams collaborate at set times in helping each other master assigned learning content. They may use memory drills, help each other to review or to understand assignments, quiz each other, and so on. In tournaments, which take place once or twice each week, teams are split up so that each student competes against students from other teams within the same ability range. Thus each of the contestants is a representative of her team and brings the score she has earned back to the original group. Scores are summed for each team, and final team standings are enthusiastically announced in a weekly classroom newsletter. In a simplified version, student teams-achievement divisions (STAD), the tournament is omitted, but the features of the team collaboration and comparison with others are retained. Slavin's (1979) research found, like the other two approaches, significant treatment effects both for the number of cross-race friendship choices and for the proportion of cross-race choices because of greater increases in the experimental groups. An additional race difference effect indicated that blacks chose more whites as friends than whites chose blacks, regardless of treatment.

Each of the three research groups was not content with having demonstrated the hypothesized attraction effects in experimental groups; each continues to study specific relationships between the several variables contained in the treatment. In Slavin and DeVries's work, the contribution of different components is particularly crucial. The function of cross-team competition has been questioned because of its likely effects of decreasing the liking of members in competing teams. If so, it is not clear that this price should be paid for increases in liking within one team only. Slavin considers interteam competition a vital part in motivating individual students; however, he concedes that "it may be time to evaluate a multiracial team approach that does not rely on team competition" (Slavin 1978). It appears that Slavin has already embarked on an experimental program of establishing the exact effects of different components. He found that the team component played a significant role in increasing nonacademic variables such as mutual concern, peer supports of academic performance and motivation, and cross-racial attitudes.

Aronson similarly took a closer look at the processes likely to bring about positive feelings toward others. Two studies reported in Aronson, Bridgeman, and Geffner (1978) pointed to relationships between collaborative interaction of the jigsaw classroom and enhancement of an empathetic understanding of others, a skill that may be needed for role enactment in cooperative conditions.

Cook and his associates (Blanchard, Adelman, and Cook 1975; Weigel and Cook 1975; Blanchard and Cook 1976) have analyzed further specific interrelationships under controlled laboratory conditions. A task was developed, presented as a management training activity, that involved the operation of a large railroad company. This task required role division into many functions, such as planning the distribution of services, moving different goods on different trains to different destinations, and making a number of other decisions designed to achieve a company profit. Members of triads were assigned different roles and functions, procedures that can be called a cooperative counterpart to Deutsch and Krauss's competitive trucking game methodology.

Blanchard, Adelman, and Cook (1975) studied young white men in the early stages of military training from small southern rural towns, where apparently antiblack attitudes were known to be considerable, using this methodology. Black recruits were trained as confederates. They acted out the prearranged executive roles, while the white subject was primarily a record keeper. Following theoretical expectations, the groups' success proved a crucial variable in the whites' liking of the black team members. In a follow-up study (Blanchard, Weigel, and Cook 1975) when responsibility for mistakes was deliberately left somewhat vague, the black workers were attributed blame. Competence proved also very important for liking and respect accorded to black workers. A high level of participation by all members similarly heightened satisfaction with the work situation and spilled over to attraction toward coworkers.

This controlled research has implications for intergroup relations in desegregated classrooms. It demonstrated clearly the consequences of a person's lack of competence in a group setting where the group's success depends on the performance of each member. In the case of integrated classrooms, which are entered frequently by less-well-prepared minority members, existing stereotypic expectations held by white group members are likely to be reinforced, often culminating in the scapegoating of minority members in the case of group failure. The TGT homogeneous ability grouping of tournament teams reduces the probability of this occurrence.

Cook's series of studies had started with a conceptual analysis of motivation and behaviors toward members of disliked groups (Cook 1969). Following a decade of research, he was able to identify a number of specific conditions under which favorable attitudinal changes are likely to occur. The important modifications emerging are that neither interaction by itself nor even success experiences within a common goal structure necessarily ensures consequent positive interpersonal relationships: attitude change favorable to a disliked group will occur when there is

> equal status contact with stereotype disconfirming persons from that group, provided that the contact is cooperative and . . . reveal[s] the individual characteristics of the person contacted and that it takes place in a situation characterized by social norms favoring equality and equalitarian association among the participating groups. [Cook 1978, p. 98]

Each of the three programs attempts to create these conditions, and evidence points to their success in doing so. However, the question may be raised as to the effectiveness of these programs in regard to pupil achievement.

Competition, Cooperation, and
Children's Learning

Several reviews appeared at this time that addressed research speaking to the effects of cooperative and competitive learning environments (Deutsch 1979; Johnson and Johnson 1974, 1975, 1979; Michaels 1977; Slavin 1977). A sense had developed that sufficient research had been amassed to justify important generalizations and that the time was ripe to do so. Deutsch believed it was time to "communicate the knowledge that we are accumulating about the consequences of different grading systems to teachers, parents, and others who are concerned about the effects of schooling on our children" (p. 400). There was almost complete unanimity on the effects of different learning structures on feelings and attitudes toward one's self and one's relationships with others. Johnson and Johnson (1974) concentrated especially on delineating the destructive consequences of competition on children's growth and development. Anxiety, fear of failure, hostility toward competitors, concern with preventing others from winning as opposed to developing intrinsic motivations, and, more generally, self-orientation and a sense of values that emphasizes winning above all else have been documented as attendant features of competitive motivations. Equally overwhelming is the evidence for positive interpersonal relationships that develop in cooperative conditions: increases in friendliness, helpfulness, supportiveness, attentiveness, respectfulness, responsibility to members, and a general attitude of openness and trust, or what Slavin (1977) calls "the building of social connectedness." More positive attitudes toward teachers, instructional activities, and subject matter were also found.

These facts are more than sufficient to justify the use of cooperative learning structures in the classroom. Deutsch ended with a flourish: "If the competitive-hierarchical atmosphere is not good for our children, is it good for us?" (p. 401). Since much of the research was based on college students, one is tempted to reverse the query: if it is not good for young adults (who have acquired skills to cope in high pressure contrient environments), how can it be good for young children?

In reviews such as Johnson and Johnson's (1974), interpersonal behaviors were treated as mediating variables between various facets of competitive or cooperative conditions on the one hand, and classroom learning on the other. By implication, negative behavioral effects of competition were said to interfere with the cognitive functioning needed to solve problems. In turn, positive gains accruing from cooperative goal structures were said to facilitate learning and bring about superior performance. But no such clear generalizations emerged from the research. Michaels (1977) summarized a number of studies in which individual competition was found to be more effective than group cooperation but it was not so in others;

group rewards proved effective in some studies but not in others. Even under controlled laboratory conditions, results are apparently situation specific, task specific, or person specific. Generalization is also made difficult by methodological noncomparability of the research.

In his review, Slavin (1977) maintained that although many studies showed beneficial effects of cooperation on performance, there was hardly any evidence to substantiate claims that cooperative reward structures benefit the acquisition of basic academic skills. He accounted for this in several ways. Competitive reward structures are efficient in that each increase in individual performance during competition pays off for the individual in ways that it may not in a collaborative endeavor. He argued further that the lack of learning under cooperative goal structures may be in part an artifact of the laboratory situation. Slavin maintained that it provides too little opportunity for pooling of intellectual resources known to improve individual learning and also believed that insufficient time was provided in controlled studies to allow the development of strong social relationships needed to motivate individuals toward a common goal or to develop norms supporting academic performance. Time to develop social connectednesses is provided in the cooperative classroom interventions under review here, and students taught by the jigsaw (Lucker et al. 1976) and TGT (Slavin 1978) methodology showed significantly greater improvements in several academic subject areas than students taught in control classrooms.

When individual acquisition of learning is not helped by cooperative learning structures, one is tempted to conclude that competitive conditions, by tapping individual self-interest, constitute the strongest motivations. But evidence does not support this inference. Clifford's (1972) discussion of research on competition as a motivational classroom technique is highly pertinent. She reviewed evidence showing that competition increases performance on mechanical, skill-oriented, or rather simple tasks. However, these are tasks that need not be taught in classrooms. Addressing herself to the learning of problem-solving tasks typical of classroom learning, she found competition to have either no effects or actually to hinder learning. Her own well-controlled research demonstrated that while a vocabulary learning task was more interesting to fifth graders under competitive conditions than in a neutral condition, contrary to prediction, neither performance nor retention was affected by competition in this extensive investigation in ongoing classroom settings.

When one adds to these facts McClintock's classroom investigation (1978) in which college students showed considerable differences in preferences among alternative distributions of their own and others' scores on a test, one can only agree once more with Deutsch (1979) that "the conclusion seems inescapable that neither system is intrinsically more motivating; however, task-requirements, situational determinants, cultural values, and personality characteristics may predispose an individual to be differentially responsive to cooperation and competition" (p. 398).

This argument is familiar, but there is a major difference between May and Doob's (1937) review and those by the reviewers of the 1970s, who have the advantage of data accumulated over forty more years. Today many of the independent variables that affect certain behaviors in either competitive or cooperative conditions can be specified. As we move into the 1980s, the need is evident for a study of their interaction in order to specify the exact mix of type of task, student, and instructional processes that will advance classroom learning. Noteworthy here is a recent attempt to develop scales that measure pupil attitudes toward cooperation and competition in classrooms (Ahlgren and Johnson 1979).

Laboratory Research on Children's Choice Behaviors

Outstanding here is the series of three studies carried out by McClintock and his associates (McClintock and Moskowitz 1976; McClintock, Moskowitz, and McClintock 1977; Toda et al. 1978), which we will refer to as study 1, study 2, and study 3. This research is a natural outgrowth of McClintock's earlier game research with adults (Messick and McClintock 1968) and with children in a different culture (McClintock and Nuttin 1969). The procedures were built on the same principle as Madsen's game series, in particular the Kagan and Madsen choice card task.

McClintock's methodology as perfected in study 3 involves the use of a two-choice decomposed game display resembling matrixes used in adult choice-game situations. Two children face each other with a game board between them. Two smaller boards are attached, each with a yellow half and a blue half, each child being assigned one color-coded side. Just like Madsen's choice cards, these boards have five holes into which a predetermined number of marbles or beads can be placed by the experimenter. Children alternate in making choices for themselves and the partner from various games that afford diverse distributions of marbles.

This general methodology forms the context for two specific procedures that help to clarify some of the relationships that could only be inferred with earlier methodologies. The first procedure is adapted from game-theoretical research with adults. Motivational orientations are studied by a systematic juxtaposition of choices reflecting various combinations of one's own and other outcomes. Four classes of games are employed to determine preferences: maximizing one's own gain (individual choices), maximizing joint gain (collaborative choices), maximizing relative gain (competitive choices), or maximizing rivalrous choices.

The games are also played within three different outcome structures in three different conditions. Rather than allowing children simply to amass the total number of marbles as a reward, three different reward structures were created that were expected to bear relationships to the choice strategies. In the individualistic reward setting, children were permitted to keep all of the marbles they gained by themselves or were given from the other. Each child had an opaque (private) jar into which her own marbles could be placed. This setting was considered unstructured in that any one of the choice strategies could add something to the final outcome. There was no need to focus on one strategy, although some might net more rewards sometimes as compared with others.

In what the authors refer to as conflictual setting, a contrient reward structure was created. Children with the most marbles were promised an additional reward (chewing gum). Both children placed the marbles they had gained onto a display board so that they could compare their relative accumulations throughout the game. To the extent that children wish to win and understand the concept of relative gain, choices that maximized the difference between one's own and other's rewards were expected to dominate in this condition.

By contrast, in the coordinative setting, children were, in Deutsch's terms, "promotively interdependent"; the reward was meted out for the combined number of marbles earned by the children. All of the earned marbles were placed into one common box to provide visual feedback of a cumulative nature. Here it was argued, choices that would maximize the total joint outcome should be conducive to winning (however, note that the actual reward, a stick of chewing gum to each player, was made to each child rather than being a common reward).

We examine findings from study 1 and study 2 together since they employed methodologies that were identical in all major respects. Study 1 involved children aged 5 to 8 1/2 years. Interestingly it could not test adequately the hypothesis of age-related increases in competitive choices in conflictual settings since even the youngest made predominantly competitive choices. To establish these important age trends, study 2 examined children aged 3 1/2 to 5 1/2 from middle-class cooperative nursery schools.

The authors were evidently concerned for the children's developmental readiness to deal with this particular task. They not only referred to previous research demonstrating that 4 year olds generally are able to make more-than and less-than judgments accurately, but prior to the game period they tested each child individually to determine whether she could perform those numerical operations necessary for expressing their own, relative, and joint outcomes.

The separation of reward structures from mere accumulation of marbles during the game served to clarify the motivation that determined different choices. As expected, relativistic (competitive) choices dominated in conflictual settings and decreased in coordinated settings, where joint or individual choices dominated. When no specific orientation concerning the goal of the game was given, children made their own or relativistic choices in preference to joint choices. These relationships take on added meaning in relation to age trends.

In study 1, the authors considered their principal finding the fact that even the youngest children systematically took into account outcomes to themselves and others in making choices. Study 2 demonstrated that older nursery school children make more relative choices than do the youngest, especially in the conflictual settings. These choices increase up to about age 6. Even in individualistic tasks, there is a steady increase in the proportion of relativistic choices from 3 1/2 to 7 years. The youngest children's orientation was primarily to maximize their own immediate gains, regardless of the implications for their own long-term gains or for the outcomes of others. Learning to give up short-term personal gains and to collaborate with others for personal long-term gain was found to occur somewhat later. In the coordinative tasks, competitive choices began to decrease only somewhere between 6 and 7 years. However, even the oldest children (8 1/2) had a large proportion (44 percent) of individualistic or relativistic choices when joint outcome selection would have been a more profitable strategy.

From these two studies, a consistent picture emerges, essentially in line with Madsen's conclusions. When the American children studied (aged 3 1/2 to 11) were given the opportunity to choose, there was a steady increase in a preference for maximizing their own relative gain, sometimes to the point of being maladaptive. These children could collaborate with others when it seemed appropriate, especially so by age 6 to 7, although they seemed to do so somewhat reluctantly in these dyadic game settings.

Study 3 of this series included older children and moved into two further directions: cross-cultural comparisons and the effects of comparative feedback. This new research investigated children in Flemish-Belgian, Greek, Japanese, Mexican-American, and Anglo-American societies. Only boys were studied, except in the Mexican-American dyads, which had to be supplemented with dyads of girls. Since the children were older than in the previous studies, ranging from second through sixth grade, procedures were only slightly modified from those used with adults. Children were presented a matrix representing the maximizing difference game. The apparatus was complete with push buttons, red starting signals, and a digital display panel showing either one's own or one's own and other cumulative scores. Every time they made a choice, half of the boys received information as to their own cumulative score; the other half additionally were given the scores of the other players. The games pitted individualistic and cooperative choices against competitive preferences in such a way that the competitive choice, while maximizing the difference in point received between oneself and the other player, netted both players less than would have a choice that accorded each player an equal but superior amount. The focus was on the development of competitive choices as a function of age, culture, and social comparison.

The major results showed that competitive choices increased with age in each culture from second, fourth, and sixth grades. Japanese boys were most competitive, Belgian boys least, Anglo-American falling in the middle after the Greek boys. This finding is interesting partly because it places Madsen et al.'s findings of competitiveness of Anglo-American children into a still wider cross-cultural perspective. More specific data on the children's urban or rural background would have been welcome here. The data also confirm McClintock's and Nuttin's earlier (1969) finding of low competitiveness in Flemish-Belgian children, although he had established in that earlier series that these children increased in competitiveness by the time they reached college, actually surpassing American students in this trait. These data begin to show the great complexities involved in cross-cultural comparisons, including caution in generalizing from one age group to the next.

The provision of social comparison feedback increased competitive choices. Social comparison effects were apparent by second grade in all cultures except the Flemish-Belgian. Also of considerable importance was the finding that competitiveness increased as the game progressed when comparison feedback from the other player was possible.

Additional statistical analyses permitted the study of a variety of effects players had on each other. One child's competitive choice tended to stimulate competitive responses in the other, suggesting a pattern of reciprocity or retaliation, which became the established procedure as the game progressed. Such locked-in patterns (demonstrated in many studies with adults) were less frequent in cooperative choices (defined here as a choice that yielded the chooser one less point than the self-maximizing choice possibility and allowed the partner the same gain in points).

Another categorization allowed the characterization of dyads into different types. This yielded the information that among the sample of Japanese boys, the most competitive group, there were a number of cooperative dyads (both partners cooperated as predominant pattern). No Anglo-American dyads showed a predominant cooperative pattern. This finding adds to our earlier warning about cross-cultural generalizations in that by one measure Japanese boys had been found most competitive but not so when another criterion was employed.

Another methodological advance during the late 1970s in the game-theoretical study of children was found in the work of Kagan and his associates (Kagan 1977, 1979; Knight and Kagan 1977). Their efforts paralleled those of McClintock in distinguishing choice situations in order to identify specific motivational bases underlying given choices. Kagan provided on a choice card four choice alternatives instead of the usual two. The four choices corresponded to his conceptualization of alternative motivations. He distinguished within competitive choices (McClintock's self-maximizing choices) those aiming to avoid absolute gains for others (rivalry) and those obtaining relative gains for self (superiority). Three types of prosocial choices consisted of avoidance of relative gain both for oneself and for the other (equality), obtaining joint gains (group enhancement), and providing absolute gains for others (altruism). These studies continued to concentrate on comparisons between Anglo-American and Mexican-American children but controlled more precisely for the urban-rural dimension as well as socioeconomic differences.

The body of work from the combined research groups led, respectively, by Madsen, McClintock, and by Kagan, has accumulated impressive systematic empirical knowledge of children's preferential behavior in game situations where limited self- and other-oriented choice patterns were possible. Unfortunately this severe methodological restriction goes frequently unheeded when these data are cited as sole evidence for American children's competitiveness without clarifying that the children were placed into a forced-choice situation that frequently allowed choice between two alternatives only. The use of different methodologies may shed different light on the children's motivations. For instance, a study requiring a verbal report of preference for either competitive or cooperative learning environments showed boys only moderately inclined toward the former and only at certain grades, while girls on the average preferred cooperative conditions at every grade (Ahlgren and Johnson 1979).

The comprehensiveness of the gaming research is enhanced by the inclusion of developmental considerations (though the only variable introduced is that of age) and cross-cultural concerns (though only the global distinction is made of growing up in different countries or urban-rural environments). Anthropological research advances this controlled, necessarily limited experimental focus by studying a variety of children's behaviors as they interact in their various cultural contexts.

*Anthropological Research on Children's
Social Behaviors*

Whiting and Whiting (1975) turned to extensive behavior observation of children in six cultures and attempted to relate differences in children's social behaviors to their social roles at home and in the larger community.

Their field study followed children aged 3 to 11 over a period of at least half a year. The occurrences of altruistic and collaborative acts were tallied during periodic five-minute observations in field settings. Three cultures were nonliterate: the Gusii of Kenya, the Juxthahuaca of Mexico, and the Tarong of the Philippines. Children who lived in these villages had a very high percentage of collaborative interactions, attributed by the Whitings to the demands for help made of children in the simple daily round of living. In the more complex cultures—the Taira in Okinawa, the Rajput in northern India, and children in a Massachusetts town—they found that children were not assigned nearly as many specific community roles other than in school settings. In these cultures, their learning roles were found to be primarily individualistic-competitive. Much less altruism and fewer collaborative acts were established.

These are the same kinds of differences suggested by gaming research between rural and urban children. One would like to see subsequent research that would relate mediating cultural variables more closely to particular behaviors. The Whitings' research points to a direction in which theoretical analysis might proceed, which has been developed further by yet another anthropologist couple in the last decade. Their work provides an example of a fairly successful synthesis of methodologies and theoretical integration of developmental and cultural variables specifically focused on the study of children's cooperation and competition.

Graves and Graves (1975, 1976, 1977) combined participant observation in a series of field studies, with laboratory research on cooperation and competition, primarily of children in the Cook Islands of the South Pacific. They made an explicit attempt to relate behavior to its cultural context, intriguing here because Polynesians are known for their communal cooperation and general helpfulness. The Graveses described the role played by mutual sharing, especially of older people, and cited instances of children's being trained to exercise generous behaviors early in their lives (in such roles as carrying food to relatives and neighbors, helping to serve at festivities, and so forth).

Their experimental work was built around games adapted to the culture from the Madsen cooperation board and the Kagan and Madsen choice card game. In the latter, pay-off options consisted of choices that they described as generous (when maximizing the others' pay-off rather than their own), equalizing (when choosing for oneself the same as for other) and self-maximizing and rivalrous. The last three categories correspond to the individual and competitive distinctions made by McClintock et al.

Data were collected from samples varying in age and social roles and along a variety of culturally relevant dimensions. For instance, an index was constructed denoting the degree of Westernization that had occurred in given individuals as a result of types of exposure to the modern New Zealand culture (Graves and Graves 1975). This index includes a category of mere exposure (dating back to the times when American troops first landed in World War II, so that even the older generation can be said to have had this minimal exposure); access to rewards of Western culture (primarily monetary in return for performance of skilled occupations as opposed to the traditional occupations), and personal identification with Western influence. As expected, degree of exposure was found to be somewhat associated with significantly more rivalry and less generosity in adults. Greater rivalrous responses also occurred in children brought up in Western-type small nuclear families rather than the traditional extended families.

In the direction of rivalrous responses were those exposed to Western technology as reflected on more specific indexes such as a possession index (including, for instance, the amount of machinery used, labor-saving devices, and other gadgets) and on an index of degree of traditional cooking methods and food preparation.

Consistent generosity was found only where there was still a strong traditional cultural pattern: older adults, living in remote parts of the islands still part of an extended three-generation family, engaging in traditional planting and fishing, having had less than average formal education, and never visiting the mainland of New Zealand.

On developmental issues, the Graveses found that children on the Cook Islands at each elementary school level became increasingly rivalrous and less generous with age. A comparison of the youngest Cook Island children (ages 5 to 7) with New Zealand children found the latter already predominantly rivalrous (Graves and Graves 1977), as was established in the McClintock and Moskowitz (1976) study for American urban children of the same age. The Graveses ascribed this trend to Westernizing influences transmitted to children particularly by the recent trend toward nuclear small families and the impact of schooling. In that connection it is noteworthy that teachers, trained in New Zealand, made the most rivalrous choices of all persons within the different occupational structures, as did high-achieving children, who competed the most for the teachers' attention and approval in the classroom and, reciprocally, were singled out most by their teachers.

In a report of these findings to the Cook Island government, the Graveses (1976) based a series of educational policy recommendations on research literature that demonstrated the social-connectedness building effects of cooperation, which they suggested should be reincorporated into the classroom in line with the way of life of the Cook Island culture.

Not content with this action research, N. Graves (1976) addressed herself specifically to the theoretical implications of their findings as they pertain to child development. She challenged the Piagetian formulation that describes children's moving gradually from egocentrism through a process of realization of their separateness from others. In fact, she found the concept of socialization through separation paradoxical. Rather she posited a basic sociocentrism that continues to grow as long as the child is part of an interdependent family group and a larger social system. Their data constrain her to argue that it is the separating and individualizing experiences encountered particularly in school that determine children's later development toward self-centeredness in this particular culture.

These anthropological studies take up where those reported by May and Doob left off, but with several significant differences. First, they are armed with a methodology that includes both observation of children's interpersonal behaviors in their daily living and with controlled laboratory techniques that had not been accessible to Mead (1937). Second, they closely relate behavioral findings to a variety of facets of the larger culture and to more specific sociological variables. And third, these relationships were examined in the light of specific relevant conceptualizations in a major theory of child development. The one omission, which perhaps also accounts for the fact that the Graveses find their own data on acculturation not quite understandable, is information from social psychological theories that can look more closely at particular influence processes in situations encountered by children.

Into the Eighties

This survey of research trends has demonstrated some consistent behavioral consequences of experiences in competitive or cooperative conditions. We end with several samples of laboratory studies that deal with variables related to these conditions whose pursuit would seem to hold great promise for progress in this field, particularly with regard to our understanding of children.

One particular study represents a culmination of several trends examined in this review. French et al. (1977) integrated several diverse features of past research and extended the inquiry in a systematic fashion. The authors started with the Deutsch (1949) conceptualization of goal structures, as applied to the research of Sherif et al. (1961) and addressed the further distinction of individual goal structures, which was made especially under the leadership of the Madsen-McClintock gaming researches. Sherif et al. had demonstrated the effectiveness of promotive goal structures in reducing conflict stimulated by prior goal contriency; French et al. inquired whether an individualistic goal structure can perform the same conflict-removing function. They addressed additionally the specific point of the comparability of behaviors under promotive and individualistic goal structures as a function of prior presence or absence of contrient goal experiences, reminiscent somewhat of similar questions asked in the social climate studies (Lewin, Lippitt, and White 1939), which, like Sherif et al.'s, were field studies; French et al. casted their investigation into a highly controlled laboratory design.

The three different reward structures were established but not within a gaming methodology. Rather a modified version of the Goldberg-Maccoby (1965) tower building task was employed. Children—first and third graders placed into triads—were rewarded with chips for their performance, but the basis of distribution differed. In the promotive conditions, each of the members received one-third of the reward, which corresponded to the total number of blocks placed by the group as a whole. In the contrient condition, the child who had placed the most blocks received that many chips, and the other two received nothing. In the individual condition, each child was given the number of chips corresponding to the number of blocks that she had placed onto the tower.

This type of methodology enables a precise determination of group performance in terms of quantity of blocks used as well as quality (the stability of the tower was used as the quality measure). Additionally the authors devised an index of division of labor within each triad. The results were unambiguous. For instance, promotive conditions that followed prior contrient goal conditions were able to improve performance but not to the level reached by groups who had not received contrient interventions.

The authors were interested in age-related differences. They attributed the fact that they found no age-related differences in behavior to the equal sensitivity of first graders as compared with third graders. However, the possibility cannot be excluded that the tower-building task required relatively few collaborative skills, masking potential age-related differences in behavior. This research thus invites replication with tasks varying in group role requirements; the Loeb (1975, 1979) transfer studies are of interest here.

Children's Social Comparisons

This area offers close linkages between social comparison and competitive conditions, linkages pursued in our own research. Social comparison also is an obvious theroretical meeting ground for rapprochement between social psychology and developmental psychology in their present emphasis on cognitive factors.

We have already examined game-theoretically derived findings (Toda et al. 1978) that simultaneous feedback information of the partner's score increased the competitive choices of children in the several cultures studied.

These researchers provided feedback to all subjects in some experimental conditions. Ruble and her associates, exploring different facets of children's comparison behaviors, designed a study to determine the extent to which children would avail themselves of the opportunity to compare (Ruble, Feldman, and Boggiano 1976). Kindergarten and first and second grade children worked in pairs on a simple speed task in high- and low-competitive conditions. Two children working at a time were separated from each other by a screen but were free to seek or not to seek information about how the other child was doing by pushing a button to observe their partner's progress on a monitor. The frequency of this button pushing was taken as an index of the strength of motivation to see the other partner's work. Children of all ages studied evinced such interest, and, as expected, social comparison interest increased with age.

Further use of this ingenious technique may be the answer to the difficulties encountered in efforts to isolate different bases of children's social comparisons. In seeking to establish the characteristics of peers who would be selected as comparison persons, Feldman and Ruble (1977) chose to explore the appropriateness of a method employed with adults in the research of Zanna, Goethals, and Hill (1975). Subjects were presented a story about various other children working on a test. Each child was asked to select one of the children whose performance she would most like to see. Their results paralleled adult findings in that all children, even first graders, used as a criterion for comparison with another sex-based similarity as well as ability.

Children's Achievement-related Motivations

Success and failure experiences are intimately linked to competition. Earlier, we noted Johnson and Johnson's (1974) dismay over the long-term effects of a sense of failure, which appear inevitable under competitive conditions where only one child is permitted to emerge as a winner. Some more recent laboratory studies address this issue directly. Children's responses to success and failure experiences were studied as they relate to their achievement striving under competitive conditions. It is significant that the method of choice tended to examine subjects alone rather than in group settings. One such study is by Parsons and Ruble (1977) who, wishing to pursue children's expectations of success as a function of degree of failure experiences, systematically exposed single children—aged 3 1/2 to 11—to one failure experience or to a series of multiple failures.

Heckhausen has researched and written extensively about adults' and children's achievement motivations (for example, 1967). In a recent study, Halish and Heckhausen (1977) focused on the obverse of the above relationships: on responses to given success or failure experiences as a function of degree of prior success expectancies. The method here involved a competitive game that required building a tower of twelve wooden rings around one's own peg. A novel stooge variant was introduced. The experimenter sat opposite the child as competitor, thus being able by his own level of performance to control systematically the child's differential success experiences. Building speed was used as a measure of performance. An index of motivation used frequency of a child's glances at the tower of the experimenter while he was still in the process of completing his own. Here again, motivation to succeed was linked to comparison behavior and performance in competitive conditions.

Within the last decade, achievement behaviors have been examined within the context of attribution models (Bar-Tal, 1978; Weiner, 1974; Weiner and Kukia, 1970). Halish and Heckhausen interpreted their results in terms of achievement-motivated theory. Lacking appropriate measures, they were able only to speculate about the children's self-attribution of their own responsibility for their success and failure. Such supplementary data were furnished in a simultaneous study by Jensen and Moore (1977), who demonstrated that respective cooperative or competitive self-attributions may predispose children to approach a task differently and thus may significantly affect performance. In this particular case, subjects were twenty-eight boys, 7 to 12 years of age, with learning and behavior problems. The modified version of the Goldberg-Maccoby tower-building task was employed (see French et al. 1977). Cooperative self-perceptions were induced in half of the children by telling them that they would work well with others. Competitive attribute boys were told they "had what it takes to be a winner." Performance was found significantly different between the two groups, in line with the induced attributions. It is also in line with Kagan and Madsen's (1971) finding that instructional sets—in one case to think of themselves as group members, in the other as separate individuals—produced differences in the expected direction in cooperative choices.

Concluding Comments

If the studies from the 1970s may be taken to prognosticate research in children's competition and cooperation yet to come, we have reason to be optimistic. There is a renewed interest in children's interactions, and attention is being paid to both group and individual factors. Attention is also being paid to a wider spectrum of social behaviors and a resulting choice of methodology that enables multibehavioral analyses. There appears to be a return to (or rediscovery of) the careful construction of a laboratory life space, with particular attention paid to task features designed to elicit children's responses. Evident also is an eclecticism, particularly in the area of competition. It includes a recognition of the context of success and failure experiences in which children's goal-directed behaviors take place. And there is a recognition of the ever-present context of social comparison as it relates to considerations of relative gain motivations in competition. The felicitous prospect is that these various strands may be increasingly combined within single investigations.

Although there exists a conceptual language for describing behaviors under cooperative conditions, it has been developed primarily in the light of group-dynamics theory in the 1940s and 1950s. These social role concepts have not been incorporated to any significant extent in contemporary social psychological theory. By contrast, much work has been done by developmental psychologists in the cognitive areas referred to as social cognition or, more specifically, role taking, which appears highly relevant for understanding children's cooperation. The integration of these two conceptual approaches may yield great theoretical advances in the study of children's cooperation.

The laboratory studies we have reviewed are, in our evaluation, examples of research that stands at the threshold of uniting sophisticated use of social psychological theory and developmental theory. The use of methodology here is eclectic, employing the most appropriate techniques from either field to obtain data equally relevant to both fields.

In this review, we have pointed to connections between the zeitgeist and direction of research concerns. There are self-evident benefits and costs in such interrelationships when the research deals with human problems. It is to be welcomed to the extent that research on competition and cooperation can shed light on the pressing problems of the day, increase understandings, and perhaps even add to more satisfactory personal interrelationships. This hope is supported in the cooperative interventions and classroom researches we have examined. There is just cause to feel encouraged not only by their results to date but also by the carefully designed action research. Investigations in this field draw freely on results of laboratory researches. The investigators themselves carry out laboratory research to pursue theoretical questions that need exact tests not feasible in ongoing classrooms. This model of interrelationships between laboratory research and action, envisaged by Lewin over a quarter of a century ago, augurs well for the future.

The problems of the day may also blind us to the important questions that should be asked or directions that should be pursued further in research. During the course of our review, we have encountered instances where ideological positions have prevented the pursuit of study in certain directions or prevented the translation of accepted findings into classroom practice. Behavioral sciences are particularly vulnerable to appeasing societal demands. Yet research is self-corrective and generates its own questions. Perhaps as particular sciences become sufficiently advanced, their research will create its own momentum that cannot easily be stopped by transient societal values. Developmental social research in cooperation and competition might be moving toward such a state.

Theoretical Orientation

The preceding review of research trends in the study of cooperation and competition touched occasionally on the theories that generated the particular investigations or on formulations derived from accumulated findings. This chapter provides a more detailed consideration of the implications of these conceptualizations, leading to what we hope will be some fruitful recastings of issues, fresh formulations, and some new understandings. This chapter concludes with an attempt to broaden our social psychological approach to encompass some basic developmental concepts that we think are necessary to understand children's behavior as they function in cooperative and competitive situations.

Some generally agreed-upon basic concepts and assumptions have emerged from accumulated research. The first is that the concept of an individual in isolation is wholly antithetical to the conditions of cooperation and competition. The two situations are, above all, social situations. They are social in two diffent senses. Different cultures, different societies, or different segments within a society place different stress on either of these social interactions. The implication here is that children are affected by these different value emphases. Competition and cooperation constitute social situations in another sense inasmuch as a person encounters a social environment in both of these circumstances.

The social character of cooperation is perhaps more readily apparent. No one can engage very well in collaborative activities with oneself. Competition, however, by virtue of its frequent association with individualism, is often deemed an expression of solitary, self-assertive, independent striving. Although individuals in competition often strive alone, they are caught in a relational network as well, although its characteristics differ markedly from those found in cooperative conditions. Perhaps one of the most important basic assumptions to make explicit is that both competition and cooperation represent conditions of interdependence.

The interdependencies derive from human purposiveness. When persons are located within a cooperative or competitive situation, they are oriented toward a desired end state (variously referred to as a goal, valence, reward, reinforcement, outcome, purpose, or central force field). Goal directedness characterizes behavior in both competitive and cooperative conditions. Individuals are made interdependent through their similar goals. However, different kinds of interdependencies are created in each of these conditions because the goal relationships among members differ in these two respective conditions.

In cooperation, interdependent goal conditions exist that are referred to as promotively interdependent. The contribution of one member affects the fate of all; any group member is potentially an asset or a burden to the group. The success of one member helps all the rest, just as the failure of one hinders the rest. This is so because in cooperation the interdependence is created by a common goal. This characteristic implies that when one person is able to reach the goal, all of the others are simultaneously moved along by that member. The goal attainment of one is the goal attainment of all. But in competitive conditions, the competitor is, by definition, an obstacle to the other's goal attainment. Persons are working not for each other's goal attainment but against each other; they are contriently interdependent. The implication is that a person in a competitive condition must eliminate the other as potential goal attainer in order to reach the desired goal.

This analysis makes it clear why research, almost without exception, has demonstrated that social relationships are strengthened by participation in cooperative work and variously strained in competitive situations. Because of this close association between one type of behavior with a given condition, the two are often used interchangeably. In spite of Deutsch's (1949a) clear distinction, there is still much conceptual confusion. All too often the terms are used to describe behaviors instead of denoting field conditions that have certain consequences for behaviors. Let us anticipate here our own conceptual position; we adhere scrupulously to the distinction. True, restriction of the terms to conditions robs us of a ready label for behavior that is found in these conditions. However, we deem it an advantage in the long run not to have global terms referring to competitive or cooperative behaviors, respectively. Behaviors in each of the conditions are not unitary. Rather we are assuming that a number of complex behavior processes characterize each of the two conditions.

Differences in goal structure between the two conditions—that is, in competition the juxtaposition of goals, the antisocial aspects, and in cooperation the benefits accruing to group members from promotive goal structures, the prosocial aspects—are of crucial importance. They determine the basic climate of interpersonal relations: hostile in the former condition and positive, friendly, and helpful in the latter. These were, to various degrees, the interpersonal behaviors found almost without exception in past research. However, behaviors along this positive-negative continuum were generally the only ones looked for. The implication pursued in our studies is that if further distinctions are made within each of the respective conditions, other behaviors become relevant.

Interdependencies derive from goal orientations. In order to reach these goals, individuals must do something. How individuals behave is to various degrees, determined by the particular task(s) that need to be performed in order that the desired goals may be reached. The activity structure—the task, for short—that requires action on the part of individuals thus becomes a second source that determines particular interdependence relations.

Relative to the precise formalization of goal characteristics that enables a specification of resulting interdependency relations, there are considerably fewer theoretical formulations devoted to the concept of task interdependence. The almost exclusive emphasis on game-theoretical models over the past twenty years may be at least in part responsible for this state of affairs. In typical gaming studies, the task demands a choice between alternative reward structures. The task, in fact, is the choice. At this point, we merely wish to call attention to the fact that competitive and cooperative conditions tend to have very different task requirements and hence create quite different task interdependencies among individuals.

Task interdependencies in competitive conditions have not been analyzed further since the early concerns with various conditions of coaction. Regardless of type of task, in competitive conditions performance is always directed toward appearing in the goal region sooner than or better than the opponent. Yet paradoxically although interaction is not required in many competitive situations, persons are exceedingly attuned to each other's actions. Theories in which the concept of social comparison is central are highly relevant to further understanding of interpersonal competition.

In cooperation, task characteristics play a key role. Since the required activities must be distributed among several people, the relationships created by the demands of the task directly affect member interdependencies. Because groups in cooperation engage in work toward a common goal as well, the vast theoretical and experimental literature on factors involved in group performance becomes relevant. Of particular theoretical importance here are attempts to categorize different types of group tasks, as well as concepts of task requiredness, task roles, and group roles. We reintroduce these concepts with the aim of enlarging the conceptualization of cooperative task conditions and related behaviors.

Competitive and cooperative conditions constitute very different social fields. The constellation of forces emanating from the goal as well as the task structure are quite different. Very different demands are made on children when placed in either of these two conditions. This assumption is fundamental to the theoetical orientation that determined our research. It implies that each of these two social conditions demands separate study, with finer appropriate distinctions made within each, and emphasis on the resulting variety of interpersonal behaviors within each. Considering the likelihood of differences in the task requirements between as well as within each of these conditions, blanket statements about the relative superiority of performance in either of the two conditions are likely to be wrong. Generalizations must be made with the greatest caution.

It follows further that concepts and theories that have been found useful in determining direction for, and analysis of, research into competitive conditions have at best a limited usefulness when considering problems of interaction under cooperative conditions. Our research has followed from this point. Only where the primary focus is on developmental trends are children's social behaviors studied in both competitive and cooperative conditions. All other studies take children within one particular chronological age and deal either with behaviors in various conditions of competition or various conditions of cooperation.

Characteristics and Requirements of Competitive Conditions

Goal Characteristics

In competitive conditions, individuals act by themselves and for themselves to obtain contrient, exclusive goals.[1] Yet goals cannot categorically be dichotomized into exclusive or nonexclusive goals; rather it makes sense to consider goal exclusivity a matter of degree. Individual goals may be thought of as varying along the dimension of exclusivity from zero—that is, conditions where A's goal attainment is irrelevant to B's goal attainment, through a range of situations where B is hindered to various degrees by A's goal attainment, to the other extreme where A's goal attainment prevents B from doing so and vice-versa, when goal contriency may be said to be absolute. Recognition of degrees of goal contriency may be reflected in recent differentiations between contrient reward structures, which distribute rewards according to each contestant's performance regardless of that of others (individualistic rewards), and those that reward only one winner (variously referred to as contrient, competitive, rivalrous, or other).

Most adult competitive relationships fall somewhere into the middle range of this continuum. Were it not so, for instance, even in the reputedly hard-headed world of business, total chaos would rule, punctuated by the constant dizzying rise and crashing fall of small business concerns and large industrial empires. The world of school children in their classrooms may be viewed in much the same way. On the whole, there is room at the top in schools, and there is no absolute bottom. As a rule, one child's brilliance does not devastate others or even deny the accomplishments of others.

Adherence to conditions of absolute goal exclusivity would make life in classrooms unbearable. This is not to say that in the minds of many students, absolute goal exclusivity does not exist, reinforced by the reality of rejection experiences from institutions of higher learning. In this light it is significant that, during the late 1960s, stimulated by student complaints about powerful achievement pressures, class ranks were discontinued in many high schools and colleges. Most examinations make it possible for more than one student to obtain the highest grade. Even the practice of marking on the curve, an evaluation procedure that comes close to employing an absolute point of exclusivity, generally makes it quite clear that those ranking close to the highest scorer are considered high achievers as well. Cutoff points were presumably invented to designate a relatively small range of scores that are unacceptable and hence are termed failures. Furthermore in most educational institutions, additional opportunities are provided to change such absolute failures to a range defined as successful entrance into the stipulated goal region of successful completion of the task.

Absolute goal contriency exists primarily in formal contests and games. Even there, the various hierarchical structures of playoffs are perhaps designed to allow the emergence of winners at different levels to forestall too many bitter disappointments and resentments. Status positions of vice-presidents, runners-up, second and third place winners, and other consolation prizes certainly are intended to bind the wounds inflicted in contests around absolute exclusive goals.

Task Characteristics

In cooperative conditions, execution of various task roles constitutes one of the major member requirements. Quite the contrary is the case in competitive conditions where task interdependence is less strong and interaction is very often not at all required. Because task interdependence is such a crucial determinant of interpersonal behaviors, we found it useful to distinguish among competitive tasks those that allow complete independence, where no interaction whatsoever is required among competitors (conditions of coaction) and those where the task dictates interdependence and hence demands interaction (conditions of counteraction).

Conditions of Coaction. In conditions of coaction, competitors are required to work by themselves, usually, although not necessarily, in each other's presence, and usually, although not necessarily, on unitary, nondivisible tasks whose characteristics are generally similar to each others'. The progress of one contestant is never deliberately impeded by interference from another. This description fits the classic definition of competitive coaction first studied in early social psychological research, of which F.H. Allport's (1924) work is an example.

In coaction, the potential for competition exists in situational and personal variables that make for interpersonal comparison. Two principal situational factors contribute singly and in interaction to coactors' competitive motivation: degree of goal contriency and degree of similarity among required activities. If conditions are such that individual success is defined independently of that of the other(s)—if the success of one person does not depend on or interfere with that of the other—no goal contriency exists. If under such independent, individual goal conditions, each coactor also engages in parallel task-required work that is so different from the other as to be practically noncomparable, such conditions constitute the most minimally competitive coactive conditions. At the other extreme are conditions where explicit goal contriency is present such that all contestants understand that the success of one prevents the success of all the others and where each coactor's task is identical to that of the other(s).

In coaction, then, we have the intriguing situation where tasks require no interaction of any kind, yet some presence to some degree of the two factors noted above nevertheless creates feelings of interdependence in the actors such that they feel constrained to pay attention to the other(s). In this formulation, the crucial intervening variable is the social comparison process.

In coaction, not only is interpersonal interaction not required, it is nonfunctional, and hence overt interpersonal behaviors may be expected to be minimal. However, as even the earliest social psychological researchers observed, coaction gives rise to nonverbal stimuli—"the sights and sounds of others doing the same thing," which Allport (1924) had found to facilitate performance of simple mechanical tasks and to inhibit more complex intellectual tasks. He noted that drives to excel others, dubbed "rivalry," went "hand in hand with social facilitation" yet often tended to have distracting effects on performance. Allport never resolved these inconsistencies, inconsistencies that plague us still today as we view competitive atmospheres charged with tension and competitors stealing uncertain glances at each other and each others' work. What does this nontask-required nonverbal interpersonal attention signify?

One contemporary theory (Zajonc 1965; Zajonc and Sales 1966) is able to account specifically for the contradictory findings of Allport and his contemporaries pertaining to conditions under which competitive performance is facilitated or hindered by the presence of others. Zajonc, like Allport, assumes that the presence of others is stimulating ("physiologically arousing"). Festinger, however, posed a prior question: why does the presence of others affect a person at all? In his 1954 social comparison theory, he posited that uncertainty about the correctness of self-evaluation and about different aspects of the external world constitutes, in the absence of possibilities for an objective testing of reality, a powerful condition for turning to relevant others to gain more accurate understandings. At bottom, one wishes to know whether one's perceptions are correct and can be trusted, whether one's values are good ones to have, and so on. Some such questions may be answered by recourse to objective tests. We can put a match to material claimed to be noninflammable and judge for ourselves, we can dig up the earth and determine soil composition scientifically, and so on. It is maintained, however, that when individuals have no way of testing physical reality—there is no way of determining the veridicality of their own perceptions, opinions, or attitudes—other individuals constitute a social reality that essentially serves the same confirming or disconfirming functions. The consequence of such comparison, according to Festinger, is that if there appears to be a discrepancy between one's own judgment and those of others, one moves closer to the position of the other. Cognitive uncertainty, then, is one condition under which a person experiences pressures toward uniformity with others.

In its basic assertion, the theory is deceptively simple, but the behavioral consequents that may be deduced from the theory are enormous. The theory in fact states conditions under which other individuals are brought into each other's life space as a central, functioning, integral part. Cognitive needs to have a correct understanding of oneself and the surrounding world constitute positive forces toward others. Festinger's original formulation referred to active attempts to seek out others who would be comparable to oneself in order to obtain accurate self-evaluations from such comparisons.

Research accumulating since the first formal statement of the theory has been summarized in two important publications (Latané 1966; Suls and Miller 1977). Attention is devoted in particular to the postulated two major motives underlying comparison: the need for accurate self-assessment as originally postulated by Festinger and needs for self-validation (to justify one's present state, almost so as not to have to change). The more research is generated, so is also growth in awareness of the complexity of processes involved in using others to establish a social reality. The range of dependent variables has been extended to feelings (Schachter 1959), including needs for self-validation (Reckman and Goethals 1973), and evaluation anxiety created in the presence of others (Cottrell 1972). Several others have begun to address needs to avoid social comparison (Brickman and Bulman 1977; Mettee and Smith 1977). The choice of comparison figures and their characteristics are examined in minute detail for clues about the particular motives involved. Here, too, the original Festingerian hypothesis about the need to compare with similar others now finds its opposite in research demonstrating uses for dissimilar others (for example Mettee and Riskind 1974).

The concept of similarity has come under close scrutiny. Goethals and Darley (1977) have proposed a somewhat more rigorous, more precisely testable definition by postulating that people will include in their comparison range and will prefer comparing themselves with "those who are perceived to be similar to themselves on attributes that are related to their opinions or performance level" (p. 265). A major study by Zanna, Goethals and Hill (1975) supports this assertion by demonstrating that when information aiding in the assessment of one's performance is sought, persons seek comparison with those who are similar to them on attributes related to performance (in their case level of ability and like sex). On the other hand, many studies show preferences for others with global similarity. For instance, when choices are given to select either associates who are relevant to a specific task or those who are broadly similar to the chooser, the latter are preferred (for example, Castore and DeNinno 1977).

The complexity of social comparison is increased still further by the presence of a postulated unidirectional drive that is present in performance situations and largely absent with respect to opinions and attitudes. Festinger (1954), perhaps wisely, has not specified this drive beyond saying that it motivates the person to do somewhat better than others and/or better than one's previous performance. These are motives that we would generally refer to as achievement-related motives that are typically found in competitive conditions. This drive, then, is thought to push comparison upward so that while one's ability may dictate choice of a highly similar other, achievement motives lead one to compare with someone of slightly superior ability, presumably in an effort to surpass him.

According to Festinger, considerable superiority over others is not desired, for in that case the original purpose of gaining accurate information about oneself is not fulfilled. Establishing great superiority of self leaves the person at a loss of knowing just how good she really is. It is likely that in actual work situations, still other sources of social comparison exist, including needs to determine rivals' progress in relation to one's own progress, needs to estimate one's own chances of winning by assessing others' progress, and so on.

These specific issues are developed further in relation to particular concerns of our research. This brief overview may have illustrated how difficult it is to isolate experimentally the many sources of forces that make for social comparison. Nevertheless where there is coaction, there social comparison shall also be. And although competitive coaction might appear calm, underneath it is teaming with action. As an example, consider the elementary classroom during periods devoted to individual seatwork. In the mind of the teacher, this is a time for independent, individualized work, with pupils moving at their own speed and doing their own thinking. More often than not, pupils turn this situation into one of competitive coaction. Typically the class is assigned identical problems, in itself a powerful condition for comparison. Add high achievement motivation in a classroom where not all can be given a top grade even under the best of circumstances, and all the essential ingredients are present to make for social comparison. As children confront new instructional material, each pupil may be said to be cognitively uncertain to some degree; highly similar and relevant others are readily present to reduce their uncertainties. Some uncertainties may be only procedural unclarities: what to do next, what page to turn to. Or they may be uncertainties about self-validation. Am I doing this right? Is my answer the same as my neighbor's? And, of course, evaluations of others may be purely competitively motivated. Is she ahead of me? Is his drawing better than mine? In sum, are they better than I? How good am I? At bottom, all of these questions in some way relate to self-evaluation and/or to an evaluation of others. Festinger's original assertion of an intimate connection between evaluational processes and social comparison may be basically correct. Furthermore evaluational processes seem to be tied to competitive motivation. Assessing another's progress stimulates an increased effort to surpass that person, and leads in turn to a renewed assessment of self and others, and so on. The cycle may be initiated at any point, and continue.

Is it any wonder that, try as hard as he may to prevent such social comparisons with verbal admonitions of "keep your eyes on your own paper," the teacher is doomed to failure. As long as these conditions remain, he succeeds only in forcing children into more surreptitious social comparisons. Furthermore what starts out in the classroom as information seeking may turn into evaluative comparisons and heightened competitiveness to surpass the other.

Social comparison has been considered an intervening variable, inferred primarily from the degree of conformity to others or the choice of comparison to others. One of the principal aims of our research was to observe children's ongoing social comparisons. We conceived of comparison as a process that occurs whenever two or more persons perceive each other relevant in some way. In competitive coaction, competing individuals are highly relevant to each other, especially as the goal structure approaches absolute contriency. The more similar the competitive task activities are to each other, the more information can be gained by comparison. We postulate three interrelated processes that comprise the total comparison. First, in order to assess oneself or another in terms of progress made, relative success, and so on, attentional processes must be engaged so that others or their performance outcomes may be observed. Second, these processes are closely followed by and often intermingle with evaluational processes, which allow inferences to be made about relative standings, about the level of opponents' abilities, strengths, and weaknesses, hidden tactics, and so on. Third, motivational processes are aroused in form of achievement-related motives as a result of conclusions drawn from the inferences. However, the comparison process may be initiated by any one of the three subprocesses. Highly motivated persons will wish to assess their competitors and in so doing attend to their performance. Yet a child's mere attending to another for some point of information about an assignment may evoke the other two processes as well.

Conditions of Counteraction. Here interaction is variously aimed to put down, weaken, overcome, eliminate, or otherwise work against the competitor(s). Almost without exception, goal contriency is explicit and absolute. Various task characteristics will determine different kinds of interaction, which may vary from minimal task-required communication or other minimal interpersonal contacts, to requirements of maximal interdependence such that each move of A requires counteraction by B. These requirements may be implicit or explicitly given in rules by which opponents must abide in their quest to eliminate each other.

An example of rather minimal interaction requirements are situations in which competitors are constrained to interact with each other around a task with many subactivities. Each person is seeking to accomplish the same task or seeking the same solution, but individual goals are dominant and their structure is contrient. Such was the case, for instance, in Deutsch's (1949b) competitively motivated discussion groups. MIT students were required to engage in seminar discussions, knowing that they would be graded on a sliding scale such that only one student would receive the highest grade. In this forced interactive competitive situation, hostile interpersonal behaviors appeared, often disguised in terms of task-role behaviors offered as well-intentioned criticism of others' performance. Evaluations here may be verbalized or remain surpressed as in coaction. Furthermore in attempts to win, others' efforts may be downgraded, one's own efforts underscored, or one's own superiority asserted.

These forced interactive competitions abound in classroom recitation periods. Here the teacher may invite pupil participation in a large group setting around question-and-answer type tasks where it is understood that correct solutions exist that are known to the teacher. An evaluative atmosphere is created, especially when children are competitively achievement oriented. Such children know their task roles well. The teacher does not even have to invite participation with "Let's see who knows x" or "Who can tell me y?" Social comparison is implied, and eager hands shoot up to win teacher approval. Wrong answers are greeted by laughter, giggles, or half-inhibited smug expressions, depending on the degree of competitive climate and suppressive classroom norms instituted.

Such task situations are midway between coaction situations in which no verbal interaction is required and comparison is taking place in a suppressed fashion, and competitive situations in which extensive interpersonal interaction—either verbal or often physical, as in sports contests—is essential in order for a winner to emerge. In the latter counteractive situations, task requirements may prescribe to various degrees the nature of the required interaction. Attention paid to others is likely to be information seeking to assess the opponent's strengths and weaknesses. Whatever the specific activity, it always contains some behaviors intended to remove restraints to one's own progress set up by competitors or to remove defenses established by the other, erect a defense of one's own, or otherwise block each other in order to prevent competitors from reaching the goal desired by both parties.

One of the few examples of laboratory research that represents counteractive conditions is the Deutsch and Krauss trucking game in which rivals may block certain routes in order to prevent the others' access to the exclusive goal. Mintz's task, requiring individual contestants to pull their individual funnels out of the container before inundating, is another example. Interestingly in both cases, implements are used to block the other rather than allowing physical contact between contestants. A curious variant of one-on-one counteraction are cockfights, where the animals are used as extensions of the self.

Sherif et al.'s (1961) robber's cave experiment examined in chapter 1, is a field study that involves complex cooperative and competitive structures and is replete with examples of deliberate acts by one group to retard the progress of the other. The frequent incidence of aggression reported would seem to be partly attacks instrumental in preventing rivals from reaching their goals and partly expressions of mounting anger and hostility in response to the others' attack.

Direct-contact sports such as wrestling and fencing require physical interactions in order for one of the competitors to emerge as victor. In all types of competitive contests, outcomes depend on three major factors: personal skill, extraneous chance factors over which the person has very little or no control (weather conditions, bad news received before the contest, sudden leg cramps), and the relative skill of each competitor. No matter how outstanding A, if B is better, B emerges as victor and A does not. In coactive sports contests—races, high jumping, throwing a javelin and all of the field and track activities that made up the ancient decathlon—relative skill is an ultimate determinant also. In counteractive contests, however, the direct contact increases interdependence considerably and hence heightens the relative skill factor. That is, the task role requirement is such that each move by A must be responded to by B, and vice-versa. By virtue of their required interaction, competitors have both more control over each other but are also more dependent on each other.[2]

Functions served by social comparison in counteractive conditions are likely to be different from those in coaction conditions. In the latter, social comparison as a rule is not required by the task and consists primarily of the information-obtaining component: determining what the coactor is doing and how, not because of objective task requirements but because of personal needs for information, curiosity, and so on. As goal contriency and/or task similarity increase and are strengthened, competitive motives and needs for assessment of coactors' progress begin to dominate, not because this information is task required but as a standard to be bested by own performance. In counteractive conditions, however, as contestants become more highly interdependent, the assessment of competitors may actually constitute part of the task requirements: opponents' vulnerabilities and strengths must be assessed, moves parried or blocked, and one's own strategies guided by an evaluation of the others' tactics.

Counteractive conditions are not restricted to contact sports. They include interpersonal games of chance such as some card games and board games, of which chess is perhaps one of the oldest and most universal. Counteractive games of all kinds abound, perhaps because each society must formalize relatively harmless occasions for competitive counteraction in order to prevent more violent uncontrolled outbreaks of such interpersonal combats.

In nonformalized activities, counteractions occur in more subtle ways. One of the most frequent occasions may be found in conditions of scarcity, characterized by situations in which the goal is generally the possession of objects rather than states of being in the goal region, which are the goals of formal contests. In sports contests, trophies are sought for the symbolic value of victory rather than as valuable objects in themselves. Scarcity can be said to exist when the number of people desirous of the same objects exceeds the number of available objects. Some of the most interesting issues in the area of competition focus on conditions under which scarcity may result either in peoples' counteractive competition or in cooperative attempts to deal with the problem. So far these questions have been addressed almost exclusively by anthropologists, as exemplified by Mead's (1951) work. Something of the American ethos is beginning to be revealed in adult responses to the gasoline shortages of the 1970s, a situation that invites field study of counteractions.

In most classrooms, competition does not reach overtly aggressive counteraction. Its occurrence is prevented by teachers in traditional classrooms who favor tasks requiring coaction, who favor individualized learning, or who create strong norms against any kind of interpersonal interaction during instructional periods. There may be an occasional outbreak such as when the class receives a limited quantity of highly desired objects (perhaps a box of colored pencils), when children may be seen to behave as do their elders on similar occasions in supermarkets. But such actions are generally quickly squelched by the teacher who is usually ready to act on a more equitable distribution principle. It is interesting that each school, regardless of its type or degree of progressivist philosophy or stance toward competition or cooperation, still provides formal opportunities for counteractive competition on the playgrounds and playing fields.

Characteristics and Requirements
of Cooperative Conditions

In a comprehensive review of children's cooperation and helping behaviors, Bryan (1975), a major contributor in the field, states that "interest in the development of cooperation among children stems more from practical than theoretical concerns insofar as theorizing is almost absent in this area of research." We certainly agree, but our conception of cooperation differs from the definition as stated by Bryan: "Cooperation is thought to be reflected when individuals coordinate their actions in order to obtain what they want."

This definition reflects the theoretical point of view in social psychology that conceives of social relationships as an outcome of contact between individuals, each of whom is motivated by a utilitarian calculus of personal gains and losses and/or inputs and outputs accruing from given interactions (see for example, Adams 1965; Thibaut and Kelley 1959; Walster, Walster, and Berscheid 1978; Kelley and Thibaut 1978). Such social-exchange theories were useful in creating methodologies for determining preferential orientation toward either competitive or cooperative relationships. And they appear appropriate for handling motivational analyses of competitive situations, since rivals may frequently consider potential gains and losses that might be consequences of their own or their opponents' competitive acts. However, a similar emphasis on individual dynamics in cooperative situations misses the central feature that is absent in competitive conditions and present in cooperation: that of common shared-group goals and promotively interdependent member activities.

Group Goals

There has been much thought, discussion, speculation, and argument about the conceptual properties of group goals and their measurement (Cartwright and Zander 1953, 1960, 1968; Shaw 1976; Zander 1971). With the shift in emphasis toward individual concepts since the early 1960s, the concept of group goal was discarded by many, along with other group concepts considered mentalistic, vague, unmeasurable, or unscientific. Others concluded that group goals were inseparable from individual goals, and since they seemed to function much in the same way, the concept of group goals was an unnecessary duplication.

We believe that group goals can be identified, that they function as an important source of member interdependence in groups, and that they play an important function in groups in cooperative conditions. The concept of group goal denotes a common, central force field that appears most of the time readily identifiable as an objective entity. The concept provides an aspect of unity, of common fate, that cannot readily be conveyed by additive individual goals.

A brief glance at research dealing with promotively interdependent goals in cooperative situations may be instructive. Almost always it entails reward structures based on the performance of the total group and distributed equally among collaborating group members at the conclusion of the work session. In so doing, the common goal conditions—to make a building, complete a puzzle, and so forth—are separated from the reward conditions. This fact has two undesirable consequences. In our view, equal distribution constitutes three individual rewards. They are equitable and equal, to be sure, but they stress the personal contribution of each group member and hence each one's individuality rather than the commonality that united them. Further the prizes or other gifts in fact constitute extrinsic rewards, generally found less satisfying and less effective than intrinsic rewards (Deci 1975).

Group Tasks

A second source of interdependence of groups in cooperation lies in the work that must be carried out, the group task. Tasks, in their broadest sense, are the reason for human interrelationships; people come together because they want to do something, ranging from fulfilling together the most basic needs—receiving nourishment from another or sleeping with another—to verbal exchanges—from grunts to military commands to prayers and blank verse—and including activities like building castles and straw huts, bridges and skyscrapers. For psychologists, tasks are important in the investigation of groups because they require various forms of interdependence. By designing specific activities around which people are asked to interact with each other, the social psychologist creates in the laboratory the basis for specific interdependence relations whose effects can be studied under controlled conditions.

Regardless of differences in task requirements, we assert that interpersonal interaction and verbal communication constitutes the essence of behaviors that characterize cooperative conditions. This means, however, that in principle, all of the work on group process—including that by social psychologists, industrial psychologists, group dynamicists, and those in related fields—becomes relevant in the consideration of cooperative task conditions. To the extent that any kind of systematic unifying framework can be said to exist in this disparate research, it is in the traditional paradigm of group interaction as mediator between input factors and performance outcomes.

An excellent overview of this conceptualization and relevant research is provided by Hackman and Morris (1975). In this model, input variables are considered variously on the level of the individual (characteristics of members, personal skills, and so forth), on the level of the group (group variables of cohesiveness, structure, and goal), and features of the wider environment (which often includes a description of tasks, outside rewards, relations to other groups, and so on). Different researchers thus may attempt to establish relationships between one or more input factors and diverse aspects of group interaction, study relationships within the interaction process itself, or relate features of the process to performance outcomes (the last generally involves quantity or quality of accomplishment but may include effects on members such as their satisfactions or attitudes toward each other).

We find ourselves in substantive agreement with Hackman and Morris's position:

> It may be unrealistic to work toward achieving a truly general theory of the relationships between group interaction and group performance effectiveness. Instead, it may be necessary to make some a priori distinctions among general classes of tasks and then to delve into process-performance relationships *within* each class. While this is not as elegant an approach as some might desire, the development of subtheories of process-performance relationships would nonetheless represent a notable improvement over current understanding of group process determinants of group effectiveness. [Pp. 58-59]

The authors base their conclusions primarily on findings of variations in relationships between performance from task to task. Close scrutiny of research on cooperation indeed yields such discrepancies both in different tasks within the same study and same tasks used by different experimenters. Thus in Deutsch's original classroom research behaviors differed somewhat as a function of tasks. For instance, the puzzle task involved fewer emotional reactions and profited less from group discussion as compared with human-relations problems. Even in as close a replication as was Hammon and Goldman's of the Deutsch study, differences in several minor procedural details apparently resulted in some discrepanices between the two findings. Yet in the study of cooperation, tasks tend to be employed all too often merely as a convenient way of getting group members to do something together. The activity itself is generally not seen as an important variable that must be considered in relation to individual skill resources required of, and possessed by, the group members who are to perform a given task.

Several attempts have been made to categorize group tasks. Most schemes readily distinguish between unitary tasks, which are indivisible and hence make mutual assistance difficult, and divisible tasks, separable into subtasks. Important interpersonal consequences follow from those task differences in cooperative conditions. Steiner's (1972) typology makes further distinctions of interest to our concerns. Additive tasks make the group's success contingent on the summation of individual products. Other tasks are singled out whose outcomes are determined principally by one member's performance. In disjunctive tasks, performance depends on at least one member's being able to carry the group, while in conjunctive tasks, the success of the group is dependent on the least effective member. Still other tasks do not demand any specific method of performance and are referred to as discretionary. These few, relatively simple distinctions between tasks point to some of the reasons for differences in performance under cooperative conditions.

Concepts for Classifying Behaviors

The lack of a language descriptive of behaviors in cooperative conditions indicates the great need in this area for theoretical advances. There is no need to invent new terms; a potential terminology exists. What is needed is its use. The terms we suggest have their origin in various branches of behavioral science and specifically in the beginning formulations of group-dynamics theory. The terms came into general use as employed by various members of the National Training Laboratory for Group Dynamics during the 1950s when some important research into interpersonal behaviors in small groups evolved around these concepts. Bales (1950), for instance, developed a categorization scheme of member interaction, the basis of most subsequent variants of methods that measure interpersonal group behaviors. One of the earliest attempts to distinguish between task roles and group roles was that of Benne and Sheats (1948), followed by Bales and Slater (1955) and Thibaut and Kelley (1959). It is unfortunate that over the years these and related terms have accumulated varied meanings so that they are either used today by some with no unitary meanings, or shunned by others for the very lack of such clarity.

We have found task and role concepts essential when dealing with interpersonal behaviors in performance situations and have adopted the following terminology that retains and clarifies some of the original meanings. General descriptions of tasks such as those suggested by Steiner (1972) are referred to as *task characteristics*. They describe properties of tasks that determine certain activities that must be performed in order for the task to be accomplished. These essential activities are referred to as *task requirements* (Hackman and Morris 1975 call the same task dimension *critical task contingencies*). Among task requirements, we distinguish activities dealing with material, nonpersonal relationships from behaviors that involve only interpersonal interactions.

The impersonal requirements are referred to as *task activity requirements*; they describe job-related manipulations, including what activities need to be performed and how they are to be done. The latter, *task role requirements*, focus on the interpersonal relationships dictated by the demands of the task that are essential to its execution. Here the concerns involve who needs to have contact with whom to perform the necessary activities.

A further distinction may prove useful; it employs the concept of *group role requirement*. This term refers to interpersonal exchanges that must occur to enable the group to function smoothly. The defining characteristics of group role requirements do not stem directly from a specific task requirement but rather derive from the internal needs of the group to maintain itself in order that any task may be performed. For instance, if a quarrel breaks out, progress is impeded regardless of the other specific activity requirements. The presence of a group role is required such that action is taken to achieve a resolution so that work can proceed. Such a group role presumably could be carried out either by the parties to the dispute themselves or by any one group member. The important point here is that this group function is needed in order for the group to reach its goal.

Categorization of Cooperative Conditions

Next we outline the skeleton of a categorization scheme for cooperative conditions based both on some of the distinctions among tasks made earlier and on our behavior terminology. In attempting to differentiate various conditions systematically in terms of their degree of interdependence, we begin with conditions that are likely to require minimal interdependence and end up with highly complex interdependent conditions.

Conditions of Colabor. In conditions with the lowest interdependence, those of colabor, each person is assigned a certain amount of work unrelated to that of others. Tasks here may be characterized as divisible and additive. Task role requirements and group role requirements are minimal. Examples of such task assignments are legion in industrial settings. Whether members see themselves at all as interdependent in such situations depends primarily on the presence and nature of the group goal. Definite production goals may exist for a group of workers and be known to the supervisor, manager, or others in charge. If the workers are not aware of the quotas or reject them, both essential sources of interdependence in cooperative conditions—goal interpependence and task interdependence—are absent. In fact, the situation conforms to the definition of coaction. When this state of affairs prevails, the situation will become an actively competitive one. Workers will work solely for their own personal gain. Comparison behaviors may make their appearance, as may covered or expressed hostility, especially if individual rewards based on individual performance are administered. The competitive situation would be accentuated if bonuses were given for maximum performance.

This analysis emphasizes the importance of group goals, for these are the powerful agents that can turn individuals into promotively interdependent members. The group goal is missing in this situation as it frequently is in factories where workers have no identification with the company, its aims, or each other. In other situations, identical but for the fact that the workers take pride in their combined work output, such a strong sense of an ultimate common group goal may be sufficient to create the interdependence needed to turn the situation into a cooperative venture. This happened in the influential Hawthorne study (Turner 1933), which obtained performance increases by the deliberate creation of a cohesive work group with a strong group goal (although later alternative interpretations were suggested for these outcomes; see Hare 1967).

Analogies may be drawn between conditions of colabor in industry and some classroom situations. In large, impersonal college or university classrooms, neither task sources nor common goals create interdependence among students. Personal goals dominate, and when a contrient reward structure is added, all of the essential ingredients are provided for the occurrence of interpersonal competition. If there is some classroom discussion or interaction of some kind before or after class, perceptions of commonalities of interest, attitudes, and the like may gradually develop. However, these social factors, being extraneous to the group as a whole, may distract or actually hinder the performance of individual students, though possibly reducing competitiveness. Common course materials or classroom experiences, while not constituting task or goal interdependencies per se, have been shown to provide a basis for interpersonal interaction outside the classroom (Feldman and Newcomb 1969). On such occasions, the task may be said to be a mediator in the satisfaction of individual goals. Situations where the central characteristic of tasks is its instrumentality in individual need satisfactions constitute the second type of cooperative condition.

Coordinative Conditions. This category comprises situations where two or more individuals come together and help each other simply as a means of reaching their own personal goals rather than working toward a common, shared goal. Goal interdependence is generally low. Tasks are generally divisible and discretionary. Whatever interdependence there is in coordinative conditions stems from particular task requirements, which may vary in the degree to which individuals need each other to reach their own goals. The label for this condition is taken from Piaget's (1950) observation that "to co-operate is to co-ordinate operations." Piaget, with a developmental focus on the individual, wants to bring out that development of a person to a level where certain interactions become possible in the physical world enables two persons with such skills to interact on that level with each other. The implication is that on this simple level of cooperation, minimal social understanding is required.

Nelson's marble pull game may serve as a prototype of coordinative work. It may be recalled that in this situation, members of a dyad each had to pull a string attached to a cup. Opposite pulls broke the cup in half and netted losses to both players. One child had to loosen her own pull to allow the other to gain a marble. Individual gain dominated with most children, except the youngest or most passive ones, who allowed the more active child to take all of the marbles. Here there was no common goal. One child's gain was another's loss. In this zero-sum game, interdependence was also created by the contrient goal structure. Yet since no child could gain by simultaneous insistence on her own need satisfaction, it was necessary to seek alternatives to sustaining losses and allowing the other to win. Turn taking turned out to be the behavioral solution that allowed each child to amass her marbles. In this situation, the goal cannot be said to have been promotively interdependent since one child's winning did not move the other child into the same position also. Group roles were not required, nor were task roles. The cooperative feature lay in the tacit agreement about a working procedure that allowed an equal distribution of individual rewards. Indeed individual operations were coordinated here according to principles of equity.

Nelson's choice of task was highly representative in the sense that it exemplifies many tasks in our culture that require engaging in positive behavior toward others in the ultimate service of one's own goals and need satisfactions. All exchange relationships based on reciprocity norms fall into this category.

The marble pull game represents cooperative conditions of minimal interdependence. Many coordinative conditions are characterized by a higher degree of interdependence. For instance, interdependence may be increased through task requirements where simultaneous interaction is demanded in order for each party to gain individual rewards. The prototypical example here may be represented by Madsen's cooperation board. The task role here requires the coordination of pointers held by two children who have to move a puck to one side into one hole in order for each to reap his own individual reward. The task role here again is barely present; only a few nonverbal coordinated movements are required. Task interdependence may be raised in such simple coordinative situations by requiring more demanding task roles, such as making prior group decisions about procedures to be followed.

One may wish to debate the extent to which getting the puck into the common hole constitutes a shared, common, or individual goal. In any case, each child finds coordinative action in this situation to his own advantage and proceeds to do so. The role of individual goals could be easily minimized and, correspondingly, commonality increased, if, for instance, successful dispatch of the puck netted rewards not to the two players but to a third needy individual. Here the common new goal would most likely increase the need for increased interaction. The task now would require common decisions about the final amount of the common contribution, how it is to be delivered to the recipient, and so forth. Both situations of heightened interdependence—increasing task role requirements or the commonality of the goal—might be expected in the marble pull game and cooperation board to result in a reduction of individual pulls and pushes and increases on turn taking or common pointer moves, respectively.

Note that increased interdependence seems to require increased role enactment. This generalization leads to the third type of cooperative condition.

Role-related Cooperation. We favor this term because the presence of roles suggests a degree of interdependence strong enough to enable a collection of people to utilize each member in action toward a common purpose. Role-related cooperation thus represents the most complex condition of cooperation.

Let us start with an example of a study carried out at the Research Center for Group Dynamics in the Group Productivity Program headed by J.R.P. French, Jr. (Pepitone 1952). Groups of four students met together with the experimenter who explained the group's project. The work task was presented as consisting of two separate parts, and two members were assigned to each part. Each pair worked in a different room; their work was to be combined at the end into the total group product. In order to hold each condition constant, each pair actually worked on the same task, each thinking the other pair was completing the other task.

Differential perceptions of task role interdependence were created through descriptions of respective member task roles. Some pairs were told that their role was highly important because the other pair was totally dependent on their task performance. If they did not complete their work and complete it correctly, the others could not proceed. In another condition, the contribution to the group success of each pair was described as equal, and in a third condition, the description was reversed in that the work of the particular subgroup was described as unimportant to the success of the group. As expected, members who assume that the other team was greatly dependent on them felt more responsible for the success of the group and performed more accurately and faster than did their counterparts who saw their roles as less essential to the group's progress.

Here the difference between coordinative and role-related cooperative groups is clear. In the latter, we are dealing with persons who perceive themselves as working members of a group with a common goal, with specific task-required activities assigned to each member. Each person understood the interdependencies among members and proceeded to carry out her task-required role in expectation of making her contribution to the group's success.

In subsequent work in the same research program, different degrees of task role interdependence were created through what Thomas (1957) called "means control facilitation." The division of labor was arranged so that in some conditions, some group members had to perform their work before the other members could proceed with their work, thus tying the roles closer to each other. These task requirements were compelling in their effects. The interdependencies created were so strong when one member provided the means that facilitated the other's work that even when workers were told to strive for individual goals, "they strove for group goals in the experiment."

Yet another example of role related cooperation is found in Aronson's jigsaw research, where member interdependence was created by assignment to each participant one part of a problem, the solution of which was needed by all of the other members. All of these three examples involved additive tasks, most likely because of the greater ease of creating in the laboratory task interdependencies by differential task role assignments. Certainly most unitary tasks that confront a group with a common activity—as, for instance, in group problem solving—fall into the category of role-related cooperation. We suspect that unitary tasks, especially unstructured ones, require more group roles than do additive tasks whose requirements are given. This seems to be the burden of Hackman's (1968) and Morris's (1966, 1970) argument when they point to the general neglect of planning phases in the study of discussion groups. On the other hand, Steiner (1972) emphasizes the important function of coordination of member activities, presumably in additive tasks. It would appear that group roles constitute key variables in cooperation, yet we know little about adult role enactments in cooperative situations and even less about the role behaviors of children.

The speculative nature of this discussion makes it evident that we have merely pointed a direction by differentiation of three types of cooperative conditions that differ in the nature and degree of interdependencies. Unquestionably new research in this area can bring about sharper distinctions in the requirements of specific cooperative conditions for specific role enactments.

Developmental Considerations

Thus far we have been concerned with making theoretical distinctions between cooperative and competitive conditions, as well as extending theoretical differentiations within each of these conditions. Essentially we have made further discriminations within the life space as it confronts the person entering either of these conditions. This situational analysis presumably helps to understand ensuing behaviors and has a generality that can facilitate empirical research regardless of the specific subjects studied. In our exposition thus far we have employed frequent illustrations of children in school settings, since this is where our concern lies. Our first studies were conducted primarily from a social psychological perspective; hence the exploration of effects of diverse situational factors was of paramount interest. Accordingly the main criteria in selection of children of a given age as subjects were concerned with their ability to interact in the experimental situation as required. Each investigation raised a host of questions, most persistently around issues of interaction between developmental and situational factors. Obviously at different ages, different motivations, understandings, and skills of children are likely to make a crucial difference in their behavior when they are faced with competitive or cooperative conditions.

A developmental perspective appeared particularly necessary because competitive situations involve behaviors oriented toward maximizing own gain, and in so doing working against others. Cooperative situations necessitate concern with others. These are two orientations that are considered in some respects diametrically opposed to each other and about which there exists much theoretical speculation, and an increasing body of research on development of behaviors likely to be relevant in these two conditions. Based on these considerations, we embarked on two of the major developmental social investigations involving two entire elementary schools, kindergarten through fifth grade, in two socioeconomically different school districts. Part II contains an account of these children's behavior and performance. Our reasons for this undertaking were echoed more recently by Wohlwill (1973):

> Simultaneous investigation of the effects of age and experimental conditions . . . can play a most important role in transcending the limitations of ordinary age-group comparisons, so as to reveal the bases for some given age change in behavior more directly. . . . This type of research is of interest not just because it allows us to sharpen our interpretation of observed age differences, but because it leads to an improved definition of the dimension of age change we are dealing with. It is thus an essential first step in our programmatic approach to the study of developmental processes. [P. 89].

Wohlwill deals here with the issue of developmental study of children's behaviors in different contextual situations from a methodological point of view. The theoretical justification for combining a developmental and social psychological approach is best expressed in Hartup's and Coates's (1970) discussion of children's peer interaction:

> The topography of peer group interaction among 6-, 7-, and 8-year olds has not been thoroughly explored. . . . Peer relations research has paid little attention to developmental problems. . . . The data consist almost entirely of age differences. . . . Consequently, there is an urgent need for integrating broad-based theories of behavioral development . . . with the classic theories of group dynamics in childhood. [Pp. 436-437]

The Development of Competition-related Motivations

Research generated by game-theoretical models has shown that children's competitive choices—at least American children's—increase between the ages of 3 1/2 and 5 1/2 and are firmly established by 5 years of age, showing small increases thereafter and being predominantly the preferred mode of interaction. The data, from several diverse sources (McClintock and Moskowitz 1976; McClintock, Moskowitz, and McClintock 1977; Nelson and Madsen 1969; Toda et al. 1978) are clear-cut and quite consistent, yet the limited methodology would seem to allow only highly limited conclusions. The inference is justified that the particular 5 year olds studied are motivated in a two-choice situation both to act so as to choose the alternative that allows them to maximize their own gain and to do so at another child's expense. But there are several problematic issues here, and each speaks to the point of the development of competitive motivations.

First, the strength of the motivation needs to be questioned. With a narrow array of choices available, repeated, even exclusively self-maximizing choices may in fact not be a reflection of the intensity of motivation, yet the research may leave the erroneous impression that competitive motivation reaches a peak at a very early age. It is, of course, hard to believe that a 5 year old's competitive choice reflects as strong a competitive motivation as is present, say, in an Olympic contestant. It may be said in reply that such research simply demonstrates preferred orientation. Still, data gathered by gaming methodology, although the major source of data on very young children's behavior in competitive situations, need to be interpreted very cautiously. They lend themselves all to easily to the interpretation that competitive motivation is inevitable, at least in American children.

This caution leads to a second issue concerning the nature of the motive itself. Since the reward is so closely tied to the response made in game situations, a child may simply choose to have a bigger reward than another child.

One may thus question whether a simply wanting more of something than another constitutes the same motivational dynamic as does competition in situations that involve expenditure of effort toward attaining a specific goal. Research and theory in the area of competition seems to have studiously avoided motivational questions, contending itself with the underlying dynamics of competitive behavior as self-maximizing. Deutsch, who focused on the structure of the social field as it affected behavior, never addressed himself directly to motivational issues in competition. Recent research that studies children's reactions to their successes or respective failures focuses primarily on the directedness of competitive motivation. Toda et al. (1978) distinguish competition as a means toward one's own gain maximization (beginning in children around 4 1/2 years) from its functioning as an autonomous social motive (around 7 years). Smith et al. (1969) consider the underlying motives in competition as part of achievement-related motives, as "factors that come into play when a person undertakes a task at which he will be evaluated, enters into competition with other persons, or otherwise strives to attain some standard of excellence" (p. 1). Their further description lays out the kinds of factors that we too would like to see considered in research on competition: "under such circumstances a variety of motivational dispositions and cognitive assessments of the situation are activated, and influence a persons' tendency to behave (e.g. his tendency to work more or less hard, to persist or to give up and turn to another activity, his thoughts of doing well or poorly, and his physical manifestations of stress" (ibid.).

Third, theories of competition must address themselves to the generality of the motive, or the breadth of situations that elicit competitive behaviors. We have delineated goal and task characteristics that constitute strong forces on the person to initiate behaviors aimed at besting another. Yet for a variety of reasons, not all of such objective competitive conditions may be responded to with such expected behaviors. Furthermore contrient goal relations may be perceived when objectively none are present. For instance, a child may devote her major efforts in school in trying to do better than another child in a variety of subjects, even though she may be in an ungraded classroom. We have already encountered cautions offered in the early days of competition research (May and Doob 1937) to the effect that competition has a psychological aspect as well, a caution that ought to be still heeded today.

We are not addressing ourselves to limitation of gaming methodologies but are raising what appear to us to be crucial questions about a child's selectivity at different ages of specific arenas for competitive encounters. Is a young child as actively involved in competitive situations at home as at school or when visiting? Even these locales are on a much too global level yet. Inquiry must extend to more specific activities in the home, in school, or at other places, which constitute competitive challenges to children at different points in their development. Whether, with age, people tend to make sharper distinctions between situations that do or do not lend themselves to competition or whether they tend to adopt the same competitive stance in a broader variety of situations is at present only a matter of speculation. We all know children and adults whose behavior would fall into extremes—those who cannot resist any competitive challenge that may come along, and turn situations into contrient goal relationships when they need not be that, those who avoid even the mere appearance of competition, and those who restrict competitive encounters only to their field of expertise. We have observed the makings of such individual differences among the many children we have studied under controlled conditions over the past years. Children's competitive styles, the areas in which a child is willing to compete, and relationship of outcomes of competition to a child's self-concept and feelings of own competencies are questions that need to be examined.

Another realm of related questions revolves around the issue of who is chosen or seen as a competitor. Is the actual contriency in the goal relationship of two or more rivals the only determinant, or does the interpersonal relationship enter into acceptance of, or invitation to, competitive challenges? Other things equal, does a child compete, or compete more readily, with siblings? with friends? with strangers? with agemates or adults? And do criteria of choice of competitor change with other developmental changes? There are no specific empirical data available, no doubt partly because in laboratory research, competitors are almost always selected by the experimenter for purposes of control.

On the conceptual level, the research and theory on social comparison gives some suggestion as to the direction in which answers may be sought. Festinger's original formulation postulated needs for an accurate evaluation of abilities, and this need is said to motivate adults to seek out comparable others in the process of trying to arrive at accurate self-assessments. The theory has received some empirical support from the experimental study of adult subjects, but there are very few directly comparable studies of children. We have referred to conditions as they exist in many traditional classrooms as an ideal field for observing children's nonverbal attention paid to each other, which presumably involve also social comparisons. When children work side by side on identical assignments, not only are the goals of the activities identical (to get the right answers) and the identity of the work allows direct comparison, but comparison is with others who are similar in many respects. Children in one elementary school tend to be generally homogeneous because of districting, which tends to receive children from similar socioeconomic backgrounds, often netting children from predominantly homogeneous cultural, ethnic, educational, religious, and political parental backgrounds as well. In school itself, grouping is based on age, and if assignment to a given section is based on ability as well, children indeed constitute similar others.

The purposes of children's social comparisons are as yet unclear. When children are given a chance to base their comparison on the ability as well as the sex of the referent, as they were in an isolated study by Feldman and Ruble (1977), they use both criteria. There was a suggestion that a number of the youngest first graders stated their preference of comparison with a low-ability other, presumably to be able to attribute greater competence to themselves. Fourth graders, like adults, showed more interest in comparing with best-off others, presumably using the other as a standard setter for the performance goal they wished to attain. If so, it would underscore Tripplett's first demonstration of the effects of pacing on children's competitive behavior. But in the Feldman and Ruble study, no competition was involved, and they noted only what children claimed were their comparison interests. What their actual behavior would be, if allowed a variety of comparisons in an actual situation, is not known. Most importantly, the motivational base for comparison was unknown as well.

Festinger has postulated an underlying need for self-evaluation, but neither he nor post-Festinger research has studied more specifically the nature of self-evaluational processes. Self-evaluation would seem to involve complex judgmental and inferential processes, culminating at some point in something akin to a self-concept with regard to the ability or characteristic in question. For children, these self-evaluation processes may be much simpler, and, in fact, the role of others in uncertain situations may be important without a self-evaluational drive. Since our earlier analysis has isolated nonverbal social comparisons as one of the major, perhaps the main, interpersonal behaviors occurring in coactive competitive conditions and since our research focuses on attentional behaviors of children as a measure of such comparisons, let us consider these behaviors from a developmental perspective.

Relative to adults or even to older children, young children are objectively less able, less certain of their abilities, more uncertain about what is expected of them (especially by unfamiliar adults in strange environments, such as constituted by laboratory settings), less clear about performance criteria or how to do what they are expected to do. According to Zigler and Yando (1972) and Ruble and Nakamura (1973), these kinds of task-related uncertainties may be expected to elicit a great deal of attention paid to others simply to solve the problem.

With age, informational dependence on others decreases across a wide range of problems, as shown, for instance, by decreases in imitation of a model with age (Hartup and Coates 1970; Zigler and Yando 1972) and by decreased judgmental conformity in Asch-type settings (Berenda 1950).

However, although older children become less information dependent on others, new variables become relevant and constrain children toward social comparisons. This may include the need for a self-evaluation of abilities, which may develop along with children's facility to engage in formal operations. Support for this interpretation is gained from the Feldman and Ruble study, which found that fourth graders attributed to story characters very strong interests in comparing with a child said to have high ability, whereas first graders did not.

We find ourselves in agreement with Hartup and Coates that very little is known about the role of peer pressures at different developmental points in children's lives. We simply do not know whether concern with other children's assessment, (the fear of being ridiculed, found wanting, ostracized, and so forth) increases or decreases during the latency years.

Finally in competitive coaction in particular, comparison has an important function of helping to determine progress en route to the goal made by the competitor. Changes with age in behaviors based on this dynamic are questionable, depending, presumably, on the developmental course of achievement-related motivations, as well as on abilities to process information obtained by gleaning at the competitor (which also should increase with age). In fact, an increase in achievement-related motives might very well heighten the information seeking from others in order to ensure being correct, even though information dependence may tend to decrease with age. In sum, social comparison, even in children, seems to comprise a variety of processes, each with its own complexities. Nevertheless, or perhaps because of this complexity, we investigated children's comparison behaviors in competitive situations in a number of studies.

Something must be said about the development of hostile behaviors, which we expect to occur in competition. If, as we assume, coaction and counteraction differ primarily in the degree of interdependence of the competitors, the behaviors are likely to differ also primarily in degree but perhaps also in mode of expression. In the former condition, hostility probably will be restricted more to verbal denigrations, while active physical combat may break out in the latter.

One of the few reviews on children's aggression and certainly the most extensive one (Feshback 1970) makes no mention of research concerned with aggressive behaviors of children in competitive conditions. There are quite a few observational studies of fighting among preschoolers, predictably noting a decrease by school age and practically a disappearance thereafter. Exceptions occur when aggression is observed in fantasy play or as vented on substitute objects, without exception inanimate. Parents and school personnel surely know better. Apparently the only researcher brave enough to dare to instigate aggression (albeit indirectly through scientific manipulation of conditions rather than himself being attributed the role of direct instigator) is Sherif and his coworkers (1961) in the robber's cave research.

Aggressive behavior, potentially one of the most harmful interpersonal interactions, is perhaps one of the most rigorously normatively controlled activities in society's attempt to protect its people from others. Normative influence processes start very early in the socialization process, at least with American children. Ironically, especially among certain subcultures in American society, this is carried out by a threatened counteraggression of adults so that aggression among many children is suppressed until they themselves reach a state or stage where their own aggression is sanctioned by the norms of their particular peer culture. While these considerations may appear to take us far afield, they help to explain why the laboratory or formal school settings are probably not the most likely places to encounter children's aggression.

Children's Motivation to Collaborate

In contrast to the voluminous theory and research on competition-related motivations in children, there is no such corresponding literature on motivation to cooperate. As far as cooperation is concerned, one is left with the impression that children must be somehow made to collaborate; that is, these behaviors must be induced by outside forces against the children's natural inclinations. Aspirations to excel over others, aside from the work on independence training that represents deliberate efforts at strengthening related motives, by contrast appear to be seen as more spontaneous, more satisfying growth experiences. Perhaps this constitutes a comment on the societal valuations accorded these respective modes of interaction in the general American culture.

Prosocial behaviors, primarily in the form of helping, are generally linked with cooperation, and there is no dearth of speculation and research on motivations to help. Included here are altruistic motives, self-gain, empathy, sympathy, and a host of normative factors as well. But the literature is silent on children's specific needs to work together. However, if the question is altered just slightly to inquire into children's needs to be with each other, not only the body of research on play but also research and theory on peer relationships and social conformity becomes relevant.

Throughout our work we have been increasingly aware that assignment to competitive conditions did not automatically or exclusively evoke competition-related motives. Rather we sensed a conflict between wanting to best others and, on the other hand, desires to be like the others, not to stand out, and hence the need to conform. Similarly in cooperative conditions, children tried to assert their individuality. Our growing conviction is that when children are placed into competitive or cooperative situations, corresponding motivations are not necessarily engaged, and certainly not exclusively so. Being asked to participate in either of these working conditions may elicit conflicting motivations, feelings, and attitudes in children of different ages and most certainly from different cultures.

On Egocentrism and Decentration

Before turning to developmental considerations of behaviors that may be expected of children in cooperative conditions, it may be useful to lay aside social psychological theories and reflect on the bearing of developmental interpretations relevant to children's interactions in cooperative and competitive situations. In particular we will concern ourselves with Piagetian theory, since it, more than any other theory, takes up the question of the development of children's understanding of other people, of crucial importance to our inquiry.

First, it is useful to picture development as a progressive differentiation of the organism from the environment, as well as within the organism. Around this basic conceptualization, there is today a striking unanimity among various child-centered disciplines. The central aspect of infancy is that it is characterized by undifferentiation. The infant cannot differentiate between herself and the environment and thus is at one with the universe in a way she will never be again during the normal course of her development. Were this separation of self not to take place, human beings would remain masses of needy protoplasm. If the person is to interact intelligently with the environment, differentiation of self from the rest of the world is essential. Thus the postinfancy years are spent differentiating the outside life space, and oneself from it, as well as differentiation taking place within the child. Flavell (1963, p. 65) puts it almost poetically: "Cognition always begins on the margins of both self and milieu, and works its way simultaneously into the inner regions of each." Here we may recall N. Graves' (1976) objection to this conceptualization as purely Westernized, arguing that children such as those living on the Cook Islands develop through and within the context of their society. This argument appears largely semantic, since Piagetian theory ascribes a tremendous role to the presence of others in individual development. However, there may indeed be cultural differences in the way that separation takes place and the way that the very young are differentiated from the outer world; and Western culture may support more a young child's differentiation from others and greater concern with her own internal differentiations. Be that as it may, a rudimentary differentiation must be present before a child can interact purposefully with another. Thus in the gaming task utilized by Graves with young children, the child could not make a choice between giving to himself or the other unless this sense of being distinct from others be present. But what determines the particular choice?

Here the concept of egocentrism, according to Flavell "perhaps the most widely misunderstood of Piagetian concepts" (p. 60), is important. As Flavell wrote, "Egocentrism . . . denotes a state in which the cognizer sees the world from a single point of view only—his own—but without knowledge of the existence of viewpoints or perspectives and without awareness that he is the prisoner of his own" (p. 60). It is not a selfish concern with one's own needs and their satisfaction in hedonistic pursuit. It is not a motivational concept but refers to cognitive processes that occur throughout different developmental periods. It is used to describe the infant in the sensory-motor stage, as well as the thought of children in preschool and early school years, and also that of adolescents, although its aspects may differ. In the preoperational period (children ages 2 to 7), one of its most pronounced characteristics is the tendency to center attention on a single, outstanding feature to the exclusion of some others: "it is . . . confined to the surface of the phenomena he tries to think about, assimilating only those superficial features which clamor loudest for his atttention" (p. 157).

How does a child come to be able to decenter, to correct egocentric distortion so as to "penetrate deeper into the fabric of reality?" (p. 65). There are essentially three ways, and all have to do with action. Interestingly Piaget accords action a more basic place than cognition, in the sense expressed in his pithy "operations are nothing but interiorized actions whose efferent impulses do not develop into external movement" (p. 83). In other words, thought springs from action. Children operate on the world, just as Dewey insisted that one learns by doing, and William James insisted that action precedes feeling. By manipulating the world, the child develops corresponding internal activities; he begins to be able to think in more complex ways, to entertain more than one thought or one action possibility at a given time, and to penetrate beyond the surface of things and people.

Second, children's behavior changes through imitation of others by simple assimilation of the acts of others in the environment. Such imitation occurs in the early periods of infancy, as well as at any other developmental period. What gets imitated at these different periods differs in age-appropriate ways. Third, children learn to decenter by interaction, principally with peers. By being exposed to different points of view and engaging in logical arguments and active disagreements, children begin to give up their own egocentric views, or, rather, they take those of others into account (not necessarily to conform, as social reality theory would be more likely to predict. However, both Piaget and Festinger emphasize the role of others in shaping persons' views of the world).

During the process of decentration, children develop the cognitive skills necessary to understand the thoughts and feelings of other people. Piaget (1926) referred to these attempts at penetrating into experiences of others as "taking the role of the other." This attempt at interpersonal understanding, which has come to be known as role taking, has been given increasing attention by developmental psychologists as a necessary ingredient in children's social development. It thus becomes a highly important concept to be examined in our consideration of children's behaviors in social situations.

Role taking is a cognitive process, concerned with making inferences about some person's features that are not directly observable. There is experimental support for Piaget's original assertion that an increased understanding of people develops parallel to the increased understanding of the physical world, being a reflection of the same underlying intellectual structures. Just as contemporary emphasis has moved from stress on discrete stages to interest in transition phases of development, so role-taking skills are also seen as developing gradually. Shantz (1975) presents a comprehensive overview of theory and research in this area. In general, just as children's mastery of concrete operations increases around 6 to 8 years of age, so does their ability to make judgments about other children's inner states, their understanding of how things look to others, or their ability to take account of the point of view of the other.

It is evident that role-taking skills are important in children's behaviors in competitive and cooperative situations. Particular difficulties are encountered in trying to bridge the gap between the behaviors of interest in these situations and the behaviors studied by developmentalists, who typically attempt to assess the age-related role-taking capabilities of one child in relation to one particular feature of the other child, and to control all nonrole-taking factors that might affect performance. Since role taking can only be inferred from performance, A is given the task—for instance, describing a picture so that B can recognize it. The task characteristic is such that it requires that A take B's perceptions into account. Ingenious designs enable an unequivocal categorization of A's description as demonstrating, or not demonstrating, role-taking skills. However, the social situations of interest to us here are on a more molar level and involve generally more complex, more prolonged interpersonal interactions. Factors are present that may be extraneous for the study of role taking but are essential for creating the kind of social environment we wish to study. Our solution has involved a three-step procedure: to analyze requirements of different kinds of competitive and cooperative tasks, to consider theoretically the task requirements in relation to the degree of decentration that may be necessary to function adequately in these various situations, and to subject these projections to empirical test.

Role-taking Requirements

In coaction where neither goal contriency nor task interdependence exists, sensitivity to coactors is not required. Interestingly among the first interpersonal peer association are those referred to as parallel play where toddlers play independently side by side. In chapter 4 we present evidence that even these very young children are sensitive to each other. The chapter offers many examples of fluid and close relations existing between the toddler and desired objects in the environment. The unrestrained wanting of the other child's toy is a classic example of egocentric behavior, foreshadowing what McClintock, Moskowitz, and McClintock (1977) call the 3 1/2 to 4 1/2 year olds' egoism in their preference of maximum gain for themselves in a simple two-person choice situation.

Let us examine, then, what is required of a child in the simplest interdependent task that uses gaming methodologies like that of the Kagan and Madsen card task. In order to choose, a child needs to have a concept of more or less, and perhaps to count. The act itself is simple; taking more for oneself than what could also accrue to the other does not require empathy with the other's feelings. In fact, the young child, who is not concerned with and is not able to reflect as yet on the other's feelings, presumably experiences no guilt when maximizing his own gain. However, children's preference for nonself-maximizing choices at this young age does not require the presence of any more role-taking skills either. It may be recalled that 80 to 90 percent of the Cook Island 5 to 7 year olds responded on a modified task of this sort with either equalizing distributions or even giving to others more than to themselves. The act of giving certainly requires no more complex motor movement than does taking. The Graves's field observations report these same children performing many community-oriented helping acts. In a culture where giving acts surround a child, modeling on the cultural ways of the elders to give to others is well within the repetoire of this age group. The crucial point here is that such giving does not necessarily mean that these children were empathetic with absent partners, or that they were able to reflect upon the deprived state of others, or even feeling that they did not wish to transgress cultural normative ways. These young children may simply have been doing what comes naturally.

Going beyond this illustrative example, we would generalize to all simple choice behaviors used as indexes of children's preferences as being essentially of such a nature that any preoperational child can carry them out, quite regardless of any progress made toward decentration. Further, in making a self-maximizing choice, the other need not be thought about at all other than in a surface fashion. Under these conditions, the dominant socialization patterns will determine the actual choices made, as the evidence suggests. Principles of generosity and sharing, giving, and other prosocial activities are certainly also prescribed in American society, even if not necessarily observed in practice. This normative knowledge, developed as part of children's socialization, is sufficient to account for increases in collaborative choices with these simple gaming tasks during the elementary school years.

In consideration of slightly more complex two-person games, such as Nelson's marble pull game, we are dealing with a coordinative situation in which each child is instrumental in helping the other maximize her gains. The task requirements here are somewhat more complex, demanding the coordination of each child's motoric movements, possibly involving also minimal needs for anticipating the movements of the other. Skills required here then, may involve rudimentary social cognitions needed in competitive counteraction, as well as in execution of task roles or group roles.

As interdependence increases in collaborative situations, requirements for role taking increase. This is also the case in counteractive situations. High interdependence, in particular if created by the task itself, implies that the other's behavior, as well as often intentions or feelings, must be understood and reckoned with. Competitors frequently must think through the consequences of their own and the other's actions (often necessitating the "lightning quickness" of formal operations, as Piaget likes to describe advanced thought processes). It means attending to surface characteristics like the expression of the opponent, the verbal messages, and the intent of both gesture and word (not necessarily the same) to make inferences from each, to plan action to block the other's move(s), and to carry it out in action, as well as to plan counterstrategies. Homeric Greeks valued the quality of cunning in their heroes, a quality that seems to describe the kind of behaviors necessary to outwit opponents through understanding the other's intentions, as well as by the use of their own prowess. Later in history, Spartan boys were deliberately taught some of these skills, supposedly beginning at their seventh birthday, just around the time when decentering processes in today's children have presumably advanced considerably. Coincidentally, also, a prototypical task in Flavell's (1968) role-taking research requires the child, in collaboration with the first experimenter, to outwit a second experimenter who knows that they are trying to fool him. The child is thus given the opportunity to match his anticipation of the other's cognitions. The measurement provided reflects the depth of the child's penetration into the other's thought and shows a steady increase in this ability between grades two and eleven.

Our argument, then, leads to the conclusion that it is not at all correct to assume that more decentration is required for functioning in cooperative conditions than in competitive conditions. It depends on the particular task requirements involved in a given condition. Highly interdependent competitive counteractions may demand as much, or more, decentering as do some relatively simple conditions of colabor. This conclusion underscores the importance of task characteristics facing children in cooperative and competitive conditions and the need to exercise extreme caution in generalizing from results obtained in any one study.

Role Taking in Cooperation

Last, we need to examine in greater detail specific sociocentric behaviors needed by children in performance tasks required in role-related cooperative conditions. The task used in much of the research examined in this volume—the simple-appearing task of constructing a design with blocks on a flat surface—is useful here. Let us assume that three children are in an unstructured condition such that they may choose what to make together. This is a role-related cooperative condition with a common group goal (undifferentiated at the outset) and a unitary task (with the potential for divisibility).

First, children are faced with the decision of what is to be represented. Second, they must develop common procedural understandings of how to do it and who is to do what. Sometimes these decisions are made explicitly in an involved group discussion, sometimes one member will simply start to work and the other two will follow and so forth. During the process of working, various disputes may flare up when different children want materials also used by others or when one child does not abide by the original group decision and goes off on a different creation. Following our previous exposition of social role theory, these and other needed behaviors can be classified into required group roles and task roles and their execution by different group members related to performance under cooperative conditions. It is clear that these roles, to various degrees to be sure, necessitate that the participants be concerned with each other and understand each others' points of view on a level that can occur only when the child has moved quite a bit away from her egocentric orientation. Furthermore one would expect an increase of these role behaviors throughout the elementary years, reflected also in the quality of the joint performance. We are led to conclude that whenever group roles are necessary in cooperative situations, there is a need for taking the role of the other also. Piaget's choice of terminology may ultimately prove to be fortunate in that it has the potential of linking up concepts and generalizations from social role theory, which is rooted in group dynamics, with concepts and generalizations of individual role taking from the point of view of developmental dynamics.

Social role requirements stem from a group member's role that involves being both a receiver and an initiator of interaction. Put differently, a child is required to be both a listener and a communicator. Underlying both is the need for a basic orientation toward the other. As a receiver, a child must try to understand not only what the other is saying but the other's intended meanings and, even more, the desires that underlie those meanings. This is the essence of role taking as it figures in Piagetian theory. As an initiator, the child's communication to the other involves not only a logical transmission of her own ideas to the other but requires concern with the other's thought processes so that her communication is understood.

There would seem to be a third basic social skill area, in which the meshing of different group members' thoughts occurs in an organized, differentiated fashion. We do not mean here that the ideas or individual accomplishments of each member must necessarily be amalgamated so that the final thought or product is better or different from any of the single outputs. Sometimes one person's contribution may be the one that finally gets accepted by all, sometimes a compromise emerges, and so forth. Rather the salient point here is that, especially in a cooperative situation, it is not sufficient that each person listen and comprehend the other or consider the other's point of view before communicating. Follow-up activities are necessary that may involve prolonged staying with or acting upon the other's point of view in a give-and-take fashion. This would appear to be a highly complex process that has not yet been examined from a developmental perspective.

Flavell (1977) isolated three aspects of role taking that mesh quite well with our own distinctions: (1) A's awareness of differences in perception, conceptions, or feelings of the other, (2) A's recognition that such differences must be taken into account, and (3) A's inferences about B's point of view. Flavell, of course, emphasizes the cognitive aspect of role taking, yet he also implies what we state explicitly as the necessity for putting these activities to active verbal and other task-oriented use in group settings.

Perhaps more than any other worker in the field, Selman (1971, 1976) seems to be building bridges from the developmental area toward the domain of the social psychologist. In broadening the concept of role taking to include feelings, motives, and moral reasoning, he has moved us closer to the possibility of relating stages of children's role taking to their functioning in various social settings. His stage description is a fitting conclusion to our attempt to integrate social and developmental factors in understanding children's behaviors in cooperative situations.

Stage 0, about ages 4 to 6, is referred to as the egocentric stage and corresponds closely to the familiar Piagetian definition of egocentrism as a period in which differentiation of self from others is possible but not that of taking points of view of the other. Stage 1, ages 6 to 8, is a period in which a child realizes differences in perspective but holds to his own as the correct view. According to our analysis, during both of these stages, children could carry out colaboring and coordinative tasks, especially if the individual ideas of partners happen to coincide. Lack of ability to execute required group roles leads one to expect periodic outbreaks of disagreement, especially where coordinative roles are required. Among the younger children, collaboration might even break up, with each child deciding to go his own way. According to Selman, the necessary skills will be available somewhat later (8 to 10 years) when cognitive role-taking skills come more easily to the child at stage 2.

It takes stage 3, mutual role taking (about ages 10 to 12), for children to be able to distinguish several group members' distinctive points of view, while they themselves can remain more-or-less objective outsiders: "In addition, each can consider a situation from the perspective of a third party who can also assume each individual's point of view and consider the relationships involved. Such an endless chain of role taking leads in the moral domain to the development of conventional rules for deciding between the claims of individuals (Selman 1976, p. 305). Clearly stage 3 cognitive skills fit precisely our specification of group roles required to function in highly interdependent cooperative settings.

According to Selman, stage 4 requires formal reasoning such as characterizes the thinking of adolescents and adults. Its distinguishing features at this stage are the invocation of a group perspective, of generalized principles of social relationships, rather than merely the interpersonal perspective of the previous stage.

The execution of task and social roles requires not only cognitive understanding but a certain know-how in execution of these roles. Selman has developed a filmstrip series based on moral dilemmas dealing with issues such as trust, fairness, property rights, and rules to be used in classrooms to stimulate children's thinking (between ages 6 and 12) toward stage 3. It might be highly profitable to give these children simultaneous training and practice in the execution of various group roles needed in cooperative work.

Summary

This theoretical exposition has developed the following major propositions with regard to competitive and cooperative conditions.

1. The nature of interdependence relations is crucial in both conditions.

2. Individuals are made interdependent by their particular goal relationships or task relationships, which differ both between and within each of the two conditions.

3. Coactive competitive conditions are characterized by an absence of task interdependence. Goal interdependence may vary from no interdependence among individual goals of coactors (no competition) to ab-

solute goal contriency (explicit, exclusive competition). Interactions are not required by either task or goal and, hence, neither are task roles nor group roles. Increases in goal contriency and task similarity heighten competitive motivation, and coactors engage in social comparison behaviors that primarily serve to gather procedural information or to assess their own or another's progress.

4. In counteractive competitive conditions, there is absolute goal contriency among competitors. Interaction is required, although task requirements may vary from minimal interaction to highly complex interdependencies such that each move of one competitor depends on the prior move of the other. Competitors engage in social comparison behaviors primarily to assess vulnerability and strengths of the competitor in order to block his access to the exclusive goal or to assess his own relative skill.

5. Cooperative conditions are defined by the promotive interdependence of members. The sources of these interdependencies may reside in the common, shared group goal and/or task and group requirements.

6. Three types of cooperative conditions are distinguished on the basis of degree and type of member interdependencies inherent in the task requirements of these different work situations. In the cooperative condition requiring the least interdependent behavior, the condition of colabor, individual tasks are not related and the amount of member interdependence is a function of the strength of particular group goals.

7. In coordinative conditions, shared group goals are minimal, but individuals assist each other in obtaining their individual goals. Various degrees of interdependence may be created by performing related task requirements that lead to the execution of task roles. Group roles tend to be minimally required.

8. In role-related cooperation, members are made interdependent through a common group goal and task-required activities. Although these conditions may vary in complexity, the execution of some task roles and some group roles is always required.

9. Studies of children's behaviors and performance in competitive and cooperative conditions must consider their skills at any one developmental stage in relation to the task requirements with which they are confronted.

10. In conditions of coaction and colabor, social role-taking skills are required only minimally, if at all. More and deeper understanding of opponents or partners is required, respectively, in conditions of complex counteraction and complex coordinative cooperation. Most role-related cooperation necessitates the presence of complex social cognitions that allow inferential knowledge of others. It also requires the ability to translate these cognitions into interpersonal interactions that are required in the exercise of task roles and group roles.

Notes

1. We are dealing here only with what Deutsch has referred to as pure competition. This excludes complex mixed competitive situations that involve, for instance, one cooperating team competing against another.

2. In team sports, all of these factors are complicated by the increased number of contestants, the intrateam cooperation and interteam competition, and the competitive conditions within each team (such as the personal records of excellence and the prestige of earning the highest pay).

3 The Research Methodology

The preceding two chapters emphasized three concerns that have direct bearing on choice of methodology. First, we presented arguments in support of the systematic study of interpersonal behaviors in working conditions characterized by competitive and cooperative goal structures. Then we outlined important social behaviors that are likely to be elicited in children when asked to function in these different performance conditions. Finally we dwelled at some length on the importance of the task structure itself as a significant, relatively unexplored determinant of children's behavior and performance.

This chapter focuses on corresponding operationalizations: the observation and measurement of the social behaviors and performance of interest to us and creation of task situations that were expected to elicit these behaviors.

Background Considerations

At the beginning of our research, the study of children within their natural classroom settings seemed imperative, primarily because these are the designated places in which most of children's learnings take place. It was not always so. In simple agrarian and urban preindustrial societies, work and social environments blended together imperceptibly, coexisting for children in an undifferentiated fashion in the family setting. It was here almost exclusively that children's needs were satisfied, and at the same time they were part of the social group that exerted its standards, defined and ascribed the roles and goals that defined children's tasks, and eventually made them producing members of the family and society at large. While children were growing up, their play environment and work environment were identical. Indeed one activity shaded into the other.

The advent of urbanization and industrialization changed this harmonious unity. Older family members left daily to work in factories and shops, and children went off to school. Historical analyses of American education have pictured the spectacular growth of free, compulsory education as a response to the need for functions that families in industrial America could not fulfill any more. Dewey in particular, in his educational philosophy of learning by doing, advocated introducing into schools activities that had been traditionally carried out in the home. His task analyses described the learning benefits accrued from woodworking or from boiling an egg in the classroom (Dewey 1966). Contemporary revisionists interpret such pedagogic strategies as deliberate attempts to include vocational training into the curriculum to fit the demands of work in industrial society. Along those lines, Violas's views (1978) are of particular interest. Singling out the subdivision of labor as the most important work pattern in the rapidly expanding empires of coal, steel, and railroads, he claimed that public schools were used as institutions to prepare the young, particularly immigrant children, for the docile, mechanical roles required by factory work. Revising the revisionists, Cremin's analyses (1969, 1970) took in a plethora of societal institutions and agencies that share educative functions in addition to family and school.

Undeniably children's understandings, attitudes, and values are shaped by their multifaceted environments. Today children, especially those of the affluent, also participate in varied outside-school activities: lessons of all kinds, games with friends, sports events and other amusements, trips, meals at restaurants, to mention just the most obvious. Yet during the school year, children spend approximately half of their waking day in school and at school-related activities. It appears still true that it is in school that the child's major task environment unfolds. Accordingly during the early stages of our research, we spent considerable time in elementary classroom observation.

At a recent symposium on cooperation in the classroom, participants agreed that almost no factual information was available about what actually transpires in the nation's classrooms. However, they disagreed completely as to their impressions regarding the extent of competitive or cooperative atmospheres in today's classrooms. Unanimously they felt more classroom observation was needed. Our own classroom observations led us to conclude that while descriptive accounts might be possible and desirable, observation alone simply did not permit a generalization about interrelationships that were of interest to us. It was clear that a measure of control was needed over the choice of children's activities and over the specific variables with which we were concerned. Therefore one of our principal aims became creating a standard task that would contain the major features found in school environments but that could be controlled and varied systematically.

We did not wish to present children with specific school tasks, primarily because their performance would have been tied too closely to prior experiences with a particular activity. We also wished to avoid tasks requiring problem solving, as individual differences in cognitive abilities would have confounded the interpersonal behaviors of interest. The other extreme of engaging children in play activities seemed equally undesirable if these activities were completely restricted to a "level of irreality" that has little connection with other activities that make up the life space of children. Lewin (1936) describes characteristics of this level such as its fluidity and the relative absence of barriers which allow the free movement characteristic of creative imagination. Piaget's conceptualization follows essentially along the same lines when he refers to imagination as "one of the two poles of thought . . . orientated in the opposite direction to logical and conceptual thought" (Piaget 1962, p. 155). Piaget here continued the analysis further than Lewin in that he made connections between specific games and the various thought processes they engage.

Helpful in our choice of a suitable task was Piaget's discussion of games in his *Play, Dreams and Imitation in Childhood* (1962). Starting from Bühler's original classification of children's games, Piaget focused on her fourth category, that of constructional games, which encompass activities like making a house with blocks, drawing and modeling. Such games, he claimed, form a special category; they involve both sensory-motor skills and symbolic representation and thus are "a move away from play in the strict sense, toward work, or at least toward spontaneous intelligent activity . . . occupying . . . a position half-way in between." These are precisely the kind of activities that we wished to capture with our task in order to reflect the developmental changes in interpersonal behavior occurring during children's work. Corroboration of our choice comes from Sutton-Smith (1979) who commented that "by the fourth and fifth year [children's] interest is focused on settings that they can construct themselves or that they can imagine with a group of friends in dramatic play" (p. 16).

Criteria for Task Selection

In the original formulation of our program (Pepitone 1971), several requirements were developed for the specific characteristics of the standard task. These requirements grew out of the intended programmatic uses to which the task was to be put. Their continued relevance suggests the usefulness of their restatement here. The task was to be employed in studies of behavior and performance under either cooperative or competitive conditions. Therefore the activity should lend itself to collaboration by several children to produce one indivisible group product. But an activity was also required with the potential for division into subtasks that each child could carry out individually to make her own product. Also the task should allow performance in all types of competitive environments, including coaction and competitive counteractions. Since the interdependence of group members was of major interest in the study of cooperation, it should be possible to manipulate this variable independently in order to create different degrees of interdependence in subactivities. Therefore the subactivities should allow for independent performance such that each child could carry out each activity wholly by herself without the help of another child, but they should also lend themselves to the creation of various degrees of interdependence, including complete interdependence such that each child could not complete her task without help from another child.

Since interest would focus in various studies on individual performance and/or group performance, the separate accomplishments of each child, as well as the goodness of the combined group product, should be measurable in quantitative terms.

Because similarity of task assignment was of major theoretical interest in the study of competition, it should be possible to manipulate this variable independently in order to create different degrees of task similarity.

The task should engage a variety of psychological functions. It should bear some resemblance to school work yet not focus exclusively on logical reasoning. It should not require possession of special abilities or require primarily the exercise of particular skills, be they sensory-motor, mechanical, verbal, or otherwise. The task should be attractive and hold the children's interest and engage their motivation, including achievement-related behaviors.

The task was to be employed in the study of behavior and performance of children of various ages; therefore all of the criteria had to be considered in relation to children's developmental states. The implications for specific task requirements were principally that the task must appeal to children ranging from kindergarten through the elementary grades and it, as well as the subactivities, must allow for the control and variation of difficulty to suit all children within this age range.

Our main interest was in children's interpersonal behaviors. This implied that the task activities must not dominate the work period to the exclusion of children's social behaviors. From our point of view, the task must remain strictly a vehicle through which interpersonal relations are made possible. The task, therefore, should allow the expression of any kind of social behavior. While working, children should be afforded the opportunity to watch each other's activities, to talk freely with each other should they wish to do so or to remain silent, to help each other, to hinder each other—in other words, to cover the range of social interaction in which they would wish to engage.

It should be possible to observe, record, and quantify the entire interaction process, both in terms of each individual child's behavior, as well as on a group level.

Although not an explicit criterion at the time, it was clear to us that if the criteria were met successfully, the task should be suitable for use with a variety of populations, including children from different socioeconomic and cultural backgrounds.

Description of the Task

Although the original requirements were adhered to, the actual form of the task underwent some changes over time. The early version consisted of a round cardboard art puzzle. It was designed for five children, each of whom worked on a pie-shaped separate section, which could be combined into a common final product. (The task is described and depicted in chapter 4 in the context of the three studies in which it was used.) The art puzzle met our major specifications. One of its shortcomings was the impermanent nature of the cardborad materials since they were easily damaged or lost, and their replacement was cumbersome. More serious was the problem-specific nature of the art puzzle because it limited severely the number of different constructions that could be created with the same parts. Further it was designed for third- or fourth-grade children and would have been too difficult for younger ones. Subsequent studies needed more permanent materials, which could be used more flexibly. Various task requirements of each study were to be created through experimental manipulations, instructions, and performance requirements that could be adjusted to different ages or different needs of children.

These early studies also helped to improve some procedural mechanics. Originally children sat in a circle, each at her own school desk, working on her own individual parts, which were put together later into the common group product. On several specified occasions during the work period, they were asked to go over to a table to see how their individual parts were beginning to fit together. This forced interaction produced the desired perceptions of commonality and opportunities for interpersonal exchanges. Still for the major part of the working period, we felt that the children were too isolated behind their individual desks. Clearly a large circular table would perform the needed function of bringing collaborating children closer together physically and psychologically. In so doing, we were following the venerable tradition initiated by the legendary Cornish carpenter who invented the magic Round Table for King Arthur so that his men could coexist peaceably. We know that such coaction in close proximity also presents opportunities for increased social comparison; hence a round table held the added potential of serving as a basis for the creation of competitive conditions.

The Pep Board Task

The Pep board is a custom-made circular board, forty inches in diameter. It is made of half-inch duraply, covered with a velvet-like substance, commercially known as Velcro. Instead of the cardboard pieces used in the early studies, blocks are used to make flat pictures on the board.

The blocks were developed by the Elementary Science Program at Education Development Center in the Boston area; they are known as Pattern Blocks, produced by McGraw-Hill Company and by Creative Publications. The set consists of 250 pieces, three-sixteenth inch thick, of six different sizes, shapes and colors (see figure 3-1). The blocks have a variety of relationships among themselves. Some pieces—the white rhombus referred to by children as the "thin diamond" and the orange square—cannot be substituted by any of the other pieces. The green triangle, the red trapezoid, and the blue rhombus ("fat diamond") can be combined to substitute for each other or for another shape, the yellow hexagonal. In fact, there are eight different ways that the area of the hexagonal may be covered by the various pieces.

The blocks were designed for classroom use in the teaching of science, arithmetic and geometry for kindergarten through twelfth grade. The manufacturer states that they are "useful for work with counting, sorting and matching, simple arithmetic problems, linear and area measurement, congruence, similarity, symmetry, angle measure and series and sequences." There are coloring books available for classroom use for kindergarten through ninth grade, as well as a variety of additional activities aimed to develop concepts of relationships, logical thinking, and other problem-solving activities (Pasternack and Silvey 1975).

Many students used the task in explorations of children's behavior. Over time "Pepitone's board" was shortened to Pep board and the name remained. Pilot work made it immediately clear that the blocks themselves have an inherent appeal for children of all ages. The sample of one design (figure 3-2) shows a certain demand characteristic that invites adding one piece onto the other. Children become so absorbed in this activity that it is often difficult to interrupt them. We exploited this creative play aspect in structuring the work task for the children. At the outset, while procedural instructions were being given, children were encouraged to play with the blocks and to explore their properties. Older children usually were able to supply the names. The youngest ones recognized the square and triangle and were fascinated by the sound of new labels for the rhombus, hexagon, and trapezoid.

While cognitive skills may be assumed to be more relevant in work with block designs than in tasks that involve primarily motor skills—say tracing star patterns with pursuit rotors or building tall towers—the cognitive aspect has been minimized in several ways in our research. If the children were to copy a model design, we pretested the level of difficulty to satisfy us that all children would be able to copy it without encountering problems. Generally the model was deliberately made to appear more difficult in order to represent a challenge, but the children were given sufficient procedural help before starting work to enable them to complete it easily. Exploration of the substitution possibilities inherent in the blocks appeared to be sufficient to reduce potential confounding effects of individual differences in cognitive functioning. In the study of second graders' reactions to a scarcity of blocks (chapter 8), considerable time and attention was given to prior exploration of the substitutability of blocks because the opportunity for

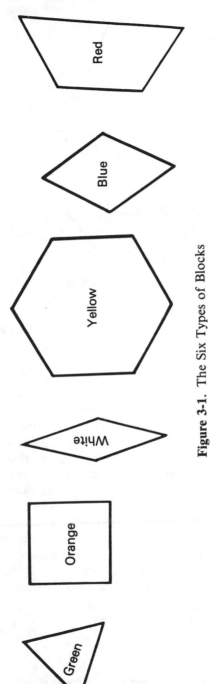

Figure 3-1. The Six Types of Blocks

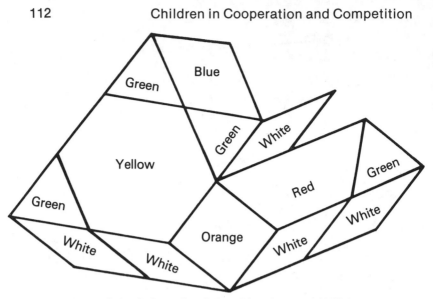

Figure 3-2. A Sample of Combination Possibilities

substitution was exploited in creating scarcity conditions and needed to be understood by the children in order for this variable to be effective. In the school in which the study was carried out, data were available on children who had been classified as intellectually gifted, defined by scores of 139 or more on the Wechsler intelligence test and by a number of additional achievement and personality tests. Comparison of performance by this group of children against the others revealed no differences in the time to completion or in interpersonal behaviors while copying a model.

The Pep board task satisfied our requirements exceedingly well. Its characteristic feature of encouraging the addition of more pieces lends itself exceedingly well to collaborative work even among the youngest children, without obscuring differences in skills needed to work together. This same feature makes it an absorbing and enjoyable task when carried out individually. In order to be able to lift the block pieces easily from one position to another on the board, yet be fastened securely, we attached small pieces of Velcro material to the back of each block. This feature facilitated the adhesion of blocks to the board, even when the board was stood up for photographing the designs for later scoring.

Experimental Procedures

The basic procedures involved several preselected children who were taken to an empty room in the school. They stood around the Pep board with a box containing Pattern Blocks at the center of the board and were asked to make a flat picture on the board.

Like every other aspect of our methodology, changes occurred over the period of ten years, mostly in the direction of simplification and procedural rigor. All of our studies still involved only like-sexed groups of children, but we reduced the number around the Pep board from the original five to three. In the family study reported in chapter 11, two parents and two children worked together around the board without being hemmed in.

The desired goal conditions of a given study were created by instructions and the promise of a photograph of the final product. Cooperative conditions were created by asking children to make one common product together. Its inclusion in our book was promised "if we like it." Care was taken not to introduce intragroup or intergroup competition by telling the children we were collecting many pictures and that we were learning something from each. Under conditions of coaction, each child was assigned one-third of the board and told to work in that space alone. In several of the studies, three thin black ribbons were used to indicate a firm separation.

Two aspects about the specific reward structures induced are important. First, reward structures were always homologous with task structures. Subjects in competitive conditions were promised individual rewards, and those in cooperative conditions one group reward that was indivisible. Second, these rewards (to have pictures of their products published in our book) were not arbitrary but were inherently related to the children's performance. Explicit competitive coaction conditions were created by further instructions, such as, "We want to see which one of you three can make the very best [picture, design, or other products depending on the needs of a given study]. We will take a photograph of the very best design from among the three of you, and include it in a book we are writing." Additional task requirements were created by further instructions.

Adaptability of the Pep Board Task

Because the task can be transformed in a variety of ways, it cannot be described as one particular type. In fact it may fit into any of the major task type categories listed by Steiner (1972). The Pep board task is made into a discretionary task simply by leaving the decision about the nature of the final product up to the children. Our instructions would simply say, "Here are some blocks. You may make anything you wish and go about it any way you wish." This freedom can be extended to a choice between competitive and cooperative working arrangements.

The task may be presented as a unitary task. In individual or competitive coactive conditions, each child is told to make an independent, complete product. In cooperative conditions, a common, indivisible product is called for.

Task requirements can be manipulated further by specifying the degree of structure. The freedom to choose constitutes the most unstructured situation; reproducing a model as exactly as possible represents the other extreme of most confining task requirements.. Within these limits, any number of task requirements may be specified. For instance, the requirement to make a balanced or unified design (as in chapter 5) places a slight restriction on performance, to make a person (chapter 6) somewhat more, and to make persons doing something together (chapter 11) places additional specifications on performance.

In cooperation, the unitary task can be subdivided either by voluntary group actions or by task requirements that may be extended into specification of task roles (chapter 5). In research reported in chapter 4, creation of conditions of colabor was desired; hence subactivities were assigned to each member who then had to combine their outputs in a specified order to make the final unified product. In that case, the task had been transformed into a conjunctive type.

In addition to manipulating requirements to establish certain goal relationships or task structures, we could also establish various degrees of task difficulty. Providing a model lowers the difficulty, as does the availability of the model for inspection during work. The model itself can be adjusted to the age-related skills of the children. Contrary to construction tasks, which must meet realistic specifications (if the task is to build a garage, the structure must actually be built to stand up and permit cars to enter), the Pep board task permits imaginative construction that does not necessarily require a comparable degree of skill (a queen's head may be represented by one child with one block only and by another with an elaborate crown). This flexibility makes it possible to extend the task at both ends of the age distribution for which it was originally intended. We have explored its use to advantage with preschoolers as well as with adolescents, college students, and adults. We are also satisfied that the task can be used successfully in research on children from different socioeconomic backgrounds (see chapter 6). Another valuable feature is its relative independence from linguistic requirements. Interesting products were obtained in an international children's village in Switzerland. Pep board methodology is in current use in Greece in studies of children's competition and cooperation, and other cross-cultural extensions are being developed.

There are many as yet unexploited potential uses of the Pep board methodology. Two specific uses are being explored currently. Children's age-related skills in group role enactment are investigated by requiring prior to the action phase a planning phase (which was referred to earlier as an important and as yet neglected area in the study of cooperation). Another direction lies in the combinatorial properties of the blocks. The study reported in chapter 8 has begun to use the substitution potential of different blocks in investigating children's reactions to scarcity. The use of the block materials (as originally intended by its commercial production) as an instructional tool in the teaching of spatial relationships opens vistas for the study of the effects of competitive and cooperative structures on the learning process itself as well as on performance, while employing the same standard task.

Performance Measurement

At the beginning of our research, each product was copied on tracing paper and the product scored later from the tracing. This laborious procedure was soon replaced with Polaroid photographs taken of the final product at the conclusion of a session with each triad. The photograph was used effectively to create success experiences in groups as well as individuals. In competitive situations, children were told that each product was highly original and creative and, hence, contrary to our expectations, we would take one photograph of all three products (occasionally this demanded much inventiveness on the part of the experimenter when one product was clearly superior and its creator had to be convinced of the value inherent in the other products). For the most part, the photograph has proved to be a highly useful debriefing instrument, enabling us to send children back to their classrooms with a glow of successful accomplishment. Under these conditions, promises were easily extracted not to divulge to classmates what had transpired. This agreement was sealed with a handshake and almost always kept.

Additionally, of course, the photograph provided a record from which quality and quantity of performance could be scored. At least two trained raters were employed in each study. Ratings were made blind. Various performance indexes were explored. The most objective ones require simple counting operations: number of pieces used and time taken to completion. When task requirements were specified or a model was provided, the indexes denoted the extent to which performance deviated from these requirements. Where interest focused on the similarity of products within the triads (chapter 6), a quantitative index was devised to reflect the degree of similarity, which varied from identity to complete difference.

Where no objective standards could be used for determining the quality of the product, various categories were devised that required rater judgments on several relevant dimensions. Scoring was based on a simple point system. Independent rater agreements varied from 67 percent agreement on the most global measure of goodness of performance, overall impression, to 80 to 95 percent for the other dimensions, and 100 percent when objective criteria were provided. The last often involved a judgment of yes or no or presence or absence of certain characteristics.

Examples of the rating schemes developed in various studies are shown here. The high intercorrelations between different dimensions have led us to use one overall index of complexity of performance, which combines elaborateness of design and of theme with quality of execution. Indexes developed in response to unique needs of a specific study are discussed as they become relevant.

Performance Indexes

Quality Category	Points Assigned
Overall Impression	
Awful	0
Poor	2
Below average	4
Average	5
Above average	6
Pleasing, well executed	8
Outstanding, creative, unusual	10
Distinctness of Theme	
Theme undistinguished in any parts of whole design of pattern	0
Theme apparently there but not clear exactly what it is	2
Theme clearly distinguished	4
Elaborateness of Design	
Board looks practically empty except for a few random patterns	0
Sparse pattern, incomplete appearance	1
Simple overall design clearly present or three separate simple designs	2
Intricate design(s), holds interest, embellished details	4
Quality of Execution with regard to Placement of Blocks	
Careless, haphazard, no attention to detail, arbitrary appearing	0
As above for some parts of the pattern; others executed with more care	2
Blocks placed carefully, colors well balanced, misses elaboration	3
As above, plus attention to fine details, subtle touches, picturesque color	4
Number of Pieces in Total Pattern	
0-49	0 (Sparse)
50-99	1 (Below average)
100-149	2 (Average)
150-199	3 (Above average)
200-250	4 (Total use)

Note: The indexes were developed in collaboration with Torop (1973).

Observations of Interpersonal Behaviors

In the first studies (chapter 4), a team of five observers was employed, each recording the behavior of two children. Observer pairs rotated throughout the research, so that reliabilities could be calculated for each observer against all of the other observers, for each category. Subsequent research employed two observers, who both observed each child within a triad over the total period of interaction. Observers participated in the process of developing and refining given categories but were told neither the purpose nor the specific hypotheses tested in a given study. Typically observers of one study became experimenters in their own subsequent research. Their work naturally built on their previous research experiences and so lent added continuity to the program.

All observers were trained by the use of simulated groups on tape recordings as well as observations of pilot groups in school settings. Daily periods were set aside during which problematic coding procedures were discussed among observers. Before the start of a study, interobserver agreement had to reach the criterion set at minimally 90 percent agreement for each category. This criterion was met easily before, as well as during, systematic periodic reliability checks among observers during the actual data-collecting stage. In general, observers can be said to have overlearned the scoring system. Their awareness that their work constituted the backbone of a study contributed to their esprit de corps and high morale, which in turn contributed to the high observer reliabilities obtained in each study.

The Observation Process

Two observers recorded the interaction among all three children within a group. Each child wore a number around his or her neck for ease of recording identification. For each interaction, both the initiator and the receiver were recorded. Thus, a continuous record was obtained of who interacted with whom and in what category throughout the fifteen-minute observation period.

The unit of verbal behavior was taken as the period of a child's speech, separated by a pause, or by another child's verbalization. Nonverbal behavior was differentiated by change from one activity to the next. Observers scanned systematically from one subject to the next around the board. Within this rhythm of observation, a unit was recorded again on the next encounter. Decisions where to place a given interaction often had to take inflection into account. For instance, "I am making a baseball player" may be coded simply as a neutral work-centered comment. But it may also be said in a tone of voice, underscoring the *I* and emphasizing *baseball player* in a drawn-out sing-song voice that left no doubt as to the self-maximizing intent of the initiator. These sensitivities developed in observers are difficult to capture in mere descriptions of the behavior categories.

The Behavior Categories

Studies that employed the Pep board methodology used a basic set of precoded interaction categories, modified if necessary to fit the focus of a particular study. The behavior categories developed followed the conceptual analysis of competition and cooperation. Thus, in competitive conditions, the major focus was on the postulated triad of attentional behaviors, evaluative behaviors, and besting behaviors. In cooperative conditions, the major interest was on a variety of other-oriented behaviors. However, the same observation instrument was used in recording behavior in either condition, since some or even all of the behaviors could have occurred in both conditions, even though most likely with different frequencies. Several of the categories were divided further into subcategories that specified the referent or detailed modes of interaction.

Attentional Behaviors

These are acts of looking. The behavior may be a silent glance or inspection (nonverbal attention) or attention accompanied by speech (verbal attention, to be double coded under verbal attention and the verbal relevant category). Referents may include the experimenter, another subject, another subjects's work, the work of the group, or a model.

Task-oriented Behaviors

These are work-oriented comments with the referents being one's own work, another's work, or the work of the group as a whole. Subcategories are all verbal. Distinctions are made between evaluative and nonevaluative modes. Neutral, work-centered acts include all factual comments about work. The key criterion is absence of positive or negative evaluation and absence of giving help to others. A child may say, "I am making blue pants" or "I can't decide whether to make my person laugh or cry." Positive evaluational acts are characterized by such statements as, "That's good, Susie" or "Those pigtails are cute." And such statements as "Mine stinks" and "This is all crooked" are called negative evaluational acts.

Besting Behaviors

The term *besting* is employed in keeping with the conceptual distinction between competitive conditions and the behavior within the condition. This category includes behaviors that move the child closer to his goal at the expense of another group member. There must be clear indicators of the presence of competitive or self-maximizing motivation. The key criterion here is the comparative feature. Behaviors may be verbal or nonverbal.

Nonverbal besting includes expressive movements reflecting besting motives (assuming sprinting stance to be the first to get needed materials, pushing ahead of others, dashing back to seat, preventing others from obtaining block pieces, looking at others triumphantly when finished first, beating chest provocatively, and so on). Verbal besting includes comparative statements that clearly raise one's own value at the expense of other(s) or lower that of other(s): "Mine is better than yours"; "I am going to win"; "Darn, Jim is going to win if I don't hurry"; or "Can't you make a better person? Look at *my* lovely girl." Statements must be clearly distinguishable from the simpler verbal evaluations. If they are not, the latter are used.

Other-oriented Behaviors

Any behavior that can be said to facilitate work and/or aid the other, either solicited or voluntarily initiated is included here. Two criteria were employed. The behaviors must be acts that can be judged to require a consideration of the other members' expectations, demands, opinions, or feelings, or those that can be construed to help other members. The naming of these behaviors was problematic. Reference to helping behaviors is too confining because it is generally restricted to more molecular behavior units, and collaborative behaviors conjures up more than we intended.

Nonverbal behaviors include manual help handing someone else blocks, placing pieces for another in his part, adding to another's pattern, completing a part begun by another, moving one's own to make room for other, and correcting placement for other. Verbal behaviors include offering suggestions, giving directions, giving information, and asking for decision. Examples are "How about if we give him a hat?" "Let's use the green blocks here"; "Can you use this yellow hexagon?" "What more do you think we should do?"

Negative Behaviors

These are antisocial acts toward other group members. They might hurt others physically or psychologically and can be verbal or nonverbal. Examples are refusal to give help or provide information, verbal insults, and acts of physical aggression. A child might say to another, "You are stupid" or "Gimme those blocks" while snatching the blocks away.

Positive Behaviors

These please or reward the other(s). A child might say, "We are having fun" or "You can do it, Jim." Most positive behaviors are likely to be codable either under positive evaluation or other-oriented, categories that have precedence.

Concluding Comment

At this stage of our work, face validity may be claimed for the major categories. For instance, the occurrence of positive and negative social interactions agrees with that found in all major investigations in competitive and cooperative conditions, respectively. Age-related increases in complexity of performance or prosocial behaviors are also in agreement with previous studies or theoretical expectations. Nevertheless we are quite aware of limitations inherent in our methodology. They are discussed throughout the volume, with emphasis on future changes to be made by us and, we hope, other researchers.

Part II
Focus on Age, Sex, and Social Class

The Role of Similarity
in Children's Coaction
and Colabor

Similarity among human beings constitutes one of the most fascinating variables underlying their interpersonal relations. It is, apparently, one of the strongest forces that unites people, yet it may also turn into a force that divides them. This chapter examines some experiments with children that speak to both of these aspects.

Social psychological literature today is replete with research that demonstrates the potent force of similarity in the liking of adults for each other. People like people with similar personal attitudes, values, interests, opinions, ages, and so forth. They also like others who share large demographic characteristics, such as national background, religion, level of education, and social class. A recent social psychology text (Freedman, Sears, and Carlsmith 1978, p. 182) concludes, "In fact, on practically every dimension except perhaps personality characteristics . . . people who are similar tend to like each other more." Of course, this is ancient wisdom, for who does not know that birds of one feather flock together? We also have the saying that opposites attract, but Freedman, Sears, and Carlsmith explain these kinds of situations—for instance, in couples where one is dominant and the other person submissive or one is talkative and the other quiet, and so forth—by pointing out that although two people may not have similar personality characteristics, they chose each other because they like what the other has or is and they are not themselves, and, in fact, they find the other complementary to themselves. The argument goes on to say that although the man and woman do not possess the same characteristics, they have the same positive attitudes toward each other's characteristics so that "if we consider basic values and attitudes as the most important aspect of personality, the similarity principle continues to hold" (p. 186).

Social psychologists have attempted to explain this apparent need for similarity by various consistency theories. One of the first and still most basic and in some ways logically most elegant and simple models is that of Heider (1958). He specified forces toward balance in social relationships, a principle that has a long tradition in research and theory in the area of perceptual processes. A long line of researchers has demonstrated tendencies to perceive coherent, organized patterns even when none exist in the perceptual field, to perceive lines as closed and ordered to appear as a good form. Accepting such data as evidence that a generalized, pervasive need for such balance exists in humans (and some infrahumans also), scientific curiosity always leads to questions about antecedents in quest for ultimate origins. Inevitably the search turns to children's development.

Organizing principles demonstrated in the perception of animals as well as infants have come to be accepted as descriptive of some kind of balance-seeking life principles such as were recognized by the earliest philosophers, including Aristotle. Studies of children's modeling behaviors, especially the work performed in the 1970s (such as Yando, Seitz, and Zigler, 1978), also underscore children's propensity, beginning in infancy, for engaging in similar behaviors as those acted out by the perceived stimulus person.

In his discussion of imitation in childhood, Piaget (1962) provides a ready conceptual scheme for understanding young children's apparent need for identity and, later on, for similarity. His description of imitative stages begins essentially with reflex schemes, becoming broadened as new elements can be integrated. Using primarily examples from his own children's development, he shows how accommodation to these new elements can be prolonged and continued "as long as the model presented is identical." He continues, "At 0.2 he imitated me as soon as I uttered sounds identical with his own . . . or even when it was merely my intonation which recalled his. He again imitated me even when he had not been crooning himself immediately before" (p. 9).

With progress of intelligence and at the point where children are able to differentiate between accommodation and assimilation, a significant difference occurs, according to Piaget's account: "Instead of appearing to be the continuation of his own activity . . . situations with which a child is now confronted . . . are now partially independent realities which are analogous to what he himself can do and yet distinct from it. Then and only then do new models have interest for the child and imitation follows accommodation" (p. 50). The explanation that follows speaks to our concerns of identity and similarity:

> There is nothing mysterious about the interest in new models which makes its appearance at this stage. It is, more than would at first appear, a continuation of earlier interests mainly concerned with the preservation of habitual behaviors. . . . In all imitation of what is already known, the interests of the desired result resides in the fact that this result provides support for the activity, and hence for its assimilation. . . . *When the subject sees objects as distinct from himself, and sees models as objects, models can no longer be assimilated wholesale; they are seen both different from, and similar to, the child himself. It is no longer only identity, but also similarity which becomes a source of interest.* [emphasis added] . . . Those models which are too remote from the child's experience leave him indifferent. . . . The interest thus appears to come from a kind of conflict between the partial resemblance which makes the child want to assimilate, and the partial difference which attracts his attention. . . . It is, therefore, this two-fold character of resemblance and opposition which seems to be the incentive for imitation. In this sense, imitation of new situations is a continuation of what is familiar. [Pp. 50-51]

The important point for Piaget is that identity and similarity to others occur in the young child's behavior not because she is motivated to do so but simply because she can do no other.

The factor of similarity as it affects children's interpersonal relationships has been investigated primarily in elementary school children. Results from these studies are well summarized by Glidwell et al. (1966): "The stable subgroups of mutual choices tend to be composed of children—usually of the same sex—who (a) have social values and attitudes that are similar, (b) are often in contact because of the proximity of their location in the classroom or home, (c) see each other as having desirable personality traits . . . With respect to . . . these bases of attraction, the children are very much like the college students studied by Newcomb . . . and the adults studied by Hall . . ." (p. 226). Although similiarity clearly emerges as an important variable, the choices of latency-aged children have been also found to be based on their desire to become like the children of their choice appeared to be (usually bigger, stronger, or in some other surface characteristics representing aspirations or ego ideals of the chooser, rather than simply matching their own traits) (Lippitt et al. 1952).

The deceptively simple statement that people like similar others has many ramifications. Since Festinger's first reference to similarity in his original statement of social comparison theory (1954), the interpretation of the concept has come udner scrutiny, most recently by Goethals and Darley (1977), who widened the meaning of similarity from literal identity with another to mean likeness by being similar or certain attributes. Further, "liking" may be operationalized by associating with or wanting to be with. Festinger's key proposition (Corollary 3A) that people wish to compare their own opinions or abilities with someone who has a similar opinion or ability implies that a person actively seeks out similar persons. Comparison with similar others also may imply the tendency to be open to influence from similar others, to imitate similar others, to be influenced by similar others, to engage in similai behaviors as similar others, to become like similar others, to want what similar others have, and most likely several other shades of different implications.

Material on the role of similarity in preschoolers' interpersonal relationships in the 4 to 5 year old range comes principally from naturalistic observational data of associative play, as depicted in the writings of sensitive child psychologists such as Stone and Church (1973):

> When children begin to do things in bunches, a flock may congregate in the sandbox, or crowd into the rocking boat, or swarm over the climbing structures, shrilling together in an expression of shared feeling. . . . Such behavior illustrates what the social psychologist calls behavioral contagion, the spread of an activity or a mood or an impulse through a group. Such

contagion is a common place in the nursery school, where one can witness
epidemics of telephoning, silliness, grotesque lurching about and collapsing
on to the floor, water play, tricycling—no sooner has one child begun
something than everybody wants to do it. [P. 264]

It appears, then, that to study children when they are beginning to
associate with other children who engage in similar behaviors, we must
move yet to an earlier age. We have seen that McClintock et al. (1977)
found it necessary to start with 3 year olds to be able to determine the
developmental course of competitive motivation. We, apparently, must
begin somewhat earlier.

An extensive literature describes the growth of sensitivity to other
human beings, to facial expressions, to familiar and strange faces, and so
forth. In the period of infancy, illuminated by Piagetian descriptions,
children begin to differentiate themselves from their surroundings. Here
research has mushroomed. A recent review (Shantz 1975) cites eight pages
of references, many documenting that social cognitions appear earlier than
was heretofore thought.

There has also been a demonstration of a parallel early development in
very young children's ability to interact with each other (Eckerman, Whatley, and Kutz 1975; Mueller and Brenner 1977; Mueller and Rich 1976;
Rheingold, Hay, and West 1976). The Rheingold et al. study reports on
partner play, consisting of giving others an object and then proceeding to
play with it while it is still in possession of the other. This behavior was
observed among 15-month-old children, mostly toward either parent, increasing up to 24 months of age.

There is much less research on the corresponding growth of interpersonal behaviors. Yet there is surprising unanimity among various experts in
child development as to the time at which children begin to initiate contacts
with other children, as well as on the manner in which it takes place. Only
recently has this stage in a child's life become of paramount interest to
social psychologists. The most detailed descriptions about this developmental period are the writings of the group of child psychologists who in the
1930s made naturalistic observations of children's interpersonal rivalries
(May and Doob 1937). They denote the period as one in which children,
beginning at approximately 2 years, play alongside each other, most of the
time not contacting each other and appearing uninterested in the other yet
often using similar toys in a similar fashion. It has been held that 2 year olds
at this point are no longer satisfied with solitary play but are not yet able to
engage each other in joint play. This is the activity referred to as parallel
play, the subject of our first exploration.

Two studies of the 1930s focused most extensively on parallel play and
provide some excellent developmental descriptions, along with some quantitative measures and data. The first of these investigations is Parten's doc-

toral dissertation (1933) submitted in a sociology department at the Child Welfare Station at the Unviersity of Minnesota, carried out in 1926-1927 under the well-known sociologist Stuart Chapin. It was concerned with constructing a developmental scale designed to measure degrees of social participation and was "based on six rather rigidly defined categories or degrees of social participation."

1. *Unoccupied behavior.*—The child apparently is not playing at all, at least not in the usual sense, but occupies himself with watching anything which happens to be of momentary interest. When there is nothing exciting taking place, he plays with his own body, gets on and off chairs, just stands around, follows the teacher, or sits in one spot glancing around the room.

2. *Solitary play.*—The child plays alone and independently with *toys that are different* from those used by the children within speaking distance and *makes no effort to get close to* or speak to the other children. His interest is centered upon his own activity, and he pursues it without reference to what others are doing.

3. *Onlooker behavior.*—The child spends most of his time watching the others play. He often talks to the playing children, asks questions or gives suggestions, but does not enter into the play itself. . . . He differs from the unoccupied child who notices anything that happens to be exciting and is not especially interested in groups of children.

4. *Parallel play.*—The child plays independently, but *the activity he chooses naturally brings him among other children. He plays with toys which are like those* which the children around him are using, *but he plays with the toys as he sees fit* [emphasis added] and does not try to influence the activity of the children near him. Thus he plays *beside* rather than *with* the other children.

5. *Associative play.*—The child plays with other children. There are borrowing and lending of play material; following one another with trains and wagons; mild attempts to control which children may or may not play in the groups. All engage in similar if not identical activity; *there is no division of labor* and *no organization of activities* [emphasis added]. Each child acts as he wishes, and does not subordinate his interests to the group.

6. *Cooperative or organized supplementary play.*—The child plays in a group that is organized for the purpose of making some material product, of striving to attain some competitive goal, of dramatizing situations of adult or group life, or of playing formal games. There is marked sense of belonging or not belonging to the group. . . . The goal as well as the method of attaining it necessitates a division of labor, the taking of different roles by the various group members, and the organization of activity so that the efforts of one child are supplemented by those of another. [Pp. 249-251]

The description of each stage is not tied to a particular age period; in fact, the authors are very alert to individual differences. Nevertheless as figure 4-1 shows, between the ages of 2 and 4.5, solitary play decreases systematically as does parallel play, which appears significantly more frequent at ages 2 and 3 than in the older children, and associative play shows a

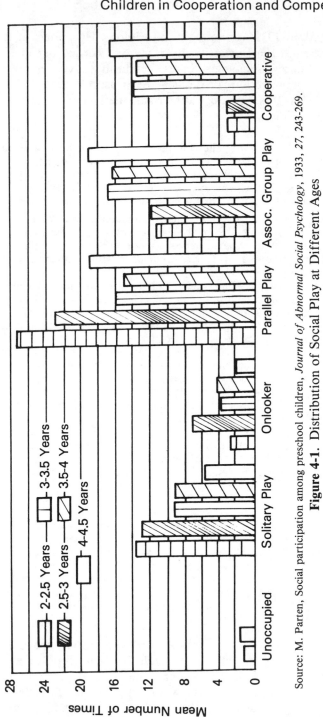

Figure 4-1. Distribution of Social Play at Different Ages

Source: M. Parten, Social participation among preschool children, *Journal of Abnormal Social Psychology*, 1933, 27, 243-269.

corresponding systematic increase. Cooperative play is practically absent until the age of 3, and even then—and until age 4½—does not occur with large frequency. The correlation between age and a composite social participation score based on the six categories of play was found to be 0.61 ± 0.08.

The second study was conducted by Cockrell (1935) with the explicit purpose of investigating the effects of different play materials on the behavior of pairs of children. She used six different types of play materials on the behavior of pairs of children. She used six different types of play materials: blocks, books, crayons, clay, houskeeping materials (such as brooms or an ironing board), and combined materials. Six nursery school children were paired each with every other and allowed unlimited free play periods while being observed behind a one-way vision mirror. Cockrell did determine various play preferences, but "the most outstanding characteristic of the division of time in this spontaneous play was that *the children were usually doing similar things with similar materials at the same time, but gave no evidence of attention to each other* [emphasis added]. This has been designated parallel play . . . to which the children devoted 74% of their time" (p. 461).

The two researchers give almost identical accounts of parallel play, with one difference: both make a point of emphasizing that children do not pay attention to each other, yet both see as central the fact that children play with similar toys. Parten states that "each plays with the toys as he sees fit," and Cockrell claims that children "were usually doing similar things." In this contradiction lies some of the fascination of this activity for social psychologists. If children are oblivious to each other, how do they come to select the same toys? Why do the two researchers' descriptions differ as to mode of play, similar in one case, different in the other? How can children appear to ignore each other yet play in the same manner? If what we are seeing here is indeed the beginning of mutual social influences, how do they happen?

There are various possible directions in which explanations may be sought. One would deny that any kind of social influence has taken place and argue for the likelihood of like-aged children having the same toy preferences. If so, they might gravitate to the same toy and play with it without noticing each other. Perhaps there is a limited number of things that can be done with, say, a broom or a book, especially by a 2 year old, so even a similar mode of interaction is explainable without recourse to social influence variables. Alternatively it is possible that no direct influence is involved in that one child starts playing and pays no attention to the other, exerting no overt social influence whatsoever, while the second child begins modeling on the first, with merely quick glances now and then that suffice to determine choice of his own play material. Finally it could be equally likely that one child in some way or another, perhaps by subtle cues or direct induction, invites the other child to play with the same toys. No doubt there are still other interpretations, and further, none of these three alternatives completely accounts for the phenomenon of parallel play. We are left with many tantalizing questions. Why do children play next to each other in the first place? Why do they not attempt to interact, or do they? What is needed is more exact, more detailed, more reliable observation under controlled conditions of the entire process and of whatever interactions which may have been involved. It is possible that children's interactions were not noticed by early observers simply because not much was known about social influence processes at that time. Our exploration tried to move in that direction. There is one other reason why parallel play is of great interest to us: it constitutes coactive conditions, presumably the first of many others encountered by children in later life. Since these situations provide a setting for social comparison in older children, an understanding of parallel play may also offer some clues as to the beginning of comparison processes.

An Exploration of Two Year Olds in Parallel Play
E.A. Pepitone and *F.H. Lloyd*

The study itself can be summarized very briefly. Thirteen pairs of 2 year olds were introduced into a playroom that contained nothing but five pairs of identical toys. Two observers kept a minute-by-minute account of the toys that each child played with and recorded their manner of playing with toys. A tape recorder caught any of the children's verbal comments. But more important than the details of the methodology is the rationale behind it. In general, we tried to control for previously uncontrolled factors that we deemed relevant for parallel play.

The Children

Previous research has studied children in nursery settings who were already acquainted with each other. To control for familiarity and liking, as well as to observe influences in parallel play of children, we studied children who had not met before. They were brought by their mothers to the experimenter's home. The mothers had been recruited by telephone specifically for this study. They constituted a rather homogeneous population: white, upper middle class, college educated, and themselves or husbands of professional backgrounds. The subjects were twenty-six children ranging in age from 21 months to 36 months. They were combined to make up nine pairs of girls and four pairs of boys. The ages in each pair were matched as closely as possible. Seven of the pairs were the identical age in months, four pairs were one month apart, and two pairs were two months apart.

The Setting

The study was conducted in the experimenter's basement playroom. This controlled home setting was used in preference to a relatively sterile, unfamiliar laboratory setting or a familiar nursery environment. The room was entered by stairs from the first floor. It was divided by a large couch and chairs on each side that acted as a natural barrier, keeping children in the part of the room where the toys were.

Number and Type of Toys

All previous studies have provided a whole nursery room full of toys. Even Cockrell, who systematically preselected different types of toys, still had a large total quantity of toys, which may have increased the difficulties of the systematic study of changing play patterns as a function of the other child's exact play choice, as we sought to do. We wanted to reduce the number of choice possibilities, yet doing so ran risks of starting fights over toys (another fascinating and theoretically related area that has been neglected in social psychological inquiry, but it was not the condition we desired to create in this study). The solution was to reduce the number but provide duplicate toys, facilitating the occurrence of parallel play and at the same time minimizing any effects of possessiveness. In this way, if a child wanted the precise object used by the partner despite the presence of an exact duplicate, it would be evident that possessiveness, rivalry, or some additional motivation was involved. Should the child seek out the duplicate toy and be satisfied with it, the social influence of peer choice of toy on one's own selection had the possibility of being more clearly established.

Our argument thus far is simple. If social influences of some kind are involved, pairs of children presented with pairs of toys should tend to play with the same pair of toys more than chance would lead one to expect, and, if there is more agreement on the choice of toy within the pairs of children rather than between the pairs, it becomes evident that the members of each dyad have influenced each other and some mechanism(s) other than coincidental liking of the same toy must be in effect.

The following toys were chosen: two play school counting frames (abaci); two yellow and red romper-room balls, ten inches in diameter; two brown stuffed teddy bears with yellow ribbons, fifteen inches high; two red and yellow Tonka dump trucks, sixteen inches long; and two Fisher-Price corn poppers (a standard push toy). The qualities considered important in choosing the toys were: (1) balance in attractiveness to the child—the aim was to have no one outstandingly liked or disliked toy; (2) familiarity—they are all relatively familiar to this population so that the excitement of novelty is minimized; (3) indivisibility—there are no multiple toys such as marbles or blocks or truck and ladder combinations, enabling simplicity of observation; and (4) variety of function—the widest possible scope of common 2-year-olds' activities were to be included. The abaci with their small beads satisfy the desire to manipulate tiny objects and also intrigue this age group with the possibility of dumping the beads from side to side. The balls are a standard favorite at this age and can be used for large-muscle play, running, kicking, rolling, and throwing. The bears allow expression of the need to cuddle and are soft and furry, allowing tactile interest in different textures. The Tonka dump trucks can be ridden or pushed, and mechanical interests can be satisfied by lifting the dumper with the lever. The poppers are a very popular toy in the park with this age group; little balls of different colors pop up when the toy is pushed or pulled along the floor.

The toys were placed in pairs on the wall opposite the stairs that enter the room. The two identical objects were beside each other in a constant location for each new pair of children. From left to right they were placed in this order: the poppers, the trucks, the abaci, the bears, and the balls.

Observers and Observation Instrument

Two observers sat on a couch at the far end of the playroom, in full sight of the children.[a] As each of the two children reached the bottom of the stairs, they were greeted by their first names and then told, "You two can play with whatever you want. We have to do some writing for a while, but we'll talk to you soon." There was no further communications with the children, and they were on their own to confront each other and the toys.

Each observer kept exact records, continuously for ten minutes, on a precoded observation chart. It featured a time line along which observers recorded continuously the toy with which each child played and the manner of playing. Two additional categories were included. Observers also kept a record of time spent simply watching another child, as well as when a child was out of field, that is, occupied neither with watching nor with any toys (perhaps playing with her shoelaces or tracing pattern of rug). The observers also kept descriptive records throughout the session of anything that would expand on the coding such as facial expressions, physical in-

---

[a]Elizabeth Schall served as co-observer.

teractions, and so on. At the end of the session, each observer wrote a general descriptive paragraph describing the emotional tone of the pair, the maturity of play, and anything else of significance. A tape recorder was used to catch the verbalizations more fully and to act as a further check on the time sequences of play.

Table 4-1 summarizes the agreement of the coding by the two observers. It shows that there was almost 100 percent agreement on the choice of toy throughout the period. In the category of watching, there was complete agreement for twenty of the children, as there was for seventeen of the children for out-of-field activity. The differences were generally a matter of seconds and occurred mostly because one observer would interpret the child as being out of field, while the other interpreted the behavior as watching, for, as the author wrote, "At times it was exceedingly difficult to judge whether for one moment a child was actually watching his companion or not, as a very finely graded continuum exists between outright staring at the peer, occasional glances, covert glances or lack of attention" (Lloyd 1970, p. 23). We include a representative sample of the play profiles. It is evident that they differ considerably both between pairs and within most pairs themselves, an interesting finding in itself that shows the likely presence of more than one uniform process. Before examining individual play profiles, let us first look at overall trends in the children's play.

Results

Choice of toy. Attractiveness was one index looked at. If the amount of time spent with a toy can be considered an index of its attractiveness, the

Table 4-1
Observer Agreement in Seconds

Observation Category	Subjects Observed		Agreement between Observers (%)
	N	%	
Choice of toy			
	15	57.7	100
	5	19.2	98.3
	6	23.1	96.7
Watches other			
	20	76.9	100
	6	23.1	88.6
Out of field			
	17	65.4	100
	8	30.8	66.7
	1	3.8	23.3

relative attractiveness of each toy can be determined by comparing the amount of time the population as a whole played with each of the five toys. Figure 4-2 shows the comparative rankings of the toys for the overall population. The abacus was played with the most, closely followed by the popper. The ball was ranked third and the truck fourth. Had the population been evenly balanced in terms of sex, these two rankings would probably have been reversed. The bear was played with least. Each toy was played with at least to some extent.

The boys, not unexpectedly, preferred the trucks (figure 4-3). They played with the trucks a third of the time and practically ignored the bears. The girls preferred the abacus and neglected the truck. In fact, they spent twice as much time on the average with the fourth-ranking toy, the bear, as they did with the truck.

To determine the role of age in the choice of toy, the four oldest pairs (ages 35 to 31 months, mean age 33.5) were compared with the four youngest pairs (ages 22 to 25 months, mean age 23.9). Since the four oldest pairs comprised three pairs of girls and one pair of boys, as did the four youngest pairs, the influence of sex in the two populations was a constant ratio. Figure 4-4 shows a tendency for the older children to spend more time with the toys that lend themselves to the more complex functions—the abacus and the balls—while the average favorite for the younger children was the popper, which is age graded for young toddlers, who have only recently learned to walk.

Trends in Parallel Play. By random chance, if the two children had no effect whatsoever on each other, one would expect that over a large sample, each would play with each toy approximately one-fifth of the time.

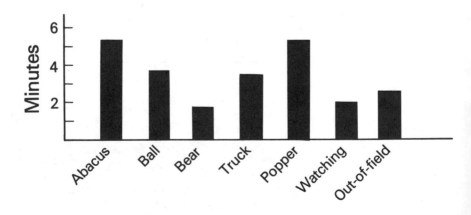

Figure 4-2. Mean amount of time in Play with Each Toy, by Total Population

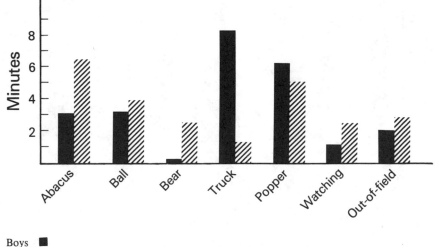

Figure 4-3. Mean amount of Time in Play with Each Toy, by Boys and Girls

Therefore the probability of the two children playing with the same toy simultaneously would be one-twenty-fifth, or 4 percent. Table 4-2 shows that the mean amount of contact with identical toys in this investigation was 204.7 seconds of a 600-second play period, or 34.1 percent. The mean time spent not only with the same toy but using it in an identical fashion was 157 seconds of a 600-second play period (26.2 percent). Put differently yet, of the total time that the children were involved with the same toy at the same time, over three-fourths of this time was spent in parallel function with the same toy.

No significant differences existed overall comparing mean contact with identical toys for boys (205 seconds) with that for girls (204 seconds), although boys engaged more in parallel functions (180 seconds on the average) than did girls (average 130 seconds). The same trends were obtained in a comparison of older and younger children. Again the average simultaneity of choice of toy of the older children (average 265.5) did not differ from the average of the younger ones (277.5), but older children had a mean average of parallel functions of 222.5, and younger ones averaged 192.5 seconds.

Another, not entirely unexpected, trend was found in the number of contacts made with successive toys as a function of age. On the average, younger children changed toys nearly twice as often (8.4) compared with the older average of 4.9. On another companion measure, older children played with an average of 2.9 toys, and younger ones investigated 4.2 toys during the same period.

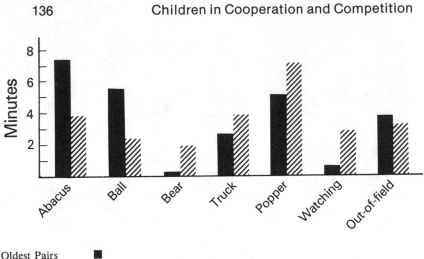

Oldest Pairs   ■
Youngest Pairs

Figure 4-4. Mean Amount of Time in Play with Each Toy, by Four Oldest
Pairs and Four Youngest Pairs

A final general trend is worth noting. Parallel play, especially with identical toys, increased with the length of play period. For the first 300
seconds, contact with identical toys was 80 seconds, as opposed to 124.6 in
the last 300 seconds. Corresponding figures for parallel function were 56.1
versus 100 seconds.

These overall trends remain only indications of tendencies that are expressed differently in different cases. Thus it is to the sequential paired play
profiles that we must turn for understanding the dynamics of parallel play.
Samples of play profiles are included for five pairs of girls and three pairs of
boys, (figures 5-1 through 5-8). Each figure was selected to illustrate unique
play relationships.

Table 4-2
**Mean Time and Percentage of Simultaneous Contact and Parallel Play with
Identical Toy**

Population	Mean Time per Pair Simultaneous Contact with Identical Toy in Ten-minute Period		Mean Time per Pair Parallel Function with Identical Toy in Ten-minute Period	
	Seconds	%	Seconds	%
Total population (13 pairs)	204.7	34.1	157.0	26.2
Boys (4 pairs)	205	34.2	180.0	30
Girls (9 pairs)	204	34.0	130.0	21.7
Older (25-31 months; 4 pairs)	265	44.2	222.5	37.1
Younger (22-25 months; 4 pairs)	277.5	46.2	192.5	32.1

The Play Profiles

Figure 4-5 is a behavioral description of the play profile for Tracy (35 months) and Shannon (35 months). Their simultaneity of contact with identical toys was 580 seconds (96.7 percent) and their parallel function with identical toys was 580 seconds (96.7 percent). The observers noted:

> Shannon and Tracy's play session was characterized by intense uneasiness, immobility, and silence. Shannon came down the stairs first and went immediately to the poppers, placing her hand on one. Tracy followed, less than a second behind, and placed her hands on the ball at the top of the second popper in the same attitude as Shannon. Both looked up at us as if to say, "Is this what we're supposed to do?" As we didn't respond, they looked at each other. Two minutes of strained silence ensued until Shannon very tentatively pushed the popper and it gave a "POP." Both were startled. Tracy followed suit by giving one pop with hers. After another pause, Shannon pushed hers making two pops. Tracy did likewise. Shannon put two fingers in her mouth, followed immediately by Tracy in the identical attitude. Soon they started a tentative duet—first Shannon pushing the popper several inches, then Tracy imitating. Tracy seemed to be concentrating very hard to go the same distance as Shannon.

> At the fourth minute, Shannon dropped her popper and started to walk over towards the abaci, all the time looking at us as if to say, "May we?" Then Shannon picked up an abacus, followed immediately by Tracy. Tracy put hers down, followed by Shannon. This was the one instance of Tracy initiating an action. Both sat in front of their abaci; then Shannon placed hers on her legs; Tracy likewise, and they started identical bead play. They

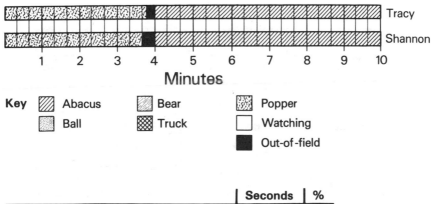

	Seconds	%
Simultaneity of contact with identical toys:	580	96.7
Parallel function with identical toys:	580	96.7

Figure 4-5. Play Profile for Tracy and Shannon

acted as if they had been trained to imitate each other. Their actions with the beads become increasingly vigorous and more at ease throughout the rest of the session. There were no verbalizations.

This profile shows the play of two children who were among the oldest. It is evident immediately that there was complete simultaneity of contact with identical toys. The transcript describes that they played with each toy in identical fashion. However, this play profile gives no further clue as to the nature of specific influences that may be operating. From the vignette description it is clear that the process here involved is imitation, with one of the children (Shannon) being almost exclusively the initiator. The transcript makes no mention of any explicit influence attempts on the part of either of the children. Shannon, child A, appears as the selector of toys, being imitated by B. There is an intriguing question as to the extent to which B's action is seen as supportive by A. The circular play sequence would be somewhat as follows in this pair and others that may show the same pattern: A selects toy, B follows suit, thus reinforcing A's play, which maintains A in the situation, playing, which reinforces B in turn, and so ad infinitum (as yet we have no clues as to causes for shifts from one activity to the next). The same cyclic analysis is possible for the smaller subunits constituted by identical functions. If this analysis is correct, parallel play with identical toys may be seen as being in some cases sustained by imitation, which provides the reinforcement for continued similar play.

Figure 4-6 presents the behavioral description of the play profile for Martha (22 months) and Allegra (22 months). Their simultaneity of contact with identical toys was 290 seconds (48.3 percent), and their parallel function with identical toys was 270 seconds (45 percent). The observers noted:

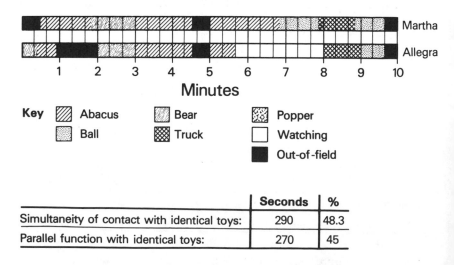

	Seconds	%
Simultaneity of contact with identical toys:	290	48.3
Parallel function with identical toys:	270	45

Figure 4-6. Play Profile for Martha and Allegra

Both girls came downstairs happily and willingly. Martha was ahead of Allegra on the stairs, but as we were almost down, Allegra said, "Bear, bear!" Both went over to the bears. Allegra was delighted with the bear and after playing with it briefly, she picked up the second bear and offered it to Martha. Martha shrugged and rejected the bear. Allegra seemed very hurt. She dropped her own bear and questioned, "Bear, bear?" Martha busily and resourcefully investigating the toys, left the abacus for the popper, then went to the bears. Allegra followed. Martha seated her bear beside the abacus; Allegra likewise. They started to push the beads back and forth on the two abaci, watching each other and imitating each other. They both pushed all the beads to the right, then all to the left. Allegra sat back at the sixth minute and watched Martha. Again she said, "Bear, bear?" Martha suddenly caught sight of the balls, ran over to them, and started rolling both of them. One hit a truck, and a short period of parallel play with the trucks followed.

Aside from the initial episode with the bears, Martha always seemed to initiate the play. Allegra's spirits had been dampened by the rejection of her offering and she was less sure of herself.

We see an interesting variant of the process described in figure 4-5. One of the children—Allegra—found the brown bear attractive from the moment the two children entered the play room. We note her direct induction attempt right at the beginning, culminating in her offer of the second bear as a prelude to joint play. However, she was rejected by the partner. Instead of positively reinforcing, rejection devalued play with a particular toy and it was dropped. Martha, who had come downstairs first, appeared more dominant, and after she commenced playing with the toy of her choice, the by-now-familiar imitative process ensued. However, the record indicates very clearly how one child's—Allegra's—liking of the original toy continued throughout the period. Halfway through the play period, she made one more tentative attempt at influencing the other child to play with her favorite choice. Alas, once more she was ignored. After the third minute, Allegra never returned to the bears, forgoing her own choice and eventually settling down to play with the toy chosen by the other partner. The dynamic here appears to be something like the following: if we cannot both play with the toy I prefer, we shall both play with the toy of the other partner's choice, but with identical toys we shall play.

Figure 4-7 shows the behavioral description of the play profile for Sheila (24 months) and Rebecca (24 months). The simultaneity of contact with identical toys was 390 seconds (65 percent), and the parallel function with identical toys was 350 seconds (58.3 percent). The observers noted:

Sheila had been very anxious when she entered the house, afraid her mother was going to leave her there. She refused to take off her coat and screamed when we tried. It was decided to let her play in her coat and let her mother sit on the stair. On entering the playroom she immediately cheered up. Rebecca entered the playroom first; both stood in the middle of the room for a moment sizing each other up, then—very suddenly—both smiled, relaxed, and went together to the dump trucks. They pushed the

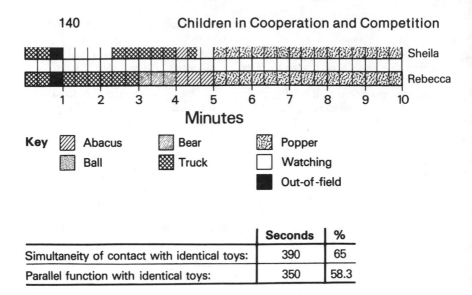

	Seconds	%
Simultaneity of contact with identical toys:	390	65
Parallel function with identical toys:	350	58.3

Figure 4-7. Play Profile for Sheila and Rebecca

trucks hard from side to side and laughed. Sheila left her truck and went to the foot of the stairs, looking up at her mother. Rebecca seemed surprised and left her truck also. Soon Rebecca returned to the trucks saying to Sheila, "Truck, truck; here truck, truck." Sheila watched but didn't join her until the second minute. Rebecca suddenly ran to the bear, looked at it, then seized the abacus, followed by Sheila. Sheila, however, was ignored by Rebecca, and stopped play altogether, looking on.

At this fifth minute, Rebecca saw the poppers and ran over to them, pushing one delightedly. Sheila chased her, got hold of the popper, and a tug-of-war started with both crying and screaming. Rebecca pulled the popper away. Sheila stood and cried. The experimenter said, "There are other toys," Sheila looked toward the toys, saw the other popper, and a pleasant five minutes of parallel play pushing the poppers ensued, interrupted only by the ten-minute bell.

In this third profile, there is yet another variant on the above themes. Once put at ease, both girls moved together at the outset and played with the two trucks. After a brief interruption occasioned by a sudden worry about the mother's absence, the direct induction of one child was this time successful in engaging the other in parallel play with the same toy. Rebecca was the initiator; Sheila modeled herself on Rebecca in a submissive fashion. Her dependence on her peer is in line with her earlier demonstrated dependence on her mother.

We have included this profile also because of another important incident that underscores that apparently many tug-of-wars over toys may not be so much a function of possessiveness but of a deeper underlying need for similarity to the other's toy. In the middle of the play period, the children had become atuned to their parallel activities when Rebecca changed activities, moving on to a new toy, the popper. Sheila automatically followed, and we were prepared for another simple imitation episode. However, Sheila did not see the second popper and tried to take Rebecca's. Realization of the existence of a duplicate immediately restored peace, as well as parallel play with identical toys and in identical function.

Figure 4-8 presents the behavioral description of the play profile for Jessica (27 months) and Laura (27 months). The simultaneity of contact with identical toys was 0 seconds and their parallel function with identical toys was 0 seconds, so their parallel function with different pairs was 600 seconds (100 percent). The observers noted:

> Jessica and Laura's session was unique. Laura entered the room first and stood in the center, a bit unsure of herself. Jessica came down, went to the *two* abaci, put them together, seated herself before them, and remained engrossed with them throughout the session, pushing the beads back and forth, lifting them and dumping the beads from side to side, and twisting the metal sticks the beads were on to make them squeak.

> It seemed to be understood that Jessica had claimed the two abaci, and Laura never approached them. She went to the two bears, picked them up one on each arm, and walked around the room chatting busily: "Look at the clock. I see a door. I hear truck." She put the bears down at the fifth minute with much ceremony, putting them to bed, and then went to the two balls. She followed this by play with the two poppers, then gathered

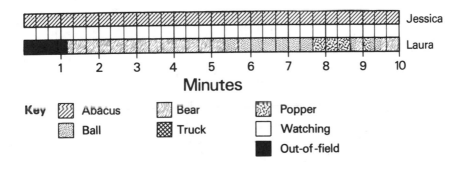

Key	Abacus	Bear	Popper
	Ball	Truck	Watching
			Out-of-field

	Seconds	%
Simultaneity of contact with identical toys:	0	0
Parallel function with identical toys:	0	0

Figure 4-8. Play Profile for Jessica and Laura

the pairs of bears, balls, and poppers together in a pile in the center of the room standing over them as if to say, "These are mine."

After Jessica's initial claiming of the two abaci, Laura also seemed to see the pairs of toys as units to be together. She never took one single toy alone, but always the pair of identical objects.

A comment on the possessiveness theme may be seen in figure 4-8. At first glance, the two play profiles are totally nonoverlapping, and so they are. However, as the record demonstrates, the parallel play is not on the particularized level of a toy but on the more global level of conception; each child played with both duplicates at the same time. Again we see the preference for an identical general pattern rather than possession of particular toys.

Figure 4-9 presents the behavioral description of the play profile of Lisa (27 months) and Mona (26 months). Their simultaneity of contact with identical toys is 40 seconds (6.7 percent), and their parallel function with identical toys is 0 seconds. The observers noted:

Both girls were hesitant to come downstairs and didn't want to leave their mothers. Mona finally came down, but Lisa would not come unless her mother sat on the stairs. Mona relaxed and started to play when she saw the toys, taking one of the poppers and pushing it in circles. Lisa got the second popper and brought it over to show her mother. She continued to hold the popper and fiddle with it near the stairs, while Mona went over to the abacus. Lisa was interested in her companion's activity but made no move

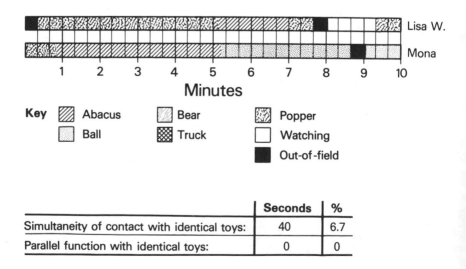

	Seconds	%
Simultaneity of contact with identical toys:	40	6.7
Parallel function with identical toys:	0	0

Figure 4-9. Play Profile for Lisa W. and Mona

to go and follow her until the fifth minute. When Lisa came over to the abaci, Mona left and started animated play with the two balls. "I kick. Look at me! I kick ball!" She continued to race around the room with the two balls for the remainder of the session, and it seemed odd to both observers that her infectious glee did not affect her companion. Lisa continued to fiddle with the abaci for two minues and then returned with the popper to her original location at the foot of the stairs near her mother.

Like the preceding pair, Lisa and Mona show almost completely nonoverlapping play profiles; the 6.7 percent simultaneous play with identical toys could have occurred by chance. This sequence is different, however, in that there was no overlap even in the general pattern of play, as had been the case with Jessica and Laura. Again we note the more passive child's reluctance to leave her mother, and, to the observers' surprise, an unresponsiveness to all stimuli from a potential peer play partner. Yet Mona's boisterous talk and play appeared more part of egocentric activity that itself was not directed at the other child. There was also the fact that she usurped both balls, thus making it impossible for her timid partner to imitate her or otherwise participate in the same activity, even had she desired to do so.

Figure 4-10 presents the behavioral description of the play profile for Stevie (36 months) and Mark (33 months). Their simultaneity of contact with identical toys was 90 seconds (15 percent), and their parallel function with identical toys was 80 seconds (13.3 percent). The observers noted:

Stevie came down happily, but Mark was reluctant and we finally had to get his mother to come and sit on the stairs. Stevie went to the popper, pushed it around the room a few times, then the abacus, then took a ball, which he bounced and rolled. He took one item each time. Mark stayed near the stairs until his mother came and then went over to the truck. Stevie continued to investigate toy after toy. There was no talking. At the seventh minute, Stevie seemed to notice there was another child in the room, and he watched Mark intently as Mark pushed the truck along the floor. Soon he joined him and both pushed the trucks, crawling after them, making "engine noises." Near the tenth minute, Mark left his truck, and the two boys played together with Stevie's truck, showing sharing and collaboration. This activity was interrupted by the ten-minute bell.

Here we see each of the two boys starting out and continuing for the first half of the period playing with entirely different toys. Mark, at first reluctant to leave his mother, engaged in unoccupied behavior or solitary play. During the second half of the period, it was Stevie, the more active of the two, who, after a brief period of onlooker behavior, discovered Mark, who had been playing almost exclusively with the other truck, and came to join him. He did not need to be induced, nor was he imitating Mark; rather the common interest in the truck, a favorite boys' toy, drew them together.

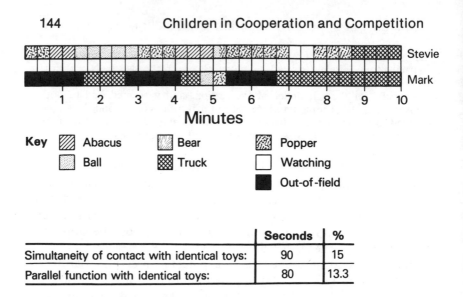

Figure 4-10. Play Profile for Stevie and Mark

Most likely they were both intimately familiar with this toy. This made it possible to culminate their play at the end of the period in more complex associative play. It is noteworthy that this pair of boys was one of the oldest.

Figure 4-11 shows the behavioral description of the play profile for Jeffrey (30 months) and Tommy (30 months). Their simultaneity of contact with identical toys was 280 seconds (46.7 percent), and their parallel function with identical toys was 80 seconds (13.3 percent). The observers noted:

> Jeffrey and Tommy came down happily, Jeffrey in front. Jeffrey went immediately over to the two dump trucks, Tommy to the two poppers. Tommy went over briefly to see the two abaci, then returned to the poppers. Jeffrey kept up a running monologue narrating his activities and talking *to* the truck: "Two wheel on it. Two wheel on it, here. I shut it. It go up, it go down. . . . Bye, bye truck. You have window?" When he left the truck to go to the balls, Tommy came over to the trucks as if he had been waiting for him to leave. Jeffrey threw and kicked the balls, then brought them over to the unused truck, put one ball in the truck, and tried to balance the other on top of the first ball. Although both were engrossed in their respective trucks from the fifth minute on, there was not much parallel function. Jeffrey lay down, squinting, looking under the wheels of his truck, still talking to the truck and to no one in particular. "This window broken? No, this window not broken. Truck has window." Tommy sat facing away from Jeffrey, raising and lowering the dumper with the lever. At the ninth minute they began to notice each other and began to push their trucks together.

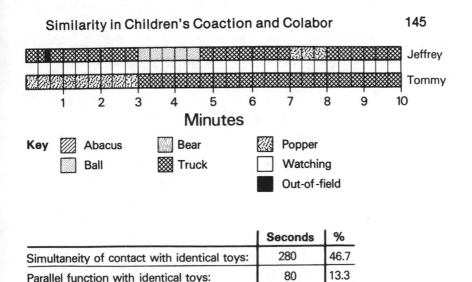

	Seconds	%
Simultaneity of contact with identical toys:	280	46.7
Parallel function with identical toys:	80	13.3

Figure 4-11. Play Profile for Jeffrey and Tommy

A pattern remarkably similar to the previous dyad's play profile is apparent. Again at the beginning was independent, unrelated play, one child engaging in egocentric behavior. Yet it appears as if Tommy had been aware of the other's presence. The profile indicates that at the very moment Jeffrey left his truck, Tommy moved in to play with one of them. We have here the interesting situation of deliberate social avoidance: Tommy was the shy one and continued to be so by facing away while playing with his truck when his partner came over to play with the other truck. Although almost half of the play period was taken up with identical toy play, only the last two minutes consisted of play in parallel function. Again the common activity and interest allowed what approaches associative activity.

Figure 4-12 shows the behavioral description of the play profile for David (28 months) and Eddy (28 months). Their simultaneity of contact with identical toys was 330 seconds (55 percent), and their parallel function with identical toys was 300 seconds (50 percent). The observers noted:

David and Eddy's play session was happy and at ease. Both came down the stairs willingly, Eddy ahead of David, with Eddy chatting busily. Eddy went straight to the trucks and tried to draw David into conversation about them. "I have truck at my house. You have truck at your house? You have truck?" David was more silent than Eddy, and when Eddy went from the trucks to the popper, he put both hands in his overall pockets, a bit overwhelmed with the volume of communication from his new friend. They went together to the abaci and fiddled with the beads briefly. Eddy was

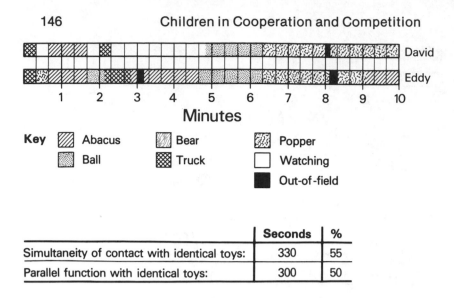

	Seconds	%
Simultaneity of contact with identical toys:	330	55
Parallel function with identical toys:	300	50

Figure 4-12. Play Profile for David and Eddy

definitely dominant in this session, and he continually tried to involve David in his interests. "See more things? Look, we could do a game. We could play with the balls. I bounce balls. You bounce balls? Want to play with the balls?" At the third minute, Eddy gathered the toys into a pile in the center of the room while David watched. He took the two trucks, then the two abaci, then the two bears, placed them all together, saying "there," with satisfaction when complete. David watched, walking around with a self-conscious swagger with his hands in his pockets. At the fifth minute, when Eddy went over to bounce a ball, David joined him, and there was parallel play in parallel function, first with balls, then with the poppers. They devised a rhythmical game with the poppers standing facing each other, each pulling his popper backward, then pushing them forward until they bumped each other, and laughed. Eddy, at the ninth minute, was concentrating hard on the balls inside the popper and said "beads, beads, beads." This reminded him of the abacus and he returned to it.

This third pair of boys is of interest in two particular respects. First, there were several direct verbal influence attempts by one boy, Eddy, inviting the other to join not only in parallel play but in associative play. The other boy, David, did not avoid him, in fact joined him off and on and tentatively played with the same toy but not with the vigor and initiative of Eddy. The latter's ingenious bringing together all toys into one place indeed accomplished what verbal induction alone could not. David joined him again in the second half for full-blown parallel play, which ended in what could almost be called associative play. The second interesting feature of this pair is that their play pattern was parallel even though it was not centered on trucks but on poppers. This was the youngest pair of boys and poppers are on the average the favorite toy of children their age.

Concluding Comments

In our small sample, not all pairs of children engaged in parallel play. In addition to the pair described in figure 4-9, there was one other girl dyad with a play profile made of up nonoverlapping play activities (not included in the sample profiles depicted here because it was almost an exact duplicate of the other pair). In both cases, one or both members of the dyad showed reluctance to leave her mother and, upon finally entering the playroom, evidenced no interest in their partners.

We have shown that given at least one member who is actively engaged in solitary play and another willing to separate, the latter will follow in parallel play activity to some degree. This may happen in several ways. We have seen that similar interests in a toy, especially among boys, are sufficient to bring about parallel play with no additional social contact before or during play. Over time, such play may turn into associative play. Parallel play may also occur through imitation, perhaps the simplest way of producing similarity through identical coaction that does not require overt interaction on part of either member of the dyad. There may also be various induction attempts that, if successful, seem to reinforce each other's activities and prolong the parallel play with identical toys. The oldest children embellish their parallel activity with rudimentary interaction, aided by monosyllabic verbal exchanges. Our brief exploration suggests that far from being a mysterious process in which identical toys get played with while children refrain from looking at each other, orderly social influence patterns are found in parallel play, patterns that appear—in skeleton, simplified form, to be sure—to contain the essence of social influence processes found in older children and adults.

In our experimental situation, coaction with identical toys was self-selective. Although we had introduced duplicate toys to maximize the opportunity for parallel play, there was no reason why each child could not have played with a different toy. The children who chose this alternative for a major part of the play period were, without exception, those who were hesitant to leave their mothers. This dependence and their unwillingness to separate seemed to prevent them from attempting to interact with a partner. Children who were able to separate appeared further along in the process of differentiating themselves from their outer environment. They appeared as distinct entities aware of their partners and, if not always eager, at least willing to establish some kind of play contact with their partners.

The last decades have given us rich accounts by developmentalists, child psychologists, and psychoanalysts of the ways in which the infant's original fusion with the mother is transformed. As delineated by Mahler (Mahler, Pine, and Bergman 1975) and documented by Kaplan (1978), this period of individuation spans roughly the first three years of life, with the period between 24 and 36 months being characterized by the toddler's increased venturing out into the world by herself. Such forays are punctuated with periodic panicky demands for closeness to her first human source of security.

One need not accept psychoanalytic thought totally as descriptive of the children whom we have studied. The children's behaviors give support to the assumption that they are variously engaged in differentiating themselves from the environment and making differentiations within the environment, which include separation from the mother and attempts to establish relationships with other persons, including their agemates. The hypothesis suggests that engaging in similar play is a transitional activity that helps a child to recognize at once separateness of self from another child by playing with a distinct, own toy but feeling also less individuated by engaging in similar or identical activities. Parallel play, especially with identical toys, makes children more similar to each other and hence less separate. Children who were not ready to differentiate themselves even to this extent from their environment stayed close to their mothers or closed themselves off in solitary play. For children who are beginning to differentiate themselves from their environment and are willing to venture out a bit further, engaging in identical activities in parallel play thus would have a reassuring function.

Similarity in parallel play is not based on some personal characteristics, as it tends to be with adults, but is created by the presence of similar or identical external objects in the environment that both children possess. Similarity as defined by the surface characteristics of toys can be comprehended even by the youngest children (their egocentrism at this age would prevent them from responding to similarities that can be known only by taking the point of view of the other as, for instance, knowing that each had older siblings, or seeing both mothers talking to each other). Additionally the toys selected for parallel play, especially in controlled research, are age appropriate, can be manipulated by all children, give pleasure, and do not frustrate any of the children. They constitute perfect vehicles around which new social interactions may be explored. The identity of the toys ensures that similarity can be maintained among the actors. To the extent that toys are sex typed, bonds are strengthened among like-sexed children.

We examined in chapter 2 Festinger's social reality theory, which starts with the assumption that uncertainty about the correctness of one's own opinions, attitudes, values, feelings, and abilities constitutes the major dynamic underlying adult social comparisons. Perhaps turning to others to reduce uncertainty has its developmental antecedents in seeking similarity in others for reassurance in early childhood. We cited evidence in the beginning of this chapter pertaining to the important role of similarity in friendship formation or mate selection among adults. Perhaps in intimate personal relationships, similarity to others has the same basic reassuring function that it gives to the very young. However, because adults have also developed achievement-oriented motivations, similar others in work situations lose their reassuring qualities and turn into potential competitors to be feared and surpassed. Hence coactive situations with adults or older children may also be seen as stressful occasions for comparison with others. Even if coworkers are friends, their reassuring quality of similarity often turns into a threatening, anxiety-producing quality as potential competitors.

Returning to our youngest population, let us remind ourselves that in engaging in parallel play, they were in fact also engaged in a coactive situation. As far as could be observed, there was not a hint of behaviors that we could have characterized as part of a comparison process; there were no evaluations of self or other of even the most primitive kind, to say nothing of evidence of besting. It would appear, then, that these 2 to 3 year olds, not yet competitively motivated, did not have to be, and at this stage of their development could as yet not be, concerned with each other's relative accomplishments. Therefore they could enjoy unreservedly the security-giving benefit of similarity with another peer. If so, it is no wonder that parallel play in identical fashion appears to be a satisfying experience at this point in childhood.

It is built into the very nature of the research process that one exploration can open numerous other questions and further directions. The Lloyd study itself raised several questions of various magnitudes. Some issues derive from the particular methodology we employed. For instance, to what extent, if any, did the feature of the exclusive presence of duplicate toys influence the nature of parallel play we observed? The possibility exists that the paired toys, lined up in a row in an empty playroom, suggested to the children that we meant them to play each with one member of a pair. Nothing in their play pattern suggests this interpretation; still it is a possibility. Along those lines, it would be of some interest to replicate the study, mixing in some single toys along with pairs, perhaps even making the singles particularly attractive to pit against the strength of attraction that we assumed to reside in identical toys.

The more important next step has to do with basic theoretical issues that relate to the hypotheses derived from our exploration with regard to specific influence processes in parallel play as well as in regard to the assumed relationship between individuation and choice of similar toys. Our field study was controlled in the sense of locale, toys, and choice of subjects. But although subjects were selected from a relatively homogeneous population and within a one-year age range and also were paired by age and sex, we had very little control over the matching of children beyond these gross variables. We had no control over the individual difference variables that seemed to determine the course of social influence. Whether, for instance, direct induction or imitation could occur at all depended on the presence of a child who was willing to initiate independent play. Next steps will require greater control by more specific preselection of subjects. If the focus is on the growth of interpersonal behaviors, one direction to pursue is to pair children of different ages with a difference great enough (say, one-half to one year, or even more, apart) for one child to be developmentally more ready to play independently, thus constituting a somewhat more controlled stimulus to which a 2 year old could react. Or in pursuit of the individuation hypothesis, we can envisage a design that would preselect children equated by age but differentiated on he basis of degrees to which they are able to separate from their mothers.

The series of studies by Mueller and his associates supports and in some regard supplements some of our findings and conclusions, although it does not touch upon issues of similarity in interaction with toys. Mueller and Brenner (1977) studied two play groups over a period of seven months. The six boys in group 1 were aged 12 months at the first session; the six boys in the second group 16 1/2 months. The groups were deliberately composed in this fashion to allow comparison when overlapping in age but varying by 4 1/2 months in amount of peer acquaintance. The setting and procedures corresponded to ours, including a small playroom with two nonparticipating teachers present, toys, and dyadic play. The six boys in each group were paired with each other on four different occasions. The resulting fifteen dyads were each videotaped separately at play for fifteen minutes. Social contacts were coded into two major categories: socially directed behaviors (visual gazes toward the other, followed by a simple single discrete act such as waving or saying, "hi"), and social interaction (several prolonged, contiguous, socially directed behaviors). We studied the former attentional behaviors only in performance situations with older children; however, some correspondence may exist between our play profile measure of continuous similar activity with similar toys and the contiguous socially directed behaviors.

Their data showed unambiguously, unconfounded by the age variable, that prolonged acquaintance permits the development of sustained, coordinated social interactions among these young children. Our findings of predominantly noncoordinated similar actions with identical toys thus was at least in part attributable to the children's unfamiliarity with each other at the first and only session. This interpretation appears particularly justified considering that our sample was older on the average, and hence could have been expected to (but did not) engage more in the slightly more complex coordinated social activity upon their first encounter.

Support for the importance of acquaintance is provided by our data, which show considerable increases in parallel and associative play during the second half of the play period. Of equal relevance to our study are the data on contact with toys. They show that in the first session of unacquainted 12 month olds (most comparable to our situation), simple, socially directed behaviors are almost exclusively in the context of toys. There is a steady though small decrease, but even at the fourth session, only 17 percent of the social contacts occurred without toys. Mueller and Brenner stress, as did we, that when the children were placed into the play environment lacking any other social input, their behavior was not to turn to unfamiliar peers but to familiar play toys. Another publication (Mueller and Rich 1976) demonstrates how several of these same young boys in the play group clustered together around a single toy. According to the authors, "Nothing seems to make a toy as interesting as its use by another child."

This research gives ample support to our interpretation of toys as facilitators of peer interactions. Mueller and Brenner concur: "Rather than showing the limits of children's social skills, parallel play is instrumental in producing peer social interactions. . . . It is the natural situation for the triggering and subsequent development of peer social relations" (p. 860).

Exploration of Comparison Behaviors
in Third-Grade Children[a]
E.A. Pepitone and *B.H. Hannah*

The first study in this series tested a simple derivation from social reality theory: we wanted to explore with children whether they will turn to each other if no external reality check is available to find needed information. From classroom observation alone, we would have been surprised had we not found the postulated comparison behaviors under these conditions. Assuming this was the case, we wanted to explore further the larger issues dealing with the role of similarity in coaction of older children.

We have proposed that social comparison can be separated into three distinct behavioral processes: attentional processes, evaluational processes, and achievement-related behaviors. We suggested further that these processes combine in a cycle of mutually reinforcing interrelationships. In early childhood, attentional processes may be expected to dominate, since achievement motivations are still relatively weak and cognitive processes engaged in evaluative behaviors are only beginning to be differentiated. Our earlier speculation suggested that under such conditions, similarity may be satisfying and reassuring to the very young. In older children, such similar-

[a]This research was supported by grant OEG-2-700026 (509) from the Office of Education, U.S. Department of Health, Education and Welfare. This section is an expanded version of "Comparison Behavior in Elementary School Children," *American Educational Research Journal* 9 (1972):45-63. Permission to quote is gratefully acknowledged.

ity may be more stressful. Attentional behaviors will evoke achievement-related motives and, in their service, besting behaviors and evaluational activities, in turn requiring more attending, and so forth. It follows, then, that the triad of behaviors comprising social comparison may be expected to occur with the greatest frequency in conditions in which children are given identical task assignments. They may be expected to occur with the lowest frequency in conditions in which children are given completely different task assignments. Task assignments of various degrees of similarity may be expected to fall between these two extremes. We also argue that if the arousal of achievement-related motives stimulates tension and anxiety (Johnson and Johnson 1974), then cooperative conditions in which individual task assignments differ may be more attractive than working conditions that require the performance of identical tasks.

Conditions of coaction and colabor are similar in that individuals in each case are working on individual tasks by themselves. If there is no interaction at all with regard to the task, then task interdependence is zero in both conditions. The two conditions are distinguished from each other only in that group goals, of various strength, are present in colabor and not in coaction. In coaction, the presence of individual goals while working on individual tasks is sufficient to set off comparison processes; if so, however, individual goals may have confounding effects on similarity of task assignments. In an attempt to reduce such potential effects from individual goals, we decided to create conditions of colabor. In the presence of a strong group goal, any occurrence of comparison behaviors could be more unambiguously attributed to the effects of the similarity of task assignments.

An unusual amount of care and attention was given to the experimental manipulations devised for this study to design a rather complex life space. The research featured a very large experimental cast, with B.H.Hannah as the principal investigator. Five observers were present at all times to observe the five children in each group. The major study represents Hannah's doctoral dissertation. She created three colabor conditions that varied in degree of task similarity. One of her observers, J. Crawford, carried out simultaneously a substudy as part of her master's thesis (Crawford 1970). She observed children's behavior in the identical task condition, varying the presence or absence of a physical model.

The Subjects

We wanted to tap the whole hypothesized cycle of comparison behaviors and assumed that third graders would have decentered sufficiently to be able to handle simultaneously these rather complex assessment processes of their own and others' work. To reduce the large number of subjects required, the two major studies involved girls only. The identical condition was later replicated by Pepitone (1972) with comparable boys. The children were studied in nine elementary schools in one suburban school district. Since no systematic differences among these schools were found on relevant variables, data from all schools were combined.

The Task and Procedures

Task Requirements. The task was designed to be attractive and intrinsically interesting to children, requiring the kinds of abilities that are common to many classroom activities. We were careful not to utilize actual class subjects, such as arithmetic or spelling, because children tend to have a clear perception of rank-ordered abilities with regard to these classroom skills.

Additionally we wanted the task to be designed so that movement toward the group goal—how far each child was from finishing the assignment—would be clearly visible and assessable at all times by each group member and by the observers. The group goal itself had to be built into the task so that it was perceived as a shared goal. Each child was to be equally responsible for success in goal attainment. The task had to be difficult enough to create the necessary information dependence but not so difficult as to be frustrating. The task had to minimize the expression of individual differences. The difficulty of the task had to be constant for all three conditions, and it had to be comparable within each condition.

Task Description. These requirements demanded much ingenuity of the task's creators. A professional artist, J. Hannah, worked with the principal investigator to create a pleasing design that would also meet the many task requirements. Equalizing the task difficulty in different conditions proved to be one of the most problematic aspects in the task development. Had this variable not been equated, it surely would have confounded similarity effects of the major independent variable. For this reason, the task was taken through many modifications after periodic testing with groups of children. Two pilot studies served as observer training sessions as well as testing sessions for task difficulty.

We refer to the task as an art puzzle. The puzzle is circular, and when completed it makes a somewhat unusual and attractive picture. Children work with precut puzzle pieces of colored posterboard that have a coating of dry wax on one side so the child can move the pieces until they decide where they are to stay. The pieces can be removed and reused with different groups.

For each condition there was a model three feet in diameter made of the same cardboard materials the children used in putting together the puzzle. All pieces used in the model were the same size as those used in the children's work. Each child received an individual pie-shaped wedge of cardboard corresponding to one-fifth of the circular model. When the five individual pie pieces are put together, they should look like the model the children have to reproduce. The models are represented in figure 4-13. The completed model is depicted on the left; a sample of the individual task is shown on the right. The models were exposed for two minutes and then removed, making it deliberately difficult to recall the exact position of the individual pieces.

In the identical condition (condition I), each of the five children worked on the same individual task depicted in figure 4-13A. The inspection of the ongoing work of other children thus could yield highly relevant and useful information. Attention to others' work in this condition was hypothesized to initiate the cycle of comparison behaviors. In the similar condition (condition S), this informational component was reduced in that each flower pair was different and the pieces were uniquely positioned (figure 4-13B). However, the parts surrounding the flowers—stems, leaves, picture inserts, and backgrounds—were in the same position in each individual task, even though they were in varied backgrounds to emphasize difference, and permit some useful comparison. In the different condition (condition D), the commonality of individual tasks was reduced still further so that the children could profit relatively little from examining others' work (figure 4-13C). Even though the individual pieces were the same as in condition S, they were positioned entirely differently. Here even the background for each individual task was different. Within the D condition, a child could gain little useful information about how to proceed with her own work by examining the work of others.

Creation of Interdependence. The task was designed to be clearly perceived in terms of both the individual and the group goals. A circular design was

Figure 4-13. The Art Puzzle Model

necessary if each child was to see the work of the whole group and if each was to have a neighbor on each side. Each individual portion, designated as a piece of pie, made a separate picture of its own, the completion of which was the individual goal. By requiring that the separate pieces be put together to complete the total design, we intended to emphasize interdependence and to remove any trace of goal contriency from the task conditions. It was essential that the group perceive itself working for a common goal since the major hypothesis to be tested asserted that similarity of task assignments in conditions of colabor is sufficient to elicit the various comparison behaviors even if there is no individual goal contriency in the objective task condition.

There were other several ways in which the perception of the group goal was strengthened. One of the most important was in the visual features of the puzzle itself. All three puzzles have a clear total unity that is evident at first glance. The children actually had to separate visually their own portion of the task from the total pattern of the model. The pattern of the group design in conditions I and S forms a star when the five pieces are combined. In condition D, there was the problem of having each part be as separate and different from every other part and yet produce the desired unity. Unity was accomplished there by a strong relationship among each of the five very different backgrounds that locked the total pattern together.

Additional aspects of the task that emphasized the group goal were the sun and the sun's rays. They could be completed only if each child completed her part: the sky in conditions I and S, the two border rings around the outside, and the black edging connecting the backgrounds in condition D. Each of these aspects required the five individual wedges to be fitted together correctly. To make sure that this unity was perceived and felt and to heighten the sense of commonality, the children were required at two points in their work to take their wedges over to the table where the five pieces could be combined to see how the picture would look. This was done for the first time after the border was completed so that a sense of unity was obtained before the different individual parts were filled in.

Other ways to emphasize commonality were the procedures intended to strengthen interaction and member cohesiveness. Pilot studies had shown that children tended to be somewhat overwhelmed by the elaborate setup to which they were introduced—five desks and chairs arranged in circular fashion, observers, materials, and so forth. Therefore a group-dynamics type of warm-up exercise was used in which children told each other their names, what they had had for breakfast, and what they liked to do best. This two-minute activity was in the spirit of fun. It relaxed them and ended in genuine laughter.

Interaction was further heightened by distributing needed puzzle pieces in different amounts in each of the five boxes of materials. Only one child received the required number of leaf pieces. Two received fewer pieces than needed, and the other two received more. It became necessary for the children to ask and to respond to requests. A perception of mutual giving and helping was created in this way.

Equalizing Difficulty within and between Conditions. A formidable challenge was posed by the need to equate the level of difficulty for the three conditions while also varying the degree of similarity. The designs were made deliberately abstract to reduce familiarity and to increase difficulty uniformly. In trying to design five different flowers for condition S and five identical ones for Condition I, we found that conventional flower patterns were too easy. In addition, some shapes were more familiar or basically simpler than others, which could make the tasks within conditions unequal. Abstract shapes could avoid these problems. Animal shapes in condition D were made from duplicate pieces of the ones that formed the flowers in condition S. This was done to make the conditions more equal in difficulty while making the tasks quite different from each other.

The degree of success in equating the level of difficulty among conditions and in making the task attractive is shown in figures 4-14 and 4-15. They represent graphically the children's own rankings on a six-point scale of their liking of the task and their evaluation of the task difficulty. Expressed liking of the task fell almost entirely on the positive side of the scale, with the mode at "liked very much." This included roughly half of all the children. Approximately one-fifth of the fifty children in each condition fell on each side of the mode. One child in each condition stated that she hated the task, and in each case this was a child who experienced difficulties in completing her assignment. Much the same picture was obtained in ratings of difficulty, with the mode at "a little difficult," and skewed a bit toward "just right." Both average ratings were exactly at the level for which we had aimed. Of course, there is no way of telling the correspondence between the children's verbal report and their true feelings. The ratings were made privately. The experimenter emphasized that we were interested in their "real feelings" and said that she would not be offended if they disliked the task. Had the task been unattractive or particularly difficult in any one of the three conditions, their answers would have probably shown some kind of irregular or skewed distribution. The children's evaluations among the three conditions are so much alike that we were satisfied that both level of difficulty and attractiveness had been equated within the three experimental conditions.

The Observation of Behavior

The Observers. Observations were made by a team of five people trained by the use of simulated groups on tape recordings as well as in actual pilot groups. The observers were ignorant of the specific hypotheses to be tested.

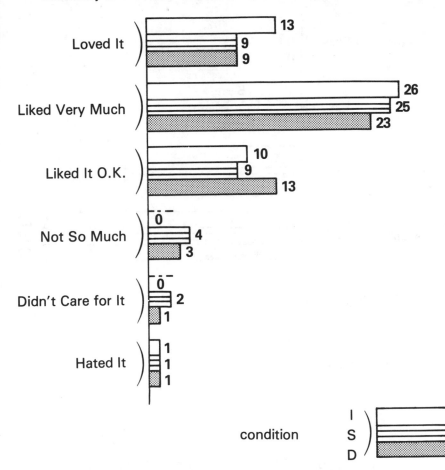

Figure 4-14. Expressed Liking for Task by Fifty Children in Each Condition

Although they thus had no voice in determining the nature of the behavior to be observed, they did participate in discussions to refine the behavior categories and their methods of observations. The total training period for each observer averaged, conservatively, fifty hours.

Each observer recorded the behavior of two children so that reliability could be determined among overlapping pairs. Children were assigned to each observer according to a prearranged schedule in which pairs of observers watching the same two children were alternated systematically. By watching two children simultaneously, observers were trained to develop a constant rhythm as they looked back and forth for continuous recording of the two children.

Each unit within the categories was recorded by indicating the number worn by the child who initiated a particular act, as well as by the number worn by the child to whom the action was directed. Behavioral acts were

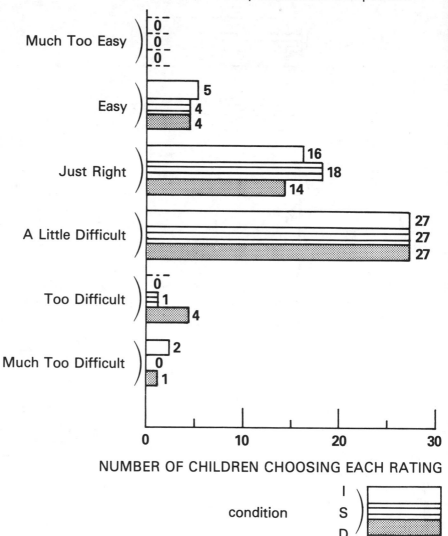

Figure 4-15. Expressed Difficulty of Task by Fifty Children in Each Condition

entered consecutively so that the sequence in which behavior had occurred could be determined. Continuous-behavior observations were employed from the point at which the group was given a signal to start until the group had assembled the total work pattern and had completed postwork evaluations.

Observation Categories. Observations included the three modes of comparison behaviors and related social behaviors.

Attentional Acts. The children's task involved primarily perceptual and cognitive functions (deciding where the pieces were to be placed, on the basis of previous inspection of the model, and positioning them accordingly). Comparison behaviors thus had to engage the visual mode of attending to others. Distinctions were made between nonverbal and verbal attentional acts. Nonverbal acts were defined operationally by the record of the child's looking activity. Distinctions were made further among the referents (own task, other's task, the objective model). Verbal attentional acts included requests for help or for information and expressions of difficulty.

Evaluational Acts. Explicit evaluative verbalizations about the task are included in this category. Distinctions were made in the mode of evaluation. Evaluations could be positive, neutral, or negative. The referent of evaluations was distinguished within each of the following categories: own work, work of specific other person(s) in the group, and work of the total group (the group product).

Besting Behaviors. These behaviors are indicators of the presence of competitive motives. Operational measurements were based on expressive movements generally associated with such motives (such as assuming a sprinting stance to be first to get needed materials, dashing back to the seat, and snatching pieces from others. Verbal statements were included from which it was possible to infer needs to excel over others (especially comparative evaluational statements, differentiated from the simpler task evaluations, such as, "Mine is better than yours").

Positive and Negative Social Behaviors. This category included social behaviors previously found to occur in competitive and cooperative conditions (Deutsch 1949b). Positive acts consisted of unsolicited offers to help or to correct others. Also included here were positive responses to requests for assistance, to expressions of others' difficulties, and to assistance offered from others. Negative acts were the obverse: hindering others' progress and negative responses to requests for assistance, to expressions of others' difficulties, and to assistance offered from others.

Reliability of Observations. Pearson product-moment coefficients of correlation were computed between the amount of behavior recorded in each category by each of the two observers who watched the same two children. The correlations ranged from .70 to .97. The lowest correlations were obtained for the categories involving answers to requests and answers to others' expressions of difficulty. Presumably observers attended only to the two children who were assigned to them and often did not realize that they were not initiating behavior but rather were responding to others. The different modes of comparison behavior were observed with reliabilities whose coefficients ranged from .87 to .97.

All of the attentional categories hovered around .90. Several sources of evidence have demonstrated the high degree of reliability with which eye movements can be recorded (Exline 1963). We found that more complex visual inspections may be observed equally reliably. Also the combined evaluational acts of the children were observed with near-complete observer agreement (the coefficient for total evaluation was .97). But only verbal evaluations were recorded, and, in all likelihood, much evaluating took place that was not expressed overtly. The techniques must be refined to include these important nonverbal evaluations as well.

The Experimental Studies

In the general procedure five children at a time were called out of one classroom to work together in a familiar room—the library, music room, or a vacant classroom—for approximately one class period. Comparisons were always made within classrooms in that each classroom was divided randomly into subgroups of five girls, which were then randomly assigned to different experimental conditions. Although these procedures involved a great deal of preplanning and coordination with the school personnel, they gave maximum opportunity to create intended variables and control such variables as classroom climate, teachers, or children's familiarity with each other.

Study 1: Social Comparison and Cognitive Uncertainty. To study the occurrence of comparison behaviors under conditions of cognitive uncertainty, the availability of a physical standard of comparison was varied (Crawford 1970). Twelve groups of five third-grade girls were assigned to two work conditions. The instructions for all of the groups included demonstration of a model of the completed design. In the model-present condition, this model was allowed to remain in sight of the children during their entire work period. It was placed in the center of the circle, equidistant from each of the five children, at a level slightly below their desk tops, thus requiring an easily discernible downward head movement. In this condition, the model can be said to have constituted physical reality in that it provided a constant source of reliable information about how the pieces should be placed, as well as being a constant standard against which one's performance could be evaluated. By contrast, in the model-absent condition, the model was removed before the children started their work. Relative to the model-present condition, the children had to rely primarily on their own memory, visual imagery, skill, and each other.

In order to create conditions that would give maximum opportunity for profiting from each other's knowledge, each of the five children in each group in both conditions worked on identical tasks. According to the theory, more need for social comparison behavior existed in the identical task, model-absent condition (IMA condition), as compared with the identical task, model-present condition (IMP condition). Table 4-3 summarizes the major behavioral findings.

Well over one-third of all interactions were spent in nonverbal inspection in both conditions. There is a highly significant difference in the attentional referent in each of the two conditions. Where no physical standard was present (IMA condition), children looked to each other; where a physical model was provided, it served as the major source of reference.

The presence of a physical standard not only decreased attention paid to

Table 4-3
Comparison and Achievement-related Behaviors When Model Is Absent and Present

	IMA		IMP		
	Mean	%	Mean	%	t-value
Independent work	108.83	32.7	46.83	14.7	3.16**
Attentional acts	127.03	38.6	151.33	54.3	n.s.
Nonverbal	120.33	36.7	146.66	52.6	n.s.
Inspects other, no work	86.33	26.7	42.83	13.2	2.25*
Inspects other, works	34.00	10.0	12.67	4.8	4.16***
Inspects model, works			91.16	34.6	
Verbal, total requests for					
information, help	6.17	1.9	4.67	1.7	n.s.
Evaluational acts	24.48	6.9	9.16	3.4	2.03
Self-evaluations	7.49	2.2	3.33	1.2	1.67
Positive	2.83	.9	.67	.2	1.58
Neutral	1.50	.4	.16	.1	2.02
Negative	3.16	.9	2.50	.9	n.s.
Evaluation of others	16.99	4.7	5.83	2.2	1.96
Positive	3.49	1.0	1.67	.6	1.86
Neutral	.50	.2	.50	.2	n.s.
Negative	13.00	3.5	3.66	1.4	1.64
Achievement-related social acts					
Besting	14.18	4.0	2.66	.9	2.79*
Negative social acts	6.01	1.9	2.17	.8	3.56**
Positive social acts	33.34	9.5	28.01	10.6	n.s.

* $p < .05$.
** $p < .01$.
*** $p < .005$.

others, it also diminished reliance on one's own abilities. As compared with work in the IMA condition, there was significantly less independent work in the IMP condition. In other words, in the latter condition, more than half of all of the nonverbal attentional acts consisted of alternations between looking at the model and working on one's task. Thus the function of the referent seems unambiguous: the model was used to obtain information. In its absence, the children depended on each other for information (Inspects other, works, 10 percent versus 4.8 percent, respectively).

In both conditions children engaged almost as much in sheer looking at each other as they did in working independently (category "inspects other, no work"). This finding, encountered in each of the subsequent studies, strengthens the inference that evidently children look to each other for additional reasons than merely to obtain information about the task at hand. In the IMP condition, children could completely ignore each other for purposes of information seeking since complete information was provided; yet 18 percent of their interactions were devoted to inspection of others.

There was a much smaller percentage of evaluational acts than attentional behavior in both conditions, but what there was was found significantly more in almost every evaluational category of the IMA condition. This held whether the referent was oneself or others in the group. Apparently attending to others stimulates evaluational activity. No simple correlation was found between these two variables, presumably because the attentional activity was followed by many different kinds of behavior as well, increasing its variability. The relationships showed up inferentially by examining other variables.

A significantly greater amount of besting behavior was found in the IMA condition. A Pearson correlation coefficient of .55 was found between that behavior and evaluational activity.

An examination of various positive and negative social behaviors throws additional light on the childrens' motivations. As might be expected, in this situation where no interaction is essential, there was relatively little overt negative behavior. When it did occur, it was found significantly more in the IMA condition. Presumably others were seen as competitive rivals and reacted to with hostility. This hostility took the form of techniques such as refusal of help when it was asked for. The correlation between inspecting others' work and offering information or help was negative in the IMA condition ($-.41$). Low negative relationships were also found between helping acts and doing independent work. In other words, comparison behavior not only elicits achievement motives but carries with it actual refusals to cooperate.

In the IMP condition, children aided each other more freely. Although there was no overall difference between the two conditions with respect to total positive social behaviors, when helping and correcting behaviors were combined, their mean was substantially greater in the IMP condition (7.00 versus 14.34, respectively). This difference may be more important considering that in the IMP condition children had been shown to be concerned more with the model than with each other. But when they did pay attention to each other, their achievement needs presumably did not prevent them from helping each other. As might be expected, correlations between inspecting others' work and offering information or correcting others were positive (offers information versus inspects others and works, .35; independent work and offering information, .25).

This study supported our major hypotheses: the absence of an objective standard by which one's performance can be evaluated does increase reliance on coworkers, as signified by more inspection of others' work. Although coworkers are not being evaluated more negatively (perhaps because their contribution to the common goal is needed), attention to others is accompanied by more besting behavior and more negative social acts.

We attributed the comparison behaviors and manifestation of competitive motivations to work on identical tasks. If this is so, then keeping the same low degree of physical reality in the sense of reproducing the model-absent condition but reducing the similarity among the activities of the five children should also lower the amount of comparison behavior. This was the object of the next experiment.

Study 2: Social Comparison and Similarity of Activity. In this experiment, the similarity of work assigned to each of the children in a group was varied systematically in three conditions. Each condition used a different model; each of the models differed in the extent to which its five parts—each child's individual task—resembled each other.

In the Identical Condition (I), each of the five children in a group were putting together exactly the same flower pair to make a completed circle of five pairs of identical abstract flowers. This condition was the same as the IMA condition of the previous study. Understanding how to put one flower pair together enabled the child fully to understand how to complete any one of the other flower pairs.

In the Similar Condition (S), each child's task involved making a different flower pair, although several comparison points existed among each of the individual tasks. Understanding how to put one flower pair together enabled the child somewhat to understand how to complete any one of the other flower pairs.

In the Different Condition (D), the same pieces were used as those of the S condition, but they were combined very differently to make five different pairs of abstract animal figures. Understanding how to put one animal pair together would not enable the child to understand how to complete any one of the other animal pairs.

Each of the tasks within a condition, as well as among the three conditions, was equated for difficulty. In all three conditions, the model was absent during the work period so that the children were made maximally information dependent on each other.

One hundred fifty children were studied. Ten groups of five third-graders were assigned to each of the three conditions.

Hannah's major findings, summarized in table 4-4, support and complement the Crawford data. The trend in the body of the data varies as predicted with degree of similarity, with highly significant differences predominantly between the extreme conditions. The greater the similarity among tasks, the less independent work was found and the more attention was paid to others while working. Significantly more total evaluations of

Table 4-4
Comparison and Achievement-related Behaviors under Three Degrees of Similarity of Task

	Mean (I)	Mean (S)	Mean (D)	t-values (n = 10) I-S	I-D	S-D
Independent work	103.6	113.9	117.0	n.s.	n.s.	n.s.
Attentional acts	120.7	83.7	84.7	2.51*	2.67**	n.s.
Inspects other, no work	82.9	66.8	70.6	n.s.	n.s.	n.s.
Inspects other, works	21.0	9.0	5.5	3.48***	4.91***	n.s.
Group evaluational acts	5.9	2.5	2.3	2.77**	3.01***	n.s.
Self-evaluations						
Positive	2.9	1.3	2.9	n.s.	n.s.	n.s.
Negative	5.0	5.0	9.7	n.s.	n.s.	n.s.
Negative evaluation of own product	0.4	1.3	1.7	−2.42*	−3.24***	n.s.
Positive evaluation of own product	2.4	1.6	1.3	n.s.	2.03*	n.s.
Negative evaluation of other product	7.4	3.5	3.0	n.s.	1.73*	n.s.
Positive evaluation of other product	1.9	2.6	1.7	n.s.	n.s.	n.s.
Besting	11.8	3.2	3.3	3.29***	2.99***	n.s.
Negative social acts	28.9	11.4	18.1	2.74**	n.s.	n.s.
Positive social acts	27.0	29.9	39.0	n.s.	n.s.	n.s.

Note: There were ten groups in each condition.
*p < .05.
**p < .01.
***p < .005.

the group were made in condition I, in which the pattern of achievement-related social acts was like that of the previous study: large amounts of besting behaviors, large amounts of negative social behaviors, and, relative to the other two conditions, fewer total positive social acts.

From the interaction pattern, it appears that identical task assignments indeed evoke increased competitive motivations, with attendant needs to examine others' work in order to profit from it. (Note the significant differences in the category "inspects other, followed by own work.") It is likely that such examination also serves the purpose of assessing other partners' progress to evaluate one's own progress (in the I condition, one's own product was evaluated most positively). The large number of total negative social acts suggests that identical conditions, even in the absence of objective goal contriency, were responded to as if such contriency existed; the other children, while in reality collaborating toward a common goal, were seen as rivals. In this highly controlled study, conditions differed only in degree of similarity; therefore we may conclude that the highest degree of similarity—identity of task assignments—in older, achievement-oriented girls is not an enjoyable, positive experience as was the case with the toddlers who chose identical toys freely. Rather it created competitive feelings with attendant expressed needs to evaluate one's own product higher, or lower that of others, as well as general expressions of hostility toward coworkers.

Although differences between conditions S and D were generally in the expected direction, none of them reached significance. Perhaps the differences were not as strong as we would expect because there are still common features among the diverse tasks within the D condition, features that were deliberately retained for the purpose of emphasizing the cooperative nature of the assigned group task. Because task requirements had to be kept constant, all three conditions were somewhat alike. Our study thus explored only a relatively small area of a possible similarity continuum that would stretch from complete identity into the other extreme of complete difference. Presumably the assignment of entirely different activities to each group member in a maximum-difference condition would reduce comparison behavior further.

Additionally, however, a unique pattern of negativity emerged in this study in condition D, in particular with regard to the dependent variables relating to evaluational processes. Although not significant, compared with the other conditions, almost twice as many statements involving negative self-evaluations were made during the work period. They involved generally belittling one's own ability or other self-derogatory remarks. In the D condition, there were significantly more negative evaluations than in condition I of one's own products and significantly fewer positive comments about own products. The picture is highly consistent in that expressions of negative evaluation of the others' products were fewest in the D condition.

A second evaluative measure was called for at the close of the work session. Children were asked to assign a numerical grade to each of the completed tasks. Table 4-5 shows the results in basic support of the behavioral trends we have discussed. Each child's own work was rated highest in the I condition, with almost half of the children (48 percent) assigning themselves a grade of A, as compared with 32 percent in the S condition and only 26 percent in the D condition. Nor did the children in the D condition simply consider their work acceptable; 34 percent gave themselves grades of C or lower, while only 8 percent in the I condition did so. Children in the D condition had significantly fewer negative evaluations about others' work, yet in grading, they graded others as critically as they judged themselves. They assigned significantly more grades of C or below to their coworkers than did children in either of the two other conditions. These are suggestive findings. Hoffman, Festinger, and Lawrence (1954) found no hostility when a low scorer compared himself with a high scorer; however, in their study, scores were objectively given and did not occur in a work setting. Perhaps in the context of performance, even if activities are relatively different and contribute to the common goal as was the case in our study, some competitive motivation is generated and manifested in lowering of performance evaluation of others.

In the D condition, children had to work independently; yet they inspected others' work as much as did those in the S condition, even though they gained only minimal work-related information. It would seem that when cognitive unclarity exists, and when children cannot obtain information through social comparison, and when they are cut off as well from any other potential sources of information, they become anxious about their work and, in the end, critical of their own finished product as well as products of others. According to Festinger, needs for self-evaluation stimulate need for social comparison, and, for comparison, comparable—similar—others are needed. It is plausible that a lack of opportunity for such self-evaluation raises uncertainties further and anxiety level as well. Perhaps this is in the nature of solitary work. Total absence of a reference group that would constitute social reality does not permit self-evaluation, which may create self-doubt and anticipation of failure. One may wonder whether activities that involve individual creativity might be the extreme point of difference on the similarity of task continuum. Much has been written, for instance, about the loneliness of the creative artist. Perhaps, creativity, almost by definition, involves a uniqueness of ability that excludes comparison with others.

As far as the role of similarity in work assignments was concerned, we concluded that in our third-grade girls, the identical work assignments seemed to create competitive tensions, while different work assignments may have left the child somewhat anxious or, at the minimum, uncertain about the goodness of her performance and perhaps anticipating failure. It would appear that our original assumption—if identical tasks create com-

Table 4-5
Mean Frequencies of Postwork Evaluations for Groups Across Three Conditions

	Mean			F(N/30)	±(N/10)			% of Individuals (N/50)		
	I	S	D	ISD	I-S	I-D	S-D	I	S	D
Q. What mark would you give? (self, positive)	2.4	1.6	1.3	2.24	1.41	2.03*	0.60	48	32	26
Q. What mark would you give? (self, negative)	0.4	1.3	1.7	4.87*	−2.42**	−3.24****	−0.81	8	26	34
Q. What mark would you give (others, positive)	9.9	11 0	8.5	1.42	−0.69	0.88	2.03**	49.5	55	42.5
Q. What mark would you give? (others, negative)	2.5	2.8	5.1	2.36	−0.24	−1.90*	−1.80*	12.5	14	25.5

Note: Questionnaire date referring to evaluation were classified in the following way: As were considered positive evaluation, Bs neutral, and Cs and marks below C negative.

* $p < .05$.
** $p < .01$.
*** $p < .005$.

petitive tensions, then different tasks should be tension free—was something of an oversimplification.

Study 3: Confidence, Competence, and Social Comparison. Our interpretation of the data has focused on the girls' uncertainty in the absence of relevant information. The next question that had to be raised focused on possible sex differences. That is, even though latency-aged girls' school performance is generally found to be superior to that of comparable boys, their expectations of success tend to be lower (Crandall 1969; Maccoby and Jacklin 1974). Thus girls' greater frequency of paying attention to each other could justifiably be attributed to their lack of confidence rather than to ability. And indeed, on Iowa tests administered previously to our third graders, the girls received significantly higher scores than the boys did on both reading and verbal ability.

Our interest in sex difference data was heightened by consideration of competitive motivations. Following our hypothesis, increased attention is expected to raise achievement-related motives, as indeed was established in the I condition with girls. Yet boys, expected to have lower levels of attentional behaviors, have repeatedly been shown to engage in more competitive behaviors. Accordingly our study compared sex differences in the I condition. This allowed pitting the level of attentional behaviors against the level of besting behaviors.

Ten boys' groups were matched with the girls from the same classrooms. Concern over the possible feminine bias of the task proved unfounded. Postwork interviews showed no differences in liking of the task among the girls as compared with the boys.

Table 4-6 presents cross-sex comparisons of interaction behaviors. The data form a highly consistent pattern. On the average, the boys expressed almost three times as much assurance about their abilities as did the girls. And the boys did, in fact, take significantly less time to complete their assignments than did the girls. Regarding errors, the boys' performance approached the 0.6 level of significance in favor of boys.

The girls, as predicted, engaged in significantly more comparison behaviors of both the attentional type and in evaluating the group as a whole. The difference is striking in the "pure attention category" of "inspects other, no work" (mean girls, 82.9, versus mean boys, 32.4), which we postulated to reflect, in part, attempts at gaining reassurance.

We have no way of deciding whether the task was actually easier for the boys or whether they had greater confidence in their ability to begin with. In either case, there would be less need for comparison behaviors, and this would free the boys to attend to their assignments more efficiently (more rapidly), as indeed they did. Not only were they free to tend to their task, but they were free to share their knowledge with each other, as shown by the

Table 4-6
Comparison of Girls' and Boys' Mean Interactions and Performance under Identical Task Conditions

Category	Mean for Girls	Mean for Boys	t-value
Expression of assurance	2.6	6.3	2.07*
Time to completion (minutes)	20.0	14.0	3.62***
Attentional acts			
Inspects other, no work	82.9	32.4	3.86***
Inspects other, works	21.0	9.8	3.01***
Evaluational acts			
Positive evaluation of group	2.3	0.6	2.93**
Negative evaluation of group	5.2	2.9	2.12*
Achievement-related social acts			
Neutral answers to requests	.0	9.0	2.26*
Offers of information	9.2	16.8	3.66***
Besting (overall)	11.4	11.8	n.s.
Besting (part II)	.08	.56	2.25*
Besting (postwork)	.9	.5	n.s.

Note: There were ten groups in each condition.
  * $p < .05$.
 ** $p < .01$.
*** $p < .005$.

significantly greater average amount of both netural answers to requests, and offers of information, as compared with the girls.

No differences in either positive or negative achievement-related social acts were found, nor did overall besting behavior differ between boys and girls. Yet at certain key points during the work period, boys betrayed symptoms of competitive motivation by their expressive, nonverbal acts. For instance, many boys assumed a sprinter's stance waiting to dash off to the table for work material to begin work in the second part of the work period. When this brief time period was analyzed, boys showed significantly more besting behaviors than the girls did.

Why, then, did the boys' competitive motives not lead to an increase in evaluative behaviors, as was found in the other studies? The answer must be sought in their greater competence and/or confidence. Boys, being both competent and confident, did not need to engage in evaluations of their own abilities, and, to the extent that they were competitive, they did not want to lose time attending to each other to ascertain the positions of others. The girls, being less confident, had a greater need to engage in comparison behaviors, and that these acts eventuate in evaluation and besting, as found

previously, can be demonstrated here too. When the girls combined their individual products at the end of the work period, there was a tendency to
evaluate and best each other more than the boys did during this brief time.

We are led to several hypotheses about the patttern of these interrelationships. The occurrence of comparison behavior is a function of a
person's level of competence, confidence in his abilities, and his
achievement-related motives. Where all of these factors are extremely
low—for instance, in some ghetto children with low school-related abilities,
very low self-confidence, and little achievement motivation—we would
expect very little comparison behavior. But we would also expect relatively little comparison behavior on the other extreme. The highly able, highly confident, highly motivated child similarly will have little need for social comparison. It is the children in the intermediate range of each of these
variables—and they constitute the vast majority of public school
children—who will show the greatest amount of comparison behavior, for
they need to rely on each other for information when they do not understand, they will doubt their own abilities and need reassurance from each
other, and they need to compare themselves with each other to gain a
realistic estimate of their abilities. Further, they may be the ones on whom
parental and other social pressures to achieve are great, leading to a perception of classmates as potential rivals to be watched in order to outdistance
them.

Implications for the Classroom

Perhaps the most important implications for teachers lie in the ubiquity of
social-comparison behavior among third graders. Our data have supported
the inference that such comparisons may serve some useful functions for the
child: reducing outer uncertainties related to immediate school tasks and/or
strengthening inner confidence in own abilities. Neither motive carries
negative connotations in itself. In fact, what teacher would wish to disagree
with instructional aims that specify that children must be given clear instructions about what they are to do and clear feedback on how well they
have done it? Is it merely a question of how this information is obtained,
and from whom it is available?

Most classrooms have extremely strong standards against a manifestation of interest in each other's work. This was brought to our attention time
and again when a child, upon catching another's glance toward her work,
responded with an angry, "Don't copy." Others attempted to cover up
their work. And the comparison seekers, in turn, had developed their skill
to a fine surreptitious art; they could cast stealthy glances at others without
betraying themselves with as much as the slightest muscle movement. These

attitudes were present in a situation where all were working toward a common goal.

In the children's attitudes, in the tones of their voices, one began to sense teachers' constant admonitions: "Eyes on your paper," "Don't copy," "Work independently," "Never mind what Susie is doing." We have discussed some data that seem to indicate the child's low self-confidence when unable to make comparison with others pertaining to own work. Because of such insecurities, a child must learn during the school years to develop skills in working independently. She is urged to do so still in too many schools from the moment she enters first grade. At the same time, she is placed in a classroom that makes comparison virtually inescapable. And, ironically, while the teacher is exhorting the child toward independence, she is unwittingly encouraging interpupil comparisons by her own evaluative comments. Some teachers may distinguish between sharing and copying, encouraging the former, although the distinction may not be at all clear to a small child. The confusion may only add to the uncertainty and guilt over copying.

What, then, are the implications of our research? We shall address ourselves primarily to the information-seeking dynamic of social comparisons. Implications, of course, must be examined in relation to teacher purpose. If a teacher is concerned with stimulating a child's inner dynamics, which involve fantasy or creativity (often the aim in the teaching of art), provision of a model is anathema. If it is there to be copied, it is believed, this will surely stifle the spark of individuality that is prized in large segments of our society. Yet even a model has its place, as is attested in its use throughout the history of education in the teaching of writing. Here we are back again to the issue of young children and the security-giving function of identical tasks. There is pleasure and satisfaction in being able to make b's with bellies to the right, and d's with bellies to the left and being able to check a model to remember which is which. Seeing that one's whole row corresponds to that of a teacher can be a firm step toward building feelings of competency. Older children studying a foreign language learn to pronounce words correctly from modeling, whether they use a record, the teacher, or some other children.

What if seatwork assignments must be identical and the teacher wishes to control the tendency to copy? Of course, it is possible for the teacher to cut down the need for information seeking simply by providing cognitive clarity and more structure. Yet the question involves more basic pedagogic assumptions about the nature of learning—for instance, the assumption from whom the child should learn and from whom she can learn. In the widest sense, the classroom may be structured as a place where learning resources are to be used. Such resources may be physical: encyclopedias, dictionaries, maps, and all of the other learning materials from which children can obtain information for themselves. Such a structure encourages the individual pursuit of knowledge and the building of self-reliance, which children need to function. Another classroom resource is the people in it—not only the teacher, ready to make himself accessible and available as a source of information, but also the pupils themselves. There is no reason for students not to utilize each other as a source of information. In fact, judging by reports of peer teaching results, there is every reason that pupils should be encouraged to become helpers and to accept help from others. Helping and sharing behaviors need to be learned and are essential in this increasingly interdependent world.

If the destructive, surreptitious aspect of social comparison is to be discouraged, classroom climates must be created in which acceptable ways of seeking information are provided. A climate that values the process of learning itself rather than merely correct answers provides the optimum learning potential. Multiple-choice tests, which are used in many high schools, are, in our view, contrary to the aims of this climate. Correct answers represent absolutes and, we suspect, function exactly as models. Multiple-choice and true-false tests tend to create needs to know one final answer but do not demand understanding. If our suggestions appear unrealistic, there are examples of learning climates like these in alternative classrooms in elementary schools and high schools throughout the country, as well as in experimental cooperative classrooms.

Implications also may be found in the evidence supporting our theory of interrelationships between different elements of comparison behaviors. If we wish to reduce attention paid to others' work, then reducing stress on evaluation should be an indirect means of accomplishing what direct rules and sanctions cannot. What, then, of the competition-related element in social comparison? First of all, what if information seeking from another reveals one's own weakness? Creating a climate as we have suggested should go a long way toward preventing a lowered self-concept, which might result from negative feedback. We had expected to find, and did find, more interpersonal besting in the identical condition. Reducing the similarity of assignments and reducing goal similarity (individualizing learning) while increasing promotive interdependence among equals (as in Aronson's 1975 jigsaw approach to learning) may help reduce competition and its attendant hostilities.

We wish to emphasize how extremely sensitive to each other children can be in experimental situations such as ours, which, after all, simulated classroom conditions. The comparison tendencies, strong as they are, have the potential of being constructive or destructive agents in children's learning and personal growth.

Perhaps the strongest implications from these studies are those dealing with the similarity of work assignments for latency-aged children. Our findings suggest that instructional practice should avoid the exclusive use of identical task assignments with its consequent competition and increased negative behaviors; it should also avoid wholly individualized work with its accompanying insecurities. Greatest pupil satisfaction, and perhaps even greatest learning, may lie in classrooms that provide for individualized, yet complementary and interrelated pupil activities, including group work, committee work, class projects, class research, small-group discussions, and encouragement for divergent as well as convergent responses.

The Role of Other-Orientation in Children's Cooperation

The research described in this chapter examined interpersonal processes in cooperative conditions that are characterized by increased member dependence on each other. Member interdependence was strengthened by requiring subjects in different conditions to act out task roles and group roles that demanded interaction. It was expected that increased interdependencies would be reflected in the group process, as well as in the group's performance. The subjects were given relatively minimal task requirements so that they were made also more interdependent by having to decide together on their specific task objective.

Our focus here was on the other-oriented behaviors that we postulated as necessary in complex cooperative situations. Just as we explored first in the previous chapter very young children's responses to similarity of activity, the independent variable under study, so here we examine first some conditions under which young children may be expected to engage in beginnings of such role-taking skills.

Sharing in Kindergarten Children
E.A. Pepitone and *C.E. Vanderbilt*

We began with the assumption that complex cooperative conditions demand the exercise of required task and group roles, which in turn rest on fundamental orientations toward the requirements (needs, purposes, and so forth) of others in a given task environment. This was detailed in chapter 2, where we also dwelled at some length on developmental processes postulated to precede children's capacity to respond to needs of others, or even situational needs. The vignettes of the children's behavior toward each other showed no evidence of one child's deeper concern for another, and, at this largely egocentric toddler age, we did not expect any. The closest expression of other orientation that went beyond immediate play concerns was that of a 28-month old boy (Eddy), persistently asking his playmate: "Do you have truck in your house too?" Significantly, he never received a reply and gave up asking.

In designing the research presented here, we started with the Piagetian conceptualization of preoperational thought as being confined to the surface of phenomena, attending only to the most obvious and strongest characteristics in a situation. Taking this conceptualization one step further, we argued that a young child's recognition of another's need is likely to be facilitated when the need can be somewhat externalized by cues in the environment. Even adults are more likely to recognize the neediness of a beggar in tattered rags, as compared to one in a top hat and tuxedo, or more realistically, one dressed in neat street clothes. Gestalt psychologists still use an appropriate descriptive Germanic term, *Aufforderungscharacteristik*. Prosaically translated as "demand characteristics," it denotes the dimension of salience of cues or, more precisely, the propensity of certain stimulus properties to intrude themselves into a person's perceptual field. It is this intrusiveness aspect of a person's need that we wished to vary. We needed some cue that would indicate to the child that another child had a lot of something, as opposed to being in great need of it.

We also needed to know whether a child is cognizant of another's need. Flavell (1968) used a child's communication as an index of her responsiveness to another's information requirements. Another procedure has been to study a child's giving behavior in response to perceived needs. The Rheingold et al. (1976) study observed children as young as 9 months old giving objects to others (mostly to mothers and fathers). One of the earliest and best descriptions of preschool children's giving and sharing was that of G. Chittenden (1947). She took the position that in order to be defined as sharing, behavior must be spontaneous and the sharer must see the results to himself and to others as satisfactory. Most of the subsequent research on sharing has asked children to divide something treasured with momentarily absent partners. Ugurel-Semin (1952) required 4 to 6 year olds to divide an uneven number of nuts, and Handlon and Gross (1959) asked that token rewards for joint labor be divided. In a study of extrinsic reward effectiveness, Fisher (1963) asked for sharing of marbles and bubble gum, and one of the favorite treasured objects asked to be shared in several studies were M&M chocolate candies (Bryan & Walbeck 1970, for instance).

Doland and Adelberg's (1967) study is important because it used a child confederate who was actually present. The confederate was given fewer pictures than the experimental child, and the child's giving responses were studied as a function of increasing verbal pressure on the child to share and as a function of modeling on the confederate's sharing. A follow-up study showed the latter more effective than repetitions without a model present (Doland 1970).

Most of this research has demonstrated an increase with age in giving behaviors, that is, the ability and/or willingness to share or to donate to others (see Elliott and Vasta 1970; Rushton 1975, 1976). The children's relative state of affluence and/or deprivation has been examined with contradictory results. Ugurel-Semin found middle-class children least able or willing to share, but Doland and Adelberg found more sharing among middle-class children than among welfare children.

In research on sharing, just as in research on competition, study has tended to move away from the central focus on the interpersonal relationship between giver and receiver.[1] Staub and Sherk's (1970) research is something of an exception because their concern was on the influence of a norm of reciprocity in giving relationships of children. Their methodology, which has certain features in common with our approach, involved the simultaneous presence of two children, each of whom had an object needed or wanted by the other. First, one child was brought into a room where she was given candy to eat while waiting; a second child arrived with a crayon that both needed to perform a task. The research determined that the sharing of candy by the first child (giver) was significantly related to sharing of the crayon by the second (receiver). The more candy the giver ate in the presence of the receivers relative to what they gave to the receiver, the less did the latter share the crayon.

In the study examined next (Vanderbilt 1971), the emphasis was not on behavior as it relates to normative reciprocity expectations; rather we sought to determine a child's giving behavior as it was affected both by the relative state of own need for specific resources, as well as the perception of needs for specific resources of another coacting child.

The Subjects

Previous research has demonstrated that most 3 year olds are not sufficiently along the decentering process to be able to respond to the needs of others, so we chose a somewhat older group of children. Subjects were 134 kindergarten children, varying within a rather narrow age range of 4.11 years to 6.00 years. They were selected from a consolidated school district in a small town of about five thousand persons in southeastern Pennsylvania. The children were taken from ten kindergarten classes, distributed among three schools, who could be matched with their classrooms according to our criteria.

Hollingshead's (1957) two-factor method was used to obtain a measure of socioeconomic status. This method uses two indexes, education and occupation, of the child's father, in a weighted relationship. Fathers in the upper-upper and upper-middle classes ($n = 22$) were professionally employed or held management positions in large industrial concerns of a nearby city. Parents from the lowest socioeconomic groups—lower-middle and lower-lower class ($n = 91$)—worked primarily as laborers in local mushroom and plant nursery industries.

The children in each classroom were matched by age, sex, and socioeconomic status. Since analyses of each of these variables showed no main or interaction effects, they are combined here.[2] (It will become evident that the situational effects were so overridingly effective as to obscure any trends that may in fact have come to the fore in a different study of the same variables.)

The members of each pair were assigned to different task conditions at random. We report here only the parts of the study that concern the single act of giving, its determinants in the structural aspect of the situation, and its cognitive concomitants.

The Task

The study was designed to determine the influence on a child's giving behavior of two primary situational factors: the amount of surplus resources available to the giver beyond what she required for her own specific task, and the degree of a partner's need for resources required to execute her specific task. The task was identical for each of the coacting children.

Contrary to much research practice, the children were studied in pairs, so the child to be shared with was present, visible, and obviously needy. Even though our focus was on interpersonal behavior that is considered a precondition for successful interpersonal collaboration, no such collaboration was required here. The pilot studies seemed to indicate that placing kindergartners into coactive identical task conditions resulted in some attention paid to the other but no visible evaluative or besting responses, especially when models were present. Children sat across from each other at a bridge table, with two observers sitting along the other two sides several feet away from the table, acting unobtrusively and apparently not interfering with the children's interactions.

A construction task was devised to enable the independent variation of levels of neediness of one child and the amount of resources in the possession of the second child. The task required both children to construct a picture following a model. One child was given too few pieces; she was the needy child (Ne). The partner was given more pieces than required to copy the picture in the model; she was the child with the surplus (Su).

The children were introduced to the study with two preliminary tasks. First, each pair was observed for five minutes in an unstructured play situation with a wooden toy train containing many pieces that could be used either individually or in associative play. Its dual purpose was to familiarize children with the setting and each other and to enable an analysis between type of play and responsiveness to the needs of others. In particular, it was hypothesized that since associative play involves more awareness of the other than does parallel play and giving to a needy child also involves more

Table 5-1
Number of Subjects and Definition of Four Experimental Conditions for House Construction Task

Item	Condition			
	I	*II*	*III*	*IV*
Number of subjects	28	32	30	44
Number of pairs	14	16	15	22
Definition of condition	Small need Small surplus	Small need Large surplus	Large need Small surplus	Large need Large surplus
Missing pieces	− 2 windows	− 2 windows	− 4 windows, − 1 door	− 4 windows, − 1 door
Surplus pieces	+ 2 windows	+ 4 windows, + 1 door	+ 2 windows	+ 4 windows, + 1 door

awareness than nongiving, children who engaged in associative play were more likely to give than those children who engaged in parallel play.

Next, both members of each pair were asked to construct individually an identical picture from a model depicting a snowman. Each child had equal and sufficient pieces to complete the picture. This activity was intended as a training task for the major experimental activity to follow. Further, the model was intended to provide children with a success experience. This was indeed accomplished because this task was considerably simpler than the next, and all children had the experience of completing it.

Then each child of each pair was asked again to construct a picture from a model. In this task, the child assigned to the needy condition had insufficient pieces to construct the picture; the child assigned to the surplus condition had extra pieces beyond the number used in the model. The task involved constructions of a house from several separate plastic pieces that could be stuck to a larger sheet of cardboard. Need and surplus were varied, respectively, by the number of pieces available for construction: fewer pieces than necessary defined need and more pieces than required by the model defined surplus. Small and large need were also defined by the requiredness of the missing pieces in the child's concept of a house. That is, a lack of two windows was defined as a small need; a lack of four windows and a door was a large need. A child could make an acceptable house with fewer windows than seen on the model, but without a door this was not possible. Similarly surplus conditions were defined as two extra windows (small surplus) or four extra windows and an extra door (large surplus).

The experimental design called for four conditions, each of which consisted of different combinations of need and surplus. The description of the four experimental conditions is presented in table 5-1. Conditions on the extreme combined, respectively, small need for Ne and small surplus for Su (condition I), and condition IV combined large need and large surplus. Conditions II and III were cross-combinations of these two extremes; CII combined Ne's small need and Su's large surplus; and CIII Ne's large need and Su's small surplus.

The Theoretical Framework

The theoretical framework extended beyond the data of particular concern here (including some personality dynamics of children and various aspects of family patterns). Our focus was particularly on the sharing behavior of the Sus. The major hypothesis in regard to Su's perception of Ne's needs and giving in relation to own surplus was stated in this way: Giving behavior is a function of the level of another's need perceived in relation to the amount of own resources. We made several assumptions and predictions concerning cognition as a function of amount of resources:

> The greater a child's need, the more likely it is to be perceived by a nonneedy child.
>
> *Prediction a*: Sus are more likely to perceive Ne's need in conditions III and IV (large need) than in conditions I and II (small need).
>
> The larger a child's own surplus, the more likely he is to perceive it.
>
> *Prediction b*: Sus are more likely to perceive their own surplus in conditions II and IV (large surplus) than in conditions I and III (small surplus).

These assumptions and predictions concerned giving as a function of cognition of magnitude of another's need.

> Unless a child perceives another's need, he does not give.
>
> The larger Ne's need (as perceived by Su), the more likely that Su will give to Ne.
>
> *Prediction c*: Sus are more likely to give in conditions III and IV (large need) than in conditions I and II (small need).

These assumptions and predictions concerned giving as a function of cognition of magnitude of own surplus.

> Unless a child notices that he has more resources than needed, he will not give.
>
> The larger he notices his own surplus to be, the more likely that he will give.

Prediction d: Sus are more likely to give in conditions II and IV (large surplus) than in conditions I and III (small surplus).

Finally, these predictions concerned giving as a function of perceived relation between the level of another's need and the amount of one's own resources (and used combinations of above assumptions):

Prediction e: Least giving occurs in condition I (combination of small need and small surplus).

Prediction f: Most giving occurs in condition IV (combination of large need and large surplus).

Prediction g: Intermediate levels of need and surplus (conditions II and III) yield intermediate levels of giving.

Observation of Dependent Variables

The observers performed the important function of recording the children's cognitions in regard to surplus and need, as well as their sharing behaviors. Both of them, female graduate students, observed the children while sitting near the table on which both children were working. They checked the children's verbalizations relating to the task and nonverbal relevant behaviors in precoded categories. There were two categories for Ne Children:

1. Recognition of own need: (a) Verbalizations ("I don't have all of mine"); (b) nonverbal behavior (looks under card, under table; counts pieces and looks perplexed; searches for more pieces); and (c) nonrecognition (happily puts on pieces; no complaint).
2. Recognition of Su's surplus: (a) Verbalizations ("She has more," asks Su for part) and (b) nonverbal behavior (takes needed piece from Su).

There were three categories for Su children:

1. Recognition of own surplus: (a) Verbalizations ("I've got too many windows") and (b) nonverbal behavior (stares at surplus pieces, leaves them on sheet and announces, "I'm done").
2. Recognition of other's need: Verbalizations ("He doesn't have a door" and then asks experimenter for parts for Ne).
3. Lack of recognition of surplus: Uses all pieces casually, without comparisons; no response to Ne's comments about his neediness).

Action on evidence of sharing was recorded in terms of both the number and kinds of pieces (door, chimney, and so forth) given or taken.

The children's action was relatively slow paced and verbalization was sparse, so observer agreement never dropped below 90 percent.

Results

The major data are presented in table 5-2. It shows the numbers and percentages of children in each condition who perceived the need or surplus situation, or both, and the numbers who gave to or took from their partners. The main results are shown in figure 5-1, which gives the Sus' recognition of the other's need and of their own surplus, accompanied with their giving of pieces to the needy partner.

The major hypothesis was confirmed. Only when the partner's need was obviously large and Su had a large surplus did the latter perceive this relationship. Condition IV thus promoted the largest amount of giving: 64 percent. In the opposite condition, condition I, none of the Sus either paid attention to their surplus or noticed the others' need. Table 5-2 shows the same relationship to hold for Nes. When the need was small, over half of the Ne children did not notice their own need, and of the Sus who had a small surplus, only one noticed the other Ne's lack. There was no giving or taking until the situation was perceived as containing the element of neediness.

One of the most interesting relationships is the interaction between a child's own surplus and perception of the other's need. When Sus had a small surplus only, 60 percent did not perceive the partner's need, even though the need was large (condition 3). What is more, in conditions of small surplus (conditions I and III), only one Su gave any pieces to the other. In conditions of large surplus (conditions II and IV), fifteen Sus (39 percent) gave to their partners. Giving was therefore related to the level of one's own surplus (chi-square $= 9.84$; $df = 1$; $p < .005$). It is clear that children do not give if they have only a small surplus, no matter what the degree of their partner's need. If, on the other hand, they have a large surplus, the degree of their partner's need plays a determining role. Of Sus with a large surplus, only one gave to an Ne with a small need (condition II), in contrast to fourteen (64 percent) Sus with a large surplus who gave to Nes with a large need in condition IV. Children with a large surplus gave significantly more to children with a large need than to those with a small need (chi-square $= 10.48$; $df = 1$; $p < .005$).

When Sus with a large surplus (which included an extra door) were matched with Nes with only a small need, Sus did not give because Nes could make an acceptable house, although it was slightly different from the model

Table 5-2
Cognition and Action by Children in Needy and Surplus Conditions

Item	Children with Need (Nes)				Children with Surplus (Sus)			
	I (N = 14)	II (N = 16)	III (N = 15)	IV (N = 22)	I (N = 14)	II (N = 16)	III (N = 15)	IV (N = 22)
Cognition								
None	8 (57%)	4 (25%)	0	0	13 (93%)	3 (19%)	9 (60%)	0
Need only	1 (7%)	5 (31%)	13 (87%)	1 (5%)	0	0	1 (7%)	0
Surplus only	1 (7%)	0	0	0	1 (7%)	9 (56%)	2 (13%)	3 (14%)
Need and surplus	4 (29%)	7 (44%)	2 (13%)	21 (95%)	0	4 (25%)	3 (20%)	19 (86%)
Action								
Gives (Sus)					0	1 (6%)	1 (7%)	14 (64%)
Takes (Nes)	0	3 (19%)	0	8 (36%)				

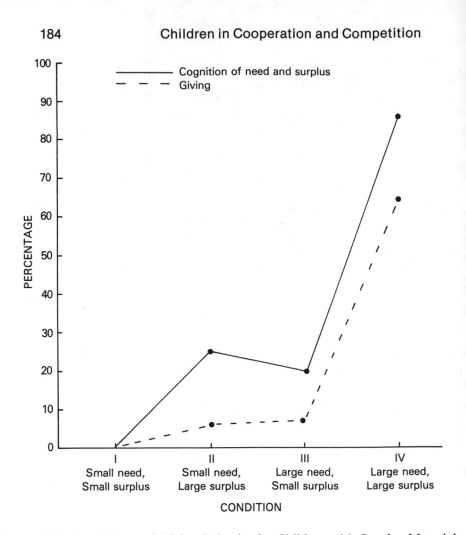

Figure 5-1. Cognition and Giving Behavior by Children with Surplus Materials

because it lacked a window. However, the surplus seems truly superfluous. The Ne child in fact did not need the door. There were no verbal or nonverbal indications as to whether the window that Ne missed was noticed. Similarly, and importantly, when Ne's need was large (including a missing door) but Su did not have the missing piece (condition III), no Su child gave her own single door, and only one gave her surplus window. In short, kindergarten children generally share only when they have a large surplus and when they are paired with a child who has a strong need for some of it.

It is evident that significantly more Nes noticed their own neediness in situations of large rather than small need situations (chi-square = 17.21;

$df = 1$; $p < .005$). However, their perception of their own need in large need conditions was independent of the amount of the partner's surplus. One's own need, like one's own large surplus, seems to be perceived in an absolute way: when the need is large, a child cannot help but notice the lack. But in conditions of small need, Nes are more likely to notice their own need when paired with partners with a large rather than a small surplus: 36 percent noticed it in condition I (small surplus) as compared with 75 percent in condition II (large surplus) (chi-square $= 3.23$, $df = 1$, $P < .05$). A partner's large surplus apparently draws attention to one's own need, even if it is small. The study thus provided an example of comparison processes in the service of providing more accurate self-evaluations, or assessments of own state of need, even in kindergartners. But it seems clear that only in condition IV, when a large need was paired with a large surplus, did the difference in resources between partners become large enough to elicit the cognitive and emotional determinants required to arouse giving responses in kindergarten children. One is tempted to explain this outcome in terms of a balance mechanism such that when the vacuum of need is large, it almost seems to suck in the needed materials, establishing or restoring equilibrium. One of the obvious factors in this result is the fact that the surplus is useless to the child and has no value. An extension of the study requires replication, with the surplus, even though not needed, having intrinsic value to the Su children.

The fact that the surplus was useless may account in part for the fact that deliberate withholding of materials was never observed. Children did not appear selfish, but it simply did not seem to occur to some of the children to give, especially in the conditions where the contrast in the respective resources was not dramatic. This illustrates clearly the differences between selfishness and egocentrism: the former is a motivated phenomenon, the latter a cognitive state, representing a lack of ability to empathize with another's state.

Vanderbilt points out another developmental factor that was important in the low rate of giving obtained in this study: the inhibition of statements of need as well as requests and demands by Nes. A number of children who were missing pieces were obviously disturbed by this fact, apparently seeing such a deviation from the previous snowman task as an indication of inadequacy in themselves. Several children, after making houses with insufficient pieces, held their cards up facing themselves so that the other child and the experimenter could not see it, saying, "I'm all done." They clearly wished to get rid of the picture; they seemed to wish to hide it from their partners who seemed better because they had more resources. Other children were able to externalize the responsibility for their need as indicated by asking for the pieces or telling the experimenter that she forgot to give them all the pieces (in effect saying, "It's not my fault, it's her's"). Along these lines it is interesting that in quite a few instances it seemed to be the Su partner who verbalized Ne's need to the experimenter, perhaps just because she could afford it, being invulnerable with a clear surplus available.

There were too few Ne children who explicitly announced their shortage, either to the experimenter, or the partner, to analyze this group separately. We assumed that they confounded the data on the giving responses of Sus relatively little. Since most Sus apparently initiated their giving responses because they noticed the large lack in their partner's resources, we speculated whether those who perceived the lack and responded to it by giving were somewhat more able to begin taking the point of view of the other and, in general, were able to interact more with their partners. Following up this argument involved analyzing these children's free play with the wooden train at the beginning of the experimental session. The Lloyd toddler study examined in chapter 4 may be recalled where parallel play was described as involving less interpersonal interaction than associative play did. If those Sus who shared were indeed more able to engage more generally in interpersonal exchanges, then more of these Sus might be expected to have engaged in associative play, as compared with Sus who did not recognize their partner's needs and did not give.

Data on Sus in condition IV only were examined since most of the giving occurred in that condition and adding subjects from other conditions might have confounded this exploration still more. Of twenty-two Sus in condition IV, ten (45 percent) engaged in associative play, while twelve (55 percent) engaged in parallel play. Of the ten who played together, eight (80 percent) also gave while the others did not. Of the twelve who engaged in parallel play, five (42 percent) gave and seven (58 percent) did not. Considering the relatively small number of children involved and the number of likely confounding factors, we may conclude that a trend exists between associative play and giving behavior (chi-square $= 1.92$; $df = 1$; $p < .10$).

By drawing the comparison between associative play and ability to give to a partner, we wanted to emphasize again that sharing occurs in an interdependent social situation. It is a response to needs and actions and/or the nature of the presence of another person in the context of one's own state. This study has incorporated the basic developmental assumption that one has to be aware of others as individuals outside oneself before one can grasp their needs, requirements, or wishes. We argued that such awareness may be enhanced by prominent emphasis on the requirements of the situation. Presumably these generalizations hold for adults as well as for children of all ages.[3] Our study has shown that kindergartners are able to share when the others' needs are made dramatically evident and when they do not deprive themselves by giving.

**Facilitation of Interdependencies in
Role-related Cooperative Conditions[a]**

In spite of our efforts to facilitate recognition of others' needs by strong
cues in the research we have just examined, it was quite evident that the
kindergartners had a long way to go not only before being able to take the
point of view of the other but also to attend and respond to several needs
and requirements at the same time. Yet these are typically the kinds of
demands made of group members who are engaged in working together
with a common purpose.

The next research was intended to demonstrate precisely how perceptions of interdependencies can be raised in the cooperative work of children
and what accompanying consequences may be expected of performance.
Our work was designed to address itself both theoretically and experimentally to "the teaching and learning of helping" (Pepitone 1971, 1973, 1977).
We wanted to make certain that we would be dealing with pupils ready to
respond to our teaching in postoperational ways, so fourth-grade and fifth-
grade boys and girls served as subjects.

The grant allowed the further development of the experimental task
used in the previous studies; the Pep board methodology was the outcome.
Major responsiblity was assumed by N. Torop who, in the course of designing her own study, adapted the Pattern Blocks for research use and designed
several of the group performance measures. Her research (Torop 1973)
followed closely upon the investigations reported in chapter 4, which explored social comparisons of attentional behaviors, evaluational behaviors,
and besting behaviors. Her focus was on independent evaluational effects—in particular, adult criticisms and helpfulness of various degrees—on
children's performance.

Both the Torop evaluation study and our facilitation study employed
identical basic methodologies. The experimental design examined children's
triads not in conditions of colabor toward a common goal but while working together. These two studies moved toward an examination of complex

[a]This study was supported by research grant OEG3-72-0007 (1-C-062) from the Office of
Education, U.S. Department of Health, Education and Welfare. Help from the following individuals is gratefully acknowledged. Carol Silberberg conducted the study and acted as experimenter and process observer. She was assisted by Jane Crawford, who was also the interaction observer and statistical analyst. Nancy Torop was in charge of computer analysis.

Some of the results have been reported in a paper, "Facilitation of Cooperative Behavior
in Elementary School Children," which was presented at the American Educational Research
Association Annual Meetings in New Orleans, March 1, 1973. A detailed account is given in
the *Final Report, 1973*, to HEW. This chapter is an expanded version of our article "Patterns
of Interdependence in Cooperative Work of Elementary School Children," which appeared in
Contemporary Educational Psychology, 1977, *2*, 10-24. Permission to quote from this article is
gratefully acknowledged.

conditions of cooperation where interdependence is created through the common goal structure and task structure. Group members were informed of certain task requirements that needed to be followed in the execution of the work. In the Torop study, this was necessary so that the children's work could be variously evaluated as they tried to meet these specifications. The experimenter directed at the group of children at predetermined time intervals critical and helpful comments, which followed a predetermined script.[4] In the Torop study, task requirements were used to serve as the basis of evaluations, which in turn allowed the introduction of negative forces into the group with which the children had to deal. In the facilitation research, we wanted to heighten interdependence through strengthening sources of positive forces within the group in addition to those created by the group's goal and the task itself.

Our intent was to increase member interdependence by tying each member closer to the other through various functions that they were to perform in order to advance the group's progress. Kagan and Madsen (1971) have demonstrated that instructing 7 to 9 year olds to assume a generalized group-oriented set increases collaboration, while individually oriented instructions that produce an "I" set heighten competition. Our study took this type of research on facilitation of cooperation one step further. Following our previous analysis, task requirements were considered the basis from which various task roles and group roles could be developed. By assigning specific roles to individual group members, it was assumed that their interdependence would be increased and reflected in increasing the kinds of group-oriented behaviors required to perform the task successfully. Accordingly various combinations of specific task requirements, task roles, and group roles were established, creating different forces toward increased cooperation in different conditions.

The Experimental Conditions

The experimental variations were created at the beginning of the session in brief group discussion with the experimenter. In all conditions, she sat in a small circle with the three children and explained the nature of the work. The children were asked to "make a big picture together with these block pieces on the board."

The Unstructured Condition (I) served as the basic control condition; no task requirements were introduced. In fact, to counter possible implications that the experimenter harbored expectations in regard to the childrens' performance, they were told explicitly that they could make anything they wanted and could do so in any way they wished. The only interdependence created was that of a common goal: "a big picture."

In the Task Requirements Condition (II), the experimenter introduced information about task requirements. The picture, she explained, needed to have some overall plan and design. It also needed to be balanced and to be unified. Children were engaged in conversation for five to ten minutes enlarging upon these requirements, making sure that they were understood.

In the Task Role Condition (III), children were told, in addition to task requirements, that they "might find it easier" if each were responsible for one specific task requirement. Each child was assigned one of the three task roles: the designer, the balancer, and the unifier, respectively. To ensure that each role was understood, each child was asked to describe his or her role assignment to the group before proceeding to work together. Any confusion was clarified until each child was clearly aware of the activities involved in his or her task and that of the other two group members.

In the Group Role Condition (IV), in addition to specifying task requirements, the experimenter elicited discussion about group process requirements. Posing questions pertaining to differences between solitary work and group work, she led the discussion to include considerations of interdependence and the benefits accruing from the sharing of ideas. The prepared script questioned whether working alone or in a group might produce superior results and brought out the point that group performance depended on interpersonal communication. Inferences were then made to behavioral guides for the work session that was about to begin, including listening to others and contributing one's own ideas.

In a fifth condition, the Combined Condition (V), conditions III and IV were combined so that each child was given one specific task role and a general group role.

The groups were terminated after maximally fifteen minutes' work, the product was photographed, and each child interviewed for a few minutes about his or her attitudes toward a variety of features of the experimental session. A summary of the salient characteristics of the five conditions, and of the number of boys' and girls' groups assigned to each condition, is presented in table 5-3.

Summarizing the underlying theoretical assumptions, it was posited that the design created different patterns of member interdependence based on the four different sources. In each case, it was assumed that such interdependence would heighten the motivation of members. If these motivations could be translated into responsible member interactions, the outcome, the group's final product, would be affected. Predictions about differential strengths of the hypothesized motives could be only speculative at this stage. Because all groups were presented common work tasks, the members in all conditions were working under conditions of goal interdependence. And as research on cooperation shows, this source of interdependence has powerful effects on member interaction. Thus pre-

Table 5-3
Description of Five Conditions of Cooperation

Condition	Description	Groups Boys (N)	Girls (N)	
I. Unstructured	Cooperative work structure, common goal No task requirements No differentiated task roles No group roles	6	8	
II. Task requirements	Cooperative work structure, common goal Task requirements No differentiated task roles No group roles	7	9	
III. Task roles	Cooperative work structure, common goal Task requirements Differentiated task roles No group roles	7	8	
IV. Group roles	Cooperative work structure, common goal Task requirements No differentiated task roles Group roles	8	8	
V. Combined task roles and group roles	Cooperative work structure, common goal Task requirements Differentiated task roles Group roles	7	8	
Total number groups		35	41	76
Total number children		105	123	228

dominantly positive social behaviors were expected under all conditions. The addition of task requirements was expected to improve performance because the requirements gave members both increased knowledge about the work and raised the perceived importance of the task. Two conditions explored the respective effects of task role assignment and group role assignment. Although there was no basis for differential predictions, performance of both roles may be deemed essential for the group's success. It would follow that a condition that created member interdependence from the combined sources of group goal, task requirements, task roles, and group roles would show the most responsible group interaction; there would be group-oriented rather than self-oriented work patterns, accompanied by superior performance.

The Procedures

In all major respects, the experimental procedures were identical to those used in our previous studies. Groups of three fourth or fifth graders were selected at random from a given classroom, taken one group at a time to an unused classroom in the school, and asked to work together on a problem requiring collaboration for its completion. A photograph was made of the completed pattern and used as a basis for evaluating group performance. The group's social interaction was recorded by an observer pair in precoded categories.

The Subjects

The sample of 228 children was made up of predominantly middle- and upper-middle-class white, fourth- and fifth-grade boys and girls from four elementary schools within one suburban school district. There were no systematic differences in pupil performance and behavior as a function of school or classroom treatment, so data from all schools were combined. Since our previous investigations had showed significant sex differences in behaviors relevant to the present study, groups were composed of like-sexed children and treated separately in the data analysis.

The children were allowed to move about freely and to converse with each other while working. Deliberate efforts were made to remove the restraints that usually exist in the classroom against displaying other-oriented behaviors. Children were given fifteen minutes maximally to work on their task.

Measurement of Performance

Scoring techniques followed the pattern outlined in chapter 3. Blind ratings were made by two independent judges who scored the quality of the group product along several predetermined dimensions. Specific ratings were made along the general dimensions detailed earlier, which included elaborateness of design, distinctiveness of themes, and carefulness of execution. Three additional indexes were developed specifically for this and the Torop evaluation study. Each of these ratings was based on one specific task requirement that had been detailed to the children in the procedural instructions, so that the degree to which the task requirements had been fulfilled could be established.

Agreement between the two raters for each dimension averaged 86 percent. These differences deviated no more than two points for a given rating and were adjusted by mutual rater agreement. For the final qualitative score, all subscores were summed; the range of the total score thus could vary from 0 to a maximum of 24 points. The quantity of work was determined, as in all other studies, by counting the number of pieces used in the total pattern (250 was the maximum score possible). There were three qualitative performance subindexes specific to the task requirements:

1. **Commonality of pattern**

   Three (or fewer, or more) indistinct, unconnected, unrelated parts: 0 points.

   Tripartite structure may still be visible, but attempt at connection of internal parts present, even though total pattern still appears unrelated: 2 points.

   Commonality present, either in form of one unified pattern where parts are undistinguishable, or parts may be present but wholly integrated into one pattern: 4 points.

2. **Unification of design**

   Circular means of unifying pattern absent (neither border nor central figure): 0 points.

   Some attempt at border or central pattern but incomplete, partial: 2 points.

   Border or central figure present, fairly well executed: 3 points.

   Border or central figure, well executed, complex, pleasing: 4 points.

3. **Balance of design**

   Points are given as indicated for any of the following features (total of 6 points possible):

   a. Balance **within design itself**

   Within given pattern or object, pieces are evenly distributed, object not lopsided: 1 point.

   Relations among several parts are harmonious, even distribution (for example, house, people, dog, all may be on one side of pattern but well proportioned): 1 point.

b. Balance of **design in relation to board**

Partial balance—a little off center but not totally unbalanced: 2 points.

Pattern is centered and evenly placed: 4 points.

Behavior Observations

For comparison purposes with other investigations in this program, one observer recorded interpersonal interactions into the basic set of molecular behavior observations categories and subcategories described in chapter 3. Categories focused on included the variants of evaluative behaviors, negative behaviors, and positive social behaviors. In this study, however, our primary interest was in the children's work patterns as influenced by differential role inductions toward contributing to the progress of the group. Therefore two additional observers kept a running documentation by checking each of the children's work patterns every thirty seconds into two mutually exclusive categories: "works for self" and "works for group."

"Works for self" was checked whenever a child worked alone with no regard for the work of the other two children. This included placing blocks into a pattern not connected physically with the group's pattern, making objects that were not in keeping with the group's decision, and ignoring or disobeying requests from the group to contribute—in other words, pursuing activities that furthered his own interests and goals, which were unrelated to or at cross-purposes with the aims of the group as a whole.

"Works for group" denoted active involvement with the aims and activities of the group. It included verbal participation in decisions about what to make and procedural suggestions as to how to make what, who was to do it, and so forth. This category was also checked when a child worked with another collaboratively on the same pattern part or worked by himself but did so with another group member's consent or request to contribute.

Results

Overall Patterns of Social Interactions in Groups. The data analysis concentrates on the molar working patterns; first, however, the molecular data descriptive of the children's behaviors during the work session may be briefly recapitulated here (for details, see Pepitone 1973). The children spent most of the fifteen minutes manipulating block pieces. Virtually absent under all conditions were any kind of negative behaviors, as were interactions characteristic of interpersonal competition, such as besting, personal comparisons, and evaluations. Most of the social exchange was friendly and helpful. The molar behaviors subsume and are in agreement with these specific molecular interactions. In all five conditions, the groups accepted the common goal to complete the task, worked in a nonevaluative climate, and displayed positive social behaviors characteristic of cooperating groups.

Social Patterns and Performance. Table 5-4 shows means for the two working patterns and for the performance of boys and girls under the five experimental conditions. In table 5-5 are found the results of tests of significance of these differences from a two-way analysis of variance. It is evident that in the case of the two work patterns, a significant interaction was obtained between sex and conditions, while significant main effects for sex and conditions were found for quality of work. Because of these significant overall effects, the data are discussed separately for boys and girls. The trends presented in the tables are shown more clearly in figure 5-2 for girls and figure 5-3 for boys.

A highly consistent trend emerged for the girls, as predicted. In the unstructured condition, the girls' work pattern showed the greatest amount of solitary work and the poorest quality. As the demands for interdependence increased over the different conditions, the girls systematically responded by increases in group-oriented behavior and by a corresponding decrease in self-oriented behaviors. The quality of performance was wholly within our expectations. Knowledge of task requirements helped to improve performance, as did each subsequent addition of roles.

Table 5-4
Work Process and Performance Means, by Sex and Condition

	Working for Self		Working for Group		Quality of Performance	
	Boys	*Girls*	*Boys*	*Girls*	*Boys*	*Girls*
I. Unstructured N Gr Boys 6; Girls 8	6.40	22.80	23.50	14.80	14.39	12.75
II. Task requirements N Gr Boys 7; Girls 9	4.60	11.20	23.60	20.67	14.86	16.56
III. Task roles N Gr Boys 7; Girls 8	16.20	9.50	18.05	22.75	15.29	17.75
IV. Group roles N Gr Boys 8; Girls 8	17.10	9.90	17.50	25.50	14.75	18.75
V. Task roles and group roles N Gr Boys 7; Girls 8	3.30	5.00	23.50	27.67	16.00	19.38

Note: Thirty-five boys' and 41 girls' groups were studied. These comprised 105 boys and 123 girls.

Table 5-5
Analysis of Variance on Process and Performance Means

Source	df	Works for Self			Works for Group			Work Quality		
		MS	F	p	MS	F	p	MS	F	p
Sex	1	258.48	1.01	n.s.	.253	0.	n.s.	220.80	7.67	.007
Condition	4	885.65	3.47	.01	344.11	1.5	n.s.	108.85	3.80	.006
Sex × Condition	4	1,087.96	4.26	.003	682.76	2.97	.02	54.75	1.90	n.s.
Significant comparisons		Boys IV vs. V $t = 3.27$ $p < .05$ Girls I vs. V $t = 3.42$ $p < .05$ Boys vs. Girls, I $t = 2.74$ $p < .01$			Girls I vs. V $t = 3.18$ $p < .02$			Girls I vs. II $t = 2.96$ $p < .05$ Girls I vs. III $t = 3.77$ $p < .05$ Girls I vs. IV $t = 4.43$ $p < .001$ Girls I vs. V $t = 5.13$ $p < .001$ Boys vs. Girls, IV $t = 2.92$ $p < .006$		

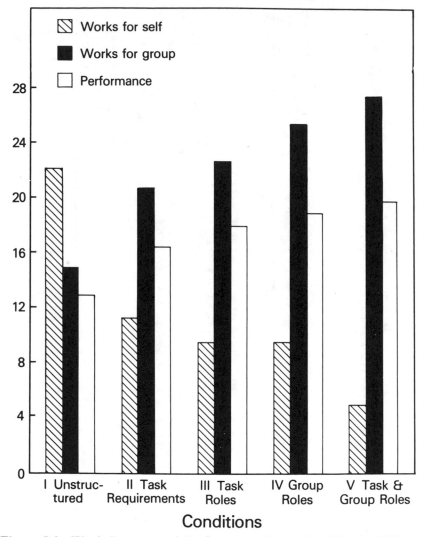

Figure 5-2. Work Process and Performance Means for Girls in Different Conditions of Cooperation

The increments over the experimental conditions were gradual, culminating in condition V, the condition of maximal interdependence. At this point, the work patterns differed significantly from those of least interdependence: the girls worked almost exclusively together for the common goal. Furthermore their mean quality of performance was highest here, approaching the maximum possible score of 24, and differing significantly from performance in the unstructured condition. While highly significant,

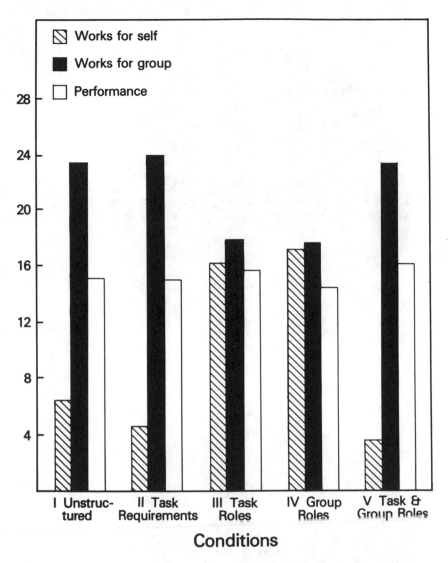

Figure 5-3. Work Process and Performance Means for Boys in Different Conditions of Cooperation

the score does not do justice to the visible qualitative constructions in condition V.

Illustrations 5-1 through 5-4 demonstrate role-related cooperation and show samples of final products made in different conditions. Illustration 5-1 represents the girls' work in condition I and illustration 5-2 represents

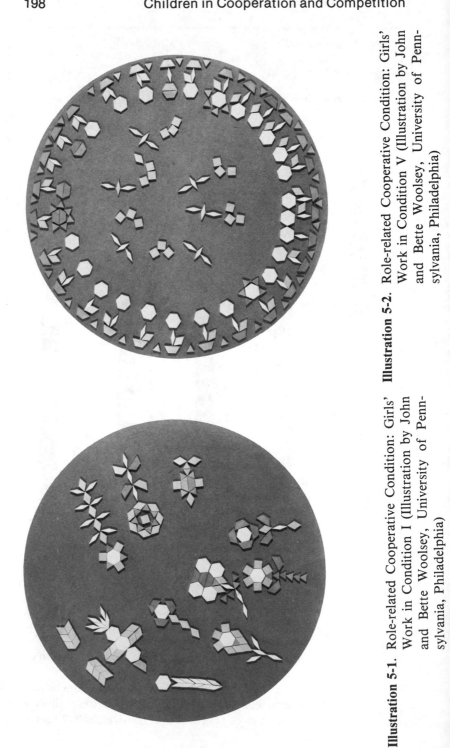

Illustration 5-1. Role-related Cooperative Condition: Girls' Work in Condition I (Illustration by John and Bette Woolsey, University of Pennsylvania, Philadelphia)

Illustration 5-2. Role-related Cooperative Condition: Girls' Work in Condition V (Illustration by John and Bette Woolsey, University of Pennsylvania, Philadelphia)

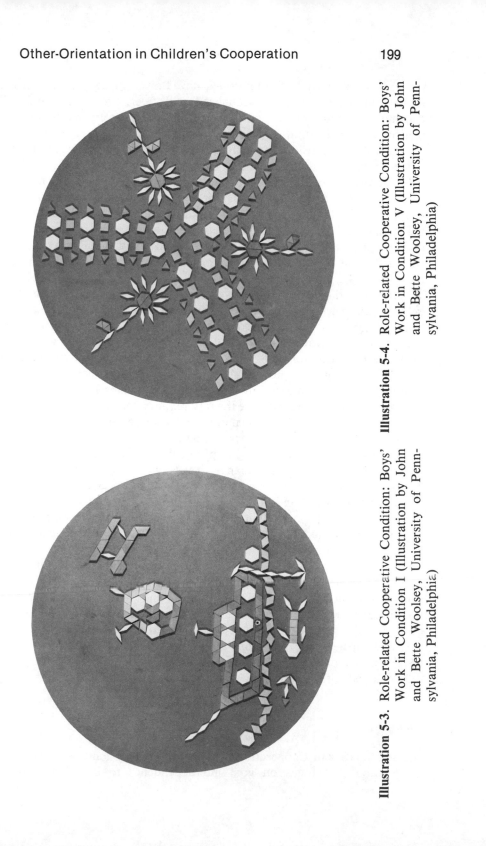

Illustration 5-3. Role-related Cooperative Condition: Boys' Work in Condition I (Illustration by John and Bette Woolsey, University of Pennsylvania, Philadelphia)

Illustration 5-4. Role-related Cooperative Condition: Boys' Work in Condition V (Illustration by John and Bette Woolsey, University of Pennsylvania, Philadelphia)

the work in condition V. Both products have flower themes; performance in illustration 5-1 is more individualized and freer, while task and role demands of condition V are reflected in more careful execution and meticulous coordination of product in illustration 5-2.

Boys show a considerably different work pattern. When given minimal structure, as in condition I, boys work significantly less by themselves than do girls, and correspondingly more so for the group. Their performance is more coordinated than that of the girls in the comparable conditions, as reflected in the sample product seen in illustration 5-3. When demands are made that work be performed to meet specified criteria, boys react in the same way as did the girls in that they reduce their individual work patterns still further, as seen in their highly coordinated work pattern shown in illustration 5-4 from condition V.

However, the boys were relatively unresponsive to role demands; their behavior and performance did not change either when required to assume task roles or to assume group roles. And, in fact, in conditions III and IV there was a trend toward a more solitary work pattern. This suggests that boys interpret their role assignments as an individual charge, which leads them to assume greater individual responsibility at the expense of working together. Even though each boy may try harder by himself, the overall performance does not improve since the task requires coordinated work for optimum performance. Only when the constellation of demands becomes massive—in condition V—do they respond by working significantly less by themselves and more for the group's goal. Once again, this change is reflected in their better performance. It was only in condition V that boys became more similar to the girls and resembled their previous performance in the Unstructured Condition.

Quality of performance paralleled a group-oriented work pattern. This improvement in quality as subjects shifted from an individual to group orientation is not surprising since the task demanded a coordinated effort. What is interesting, however, is the sex difference in the particular conditions that elicit this coordinated effort. The boys worked together most when left to their own devices (condition I), and the quality of their work was better than the girls' under similar conditions, although not significantly so. The girls' work became better than the boys' as their tasks were specified further, and their work quality was significantly better than the boys' only in condition IV. It was in this condition that they were specifically charged with group roles, which require attending to each other.

Analysis

Social Climate and Cooperation. We attempted to extend the analyses of cooperation that focus on goal interdependence to include additional sources of interdependence in groups. The determinants of interdependence among group members must include the climate of the culture in which the groups are working. More particularly, one must look for group standards in regard to competition or cooperation or, put differently, in regard to individuals working independently or together. Consideration of this type of ideology seems particularly relevant in school settings where strong standards fostering independent individual effort are the rule. Often school standards may implicitly or explicitly discourage sharing of information. In our study, children were placed into a situation where social interaction was valued quite explicitly. The children were encouraged to work together, and the experimenter tried actively to remove remnants of classroom restraints against social exchange while at work. Such a positive climate seems a precondition for cooperation; its impact cannot be assessed here because it was held constant in all conditions. Repetition of this study in an atmosphere less conducive to interdependent work may show different results.

Thus two of the most important variables known to stimulate cooperative behaviors were present in all our conditions: a climate that fostered member interaction and a requirement of all group members to work toward a common goal. The fact that task and role requirements had sizable effects in this study attests to their importance as additional determinants of cooperative behavior.

Interrelationships of Task Requirements, Task Roles, and Group Roles. In this study, task roles were described to the children on a very general level, which coincided with general task requirements for purposes of experimental control. That is, since task requirements define what needs to be done, they may be expected to have main effects on interpersonal relations and on the nature of the group product as well as on their interaction. This was indeed the case in the control condition for girls. The largest differences in quality of performance were found between condition I where the experimentally created task requirements were absent and all other conditions. The possibility cannot be excluded that differences between the remaining conditions were systematically reduced by the constant presence of task requirements.

In the creation of task roles, the only specification added to task requirements concerned division of labor. Thus, following the above reasoning, it may be argued that because task roles were defined primarily in terms of task requirements, the differences between conditions II and III did not reach statistical significance. The task roles were deliberately left relatively unstructured; the roles of balancer, unifier, and designer were created without explicit instructions of what each person in a given role was to do. Had such details been given, stronger task role effects might have been obtained. But this procedure would have made interpretation of performance data difficult because it would have confounded interdependence effects of formal task role assignment with effects due to the content of the assignment.

This exploration concentrated primarily on the function of task roles in increasing member interdependence. In order to have a balanced, common, or unified design, each member's performance had to be related to that of the others. The interdependence created here was considerably greater than that created in the studies examined in chapter 4. Task role interdependence may be increased still further, as, for instance, in Thomas's (1957) study in which each person's working step was a prerequisite for the other member's task role execution. This analysis indicates directions for further study of task roles: variations in the number and detailed specifications within the task role assigned to each member and variations in the required interrelationships among the task roles assigned to different members.

Much the same generalization made with respect to the experimental creation of task roles may be made regarding the methodology of group role induction: only a few minimal expectations were laid down. Following our assumption that group roles variously orient members toward each other so that task-required activities may take place, we aimed merely to highlight behaviors in the area of attending to others and communicating. We did not even attempt assigning different types of group roles to different group members; it would have required an overwhelming amount of additional instruction that would have had to be transmitted to, absorbed by, and acted upon by children. In condition V, such individualized group role assignments would have yet had to be combined with individualized task role assignments. We see this research in part as a demonstration of the importance of helping children to perform different group functions in cooperative work. Here too, then, this research may serve to stimulate further study of children's specific group role functions. We noted with interest Flavell's (1977) emphasis on children's cognitive role taking, which involves awareness of others' differing perceptions, cognitions, or feelings that must be taken into account in own behaviors during interpersonal interactions. These are the kind of cognitions we tried to activate in our generalized group role inductions. We see such cognitive readinesses to understand others as a basis on which to build skills in a child's enactment of specific group roles in cooperative settings.

Some of the findings of this chapter speak to several theoretical issues that have a generality beyond developmental concerns. Of major importance in regard to group roles is the persistent question of whether performance of certain group roles is essential for work under cooperative conditions. Even if required group roles can never wholly be separated out from specific characteristics of a task, certain group roles may be required within specific types of tasks. For instance, additive tasks may require certain group roles not essential in unitary tasks, and vice-versa.

We suspect that it is in part the presence of required group roles that reduces individual competitive motivations under cooperative work conditions. It would seem likely that some kind of group roles are essential that maintain the force of the common group goal alive in members by periodic reminders of the group's purposes, exhortation to continue, evaluation of progress made, and so forth. The task requirements for balance and unity in this study may have helped to stimulate such behaviors, a hypothesis we did not test.

Without the presence of some group roles that emphasize commonalities, task roles may be perceived as a personal charge and, while heightening personal motivation and responsibility, may lead only to individual effort rather than to greater interdependence. This may have occurred in condition III, where the boys showed a considerable reduction in working for the group (though the same trend in condition IV is not so readily explained). It is, however, also likely that exclusive enactment of some group roles, at the expense of task role performance, may hinder the group's accomplishment. For instance, concern with opening communication channels or with maintaining satisfactions of individual members may actively interfere with the execution of some tasks. Most everyone has encountered situations where group-building roles were so successful as to increase individual member attraction to the point where enjoyment of interpersonal interaction prevented the completion of a common task. This did not happen in conditions IV or V, probably because of the presence of task requirements so strong as to create some kind of task role expectation to be fulfilled by each member. Where groups are composed of achievement-oriented individuals, task roles are likely to dominate group process. We would posit the necessity for maintaining a delicate balance between these two sets of roles to satisfy both the needs for positive interpersonal relations and for successful completion of the task assignment.

We deliberately did not consider individual differences in skills available for execution of required tasks or skills in ability to respond to role demands. Obviously provision of optimum conditions will come to naught unless the skills needed for their execution are present. It was beyond the scope of this study to include observation of the manner in which individual children were able to respond to the different role requirements. Next steps must move in that direction.

Sex Differences in Behavior and Performance. It might be argued that our task favors boys, perhaps because of their more frequent experiences with cooperative block building in preschool (while girls gather in the doll corner) or perhaps because of allegedly better-developed spatial factors relevant in our particular task. Indeed the generality of our findings needs to be explored with a variety of tasks. However, Maccoby and Jacklin's (1974) review would lead one to minimize this task as a variable that may account for obtained sex differences. The authors cite twenty different studies that include tasks involving spatial abilities such as identification of geometric figures by touch, shape identification under different orientations, assembling puzzles, and so on. No sex differences were found for ages 5 to 11 in eighteen of the twenty studies, and of the remaining tasks, one favored girls and the other boys.

Yet sex differences emerged as one of the most interesting, consistent, and strongest findings. Girls responded to the role demands created in the different conditions, whereas boys did so minimally. And when no task requirements or role demands were made (condition I), the boys spontaneously engaged in significantly less individual effort but worked together more. In so doing, their performance surpassed that of the girls. These sex differences are in general agreement with Hoffman's (1972) integration of diverse earlier studies in a theory that relates girls' task performance to dependency and affiliation needs and that of boys to their orientations toward mastery. Following this interpretation, in our study girls were presumably more open to the experimenter's role inductions because they sought her approval, which they expected to receive as a reward for their successful execution of the task as was required. The boys, on the other hand, were challenged by the task itself, strove for mastery, and were confident of their ability. They worked best when given independence (condition I); extrapolating, one might infer that they would resent and resist constraints from task and role requirements (conditions II, III, and IV) and conform to the requirements only when strong force is applied (condition V).

The validity of this line of interpretation is supported by data from several of our related studies. In our replication of Hannah's study with boys (chapter 4), they expressed greater confidence in their abilities than did comparable girls. In the scarcity study (chapter 8), when asked to vote for the best product, 74 percent of boys chose their own, while only 28 percent of the girls did so. Strongest corroboration is found in Torop's evaluation study, which used the same basic methodology employed in the study under consideration. The experimenter made periodic critical remarks of various degrees of severity about the children's work, and these negative evaluations were accompanied in some conditions by helpful suggestions from the experimenter. Both boys and girls were affected by strong criticism in that they rated their own performance as well as that of their partners lower in conditions of strong criticism; however, they reacted to criticism very differently. The girls started working more for themselves when strongly criticized, and the quantity of their performance deteriorated. What we referred to as strong criticism was agreed by school personnel, including the district superintendent, to be mild as compared with usual teacher criticism. It included comments such as, "You didn't get off to a very good start,"

"That's not too good," or "Is this the best you can do?" Girls appeared to recoil from such criticism, withdrew into themselves, and appeared at a loss what to do next. But the boys worked together more, showed more positive behavior toward each other, made defensive comments to the experimenter, or actively defied her. Boys appeared to be able to protect themselves better and to draw support from each other, although under strong criticism, their performance deteriorated also. Several boys' groups became so angry at what they apparently perceived as constant nagging criticism that they cleared off the Pep board completely, demolishing whatever construction they had made. Nevertheless, they gave each other the strength to start again, even though overall performance suffered.

Implications for Educational Theory and Practice. This study, perhaps more than any other research reported in this volume, speaks primarily to educational theory by elaborating certain concepts that may highlight several pedagogic issues. Curriculum design, lesson plans, and even homework assignments and any other structuring of classroom activities deal in fact with task requirements. Seeing learning activities in this context may help educators move from decisions based on considerations of learning content to consideration of cognitive requirements inherent in the learning task. An emphasis on the specific activities demanded by an assignment allows consideration of learning gains accrued to individual students, rather than dwelling, as is often the case, on practical matters such as the availability of materials, length of assignment, entertainment value, and so forth. It also poses more general questions of best fit between the nature of the learning task and the structure of the medium by which mastery is to be attained.

Teachers tend to question more often the fit between learning activities and age or abilities of pupils and less so the procedures by which these learnings are to be accomplished. Specifically questions must be directed to linking task requirements to procedures by which they may be accomplished. Chapter 2 in its discussion of task typologies may provide some guidance to determine where individual work is most indicated, and where work may gain if performed in cooperative conditions. If the latter procedure is chosen, the theory and research presented in this chapter should have made it abundantly clear that assignment of a group project is only the first step in initiating a highly complex group process. In effect, the pupils are placed into a task situation that demands competence in the exercise of task roles and group roles. The teacher may well ask where in the curriculum there is a place for the instruction of pupils in the necessity for and use of group roles.

One of the most interesting issues and perhaps one of the most important ones confronting educators today is raised by our data from the unstructured conditions. Educational psychologists have offered a number of theoretical models descriptive of congruence between characteristics of instructional materials and learning processes. Scandura's (1977) structural approach to problem solving is perhaps among the most explicit rational models. But relatively little attention has been paid to the amount and type of guidance to be provided by teachers in specific learning situations. We note with interest studies such as Slavin's (1978) whose main focus was not on learning structures but who attributes equal gain in pupil achievement in all conditions of differential reward possibly because of "a highly structured intensive schedule of teaching, studying and testing."

Chapter 4 pointed to some problems of interest to educators that may be inherent in solitary work and problems inherent in work with others as well. The effects of providing more- or less-structured learning tasks bring out yet another set of problematic issues.

It apparently takes considerable time to resolve fully the legacy of the 1960s that called for alternatives to traditional schooling. The combination of variants of the self-motivated, self-directed learning child described in A.S. Neill's *Summerhill* (1960) and other critics of the period (such as Goodman 1960), quickly found its way into student demands for choosing their own activities. Free choice all too often still is translated as meaning provision of no structure at all by those responsible for children's growth and development. We know that human beings need a certain amount of structure to function in their environment, but the parameters of how much, when, and under what conditions are still largely unexplored. Social psychologists, from Sherif's classic study (1936) to post-Festinger research, have demonstrated that the potential for social influence is greatest in unstructured situations. Should not those who are most qualified to provide learning structures do so? If they do not, someone else probably will. As Jones and Gerard (1967) summed up so aptly in listing among the attributes of influential persons, those who get there first may influence most.

These issues are still with us. As we discover increased illiteracy among today's high school graduates and lower averages in national achievement scores, loose learning structures are blamed as one of the chief causes, and the call for a return to basics is heard once again. We shall remain victims of this pendulum, and the problem will remain with us until it is squarely faced.

The classroom is a natural laboratory in which educators may freely experiment with curricula in order to determine the effects of different degrees of structure on pupil learning and performance. Our exploration as well as Torop's study showed significant positive effects on third-grade girls' performance accrued from a firmer structuring of task requirements and increasing the task-relevant information.

We would caution against wider generalization from these findings before they are replicated with different tasks and different populations.

Structure, for example, may be more needed at some developmental periods than at others. We have pointed to individual differences in the data from boys, who appeared to demand independence. They saw firmer structures as interference which they resented and under which they performed less well. However, the implications for teaching practice of these sex-related performance differences are not at all clear-cut. Whether girls ought to be provided with more-structured learning experiences because they apparently thrive on them or whether a deliberate effort ought to be made to reduce their needs for structure is a value question that cannot be answered here. Whatever one's values, however, our position is that before such questions can be addressed fruitfully, more data are essential. It is, for instance, not at all certain that the consistent and significant behaviors of our third-grade boys may be generalized to other boys. In part, their apparent needs for independence may be determined by social class. The next chapter includes an exploration of this hypothesis.

Notes

1. The most recent research has increasingly divorced the act of giving from cooperative situations, following research in social psychology focused specifically on helping behaviors.

2. The only significant difference was in the preexperimental task of copying a model of a snowman to acquaint the children with the type of materials to be used subsequently in the experimental task proper. In this situation, each child received all of the needed pieces. Ratings of the degree of exactness with which children could copy the model revealed that combined upper-upper- and upper-middle-class children (N = 40) made significantly better copies than did the ninety-two lower-lower- and lower-middle-class children (chi-square = 6.51; $df = 1$, $p < .01$).

3. Subsequent to this investigation, several studies of adults have also addressed the question of how helping behavior is affected by the degree of personal need and environmental cues. In a series of studies Staub and Baer (1974) showed that a confederate collapsing on the street received more help when he held his chest (presumably indicative of a heart attack, a strong cue for helping) as opposed to holding his knee (a less serious injury). Further determinants of helping were various other situational stimulus characteristics, such as degree of difficulty of escape from the scene of the accident.

Other recent research presents some evidence supporting assumptions of a linear relationship between degree of situational arousal and motivation to make some response to the emergency to reduce the arousal (Piliavin and Piliavin 1972); other evidence (Ashton and Severy 1976) points to a curvilinear relationship between degree of need perceived and helping. These studies focus additionally on personal costs and benefits accruing to the helper, rather than on their social cognitions. Some of our findings could be subsumed under the Piliavin model inasmuch as children were found to give when costs to their own work were zero.

4. Torop's research had its source in the literature which reports highly contradictory effects of negative evaluations such as disapproval or criticism on children's learning or performance. She developed a two-factor theory that separated information-giving (cognitive) components from the affective components of negative criticism. Her model predicted that when the affect created by criticism is strong, the child will not be able to use any information offered; when affect is mild, albeit negative, children will be able to use the information provided.

6

Age and Socioeconomic Status in Children's Behavior and Performance in Competitive and Cooperative Working Conditions

E.A. Pepitone,
H.W. Loeb, and
E.M. Murdoch

The studies described in chapters 4 and 5 provide some indication of developmental trends in children's social behaviors; they were, by and large, in accord with expected theoretical accounts of children's growth and development. Toddlers played with familiar toys and began to imitate each other's play. Kindergarteners in dyadic situations helped each other when they themselves clearly had a surplus of materials that they could not use and the other definitely needed. Both studies gave support to the basic egocentric orientations of preschoolers. However, they also showed that this egocentrism could be modified by very strong cues so that even these youngest children, under special conditions, could take account of their partners' state and be influenced by it in their own behavior. While our interest in third- and fourth-graders' interpersonal relations in cooperative conditions stemmed primarily from social psychological theoretical concerns, it was evident that these older children had grown in competence and had acquired a variety of skills, including manipulative abilities, verbal facilities, and increased capacity to respond to each other. Such growth was reflected in their paying a great deal of attention to each other, evaluating each other's performance, and trying to best each other even when working for a common goal. We also showed that basic other-orientations, once present, could be built on by increasing postoperational children's interdependence in cooperative situations to further their collaborative behavior.

This study was partially supported by research grant OEG 3-72-0007 to the senior author from the Office of Education, Department of Health, Education and Welfare. The observers were C. Diaco, K. Whyer, J. Roberts, and B. McGonagle. We gratefully acknowledge their contributions. We are also grateful for the assistance in data analysis provided by R. Heiberger and F. Rothbaum.

Among the many new questions raised by our research, two persisted. The first centered on our sample, which had been consistently suburban, white, and in school districts located in the affluent Main Line outside of Philadelphia. To understand the generality of our findings, it seemed imperative that we extend our inquiry to include children of different socioeconomic backgrounds. Second, in those first studies, we had deliberately taken samples of children who were at very different developmental points; yet some of the most interesting questions, especially in the light of familial socioeconomic background differences, had to do with gradual changes in comparison behaviors, helping, evaluation of self and others, and the like. All forces seemed to point toward next steps that would involve children from kindergarten up and through all elementary grades. Therefore, a study of children from two different elementary schools differing widely in socioeconomic status of the parents seemed indicated.

We did not wish to study children attending a center city Philadelphia school because these schools included black and other minority group children, which would have confounded the data when compared with our almost exclusively white, affluent, suburban sample. Therefore our choice for a companion school fell on an elementary school located in a white working-class school district in a North Philadelphia industrial area. In each of the two respective schools, all children, kindergarten through fifth grade, were studied. In each classroom, half of the children were assigned randomly to like-sexed triads to work under competitive instructions, while the other half were assigned to cooperative conditions. Their interpersonal behaviors and performance were observed, recorded, and analyzed.

The two studies were planned and executed simultaneously in the two different schools. Each methodological step had to be standardized and coordinated, so that the research procedures in themselves could have constituted a study in cooperation (and occasional competition).

The Children and the School Setting

The study involved in both schools the total population, kindergarten through fifth grade, excluding only children designated as behavior problems or those in special learning classes. Four hundred sixty-eight children were from a city school whose parent population was white, and, according to the 1970 census information for the district in which the school was located, over 80 percent of parents were classified as blue-collar workers and only 7 percent as professionals. We designated this sample as working class (WC). By contrast, 450 children came from a suburban school district with white parents, over 90 percent of whom were employed in professional and managerial positions and hence were designated as upper middle class

(UMC). Mean ages of children at each grade level and number of groups assigned to cooperative or competitive conditions are given along with the basic data in tables 6-2 and 6-3.

Classification of each particular child by parental status might have been preferable, but school policy did not permit access to the children's records. The census data may not be as convincing of the highly significant differences in the two populations and in their life-styles, as would a visit to the respective schools. The following description represents some informal observer impressions of both schools and should be read as such. The observers differed considerably among themselves in their own social origins.

In suburbia, the school building was a modern cinder block and glass structure set in the midst of three rolling acres of green landscaped grounds. It was constructed in the shape of a square with an open garden area in the center. Doors opened onto it from each classroom. Each classroom had glass walls looking out on both the garden area and the surrounding countryside. The classrooms were built so that they each had only three walls and were open to passersby in the school corridors. Teachers and children felt free to move about, alone or in small groups, within a classroom or visiting another, often for some additional enrichment experiences. Most of the children were bused to the school or brought by car. At the end of the school day, the parking lot was filled with oversize station wagons, driven by housekeepers, maids, or brightly dressed mothers, chatting with each other while waiting. Sometimes there was a young child present, often with his own steering wheel in the carseat into which he was strapped next to his mother.

The working-class school gave the impression of a miniature fortress. It was a grey stone and brick structure with a fenced-in, paved yard, and not a tree or shrub in sight. Contrary to the frequent stereotype of rowdy, undisciplined classes in lower-class schools, when classes were in session here, the school had more of an appearance of a morgue than a school for small children. The halls were empty, and no voice was heard except the droning or occasionally sharp voices of a teacher. Upon occasion, we stumbled upon a child sitting—perhaps indifferently or dejectedly—on the floor outside the classroom door, obviously being punished.

When the bell sounded, children lined up silently to move somewhere else. It was only on the playground that bedlam broke loose, and there was a constant hum in the air. Pushing, shoving, and running games that did not seem to pit peer against peer in terms of skill as much as sheer brawn. At the end of the school day, the older ones escaped noisily for home, stopping at pretzel or ice cream vendors on the way. The younger ones were often picked up by the mothers, who many times pushed a baby carriage and/or had a toddler at their side, sometimes wailing from a motherly slap or two.

Home and school appeared rather harmonious in purpose and practice when the data were collected in the early 1970s, contrary to assertions of some radical writers of the time. Disagreements between school authorities and parents did exist in suburbia, but they tended to be between parents and school boards (the latter themselves consisted of parents as community representatives). They generally involved financial disputes. In some schools in the district, strong disagreements existed over instituting open classrooms in elementary schools. These issues were generally resolved by various compromises, usually giving parents the option to choose learning structures deemed suitable for their own child, often with advice from teachers. According to several suburban principals and teachers, the concerns of parents centered on their children's performance and achievement. One of the most frequent questions involved why their child had not been placed into an advanced, or enriched, section. School personnel seemed quite sensitive to these parental needs.

Because of the increasing numbers of the population that were completing high school and attending college in the 1970s, the educational level among the young parental working-class generation was rising, so the distance that was said to exist between these parents and school authorities was diminishing. This may well be accompanied by increasing concern for, and involvement with, their children's education. If some highly publicized media reports that depict irate parent-teacher meetings are correct, this may be true for some segments of the population. Still, in the working-class studied, we observed teachers exercising strict authority in the classrooms and halls. On several occasions, we noted parents listening to teachers with considerable respect: teachers held forth, parents nodded vigorous assent. When queried, several of these teachers claimed that the chief reasons for meeting with parents was because they had called them to discuss a child's unruliness and general deportment. One teacher said, "If a child behaves, I don't need the parent. Just leave him to me and he'll learn."

What might one expect from a comparison of children from such diverse social environments? A host of variables have been isolated in theory and research, and from practical experience as well, as being influential in socialization: from physical nourishment to affective nurturance, degree of control and type of control, exposure to diverse experiences, presence of uniform codes of ethics, factors inherent in the familial structure and factors in the peer group structure, and so on.

As far as class differences are concerned, there are not only differentiating but also powerful leveling and homogenizing forces in any society, and perhaps especially in the still relatively young and affluent United States. And who can tell the pertinence today of even as broadly conceived an analysis as Bronfenbrenner's influential "Socialization and Social Class through Time and Space" (1958)? Social scientists assert that we live in a transition period with regard to social values, and parents are likely to be the first to agree from their personal experiences in raising children. Today everyone encounters problems that in some way reflect basic reevaluations of role-appropriate behaviors for women and men and of social standards pertaining to general life-styles. No one can tell whether, and how much, changes in values extend to various subgroups. One wonders what can be said today with any degree of assurance about socialization practices of any subgroup in American society.

Still it would appear that for those dealing with the young, many fundamental issues today evolve around the distribution of authority and, by implication, assuming personal responsibility and freedom of individual choice. Although these issues may peak during adolescence, they color parent-child relations from early childhood on. They are also reflected in normative standards and regulations of schools. On an authoritarian-permissive distribution, our impressionistic observation of the two schools would place the WC population clearly leaning toward the former end, with firmer, stricter rules, on insistence on adherence, and punishment for their infraction. The UMC population clearly belongs on the more permissive end, supportive particularly of children's achievement-oriented endeavors, ever ready to supplement school enrichment with yet more enriching home experiences.

Here it becomes necessary to consider the well-known intercorrelations of occupation, income, and education. These relationships are by no means simple to disentangle in any kind of causal sense, especially so in the 1970s, which saw a widening of educational opportunities for those who had been denied such access or had not been able to afford it earlier. It still seems to be true that parents who are higher in the occupational structure, who are well off, and who are highly educated themselves—parents like those of our suburban children's sample—are most able and willing to provide such advantages for their children. They are most concerned that their children aspire to and achieve high personal goals.

The sociologist Kohn (1963, 1969) is one of the few recent behavioral scientists who has pursued this line of analysis both in his research and theory. Following a sociological tradition that can be traced as far back as Marx and Weber, he linked parental values to different occupational demands, reinforced by differences in general conditions of life. According to Kohn, upper-middle-class occupations are likely to be free of close supervision and require personal responsibility and initiative; therefore parents of this population will tend to stress self-direction in their children. As taxpayers, they are usually quite vocal in insisting that the schools instill the same kind of individual achievement-oriented values in their children, and they are usually successful in obtaining what they want.

By contrast, working-class occupations are more subject to standardization and direct supervision, which requires conformity to rules and procedures established by those in authority. Hence the emphasis in the socialization pattern of working-class parents is on conformity to externally induced proscriptions. Teachers in their schools, being predominantly middle class themselves, agree with their values and seek to perpetuate them in the classroom. In fact, working-class parents see schools as places where their children will learn to obey.

Assuming that this differential training is effective, UMC children's individualistic achievement orientation should lead them to be more strongly motivated to compete in competitive situations than are WC children. Analogously WC children, having learned to be more attuned to the wishes of adults, may also be more attentive to their peers and hence function better in cooperative situations. As far as middle-class children's achievement orientation goes, there is much anecdotal evidence but only a few definitive studies, the strongest being those of Winterbottom (1953) and Rosen and D'Andrade (1959).

As far as class-determined behavior in competitive and cooperative situations is concerned, the Madsen series is useful. Although the urban-rural dimension confounds to some extent the class differences, that research indicated that lower-class rural children generally make more cooperative choices, while urban middle-class children tend to compete more (Madsen 1967; Shapira and Madsen 1974). However, this research related only to choice behavior (motivational preferences) and did not speak directly to the point of the interpersonal behaviors in which children from different backgrounds will or can engage when asked to work competitively or in situations that involve more complex and extensive collaboration than letting go of a string or distributing coins to another.

Furthermore it is evident that interactions may be expected between effects due to socioeconomic influences and effects attributable to variables related to the age of the child. With all of the reservations indicated earlier, the following expectations with regard to the children's behaviors were formulated as guiding themes in the two parallel studies.

1. If collaboration depends on the development of other-oriented cognitions, neither UMC kindergartners nor their WC counterparts will engage to any substantial degree in the other-oriented behaviors required by the cooperative situation in which they will be asked to work. There is contradictory research evidence on this point. As far as simple sharing was concerned, Ugurel-Semin (1952) found less sharing among young middle-class children and Doland and Adelberg (1967) found more. When simple cooperative acts were required, Brotsky and Thomas (1967) and Nelson and Madsen (1969) found no differences in cooperation between middle-class and lower-class 4 year olds.

2. Somewhere between the ages of 7 and 9, a significant increase in other-oriented behavior in children of both social classes was expected,

assuming that by then children from both classes will have decentered and developed the listening and communicating skills needed for collaboration, as suggested by Selman's analysis (1976). McClintock, Moskowitz, and McClintock's (1977) studies established rapid rises of collaborative behaviors in coordinated settings somewhat earlier, between ages 6 and 7. This is to be expected considering the choice behaviors called for, a much simpler response than the interactions required here.

3. If performance in cooperative conditions requires responsiveness to others and if conformity training strengthens such sociocentrism, working-class children of approximately 8 years and older will engage in significantly more other-oriented behavior and perform better than will their upper-middle-class counterparts.

4. If middle-class independence training strengthens the ability to work alone and heightens achievement motivation, UMC children will perform better and pay more attenton to their competitors, and they will engage in more evaluation and besting than will their WC counterparts. Since coactive competition of the kind required of the children does not necessitate understanding the others' perspectives and since children will be concerned with individual goal attainment, motivation for which has been shown to develop during preschool years (McClintock, Moskowitz, and McClintock 1977), these class-related differences were expected to appear in kindergartners' behaviors and performance under competition and to continue throughout the elementary years.

The Experimental Task

Pattern Blocks and Pep board were used as described in chapter 3. The task requirement was to make a flat picture of a person on the board. Because of the developmental emphasis of this study, children were not given free choice as to the block picture they wished to make, since cross-age comparisons and contemplated future cross-cultural comparisons would otherwise have constituted a formidable task. We wanted to choose a performance content that would be meaningful to, and that could be handled by, the youngest children, as well as by the oldest, each at their own particular skill level. These task specifications coincided closely with those that had led to Goodenough's (1926) introduction of the draw-a-man technique into the study of children's drawings. In selecting the criteria for choice of drawing content, Goodenough had pointed out additionally that the subject must be one of generally high interest and appeal so that children's motivation could be maintained across age levels. Further, she argued that the subject to be drawn must also show a number of constant characteristics against which a given drawing could be evaluated. In his extension of Goodenough's test,

Harris (1963) argued convincingly that "because the human being is so basically important [to the child] . . . affectively as well as cognitively, it is probable that the human figure is a better index than, for example, a house, or an automobile. . . . The human figure both in its parts and as a whole must come to include a richer store of associations, or 'meaning', than most other complex objects." (p. 7). Both Goodenough's and Harris's rationales gave further support to our decision to choose a block person design as the required product to be made in this developmental study. Girls' objections during pilot work convinced us very quickly to request a picture of a person rather than that of a man.

Both Goodenough and Harris considered children's drawings of the human figure primarily in relation to children's cognitive development. Other clinicians—among them the most recent and well-known work of Koppitz (1968)—consider drawings more broadly indicative of children's emotional states, including specific attitudes toward themselves, their families, important events in their young lives, and so on. Pilot work with blocks confirmed our belief that drawing human beings is a more difficult task than making a block person. The former starts with a blank page and a pencil and requires that each part of the person be generated wholly by the child's knowledge, imagination, and skills. When blocks and their definitive shapes are given, they impose limits on children's imagination and provide some structure from which to build. A child can put a hexagon on the board and call it a head, place a block below it and call it a neck, and lead off two "skinny diamonds," which he calls arms. In drawing a figure, these all have to be produced from scratch.

As a working hypothesis, then, we assumed that developmentally, children's block products would become more differentiated with age. We also believed that they could be considered as an index of children's growth in cognitive and motoric skills, reflective of their total experience. As such, children's block persons are of interest in relation to parallel development of their social behaviors.

The Experimental Conditions

Children within each classroom were assigned at random to like-sexed triads. Subsequently half of the triads were assigned randomly to the cooperative condition and half to the competitive condition.

In the competitive condition, conditions of coaction were created. The Pep board was divided by a black ribbon into thirds, and each child was told to work on her third. Each was asked to use the blocks to make a flat, big person and to try to make the best person she could, because a photograph would be taken of the best product.

In the cooperative condition, conditions of role-related cooperation were created. Divisions were absent. Children were asked to make one flat, big person together and told that a photograph would be taken of their product. Exact instructions were adjusted to particular age levels. With the youngest children, it was essential for the experimenter to make sure that each child understood the task instructions; therefore, each child was made to repeat what it was she was to do, and the children were not permitted to start until each had satisfied this verbal requirement (even under these conditions, their actions did not necessarily follow what they had said they were to do). With the older children, more emphasis was placed on the purposes of the study, emphasizing children's imagination and creativity. Their interest generally increased when the experimenter said that their design might be included in a book.

The picture taking was important as a successful debriefing method, and it sent children back to their classrooms proud and satisfied. Especially with the youngest children, the ritual of who was to stand next to whom and in front of whose picture was in itself worth another study.

Productivity Indexes

The children's products were scored from the Polaroid photographs on sixteen separate indexes. The measures were quantitive and required either a dichotomous scoring of presence or absence, or addition of separate parts. Rater agreement was 100 percent for the most part and never fell below 90 percent.

The most inclusive measure of performance was an index of the amount of differentiation achieved in the person product. This served as the measure of performance examined in our major statistical analysis. It was obtained by adding separate elements of the human figure, including major parts of the body (head, neck, arms, legs, hair, fingers, and so on) and embellishing details (hair ribbons, hat, trousers, and assorted objects added to the person such as baseball mitts or bats, hockey sticks, pocketbooks, beads, and so on). Points were assigned for each detail. The total score thus obtained correlated highly with several other separate measures: total number of pieces used and length of working time (a fifteen-minute maximum was allowed). The assignment and accumulation of points for each part of the figure resembles to some extent scoring methods employed by the major systematic methodologists in the area we have mentioned. Their procedures differ, however, in that they developed various normative scales by assigning points only for certain bodily parts expected to be drawn at a given age level.

Several additional indexes were used. Two measures were concerned with children's ability to follow instructions. The measure-of-condition direction determined whether in each group each child who had been assigned to competitive conditions worked by herself as requested, and a child assigned to cooperative conditions worked with the other two group members. The measure-of-ability-to-follow-task directions determined whether each child had made only one person as they were asked to do, or whether they disregarded these instructions by either making several persons, or other objects such as a cat or flowers. Both of these measures demanded a Yes or No score for each child by the raters.

A measure of figure complexity consisted of four categories into which person products could be placed. Stick figures denoted a person consisting of a minimum body width and one block width legs and arms. A second category was reserved for products that consisted only of a head with variously developed facial features but the rest of the body missing. A third category included products consisting of a head and partial body. Completed figures consisting of all essential parts, and more elaborate than one block wide stick figures were placed into a fourth category.

Behavior Observations

Two experimenters, Loeb and Murdoch, each in charge of data collection at one of the two schools, jointly developed the observation scheme. Prior to the execution of the study, the two experimenters and four observers worked together in pilot studies over a period of three months. Approximately thirty groups were tested while the behavior categories were refined and observers trained in their use. Before the start of the study, interobserver agreement reached the criterion set at minimally 90 percent for each category. Throughout data collection, each experimenter worked with two observers at one school for two weeks at a time, followed by one week during which the observer pairs were broken up and systematically rotated to work with the other observers at the other school, including observations from each grade and from each of the two conditions. Five such observer exchanges took place throughout the study. The criterion of 90 percent was met easily during each of these rotation periods because the observers had developed almost machine-like precision.

Behavior observations utilized the basic interaction categories defined in chapter 3. They included: nonverbal attention, besting behaviors, task-oriented behaviors, and other-oriented behaviors.

The Major Findings

The data collected for the 918 children were analyzed in various ways. First, data from each school were treated separately by each of the experimenters for their respective dissertations. Loeb devoted one of her chapters to an exploratory cross-socioeconomic analysis that included only kindergarten and first and fourth grades. Based on our knowledge of results from these prior analyses, we carried out statistical treatments of what we considered the most important trends in the data. This analysis constituted the main data base for this chapter, rounded out as needed with information from the other analyses.

The major analysis considered the separate and joint effects of the independent variables of working condition, social class, grade, and sex of children as they related to each of the behaviors of interest to us. Because of the complexity involved in a simultaneous statistical treatment of the dependent variables, a separate 2 (social class) × 2 (work condition) × 6 (grade) × 2 (sex) ANOVA, corrected for uneven cells, was performed on each of the four dependent variables: nonverbal attentional behaviors, task-oriented behaviors, other-oriented behaviors, and performance. As a protection against gaining significance by increasing the number of analyses, a conservative level was adopted: $P = < .01$. All post-hoc comparisons used the Newman-Kuels procedures.

The Competitive Condition

Interpersonal Behaviors. The mean amount of total behavior in the competitive condition for both samples was around fifteen interactions per session. This level of interaction—on the average five exchanges per child during each session—did not change significantly over the grades. Also practically absent within this sparse interaction pattern were negative evaluations and other negative behaviors generally reported in competitive situations. They made up less than 2 percent of the overall interactions. Positive interaction was absent altogether. The mean amount of besting behavior reflected the same trend: at any one grade level, besting constituted most frequently a fraction of one interaction in a given group, too little to be included in an ANOVA treatment. The only substantial social interaction took place on the nonverbal level. It made up almost 90 percent of kindergartners' behavior and somewhat less (67 percent) of all behavior engaged in by fifth graders.

Such overwhelmingly consistent and strong effects showed that in our attempt to create conditons of coaction we had not set up the conditions too poorly, but too well. We had created coacting conditions that did not require interaction. We had staunchly maintained that competitive conditons are different from cooperative conditons and had demonstrated exactly that.[1]

Table 6-1 presents overall means for the four major dependent variables for the three grouping factors of working condition, sex, and socioeconomic status. It is evident that behavior in cooperative and competitive conditons, respectively, was completely different.

Table 6-1
Mean Behavior and Performance, by Condition, Sex, and Social Class

Behavior and Performance	Condition				Sex				Social Class			
	Cooperative	Competitive	F^a	p	Boys	Girls	F^a	p	Upper Middle Class	Working Class	F^a	p
Nonverbal attention	13.48	30.84	45.40	< .001	22.37	21.96	0.03		18.67	25.66	7.37	< .008
Task oriented	24.10	11.64	26.05	< .001	19.40	16.34	1.57		18.73	17.01	.49	
Other-oriented	19.11	0.90	152.05	< .001	10.41	9.60	0.30		6.50	13.60	23.08	< .001
Performance	32.26	25.16	41.04	< .001	28.21	29.21	0.83		31.15	26.28	19.35	< .001

[a]df (1,258).

There was a significant condition difference for other-oriented behaviors. They were also virtually absent in competition, not surprisingly so. Twice as many task-oriented interactions occurred in cooperation. Even though this category constituted the largest verbal category in competition, the mean of 11.64, distributed over interactions of three children, amounted to very little discourse. As additional experimenter process notes documented, this type of interaction consisted mostly of monosyllabic neutral comments about a child's own work and that of others. Some groups talked a little more, contributing to the overall mean and balancing the many triads who worked in uninterrupted silence throughout the whole session. We had explicitly removed restraints against interaction at the beginning of sessions. Children in each group were told that they were free to talk with each other as they worked. Their silence, coupled with the large amount of nonverbal interaction, signifies to us that it was not simply that interaction was not required but rather, that children seemed actively to suppress such interaction.

Table 6-1 also documents that nonverbal attentional behaviors occurred with significantly greater frequency in competition, almost twice as much on the average as in the cooperative condition. Nonverbal attention can be generated by a variety of motives. When children are working on a common product, looking at another's work is accompanied with much other-oriented interaction and thus is likely to assume quite different functions. Table 6-1 discloses no more than that, overall, boys engaged in this behavior as much as did girls and that WC children engaged in significantly more nonverbal attention than did UMC children. The fact that WC children, additonally, made less complex products than did UMC children (see table 6-1 for class differences in performance) suggests greater procedural uncertainty in WC children. Tables 6-2 and 6-3 advance our analysis further; they break down the same behaviors and performance for each of the two conditons by grade level and socioeconomic status.

Table 6-2, which deals with the competitive condition, shows, surprisingly, that nonverbal attention did not differ appreciably with age. Fifth graders still paid as much attention to each other as did kindergartners. The grade-related decrease in percentage of nonverbal behavior thus was not due to a decrease in these behaviors but rather to an increase in some other behaviors. Table 6-2 suggests that these behaviors were task-oriented communications, which rose steadily over grades in both samples.

Performance Complexity. Performance trends for both UMC and WC children at different ages are shown in table 6-2 and, perhaps more clearly, in figure 6-1. The data show that children from both schools made increasingly more complex products with age up to second and third grade, where the asymptote was reached. And at each grade level, UMC children scored

Table 6-2
Mean Behavior and Performance in Competitive Condition by Grade and Social Class

	Grade					
	K	1	2	3	4	5
Mean age						
UMC	5.8	7.0	7.8	8.8	9.9	10.8
WC	5.8	6.9	7.8	9.2	9.8	11.0
Nonverbal attention						
UMC	30.88	24.75	28.33	31.99	23.10	34.85
WC	26.36	33.93	41.86	36.60	34.38	23.10
Task oriented						
UMC	1.13	9.25	11.08	12.86	17.98	15.77
WC	2.02	15.43	13.29	10.63	3.54	26.70
Other-oriented						
UMC	0.38	0.19	0.38	0.27	0.60	0.54
WC	0.0	0.64	3.07	2.33	0.75	2.68
Performance						
UMC	19.50	23.13	30.38	31.16	31.08	31.23
WC	12.54	20.29	22.21	28.22	26.04	26.20
Number of groups						
UMC	8	12	10	15	9	17
WC	15	14	14	16	10	10

higher than did their WC counterparts. This performance difference is in line with generally accepted variants of social advantage hypotheses. The largest performance differences occurred among the youngest children. Similar findings of decreasing differences with length of school attendance are often cited to support arguments of the "school as the great social equalizer."

More insight about the nature of these differences is gained by examining the type of products made by children from different socioeconomic backgrounds at different ages. Data from prior separate analyses are highly pertinent here. They demonstrate that all kindergartners, regardless of socioeconomic background, can and do follow the directions to work by themselves (contrary to following directions to work together in the cooperative condition). Not surprisingly, considering the meaning of egocentrism, working alone is easier for all kindergartners than working together.

Differences related to socioeconomic background already begin to

Table 6-3
Mean Behavior and Performance in Cooperative Condition, by Grade and Social Class

	Grade					
	K	1	2	3	4	5
Mean age						
UMC	5.8	6.9	7.9	8.6	9.9	10.8
WC	5.7	6.8	7.8	8.9	9.9	10.9
Nonverbal attention						
UMC	14.73	8.43	6.54	2.46	14.38	3.53
WC	33.07	34.83	17.57	14.98	7.33	3.91
Task oriented						
UMC	19.70	29.01	18.89	19.9	22.93	25.64
WC	9.51	17.64	19.13	26.84	28.50	51.50
Other-oriented						
UMC	3.70	7.61	13.23	13.52	14.96	22.14
WC	7.38	12.19	11.90	39.63	36.83	46.17
Performance						
UMC	18.70	33.39	35.83	38.12	42.07	39.19
WC	9.75	21.48	25.10	45.98	37.50	40.00
Number of groups						
UMC	8	13	12	15	13	18
WC	15	13	12	13	12	12

emerge in the nature of the product made. In table 6-4, all UMC children, beginning with kindergarten, made recognizable persons, while only 75 percent of WC boys and 95 percent of WC girls did so. It was only at third grade that all of the WC boys' groups could make recognizable figures.

Following trends in children's human figure drawings, we have assumed that stick figures are developmentally easier to make than complete figures. And indeed, as table 6-4 shows, none of the kindergartners of either class or sex made a complete figure. Instead stick figures dominated in the primary grades. For class differences, 100 percent of the UMC kindergarten boys' groups and almost all kindergarten girls made stick figures. Among WC children, only about half of the kindergartners were able to make recognizable stick figures. WC children's performance complexity dovetailed that of the UMC children by about two grades: the peak of UMC children's stick figures occurred at kindergarten and first grade, and then this type of figure decreased over the grades. Illustrations 6-1 and 6-3 show differences in complexity between kindergartners and second graders. The

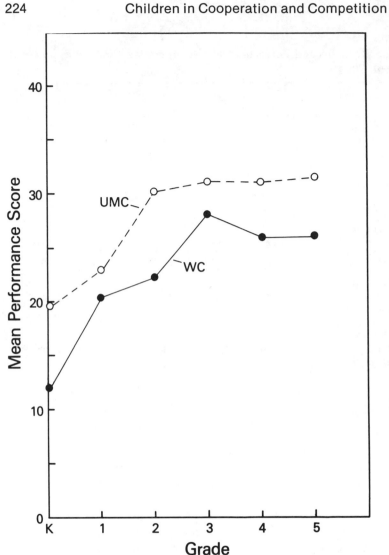

Figure 6-1. Competitive Condition: Mean Performance of Working-Class
          and Upper-Middle-Class Children

peak of WC children's stick figures occurred at second and third grades,
reaching the same low as their UMC counterparts from fourth grade on. A
corresponding increasing trend in complete figures was found in both
samples, although WC children tended to continue to make less-complex
figures in the upper grades as well.

Table 6-4
Percentage of Children Making Stick Figures and Complete Persons, in Competitive Condition, by Grade

		Grade					
		K	1	2	3	4	5
Stick Figures							
UMC	Boys	100%	83.3%	72.2%	62.5%	60%	16.7%
	Girls	83.3	83.3	58.3	94.1	75	45.8
WC	Boys	48.3	50.1	81	80	53.2	20
	Girls	53	85.7	77.4	77.8	73.3	60.7
Complete figures							
UMC	Boys	0	12.5	27.8	37.5	26.7	66.7
	Girls	0	8.3	33.3	0	16.7	37.5
WC	Boys	0	14.3	4.8	20.0	40.0	20.7
	Girls	0	0	19.0	16.7	6.7	33.3

Note: Where percentage figures do not total 100 percent, products fall into the additional categories of nonrecognizable or incomplete figures.

One phenomenon was present almost exclusively in WC children's performance: a tendency to duplication of figures, especially at second and third grade (see illustration 6-2). It appears as if WC children at this age equate best with quantity, while UMC children make one person but tend to embellish it, suggesting equation of best with quality. The former maximizing attempt is reminiscent of the youngest subjects in the study of McClintock, Moskowitz, and McClintock (1977), who opted for the greatest number of marbles they could obtain for themselves, without being concerned with more complex issues of relativity of rewards.

Under coactive competitive conditions, UMC children, and especially boys, were able to perform this particular required task earlier, and perform it more elaborately, than their WC counterparts, and they continued to do so as they grew older.

Performance similarity. A final issue pertaining to performance under coactive competitive conditions is that of the similarity a child's performance bears to that of other children in the same group. The study reported in chapter 4 focused on similarity among group members' subtasks as an independent variable as it affected children's interpersonal relations and, in particular, their comparisons with each other's performance and ensuing achievement-related competitive behaviors. Here we are concerned with the similarity of children's performance as a dependent variable in the light of postulated comparison dynamics.

According to Festinger's (1954) social comparison theory, in order to

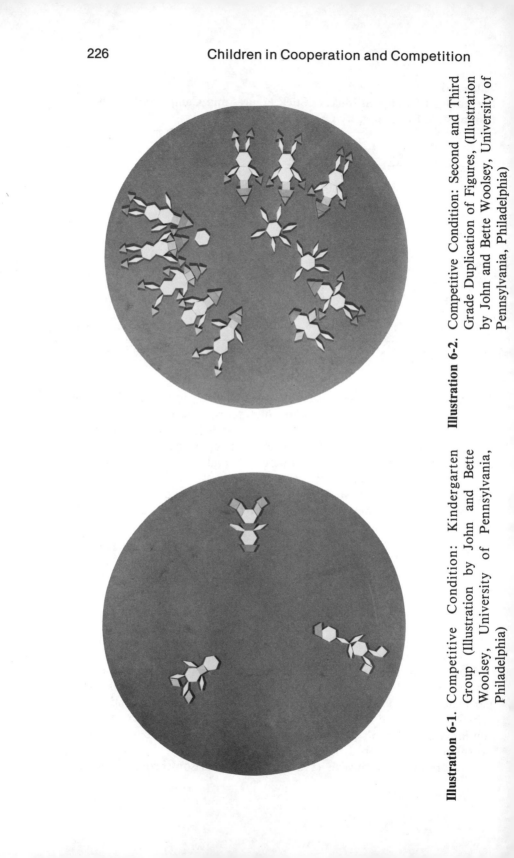

Illustration 6-1. Competitive Condition: Kindergarten Group (Illustration by John and Bette Woolsey, University of Pennsylvania, Philadelphia)

Illustration 6-2. Competitive Condition: Second and Third Grade Duplication of Figures, (Illustration by John and Bette Woolsey, University of Pennsylvania, Philadelphia)

evaluate one's abilities (by determining the meaning of one's performance, the significance of one's accomplishment, its correctness, its goodness), standards of judgment are necessary. In the absence of objectively given physical standards, similar others are chosen as comparison standards. It is implied that, in case of discrepancy between own and other performance, own uncertainty will determine a closer move toward the performance of other.

Much of recent research and theory has focused on the exact meaning of similar others: their definition, functions, and conditions under which they will be chosen as referents (Suls and Miller 1977). We need not concern ourselves with these issues here because it is clear that in this study, the children's choice of similar others was limited to the two coactors provided by the experimenter. There is no question but that coactors were similar on related performance attributes; the most salient included their same age, sex, classroom, teacher, learning experiences, and so forth. No performance standards were given; the children were not told what the experimenter's criteria were for producing the best figure of a person. This absence of task requirements and general lack of structure created uncertainty about their performance, another precondition for social comparison. Thus the stage was set for this behavior to occur.

Taking coactors' performances as standards would lead to accommodation and assimilation of each other's creations, leading to generally similar products within given triads. Post-Festinger research and theory has isolated additional motives for comparing with others, which cluster around the need to validate one's performance (to receive approval and agreement from similar others to maintain or gain self-esteem). As applied to our situation, such motives may be further forces toward making products more similar.

One of the difficulties encountered with Festinger's theory is that comparison of abilities may refer to several distinct processes: In one sense, it refers to the person's actively seeking out others of the same level of ability, irrelevant here because children had been assigned to groups. In another sense, it may refer to the process of attempting to influence others to make their own performance comparable, also unlikely here because goal contriency existed. In our performance situation, then, social comparison must also be in the service of competition-related motivations. Festinger would concur for his tenet was that what sets off ability comparisons from comparisons of opinons or other personal attributes is the presence of a unidirectional drive. It motivates the person to do better than others and/or better than one's previous performance. It thus denotes competitive achievement motives.

Competitive achievement motives constitute forces toward individual distinction. Rather than making for similarity, such forces stimulate the creation of differences between oneself and others. In other words, people seek similar others so that they can compare themselves with them meaningfully, obtaining useful information that may be employed toward making similar products. But in performance situations, they also wish to surpass similar others in order to do better. This is what achievement motivation is all about; this is the motive identified by McClintock et al. as maximizing differences while making relative choices in competitive games.

Festinger argued that when such motivations are absent, complete uniformity would exist in peer groups, and a state of social quiescence would obtain (occasionally noted in groups who attained total unanimity of opinions with respect to given issues). Presumably where both uniformity and achievement pressures exist, "the resolution of these two pressures, which act simultaneously, is a state of affairs where all members are relatively close together with respect to some specific ability, but not completely uniform" (p. 125).

Applying the above reasoning to competitive situations, we suggest that there exists an essential conflict between competitors' striving to distinguish themselves from each other and at the same time not wanting to stand out from among each other. In contrient goal conditions, one person's performance must be better than that of others. The winner must distinguish herself from the others by making her performance outstanding, that is, different from that of everyone else. In addition to self-evaluational and self-validational forces, which make for performance similarity, public coaction (such as happens in the classroom) evokes further social dynamics that constrain a person to be more alike to others. Chief among these forces would be fear of failure or fear of ridicule for inferior products, fear of retaliation or ostracism for superior performance, and other specific fears related to being different. Since such fears are particularly strong in children, this conflict analysis appears highly relevant to our study.

Following this argument, our competitive condition may be analyzed as follows: the absence of objective achievement standards and specific task requirements creates uncertainties that stimulate comparison behaviors. Similar performance reduces such uncertainties and other fear-related forces. We have seen that among the youngest children, some were unable even to reproduce a model as represented by a coactor's products. Once children are able to imitate each other, the resultant forces toward similarity, which may be assumed to be strongest among the younger children, and their relatively weaker low achievement motivation would lead us to expect greatest product similarity in the primary grades.

We have also shown that older children have the ability to make comlete, differentiated, and embellished products. They may also be assumed to understand that the probability of winning is increased by maximizing discrepancies between self and others. Therefore, we may infer an age-related decrease in performance similarity within groups. The degree of difference among products of these older children might be taken as an indication of the relative strength of their competitive motivations.

Exact predictions as to the degree of similarity depend on the level of the various forces involved. Because UMC children are able to make more differentiated products and have a likely history of past school successes, they may be assumed to be more confident in their abilities and less dependent on their neighboring coactors as models. These relatively low pressures toward uniformity, coupled with strong achievement needs, may be expected to result in attempts to distinguish their performance from those of competitors. Reasoning thus, we concluded that UMC children, especially the older ones, may be expected to make more dissimilar products than did their WC counterparts. Within each group, the greater the difference among products of each of the three members, the stronger their individual competitive achievement needs.

Because this analysis promised to give important additional information about the motivation of children in the competitive condition, the rough dichotomous similarity index originally designed was revised to measure a wider range of difference.

The Similarity Index: Rules for Construction. Within each triad, each child's product was compared from the photograph with one other child's product that appeared most similar to it. The comparison included two criteria: similarity of figure outline and commonality of blocks. Points were assigned according to these criteria, as follows:

Identity: 9 points (outline identical, 0-3 blocks placed differently).

Very similar: 6 points (outline identical, 4-6 blocks placed differently).

Similar: 3 points (outline similar, 4-6 blocks placed similarly).

Different: 0 points (outline different, 3-0 blocks placed similarly).

If three children in a group made identical products, the similarity score was 3×9; thus 27 was the highest score possible, signifying identity of product among all three members of a given triad. The indexes thus obtained could vary from 27 to 0, in the following order of degree of similarity:

27:    three identical products.

24:    two identical products, one very similar.

21:    two identical products, one similar.

18:    two identical products; one different; or, three
       very similar products.

15:   two very similar products, one similar.

12:   two very similar products, one different.

 9:   three similar products.

 6:   two similar, one different product.

 0:   three different products.

Independent coding by two coders showed 84 percent agreement; 100 percent agreement was found on products scored as identical or different. Disagreements occurred in the very similar or similar range and were adjusted after further inspection and discussion.

Results. The mean product similarity (table 6-5) is shown for boys and girls separately for each of the two socioeconomic distributions and at each grade level. We also depict these trends graphically in figure 6-2 for boys from both socioeconomic status distributions only because they accentuate the general trends shown in the table. Differences between UMC children and WC children, as well as at different grade levels, are apparent.

Age Trends in Performance Similarity of UMC Children. It is evident that UMC kindergartners and first graders within each group made, on the average, persons that were very similar to each other. The group means of these young children ranged from scores of 18 and above to 27. This range reflects three identical products or two identical products and the third very similar or similar within a given triad. A sample of such highly similar performances is shown in illustration 6-1. Again, numbers cannot convey the full reality and even one illustration cannot quite demonstrate the precise identity achieved by these children within their groups. Just like the toddlers studied in chapter 4, the parallel play here was not merely limited to choice of identical toy; it included identical function, with blocks placed in the same position. If one child used a red block symbolically as a shoe, so did the rest of the members of that group; if it was turned up or one shoe was up and the other one down, this pattern occurred three times in the exact fashion. It could be objected that since all kindergartners made stick figures, great similarity is to be expected, but that protest simply does not hold up in the light of between-group variation of stick figures and exact copies of unique features within groups.

It seems to us that such deliberate similarity indicates the same security-giving function of identity we referred to earlier, a security that is arrived at by social comparisons that produce similarity of attitudes, behaviors, possessions—or products.

Table 6-5

Mean Product Similarity in Competitive Work, by Grade, Socioeconomic Status, and Sex

Grade	WC		UMC	
	Boys	Girls	Boys	Girls
K	7.88	11.57	23.25	20.25
1	14.57	9.86	21.00	18.75
2	14.57	20.57	15.00	12.50
3	20.57	14.50	13.29	18.00
4	18.00	8.25	12.60	15.75
5	14.40	17.25	6.00	15.33

The findings of such similar products among the youngest children are important also in the light of previous research that demonstrated the presence of competitive motivation in 4 year olds from populations comparable to our samples (McClintock, Moskowitz, and McClintock 1977). This motivation was inferred from their choice behavior, which involved taking more for oneself relative to the partner, even if it meant less for oneself in absolute terms. Our interpretation would be that these children understood, perhaps only dimly, the concept of getting more than the other. Our data suggest that 5 and 6 year olds do not understand the meaning of competitive performance in the sense of having to produce something different from others. It is also possible that these young children understood competitive requirements, but were unable or unwilling to risk differentiating themselves from others.

Data from the older UMC children support the assumption of a steady growth in cognitive understanding of the behavioral requirements of competition and a willingness to take up this challenge, especially for the UMC boys. By fifth grade, their group mean of 6.00 signifies that, on the average, at least one boy in a triad made a completely different person from those of the other two group members. In several groups, the three products are wholly dissimilar, as shown in illustration 6-4. This difference was deliberately produced. We frequently observed that one of these boys started out with an idea, and when he noticed a competitor reproducing it, immediately altered it to make something different. We suggest that embellishments are means, for the boys most particularly, of differentiating themselves from each other with a unique product that they hoped would appeal to the experimenter, who selected the winner.

Age Trends in Performance Similarity of WC Children. WC kindergartners' low similarity score is to be understood as a function of the considerable numbers of children (33 percent from their sample) who were not

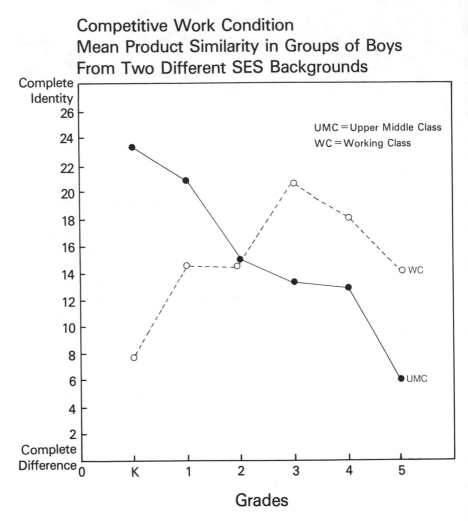

Competitive Work Condition
Mean Product Similarity in Groups of Boys
From Two Different SES Backgrounds

Figure 6-2. Mean Product Similarity in Groups of Boys, by Socioeconomic Background

yet able to make a recognizable person. Even though they looked to each other, they lacked the skills to imitate. As their manipulative and cognitive skills increased, so did their ability to imitate, and their products correspondingly increased in similarity.

WC boys' similarity index followed the same course as did their stick figure score noted earlier. By third grade, their similarity index was the same as was that of the UMC boys at first grade. From then on, the downward trend of their curve paralleled that of the UMC boys with a two-year lag, never quite reaching the low of fifth-grade UMC boys.[2]

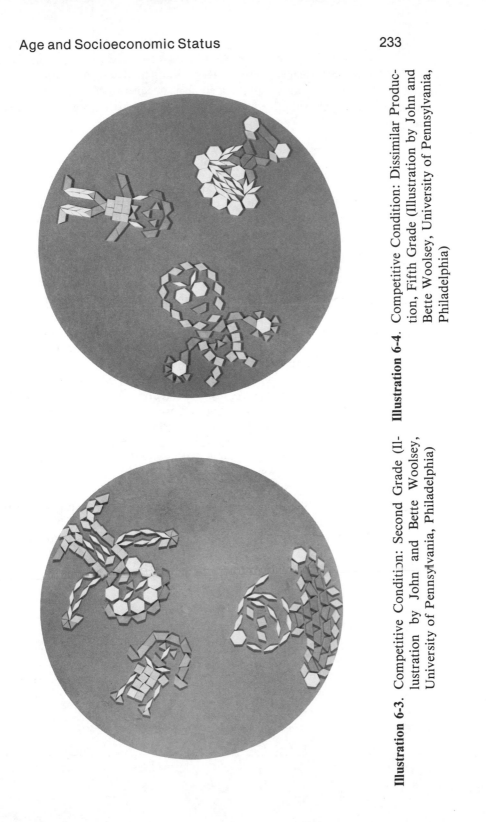

Illustration 6-3. Competitive Condition: Second Grade (Illustration by John and Bette Woolsey, University of Pennsylvania, Philadelphia)

Illustration 6-4. Competitive Condition: Dissimilar Production, Fifth Grade (Illustration by John and Bette Woolsey, University of Pennsylvania, Philadelphia)

Girls from both socioeconomic backgrounds tended to have somewhat more similar products, although the trend was not pronounced, with the exception of the highly significant difference between fifth-grade UMC boys and girls.

The Cooperative Condition

Two overall findings with regard to cooperative conditions stand out (see table 6-1). First, illustrating our basic assumptions about the nature of cooperation, a great deal more interaction around the task took place in that condition, involving both verbal exchange about the task and active collaboration in its construction. Second, and not necessarily to be expected, was the fact that, overall, significantly more complex products were made in the cooperative condition than in the competitive condition.

Performance. The overall trend shown in table 6-1 may be quite misleading. It needs qualification in the sense that there are several main effects and interaction effects, which tell a much more complex story.

The mean performance in cooperative conditions, 32.26, was superior to the average performance in competitive conditions, 25.16, a highly significant difference. A main effect for performance was also obtained for grade (F (5,258) = 33.99; $p<.001$), showing that, regardless of condition and regardless of socioeconomic status, all children's performance differed, on the average, as a function of age. Additionally there was also a significant interaction for performance between grade × condition, F (5,258) = 40.4, $p<.002$).

This statistical information is reflected in table 6-6, which shows performance means at each grade level for each of the two conditions. The trend of a steady increase in quality of performance roughly up through third grade,

Table 6-6
Mean Performance in Cooperative and Competitive Conditions, by Grade

| Grade | Mean Age | Mean Performance | |
		Cooperation	Competition
K	5.8	14.23	16.02
1	6.8	27.44	21.71
2	7.8	30.46	26.30
3	8.8	42.05	29.69
4	9.9	39.79	28.56
5	10.9	39.59	28.72

already noted for the competitive condition, holds here also. It is also apparent that throughout the first three grades, there was no statistically significant difference in average performance under the two conditions. Only from third grade on did differences become large and significant in favor of more complex products being made in the cooperative condition.

There are some other noteworthy differences in performance, especially in the early grades. None of the kindergartners in the two samples could make a complete figure when working alone under the competitive condition. But when they worked together, several groups within both samples were able to make a complete figure (table 6-7). The number of such groups increased throughout the primary grades. With two minor exceptions, children in both samples at each grade level made more complete figures in the cooperative condition than they did in the corresponding competitive condition. Illustration 6-5 shows a rare product by a kindergarten group unable to make one complete person. Illustration 6-6 shows a fairly complex head made by a group of first graders. Illustration 6-8 gives an example of a highly coordinated, complex, and imaginative person product never found in corresponding competitive conditions.

Along the same lines, additional data are relevant from the performance index scoring of figures in role. In the upper elementary grades, figures were often embellished by placing the person into a specific role enactment, such as a hockey player, dancer, or other sports figures. (See illustration 6-7.) These effects were completely absent in the competitive condition. Interestingly in the UMC samples, figures in roles were found only in the products of fourth-grade boys (16 percent), who cast their male figures into sport poses. In the WC sample, these figures appeared in both boys' and girls' products, beginning with third grade and continuing into fifth grade. Approximately 15 percent of the girls at each upper grade level showed such role enactments. The frequency for boys was 11 percent at third grade, 50 percent at fourth, and 33 percent at fifth grade. These performance data point to the conclusion that employing the Pep board task in cooperative conditions is conducive to the creation of more imaginative, richer products at all grade levels than those found in corresponding competitive conditions.

Yet another set of data lends support to this generalization. The research in question deals with transfer effects studied in the UMC sample only (Loeb 1975, 1979). Loeb determined that when children first experienced a cooperative work condition that was then followed immediately with work in the competitive condition, there was a subsequent decrease in stick figures at every grade level. Experience in the cooperative condition enhanced the product even for kindergartners, although positive transfer effects became increasingly stronger with grade level. When first exposed to the competitive condition, 60 percent of the boys and 75 percent of the girls were still making stick figures at fourth grade (see table 6-4). Prior ex-

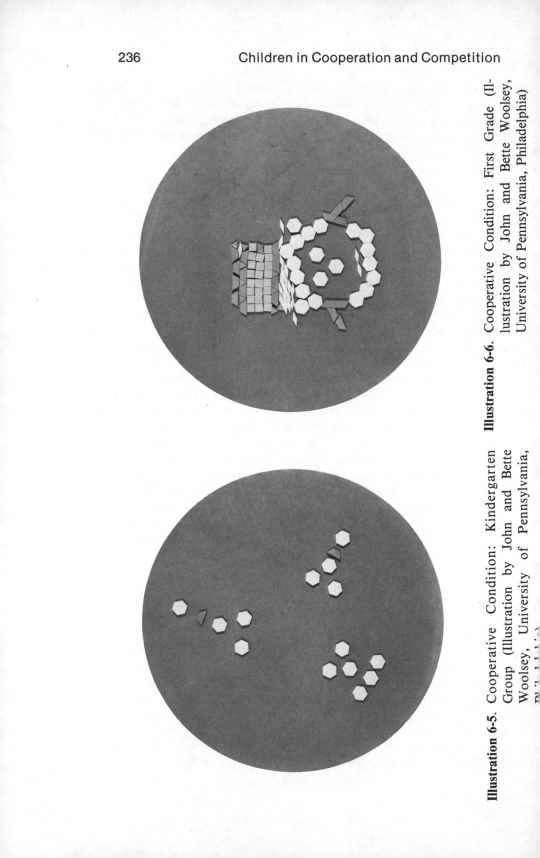

Illustration 6-5. Cooperative Condition: Kindergarten Group (Illustration by John and Bette Woolsey, University of Pennsylvania, Philadelphia)

Illustration 6-6. Cooperative Condition: First Grade (Illustration by John and Bette Woolsey, University of Pennsylvania, Philadelphia)

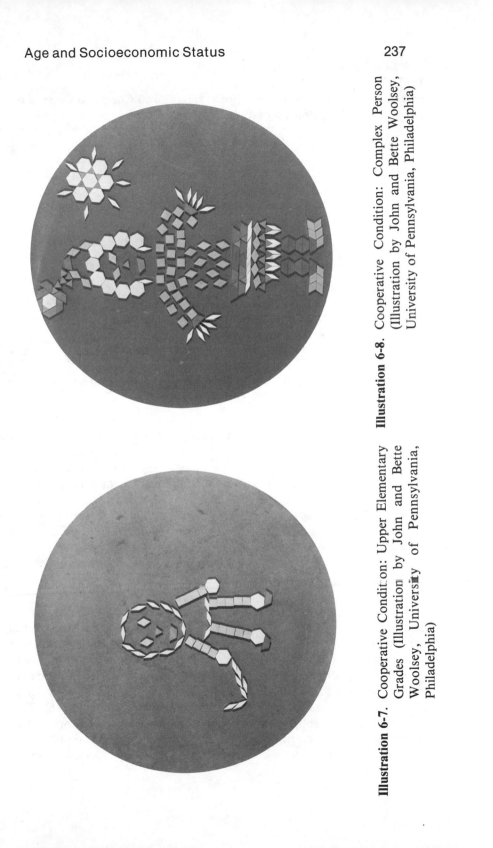

Illustration 6-7. Cooperative Condition: Upper Elementary Grades (Illustration by John and Bette Woolsey, University of Pennsylvania, Philadelphia)

Illustration 6-8. Cooperative Condition: Complex Person (Illustration by John and Bette Woolsey, University of Pennsylvania, Philadelphia)

Table 6-7

Percentage of Children Making Stick Figures and Complete Persons in Cooperative Conditions, by Grade

	Grades					
	K	1	2	3	4	5
Stick figures						
UMC						
Boys	60%	0%	14.3%	50%	0%	0%
Girls	33.3	66.7	22.7	20	16.7	6.1
WC						
Boys	16.7	66.7	28.6	15.4	16.7	16.7
Girls	33.3	47.6	64.3	22.2	16.7	16.7
Complete figures						
UMC						
Boys	0	100	71.4	33.2	71.4	62.5
Girls	33.3	16.7	66.7	40	50	66.7
WC						
Boys	8.3	0	28.6	65.4	50	83.3
Girls	14.3	28.6	21.4	77.8	83.3	22.2

Note: Where percentage figures do not total 100 percent, products fall into the additional categories of nonrecognizable or incomplete figures.

perience with making one figure in the cooperative condition resulted in the complete disappearance of such figures in subsequent individual competitive work. By contrast, prior work in the competitive condition actively interfered with performance under the subsequent cooperative condition for both fourth graders and first graders. For kindergartners, prior performance under the competitive condition was not found to interfere but in fact actually facilitated following cooperative task directions and aided somewhat in the execution of complete figures. Loeb argues that for these youngest children, prior work in the competitive condition constitutes task practice rather than eliciting competitive motivations, as yet relatively weak at that age.

In reflecting on the overall performance trends under the cooperative condition, the highest priority is indicated for replicating this type of study with a variety of tasks. The tasks would have to be carefully selected to disclose which task structures do or do not enhance performance under cooperative conditions. There is a body of research on small discussion groups that shows that problem solving in small discussion groups permits the emergence of more, and more variable, solutions (Shaw 1976). Tasks that require such collaborative exchanges thus have the potential for enriching the final performance. We believe that the Pep board task falls into such a category by virtue of the fact that the final product is capable of reflecting a variety of individual contributions, if the group is able to incorporate them. In our view, it is not only an oversimplification but wrong to take for granted that three children will make a more complex product together than will one child working alone.

Comparison of Performance of UMC and WC Children. In the competitive condition, the overall performance of UMC children exceeded that of WC children significantly at each grade level (see figure 6-1 and table 6-2). In the cooperative condition, there was also an overall significant difference that favored the performance of UMC children: UMC mean performance was 34.55 and WC mean performance was 29.97 ($F (1,132) = 6.47, p<.002$). Additionally there was an interaction of grade × socioeconomic states ($F (5,132) = 3.02, p<.01$, one that was absent under the competitive condition. It was crucially important in cooperation (see table 6-3 and figure 6-3). The superiority of UMC children is apparent, just as it was in the competitive condition, but with this difference: it persisted only through second grade. Under cooperation, by third grade and thereafter, WC children performed as well as did UMC children (from third grade on, differences were not significant).

Interpersonal Behaviors. Since performance is a function of what the children do and since collaboration was the central feature in our cooperative condition, it would seem most likely that the social interaction pattern should in some ways reflect the performance picture just sketched. Following our theoretical analysis, successful performance in this cooperative condition was expected to depend on the exercise of task-oriented and other-oriented behaviors.

As far as verbal exchange about the work was concerned, we have established already that task-oriented verbalizations occurred with significantly greater frequency in the cooperative condition (table 6-1). Table 6-3 shows an ascending order of increase over the grades. The increase was found steady and particularly large in WC children. Schette's test against a linear contrast was significant for WC children only ($F = 23.51, p<.001$). Here, too, a significant interaction between socioeconomic status × grade was found ($F = 19.35, p<.001$). Table 6-3 shows a pattern in which UMC kindergartners and first graders engaged in more task-oriented behaviors than did WC children. The trend began to reverse itself at third grade, when WC children showed more of this behavior. By fifth grade, this difference reached statistical significance by the Newman-Keuls test.

Thus far, our expectations were confirmed inasmuch as UMC kindergartners and first graders showed more task-oriented behaviors in line with their superior performance at this age, and WC children showed a

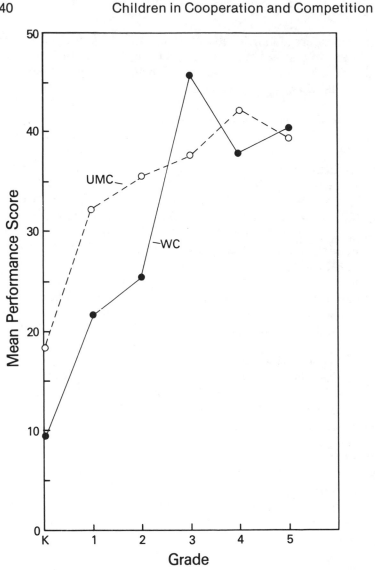

Figure 6-3. Mean Performance of Working-Class and Upper-Middle-Class Children in Cooperative Condition

dramatic increase in these behaviors throughout the grades, also commensurate with their performance.

We have already established the significantly more frequent occurrence of other-oriented behaviors in the cooperative condition (table 6-1). Table 6-3 and figure 6-4 show mean other-oriented behaviors by grade for the two

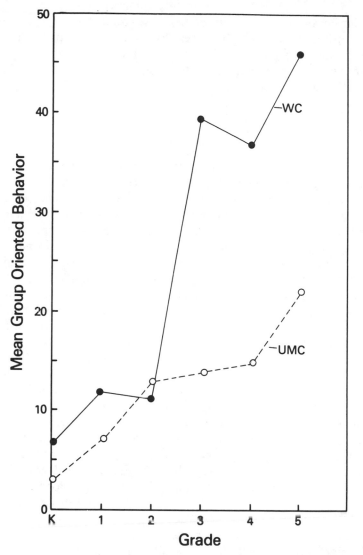

Figure 6-4. Mean Group-oriented Behavior of Working-Class and Upper-Middle-Class Children in Cooperative Condition

socioeconomic samples. The data parallel the respective children's performance. The statistics support what the eye tells at a glance. There was a significant increase with age ($F(5,258) = 10.23, p < .001$) and a significant interaction of socioeconomic status $\times$ grade ($F(5,258 = 2.85, p < .017$). Newman-Keuls tests of the significance of the difference at each grade point between mean behaviors of children from the two different socioeconomic groups confirm the strong trend evident by inspection: the differences were not significant throughout the first three grades. Thereafter at each grade point, WC children had significantly more other-oriented behavior than did their UMC counterparts.

Class Differences

Assuming that the differential socialization practices of the two populations make a difference in children's relative degree of self-confidence, competence, and competitive achievement orientation, differences in the behavior and performance between the two samples of children fell into the coherent pattern reflected in the data. Let us suppose, then, that UMC parents and schools reinforce each others' attempts to instill strong achievement motivations in their children. By the time they reach kindergarten, such children have already been given a firm foundation not only by establishing needs for independence and competence but also in skills that allow a small child to meet those goals. Thus they will have had a number of success experiences, which in turn help to strengthen their self-confidence.

When it is time for kindergarten, the children who have had such preparation are quite able to function well in coactive, age-appropriate tasks, as well as when asked to work together (contrary to their WC counterparts, who were less well trained in competencies required in school settings). To be sure, in the cooperative condition, these youngest UMC children are indeed not very much concerned with wishes of the other triad members (as indicated by the low level of other-oriented behaviors). Still they managed by first grade to make one single product together that was quite coherent and recognizable and clearly required some degree of simple interpersonal coordination. In the competitive condition, having to work by themselves and with very little direction, they were still unsure as to what was required of them and looked to each other just as their counterpart WC children did. However, having the skills to imitate each other, they came up with three acceptable, simple, highly similar products.

At each grade, their competence increases, as does that of their counterparts. However, having the added thrust toward independence and the added confidence gained from rewarding results reaped in a variety of situations, at each grade level they can function better by themselves in competitive conditions than can their WC counterparts. The older children have learned the meaning of competition well. They understand that in order to win, one must excel, and excel at the risk of being different from one's neighbor; they forsake the security that comes from alikeness, nondeviance, and general conformity. Thus it is that older UMC children's products, especially those of boys, become steadily less similar.

The last question posed is this: if UMC older boys are as competent, as confident, as achievement oriented, as attuned to each other's progress, why are they not doing outstanding work as a cooperating group? Considering especially that they have been able to work together since kindergarten, their combined strength toward one common group product could be spectacular. Yet it is not. At least it does not excel in creativity or complexity that of their WC counterparts, as we would have been led to expect both from their earlier performance and especially from their performance in competitive conditions. The answers may lie in their continued individualistic orientations. UMC children's greater task-related skill and potentially superior performance was not realized, we would suggest, because of their insufficient exercise of other-oriented behaviors needed in cooperative work. In collaborative work, UMC children pay the penalty of individualism when it is not tempered by concern for others. This individualism was encountered in the previous chapter among UMC third-grade boys, whose cooperative performance declined somewhat when they were assigned task roles that increased their individual function. There is also ample support in the Madsen series, which has shown the persistence of competitive choices to the point of being maladaptive (Kagan and Madsen 1972a), especially among middle-class children (Madsen 1967).

Thus upper-middle-class independence and achievement training may accomplish its aims of creating children who are self-sufficient, competent, and highly goal oriented. However, by praising children's independent pursuit of personal goals, parents and teachers may be unintentionally reinforcing their youngest children's egocentric ways of thinking and behaving. UMC training may be accomplished at the expense of children's development of other-orientations. Ironically in this age of large organizations and mammoth corporate structures encountered particularly in the occupations of the adults in this population, such individualism, if extreme, may be a severe disadvantage.

In emphasizing this individualistic extreme, we have spelled out its obverse as it applied to the WC children. If the very recent, almost ubiquitous strikes of workers throughout American society may be taken as an index of increasingly greater self-assertiveness among this population, we may be witnesses to considerable changes in values right now. Our data were collected in the early 1970s and thus may reflect earlier values. Of course our data cannot tell whether these children have simply less of the kind of individualistic achievement orientation we have assumed dominant in UMC children or whether they, because of their particular socialization, are actually more other-oriented. The latter interpretation would have to assume that WC emphasis on obedience to authority results in children's greater openness to adult social influence. This socialization practice may have the unintended effect of creating in children greater dependency not only on adults (including parents, teachers, and future employers) but also on age peers. It may have the additional unintended effect of creating greater responsiveness to others, as reflected in their heightened other-oriented behavior toward each other when asked to work together. In cooperative situations, they are able to utilize each other's contributions and to come up with products that equal, if not excel, those of their UMC counterparts.

These patterns of behavior are in line with the hypotheses pertaining to social class differences in respective degree of self-orientation and other orientation fostered in children.

The strongest and most recent support comes from Knight and Kagan (1977). Their sample of children paralleled ours fairly well. The ages of their urban Anglo-American children ranged from 5 to 9 years. Their upper-middle-class population was on the whole somewhat lower than ours, which was predominantly professional, while their sample contained only 35 percent in this category, with skilled labor represented most heavily. Their lower socioeconomic sample contained practically no families from the professional category and mostly working-class families, wholly in agreement with our working-class sample. They found working-class children making significantly more prosocial choices than did upper-middle-class children, regardless of age. This result underscores our argument that age-related differences in prosocial behaviors are in part a function of task requirements, game-theoretical tasks being less demanding of the presence of prosocial skills.

As far as our interpretation of interference by individualistic orientations is concerned, there is also considerable supportive evidence. We have discussed findings from game-theoretically based research showing that when children are disposed to make self-maximizing responses, they continue to do so even if it is maladaptive (Madsen 1967; Nelson and Madsen 1969; Madsen and Shapira 1970; Toda et al. 1978). The most direct evidence of the interfering effects of individualistic orientations is provided by Kagan and Madsen (1972b), showing that induction of a self-oriented set greatly increased competition, which interfered with the amount of the reward children could have obtained otherwise. This is also in line with the Loeb (1975, 1979) data that prior individual experiences with our task resulted in a negative transfer in terms of less complex figures produced in subsequent cooperative work. French et al. (1977), shifting their 7 and 9 year olds from contrient to promotive goal structures, obtained subsequent lower performance levels also but, on the basis of additional evidence, ascribed differences to practice effects.[3] The Kagan and Madsen (1971) and Loeb studies round out the pattern still more in that both obtained these results only with older, postoperational children. Kagan and Madsen reported 4 to 5 year olds unaffected, whereas Loeb's kindergartners showed positive practice effects.

The evidence justifies the conclusion that when children have developed necessary collaborative skills, self-orientation, be it individualistic or competitive motivation, inhibits working constructively with others. We suspect that this effect may be stronger the more role determined the cooperative task and the more numerous the group requirements. Our data support and our overall conclusions agree with Bryan (1975): "while the socialization of children into competitive response styles may well enhance achievement, mastery of skills and general success within a competitive society, it may have at least two negative consequences: first, competition may become an end in and of itself. . . . Second, competitive styles may attenuate cooperative activities" (p. 139).

Conclusions

First of all, we call attention to the coherent pattern of the data, rather rare in research of this magnitude. In particular, our demonstration of the course of development of other-oriented behaviors, with its considerable increase somewhere between second and third grade (around 7 to 9 years), is in agreement with many data supporting theories of social decentration. Our data certainly are in line both with the Piagetian assumption that abilities to take various points of view of the other emerge particularly during middle childhood and with research supporting this assumption (Flavell 1968; Selman and Byrne 1974; Selman 1976; Glucksberg, Krauss, and Higgins 1975). Recent research in developmental psychology is beginning to demonstrate the relatively early appearance of the ability in younger children to identify simple feelings or thoughts in others (for example, Borke 1971; Deutsch 1974). Along with such development of social cognitions may develop also rudimentary skills of role enactment. This seemed to be the case with many of our preschoolers who were able to make one common, albeit simple, product together.

Since our data stem from children's interaction around a role-related cooperative task, they bring to light some different aspects of cooperation from those obtained with different methodologies. Thus, other findings of an increase in joint choices to 44 percent frequency by age 8 must be juxtaposed with our data showing that 100 percent of UMC first graders were able to collaborate on a simple joint product. Or again, game-theory-based research found that older children on the average do not prefer making choices that offer joint gains. Yet we found that when they were placed into a cooperative situation where joint action was required, they all functioned in it and enjoyed it. All of this underscores our argument that making inferences from children's preferences in choice situations to their behaviors in cooperative conditions can be quite misleading. Our conclusion is that children are able and willing to work together in cooperative conditions throughout the elementary grades if certain conditions are met: (1) the task is appropriate to the cognitive and motoric skills at the children's disposal; (2) the children are not seduced away from collaboration by the irresistible promise of greater individual gain; and (3) the children are helped to work together.

The study of coordinative preferences is also likely to lead into quite different directions from the study of the social role behaviors we advocate. Our top priority calls for analyses of specific task role behaviors as well as group role-related behaviors instead of the global other-oriented measure we developed as a first approximation. Our methodology might be extended to setting up more specific task requirements during the process of collaboration that would demand, unequivocally, an understanding of collaborators' intentions, wishes, feelings, or other internal dynamics in order that a required group role could be executed in cooperative settings.

Our data on competition appear also to support and extend other research. Self-maximizing preferences have been shown to develop during the preschool years and to increase steadily thereafter (Toda et al. 1978). Yet our methodology revealed a very large percentage of young children—and persisting well into upper elementary grades—who made highly similar products. We argued that in a competitive condition, making similar products is counterproductive to winning and that, therefore, strong forces are likely to be present that operate against wanting to distinguish oneself from others. This interpretation is of necessity speculative; it can be said with greater certainty that there was very little, if any, evidence of the strong self-maximizing motivations presumably expressed in children's preferential choices.

Our studies did not note any of the devastating effects said to be experienced by children in competitive conditions, including anxiety, feelings of inadequacy, and so forth. Ames and Ames (1978) attribute such results mainly to the affective significance of failure in competition, and, we might add, most likely failures that occur repeatedly over time. In our instructions, success and failure were not mentioned; rather, the emphasis was on being the best. The two children in each group who did not end up as winners may have felt envious of the best performer, disappointed that they themselves did not finish first, but may not have considered themselves to be losers or actual failures. This may turn out to be an important distinction. It suggests that some of the negative effects attributed to the goal contriency of competitive conditions may be results of failure experiences rather than resulting from engaging in competitive contests.

One difficulty in making the suggested distinctions stems from the fact that the battlefield in coactive competition is internal. Its partial operationalization through measures of attention paid to others shares the same difficulty: it is complicated to identify particular motivations. What makes a study of social comparison important and yet problematic is that it may engage several motives, including their opposites. Wheeler and Zuckerman (1977) conclude that "looking behavior seems a promising measure of social comparison" (p. 361). After ten or so years of experimenting with this measure, we are somewhat more skeptical. True, we found that attentional behavior can be measured with great reliability. We have also shown that attentional behaviors occur in competitive situations with great frequency, equally between the ages of 5 and 11. It is evident that the behavior here too represents different motivations. Younger children, presumably less competitive, pay exceedingly much attention to each other, probably because they are motivated by procedural uncertainties. They appear to be at a loss when they look at each other and start imitating others. Older children's equally frequent attentional behaviors may represent attempts at assessing their competitors' progress, perhaps in order to differentiate themselves from others. Then again, they may pay attention to receive validation that their own performance is acceptable. But we could not tell from our data.

Perhaps in addition to attentional behaviors, recording simultaneous other behaviors might help, but we do not hold out much hope for that. We feel that progress may come about by the creative invention of methodologies that can match the recent theoretical advances in consideration of social comparison processes. For instance, coactors could be selected in terms of their known differential attributes—for example, one child being known as the smartest in class, another as barely passing, or being gifted in art, and so on—so that unambiguous interpretation could be placed on attention paid to coactors.

Our data, and some of others, contain suggestions that changes occur in the cognitive categories on which age-related relativistic competitive orientations may be based. Such categories may correspond at least in part to developmental changes in children's comprehension of number concepts. If so, the type of social comparisons made by children may go along with, be a function of, or in some ways reflect their level of cognitive development.

Cognitive processes studied in conservation experiments may be said to constitute studies in physical comparison (see especially Piaget 1965; Inhelder and Piaget 1969). As such, they provide much of interest to social-developmental psychology. The notion may be entertained of development of social comparisons parallel to growth in physical comparisons. These notions appear to be a promising approach to the study of children's social comparisons.

Piaget postulates global qualitative comparisons as one of the earliest steps in the process toward logical classification. These comparisons, he maintains, concentrate on general configurations rather than on specific items within stimulus figures. He argues further that such judgments may not require conservation, making their appearance perhaps even at the sensory motor stage when, for example, children are able to place three blocks in terms of order of size. Later development of physical comparisons is said to proceed through the ability to compare specific elements and to judge correspondence among all analogous parts, culminating eventually in the capacity to estimate equivalence and difference. These abilities are said to develop fully when children make use of numeration (using constructs susceptible to seriation and eventually more complex classificatory processes).

Along these lines, McClintock, Moskowitz, and McClintock (1977) presented evidence that 4 year olds apparently can and do define competition in terms of having more than others. Their responses may well be based on the early configurational processes that Piaget described. Some of our WC second and third graders replicated their products twice or several times when only one best product was required to win. Our interpretation was that "best" to these children seemed to mean "most" (that is, the greatest number of identical products), a judgment apparently based on simple counting operations and perception of equivalence. Older children's increasingly different products could reflect—in addition to their ability to understand that competition necessitates differentiation of self from others and willingness to do so—mastery of estimating concepts of equivalence and difference.

A similar developmental perspective may be fruitful in considering the choice of comparison others. Young children's choice of others for comparison may be based on global judgments, involving, for instance, others who happen to be playing with the same toys. Analogously, somewhat later, social comparison may be based on a number of discrete elements. Children still predominantly in the egocentric stage may base these judgments on easily noted surface qualities of similar others—sex, age, dress, even hair color. The development of social cognitions may lead to the ability to choose increasingly comparison figures whose similarity needs to be judged quite abstractly (for example, similarity of future goals) or inferentially (for example, she is as idealistic as I am). At some later time, children may acquire needs and abilities to compare with others who are different, and different even on several dimensions of considerable complexity.

We are in no way implying an invariable sequence in choice of comparison figures. It stands to reason that comparison figures are chosen within a child's cognitive limits at a given time. Additionally affective needs and motives will be dominant determinants.[4] In our view, comparison is a lifelong process. Young and old compare themselves to others as their needs and life situations change.

The next chapter is written from much the same perspective. It recognizes the vital role of comparisons with others in adolescent lives and attempts to understand them from a consideration of needs and goals that may dominate the adolescent life space, including the reference-group context available to adolescents. Since one of the main means that adolescents use in dealing with their concerns is that of verbalization among peers, adolescent social comparisons are studied within discussion group settings. This methodology enables Seltzer to advance from our global nonverbal measure of social comparison to a determination of several different types of verbal comparisons which are analyzed against the needs of the adolescents.

We may imagine our highly achieving fifth-grade boys from both schools seven years later turned into the high school seniors whom Seltzer studied. Her boys' sample from an urban public school was more varied socioeconomically and, on the average, was somewhat less affluent as compared with our suburban sample. The school has a reputation for excellence, and her subjects were taken from the top third of the class. Their active involvement in achievement-related discussion topics leaves little doubt but that they attach positive values to achievement and continue to have high aspirations for their future. Yet the extensive data Seltzer collected presents a convincing picture of young men who are almost deliberately intent on avoiding conflict within their peer groups and in fact fostering harmonious interpersonal relationships. Her study contributes further evidence for our conception of groups presenting to their members conflicting force fields between individual personal needs to excel, and hence to distinguish themselves from others, and the needs to be accepted by and be part of relevant others. As Seltzer documents, in early adolescence this conflict is often resolved in favor of remaining consonant with the peer group.

Notes

1. One might ask why besting occurred in the Hannah research in the preceding chapter. After all, it involved also coacting children. What is more, they were working toward a common goal, hence, even less, or no besting might be expected. The point is that the common goal changed the situation from one of coaction to one of colabor; interaction was deliberately required by task roles and group roles in the coordination of individual tasks. Interaction was further facilitated by common concerns deriving from the common goal. The commonality between task assignments, especially in the identical condition, was sufficient to elicit the triad of com-

parison behaviors. These achievement-related comparisons could be expressed behaviorally during the required interaction in the Hannah study. The present design created coactive competitive conditions without interdependencies other than those created by contriency of individual goals; hence, next to no interaction took place on the verbal level, and whatever competitive motivations may have been generated were not expressed behaviorally.

2. The relationship between attentional behaviors and product similarity was of considerable interest also because it was hoped to give some clues as to the function and meaning of attentional behaviors at different ages. Product moment correlations for these two variables, calculated separately for boys and girls from the two populations, showed the following relationships at different grade levels. At kindergarten, except for UMC boys, there was no relationship (UMC girls, .02, boys, .48; WC girls, .05, boys, − .03). At first grade, all correlations were positive and fairly strong (UMC girls, .56, boys, .44; WC girls, .26, boys, .55). From second grade on, the relationship at each grade level for UMC children was negative (girls, − .12, − .47, − .54, − .82*; boys − .62*, − .20, − .60, − .32). For WC children such a clear relationship was absent (girls − .16, − .05, − .59, − .97*; boys .01, − .23, − .03, .26) (level of significance * = .025).

The data for WC children are ambiguous. The positive relationship between attending to others and subsequent similarity of product for the youngest UMC children suggests that they examined each other's product for imitative purposes, and indeed, succeeded. After second grade, their attention to coactors has the function of distinguishing their products from those of the coactors in the triad.

3. We are inclined to think that the French et al. (1977) block building task was more structured than our task and required the execution of fewer task and group requirements. Thus their less difficult task might account for both their findings of practice effects rather than interference and an absence of age differences.

4. This latter consideration is one cause of our skepticism as to the generalizability of social comparison data that are gathered almost exclusively from a subject pool constituted by college students. Many, if not most, of these students may be at a point in their lives and in alien surroundings where congenial ("globally similar") companions may be most important to them and may be so chosen in total disregard of the choice alternatives provided by particular experiments.

Part III
Focus on Situational Variables

Social Comparison Behaviors of Adolescents

Vivian Center Seltzer

The earliest period of intellectual development, according to Piaget (Inhelder and Piaget, 1958), is characterized by a utilization of the five senses in what is referred to as the sensory motor period of intellectual development—sight, hearing, touch, taste, and smell—or sensory motor intelligence. The infant uses her five senses to get to know the strange world into which she has thrust herself. With the continuum of development and the achievement of the ability to conjure up and retain mental images, sense impressions can be stored and then retrieved for use. The advent of language is dependent on this storage. Verbal communications move into prominence as the way human beings expand their capabilities of learning more about their world. As development continues, the individual moves further and further with a complex ladder of skills by which socialization takes place and the child takes her role as a member of society. The senses cease their exclusive functioning and operate in conjunction with more complex and intentionally inaugurated strategies for coping.

The study of comparison behavior brings us again to regard with respect the role of basic senses, specifically sight and hearing, behaviorally distinguished as looking and listening. Social comparison theory has delineated specific components of this looking and listening to others when an objective reality is not present and has identified its invocation when a frame of reference is sought for some evaluation of abilities and/or opinions. Further development of social comparison literature has delineated both the reinforcement and the motivational components.

When we regard the circumstances that call forth comparison with others in periods of relative insecurity or doubt, how logical and how appropriate it seems to rely on foundational life-promoting skills. How logical that individuals, as it is said, might fall "back to basics," utilizing those abilities that introduced the outer environment and that were instrumental in handling earliest survival forays.

Inasmuch as the literature suggests a second intense period of insecurity and doubt during adolescence, it seemed natural to speculate on the fundamental function of the senses, specifically the eyes and the ears, in the period when the developing individual is once again assaulted abruptly from within (emotionally, physically, cognitively) and from without by the shock of new and insistent stimuli. The infant utilized what equipment came with birth, the basic senses, to acquaint herself with a new environment and to begin to handle herself in it. In like fashion, as a result of emotional and cognitive changes, adolescents are called upon to learn to handle an abrupt new environment of themselves, and themselves in relation to others. The key word here is *learn*. Coping with the demands of societal membership is not an automatic process. Yet old teachers do not suffice in quite the same way as they did before. For example, the acceptance of parents as guideposts, as in prior years, is no longer the case. Biological change, for one, has interfered. New strategies must be identified and new directions must be achieved. Where does an adolescent go in a frameworkless world?

The study we embarked upon attempted to offer an approach to this question. The formulation that follows sees adolescents in concert with the description in the literature as bombarded by new stimuli but lacking a framework, and it therefore offers the notion that adolescents move between periods of regression and integration. They regress to the first helpers, the senses, and then integrate information yielded by those senses. But cognitive skills acquired in the course of development are now fast advancing to completion. Cognitive growth has advanced to a point where adolescents can incorporate the concepts of past, present, and future. The sensory motor skills are utilized in connection with a cognitive awareness of the necessity not only to cope in the present, but that a future lies ahead and that they must establish a place in it. The look-and-listen process differs from the immediacy of satisfactions of the infancy period. Adolescents have moved beyond the concrete of the immediate to a conception of the present that incorporates the future.

Social comparison that is invoked in a period of uncertainty and change and is grounded in use of the senses also posits an internal looking that works in dialectic fashion with the external looking and moving back and forth in a series of speculations and assessments. (Intentionality and striving are essential components.) How natural it is for adolescents to engage in comparisons with others as they strive toward achieving knowledge of self and direction in life. Yet a review of the literature revealed that these theoretical connections had not been heretofore made. In fact, little has been done with exploring the function of social comparison in the adolescent developmental period. The theoretical structure from which this pioneer study draws its hypotheses incorporates notions from two discrete branches of theory: adolescent developmental theory and social psychological theory. Hypotheses have been formulated to investigate the dynamics of adolescent growth operationally.

Perspectives on Adolescents

The word *adolescence* is derived from the Latin verb *adolescere*, which means "to grow into maturity." The concept of adolescence generally goes beyond biological and physiological change to which the Latin words *pubertal* ("age of manhood") and *pubescere* ("to grow hairy") refer. Adolescence is considered to be a broader, inclusive concept that also refers to changes in behavior and social status. G. Stanley Hall is considered to be the father of the field of adolescence and is credited with moving the science forward from philosophical formulations to embracing the scientific method, but antecedents of current theories of adolescence can be traced to developmental notions implicit in the theories of Plato and Aristotle, to theological conceptions of homoncular man, to John Locke's doctrine of environmental determinism, and to Rousseau's eighteenth-century naturalism. These antecedent notions may be seen as falling within the framework Ausubel (1954, and Ausubel and Sullivan 1970) developed for the regard of developmental theory: preformationist theories, which represent the theological proposition of man's instantaneous creation (for example, the doctrine of innate ideas and Jung's "racial unconscious"); predeterministic approaches, which postulate the unfolding of invariant stages of development (such as Rousseau's internally regulated sequential stages, G. Stanley Hall's doctrine of recapitulation, Gesell's theory of maturation, Piaget's theory of intellectual development, Darwin's biological evolution, the field of embryology, and the field of genetics); and tabula rasa theories, which emphasize environmental determinants' minimizing genetic and biologic factors (humanism, behaviorism, situational determinism, varieties of cultural relativism). The current literature on adolescent development generally falls between one set of theoretical propositions derived from preformationist and predeterministic theories, which consider adolescence to be a specific stage characterized by storm and stress ("sturm and drang") that is pathological or near pathological in character, and another set of notions derived from the tabula rasa theories, which deem the vicissitudes of the period as not much different from the general ebb and tide of any period in the developmental span.

Exemplary formulations can serve as a framework by which to comprehend the potent forces underlying the outwardly observable erratic behaviors and associations that seem to characterize an age group more so than an occasional individual. Proponents of the stage formulation identify the onset of adolescence in the pubertal awakening and postulate a turbulent course incorporating a second psychological separation from parent in the service of individuation. This disengagement and subsequent self-definition culminates in an ability to unite intimately with a permanent mate and to fill a functional role in society. Psychoanalytic formulations offer views of adolescent development that seem to dovetail with external manifestations, observable in behavior, associations, and interests. Sigmund Freud's original formulation (1949) posited that pubescence heralds the onset of adolescence with a reawakening of sexuality repressed during the latency period of development. This sexual tension revives incestuous objects of the earlier oedipal period toward whom libido (love feelings) are directed. Paradoxically tensions further increase. An unconscious process of resolving the reawakened conflict in order to transfer libido to an appropriate object comprises the major task of adolescence. Vicissitudes of adolescent moods—perhaps the erratic, impulsive, hostile behavior of a previously compliant offspring—are often manifest as resolution is sought.

Anna Freud's concentration on the dynamics of adolescence within the framework of biologic drives and societal precautions advanced by her father may have been stimulated by her work with the pathological and her recognition that the adult personality is markedly determined by the mode of resolution of adolescent conflicts. She theorized that upon pubescence, the developing adolescent is catapulted into a position of extreme vulnerability by assaults to a weakened ego from strong id drives released from repression and by the rigidity of the newly structured superego. Adolescent turmoil is considered natural; adolescent equilibrium is not and may itself be pathological. For Anna Freud, there was no question that the task of adolescence is the reestablishment of harmony between and within the systems of the id, ego, and superego at the least psychological cost.

Anna Freud's (1948) development of ego psychology and the mechanisms of defense called into play to assist the ego affords insight into some of the often mystifying, outwardly erratic, and idiosyncratic behavior of adolescent youth. Two defense mechanisms are set forth to be particularly active in adolescence to assist in containing the anxiety signaled by the reawakening of oedipal fantasies. Asceticism and intellectualization serve to reverse the unacceptable libidinal impulses into action against the self rather than in service of self-desires. (Thus guilt is relieved.) Asceticism wages total war against the pursuit of pleasure, going beyond just the sexual impulse into eating, sleeping, and dressing habits, while intellectualization, often seen in theorizing and philosophizing and excursion into exotic philosophies moves the adolescent away from concrete satisfactions to abstract interests. Observable behavior masks the unconsciously desired behavior; often it is the complete opposite. For example rigidity and/or an uncompromising attitude can cover an unconscious fear of "giving in all the way" if precautions are relaxed even somewhat (Freud 1958).

The concept of the ego ideal is introduced by Blos (1962) as a route selected by adolescents to handle the changes set into play as they sever former guideposts. Blos's five-stage formulation offers an insight into the adolescent peer relationships that are observed to reach a crescendo in early and middle adolescence. Blos argues that in early adolescense, a peer viewed as just like the self is selected to function in loco parentis as a substitute support. He argues that psychological maturity and equilibrium is achieved through the freeing of libidinal ties with parents by way of transfers of the libido to a series of peers and models.

Theorists who subscribe to the societal (tabula rasa) rather than the biological end of the theoretical continuum do not see either adolescent turmoil and/or the turn to peers as inevitable and normal but rather, if present, as embedded within a cultural context and a societal climate that may reinforce these behaviors. This group of theorists contends that adolescence is but one period within a continuum of developmental periods and not one of essential or characteristic difference. Rather it is a continuity of social learning from childhood to maturity, both in and out of the home, which is seen as the elicitor, shaper, and maintainer of behavior patterns evident in modified terms even in later years of life (Bandura and Walters 1963b). Positively reinforced behavior remains in the repertoire; negative reinforcement, of course, is not encouraging of maintenance. The processes and vicissitudes of adolescent behavior are seen as externally, not internally, based. In fact, the structure of Western culture that compartmentalizes adult and child and continually reinforces this separation is considered by some subscribers of this view to stimulate the adolescent behavioral response.

Psychological theorists offer formulations that interlace societal factors with psychoanalytic constructs and, in a sense, bridge the theoretical gap between stage formulations that stress internal determinants and those of continuous development that stress external factors. A primary psychosocial exponent, Erik Erikson, modified Freudian theory in light of findings from the field of cultural anthropology and shifted the emphasis from only sexual conditions to include social conditions and organizations in which the ego must be rooted in order to develop normally (1950). Erikson's developmental model of eight life stages, each of which has its own conflict and crises to be resolved through a dominant task, cites adolescence as the fifth stage. The task is to establish an identity—a continuity between what the person was, is, and wishes to become—and to escape identity diffusion. Resolution, an unconscious process, is held to be rooted in and dependent upon the society of immediate people and accepted values; identity does not develop in isolation. Erikson contends that Western society makes no provision, as do primitive societies, for adolescents to fill functions and thereby try out roles in the process of identity formation. Therefore the peer group forms out of a necessity to provide a substitute structure where the process of identity seeking can commence, through interaction, diverse discourse while functioning as source for emotional support. Of particular pertinence to social comparison behavior is that Erikson did not specify, as did Blos, a peer stand-in who provides substitute parental functions; he sees, rather, a peer group. Erikson contends that by projecting one's own diffused ego image onto other peers and seeing it reflected, data are yielded to be used for self-clarification. While Erikson does not explicitly specify a state of tension among peers (other than the sexual tensions and their outward manifestations, which psychoanalytic theory posits as present in the adolescent), the formulation appears to imply a tension of another sort that accompanies evaluating and being evaluated—a reciprocal process rooted in one another as object.

Not only is biological change manifested in adolescence, but cognitive development, with its expansion of mental powers, also accounts for behavioral differences. According to Piaget, in infancy intellectual activity is involved with sensory motor activity, in eary childhood with the ability to hold the concrete image in mind, and then in later childhood to abstract upon the concrete image. The advent of adolescence heralds the development of inellectual structures that abruptly expand intellectual powers and scope. Achievement of formal operational thought enables adolescents to think in abstractions of all possible combinations; they are no longer tied by a need for the concrete image. And it becomes possible to conceptualize not only their own thought but that of others. However, in the initial period, there is a failure to distinguish between one's acts and those of another. The adolescent assumes that others are as obsessed with his behavior as is he. Behaviors are therefore stimulated to cope with this imaginary audience, which Piaget proposes as one of two mental constructions of adolescence. The other of the two constructions is a personal fable of uniqueness and immortality, which gives rise to an increasing sense of power and ability (which may be subject to limitation in expression by the pervasive sense of being in the limelight). A cognitive component is added in adolescence to the already active affective forces. According to Piaget, the interactions of both of these developmental domains give rise to unstable behaviors as the youth alternates between dreamer and innovator, recluse and socializer, extreme self-involvement and outward egotism and altruism. The task of the adolescent for Piaget is to decenter, a process begun in childhood but now involving a "continual refocusing of perspective and acquisition of multiple perspectives" (1958).

Piaget, like the theorists of the affective domain, sees the peer group as the available arena for working at this task. In contrast to the imaginary audience, the peer group functions as a real audience, projecting an interim reality. The actions that are accompanied by slow reconciliation of thought and experience transform a youth from idealistic dreamer to achiever. Strength or fragility may be discovered as they test out, one in relation to another. Piaget sets forth the adolescent cognitive condition, its manifestations, and the task.

Adolescent Peer Group Functions

Adolescence is seen as a period of acquisition of a new sense of physical and intellectual capacities and as a period when these new characteristics must be integrated into a self-perception which begins to fit into the immediate society. Few former guides or guideposts retain relevance during this period. The literature suggests that in sophisticated, age-segregated, technologically oriented Western cultures, the peer group is the only arena where important adolescent needs are met. Theoretical formulations in the literature generally divide between the notion of the peer group's serving one of three major functions. Some investigators focus on its affective environmental function: as an island from which to escape the tumult from without and from within (Josselyn 1952), as the only arena provided by an otherwise rejecting society (Friedenberg 1959; Goodman 1956; Bronfenbrenner 1970), a way station on the path to maturity (Keniston 1965), or a family substitute where libido can be transferred in the process of sexual identity resolution as well as an atmosphere for social play and an arena for external control (Erikson 1950). Other theorists emphasize its interactional function: an arena for discovering one's own limits and powers and assessing new value systems (Inhelder and Piaget 1958), a setting in which to try out new roles (Erikson 1950), a place to carry out functions of resatellization through the process of desatellization (Ausubel 1954), a source of intellectual decentering with the opportunity to experience feedback on emerging concepts and actions (Piaget 1958). Yet others focus on its end function: a place offered to work out self-definition (Friedenberg 1963), the setting to work through the developmental tasks of identity in love and work (Erikson 1959; Blos 1962), the arena within which one becomes free from the bondage of egocentric thought (Piaget 1958), or a subsociety that can serve the needs of a transition period with interests and responsibilities far removed from real responsibility (Coleman 1961). Within this variation of emphases, there is general agreement that the peer group society serves the transitional needs of adolescents and provides a framework within which they can move toward separation from their parents and independent functioning and away from the protective and sometimes intrusive environment of childhood.

The formulations referred to above describe the functions of the peer group. But a review of the adolescent literature found little or no attention paid to the interactional processes occurring within the congregations of peers and through which these functions may be enacted.

Relevant Social Psychological Theories

The field of social psychology, an area of theory quite separate from the concerns of developmental psychology, offers selected theories that deal with interactional processes and dynamics. A review of this literature yielded a rich area that seemed to hold particular relevance for application to the interpersonal dynamics of adolescents. As an example, Jones and Gerard's (1967) discussion of reflected appraisal offers an analysis of interactions that is directly applicable to what Erikson, in his discussion of identity formation (1968), details in his reference to the self-reflective aspect of growth. Earlier we established the adolescent literature as supporting the notion of adolescent frameworklessness where stable guideposts are no longer functional and where, in Lewinian terms, the adolescent feels like a marginal person between the psychological fields of childhood and adulthood. Festinger's (1950) theory of informal social communication provides an approach that may help to deal with the processes involved in adolescent attempts to assemble a structure for his own world. A primary premise of Festinger's communication theory implies that in the absence of physical reality, people communicate in order to establish a social reality. If we apply this specifically to adolescence, the exaggerated need of adolescents to talk and to discourse links directly with a need to communicate arising when traditional guideposts are absent. In order to communicate, it is necessary to have individuals one wishes to communicate with. Festinger emphasizes the need for similar others. The need for peer group affiliation fits.

Further support and further linkages come from Schachter's study of affiliation and uncertainty as well as Leon Festinger's theory of cognitive dissonance. Schachter's (1959) investigation disclosed that a state of uncertainty about one's emotional state heightens the need to affiliate while Festinger's (1957) theory posits a need to reduce dissonance and achieve consonance. Certainly the state of adolescent uncertainty and its affective component of insecurity fits. Adolescent uncertainty may indeed manifest itself in affiliation in hopes that contact with others who may be experiencing similar bodily, emotional, and intellectual change will be reassuring and will reduce feelings of aloneness and insecurity. Once the adolescent finds himself in a group of selected peers, not only is the existence of others who are alike reassuring, but there is also an awareness of other immediate, gross similarities.

Here, too, theory from the social psychology literature seems appropriate. Festinger posits in his theory of social comparison processes (1954) that when one wishes to evaluate one's abilities, an individual who is perceived as similar is selected for comparison. A community of peers who are in a similar stage and state of life do indeed provide the potential for more discrete comparisons. Peers are particularly pertinent comparison objects for the adolescent who is so acutely aware of having gone beyond childish identifications but has not yet attained adult status.

The easy blending of theoretical formulations from the social psychology literature dealing with forces for affiliation, communication, dissonance reduction, and comparison with those of developmental literature dealing with adolescent change, needs, and processes appeared to offer a dialectical field of reference quite natural to the study of adolescent interactional processes in a peer group. The decision to examine the interactions of adolescents one with another in a peer group setting grew out of a strong conviction that these interactions were not casual or ends in and of themselves but that they were instrumental to the adolescent developmental process—to unique self-definition and self-direction. A basic assumption of the study, therefore, was that the adolescent peer group is an arena in which growth-producing work is accomplished and that within this setting, adolescents assess their own status and progress through an examination of self in relation to others.

Before looking more discretely into the interactions within the group, we felt that a broader frame of reference within which to place the importance of the peers was necessary. Just what was the influence position of the peer group relative to other important reference groups? It seemed that the peer group could not be independent of the immediate or the greater social context. For example, to know only that the adolescent pays a lot of attention to a friend's advice on what college to attend was not enough. This information needed to be viewed within a general framework that told us also how much heed the adolescent pays to the opinions of a variety of other reference groups on the same question—parents and teachers, for example. Other than many studies that dealt with a peer-parent dichotomy, a further review of the literature revealed no study to date that dealt with the actual reference field of the adolescent.

Some brief discussion of some concepts in reference group theory seems foundational to picturing the topography and shape of the complex psychological reference field of adolescents. Reference group theory and research may best be seen as directed toward an understanding of the processes by which people refer themselves to groups. Reference group theory highlights the social interaction of most individuals with a diversity of persons who make somewhat contradictory demands. It takes into account that one can be influenced by a group without becoming a member of it. According to Merton and Russi (1937), one did not have to hold membership for it to be a reference group. They delineated two types of refrence groups: membership groups and nonmembership groups. In the former, the individual is a member of the group; in the latter, he is not a member but uses it as a referent and is influenced by its values. Kelley (1952) defined two functions of reference groups. A normative reference group sets and enforces standards. The function of a comparative reference group is that of being a standard or comparison point against which the person can evaluate himself and the other. These two functions may at any time be served by the same group and it can be either the membership or the nonmembership group. Positive reference groups as well as negative reference groups exist. Not only reference groups exist; so do reference individuals, who serve the same functions. Individuals may have multiple reference groups. Some reference groups may serve as stepping-stones (or tryouts) for other reference groups. The reference field itself is dynamic. Certain reference groups occupy a position in the reference field over a long period of time; others may be far more temporary.

The first pioneering studies in reference group theory are especially pertinent to the investigation described in this chapter. Hyman (1942) first explored the concept of reference group in investigating the question of self-ranking in terms of comparison with other figures. In 1943, Newcomb's Bennington study explored the effects of various influence sources (reference groups) in determining the extent to which female students allied themselves with the prevailing college political attitudes. Sherif (1948), Hartley (1952), and Stouffer et al. (1949) each contributed to the development of the concept of relative deprivation: an assessment of one's own condition that went beyond the observable facts to encompass the psychological components.

The peer group can be conceptualized in and of itself as a reference group. It can be either a membership or a nonmembership group; it can function as a negative reference group or a positive reference group; it can provide a normative or a comparative function or both; it may be the primary reference group or not; it exists in relation to varying degrees of strength of other groups or figures. It is vital not to lose sight of which factors are operative in the final status role that any reference group holds. Its selection is a product of individual needs, the social situation, social demands, and the potential for secondary reinforcements. The investigation of the adolescent reference field was structured within the context of these theoretical formulations.

A Study of Adolescent Reference Fields

The view of adolescence in the literature is of a transitional stage between childhood and adulthood. Adolescents are conceptualized as occupying a marginal position that has grown beyond the structural model provided by parents or guardians and seeking to structure their own framework. They exist in a state of biological change and consequent emotional fluctuation. The conceptions about themselves and the world are jarred loose from traditional representations, and the conceptual world confronts dissonance with regularity. Thus conceptualized as a marginal person, the adolescent literature portrays the adolescent as turning to and/or being torn between one of two major influence sources, parent and peers. The former has been a part of the social context. The second is newly arrived in time but strong in power and potential and many times seen as a rival to parents.

The conceptual model on which the study to follow was developed extended the potential sources of influence to include a broad range of reference groups. Within the context of a reference group perspective, the peer-parent dichotomy appeared to offer too limited a formulation. Since the literature on cognitive development portrays adolescents as being in possession of new cognitive structures, they are able to focus attention on issues that are not necessarily present-oriented or concrete in nature. It follows that with an expanded intellectual scope, adolescents would search out a number of influence sources and not limit themselves to only parents and/or peers and that each source of influence might vary according to the specific concern and the dilemma posed. In view of the developmental concerns, the newly expanded physical and cognitive skills, and the larger social context in which modern adolescents move, larger number of reference groups than is customarily found in adolescent literature seemed more logical. Therefore this theoretical model provided for an adolescent influence field. Parents and peers were seen as but two elements in this field of elements. Peer influence was seen relative to a number of other sources of influence pertinent to interests and age-appropriate concerns. Embodied in this approach is the notion that the adolescent cognitive field is labile and elastic and can incorporate a variety of elements. The model includes sources of influence that have been active most of the adolescent's life, others that relate to the concerns of this specific period, and others to the concerns of the moment. The model allows for the possible fluctuation in strength of each source of influence varying in accord to the number of other possible influence choices and/or their relevance to the issue at hand.

A review of the literature disclosed a paucity of reference group measures in general and little attention to the specific question of diverse reference groups for adolescents. Therefore it was necessary to design an instrument relevant to adolescent concerns incorporating potential influence sources. The theoretical position was restated in the form of six predictions.

1. Adolescents will utilize a number of reference groups, not just one or two.
2. Parents will constitute a major source of influence.
3. Peers will constitute a major source of influence.
4. New reference groups will be strong influence sources.
5. The percentage of influence accorded each reference group will vary dependent upon the specific issue.
6. The same reference group will be accorded differing amounts of influence relative to the specific issue.

The Sample

Since the purpose of the study was to identify reference group preferences of adolescents who were progressing along normal developmental lines, the sample included sixty-six adolescent males drawn primarily from the top one-third of the senior class of an academic high school for boys in a large eastern seaboard city. The school was selected because it drew from a city-wide rather than a neighborhood population and could therefore offer variance in background. The subjects did, in fact, represent major differences. Socioeconomic background ranged from professional and business class to unskilled labor. Three racial groups were represented, as were four ethnic backgrounds and five major religions. The subjects were similar in stable home backgrounds, normal developmental progress, and goal orientation. Seventy-two boys were invited to participate; sixty-six accepted.

The Instrument

In the absence of a suitable measuring instrument, the adolescent reference group index (ARGI) was developed. ARGI included fourteen discrete categories of reference groups. In the interests of mutual exclusivity and total inclusivity, the popularly conceptualized broad category of peers was refined into a subset of five peer reference groups that were conceptualized as serving distinctly separate influence concerns, as well as more global common concerns: school friends of the same age, neighborhood friends of the same age, friends two to five years younger, friends two to five years older, special friend. Nonpeer categories were: older brothers and sisters, younger brothers and sisters, media, clergy, parents, older relatives, school personnel, and a composite category of "other."

The index presented ten issues, which included concerns ranging from relevant political, social, moral, and educational issues to practical concerns such as fashions and hair style. An eleventh summary-type question was structured to provide an index of influence perceived by each respondent to be attributed to each reference group to be analyzed in relation to what percentage of influence actually was attributed. Three months of pilot studies with ninety-eight eleventh- and twelfth-grade normal, achieving adolescents drawn from public and private school populations in the city and surrounding suburbs were devoted to refining issues and reference group categories. Ninety of these subjects were male, and eight were female.

The Method

ARGI was administered to the entire group at one sitting in the school auditorium. Each index, in the form of a questionnaire, included eleven separate pages plus a cover page of instructions with an example. Each issue, in the form of a question, appeared at the top of a separate page. Each of the fourteen categories of reference groups appeared below the question. They were listed vertically. A blank, underlined space beside each category was available in which the respondent could write the amount of influence attributed. For each issue, the subjects were asked to select the category of reference group (as many or as few as appropriate) he would choose to consult in the course of reaching an independent decision on the specific issue or concern. Respondents were clearly instructed that influence accorded over all groups for each issue (one per page) was to total 100 percent. After the selection was made, the subject was instructed to assign and then record the percentage of influence he would accord to the opinions or information of each of these separate reference groups.

Results

The responses were collated according to the percentage of influence accorded each reference group per issue and over all issues. Four separate analyses were computed. Analysis I included responses of all students on a per-issue basis and an overall (totaled) basis. Percentages and rank were computed. Analysis II, a cluster analysis, combined data to reflect three traditional sociological clusters: family (parents and siblings), peers (five categories), and agemates (siblings and peers).[1]

Findings 1-12 were a result of analysis I, which was based on data from the entire group of sixty-six and over all issues. Item 13 was drawn from the cluster analysis, analysis II. Our predictions were confirmed. The data disclosed the following:

1. An adolescent reference field, not a peer-parent dichotomy, existed. Thirty-nine percent influence was accorded groups other than parents or peers (table 7-1).
2. Parents constitute a major source (20.5 percent) of influence (table 7-1).
3. The combined peer influence categories constitute a major source (41.4 percent) of influence (table 7-1).
4. Previously unrecognized reference groups were strong. Older siblings constituted one of these groups (9.5 percent). (Table 7-1.)
5. The percentage of influence accorded each reference group varied according to the issue considered (table 7-2).
6. The rank order of influence accorded each discrete reference group varied according to what the issue was (table 7-3).
7. Distinct peer issues exist (table 7-2).

Table 7-1

Mean Percentage of Influence, Standard Deviation, and Rank Accorded Fourteen Categories of Reference Groups across Ten Issues

Category	Mean %	Standard Deviation	Rank
1 Brothers and sisters, older	9.5	14.85	3
2 Brothers and sisters, younger	. 1.6	5.83	12.5
3 Friends 2-5 years younger	1.1	4.34	14
4 Friends 2-5 years older	7.3	10.77	7
5 Friends over 5 years older	4.7	10.38	9
6 Media	8.1	15.06	6
7 Clergy	2.4	7.63	11
8 Neighborhood agemates	9.2	15.76	4.5
9 Parents	20.5	20.01	1
10 Relatives, older	2.0	5.59	12.5
11 School agemates	14.4	18.05	2
12 School personnel	6.3	14.36	8
13 Special friend[a]	9.4	18.04	4.5
14 Other (please specify)[b]	3.5	14.65	10

Note: There were sixty-six subjects in the group.

[a]Subjects were requested to specify who the special friend was. Two-thirds of the responses referred to "girlfriend," 20 percent to best friend or buddy, and the remaining 14 percent to miscellaneous parties: intimate relation, cheater, far-away friend, another member of the discussion group, partner, person involved, male, female, close friends. The issues that elicited the most frequent listings of girlfriend were "living together before marriage" and "what to do with a day off from school." Also popular for the listing of girlfriend were "haircut" and "where to buy a jacket."

[b]Subjects were also requested to specify whom they meant by "other." Sixty percent of the responses referred to "myself" (notwithstanding the fact that the directions made it clear that the ultimate decision on each issue was most certainly the subject's). Apparently the issue stimulated a need for some to emphasize independence of thought. The three issues that elicited the majority of the "myself" responses were "haircut," "drug legalization," and "peer cheating in a test." The remaining 40 percent of influence was distributed among the following: acquaintance, political contacts, veterans, employer, scientific information not in the media, the cheater, married couple, psychology, computer, philosophy, God, people in general.

8. Distinct parent issues exist (table 7-2).
9. Older siblings penetrated both subfields of peer and parent influence (table 7-2).
10. Objective influence sources were preferred for informational concerns (table 7-2).
11. Authority figures (such as school personnel) were attributed little influence except in specific instances where they were presumed to have knowledge (table 7-2).
12. Constancy of parental influence was disclosed. They occupied ranks 1 or 2 on eight of ten issues (table 7-4).

Table 7-2
Mean Percentage of Influence Accorded Reference Groups per Issue

Category	Amnesty	Haircut	Year Off	Cheating Friend	Shop for Jacket	Drug Use	Living Together	Qualities to Look for	What College	Day Off
Brothers and sisters, older	9.6	8.7	13.4	8.4	9.3	10.0	10.3	10.0	10.8	4.2
Brothers and sisters, younger	1.2	5.2	0.6	0.7	3.1	0.7	0.9	1.2	0.5	1.7
Friends 2-5 years younger	0.9	1.5	0.7	0.8	0.9	1.3	1.0	1.5	0.8	1.5
Friends 2-5 years older	9.6	5.9	10.4	6.2	8.9	7.3	5.9	7.0	6.5	5.2
Friends over 5 years older	4.2	1.4	6.4	1.9	2.6	7.8	9.9	7.2	5.3	0.5
Media	25.5	1.1	4.3	1.2	7.8	21.0	5.6	3.6	6.8	4.5
Clergy	3.9	0.4	1.2	1.6	0.0	4.2	7.4	4.6	0.6	0.0
Neighborhood agemates	5.0	9.8	4.2	7.2	16.1	10.1	6.5	8.2	1.8	23.1
Parents	17.8	27.1	29.7	14.2	22.5	11.8	18.4	27.5	25.8	9.1
Relatives, older	2.6	1.4	2.4	0.3	1.7	1.2	2.0	4.1	3.6	0.2
School agemates	9.7	12.7	6.2	34.5	20.0	14.1	9.2	10.4	8.8	18.3
School personnel	5.0	0.3	14.8	8.7	0.1	3.1	1.9	3.6	25.2	0.8
Special friend	2.0	17.3	2.4	7.2	6.5	3.2	18.6	9.0	2.7	24.7
Other (please specify)	2.9	7.3	2.0	7.0	0.5	4.1	2.6	1.5	0.8	6.1

Table 7-3
Rank Order of Influence of Fourteen Reference Groups per Issue

Category	Amnesty	Haircut	Year Off	Cheating Friend	Shop for Jacket	Drug Use	Living Together	Qualities to Look for	What College	Day Off
Brothers and sisters, older	4	5	3	3.5	4	5	3	3.5	3	7.5
Brothers and sisters, younger	13	8	13.5	12.5	8	14	13.5	13	12.8	9.5
Friends 2-5 years younger	14	10.8	13.5	12.5	11.5	12.5	13.5	13	12.8	9.5
Friends 2-5 years older	4	7	4	8	5	6.5	8.5	6.5	5.5	6
Friends over 5 years older	8	10.8	5.5	10	9	6.5	4.5	6.5	7	11
Media	1	10.8	7.5	10	6	1	8.5	10.5	5.5	7.5
Clergy	9	13.5	11.5	6	13.5	8.5	6	8.5	12.8	14
Neighborhood agemates	6	4	7.5	6	3	4	7	5	10	2
Parents	2	1	1	2	1	3	1.5	1	1.5	4
Relatives, older		10.5	9.5	14	10	12.5	11.5	8.5	8	11
School agemates	4	3	5.5	1	2	2	4.5	2	4	3
School personnel	7	13.5	2	3.5	13.5	10.5	11.5	10.5	1.5	11
Special friend	12	2	9.5	6	7	10.5	1.5	3.5	9	1
Other (please specify)	10.5	6	11.5	6	11.5	8.5	10	13	12.8	5

Table 7-4
Rank Order of Influence per Issue, Mean Rank, and Ordered Rank for Five Clusters of Reference Groups

			Cluster		
Issue	Peer[a]	Parent	Sibling	Authority	Other
Amnesty	2	3	5	4	1
Haircut	1	2	3	5	4
Year Off	3	1	4	2	5
Cheating	1	2	4	3	5
Jacket	1	2	3	5	4
Marijuana	1	4	5	3	2
Live together	1	3	4	2	5
Qualities	1	2	4	3	5
College	3	2	4	1	5
Day off	1	3	4	5	2
Mean Rank	1.5	2.4	4.	3.3	3.8
Ordered Rank	1	2	5	3	4

[a]Peer cluster includes five categories of peers.

13. A clustering of influence categories revealed the pivotal power of various groups. When peers were clustered, they were accorded the top influence position of seven issues; parents occupied rank 1 on one issue. However, when a family cluster was introduced, peer occupancy of rank 1 was reduced to six issues and family-occupied or shared rank 1 on four issues (supplanting other groups) (tables 7-4 and 7-5).

Discussion

The findings of the reference group study lend support to the existence of an adolescent reference field rather than to a peer-parent dichotomy that has been reflected in the literature previously. Within this broadened frame of reference, which includes a breakdown of the global peer group, it is also possible to discriminate areas of distinct peer influence rather than being caught in a more abstract notion of a global peer presence. Five discrete peer categories provided information as to the sphere of influence that specific peers occupy. For example, living together before marriage was discussed most often with a "special friend" (often for the boys in this sample, the special friend was a girlfriend) and with a parent, not with peers. From another vantage point, peers were overlooked in favor of the more direct information route—the media or informed professionals when these groups appeared most pertinent. The areas of strongest influence for

Table 7-5
Rank Order of Influence per Issue, Mean Rank, and Ordered Rank for Four Clusters of Reference Groups

Issue	Cluster			
	Peer	Family[a]	Authority	Other
Amnesty	3	1.5	4	3.5
Haircut	1	2	4	3
Year off	3	1	2	4
Cheating	1	2	3	4
Jacket	1	2	4	3
Marijuana	1	3	4	2
Live together	1	2	3	4
Qualities	2	1	3	4
College	3	1	2	4
Day off	1	2	4	3
Mean rank	1.7	1.75	3.3	3.25
Ordered rank	1	2	4	3

[a]Includes parents and siblings.

peers related to style, leisure, and moral issues involving peers. Parents, by contrast, were generally accorded positions of consultant on future-oriented issues and as caretaker for concrete matters. The cluster data highlight the importance of the issue in the adolescent selection of reference group. Tables 7-1, 7-2, and 7-3 show that different influence groups were selected for different issues. Tables 7-4 and 7-5 disclose that the influence position of the clusters of reference groups also varied relative to the specific issue.

The data lend support to the evaluational and upwardly mobile orientation of the developing youth. They imply that adolescents move out with directed precision to that reference group or figure considered to be most relevant, having most information, and/or whose view is perceived as most pertinent to the issue in question. The findings revealed a discriminating student selectively seeking influence from the source he had determined to be functional to his goal.

The existence of an adolescent reference field rather than the peer-parent dichotomy has been supported. The continuing primacy of parent and family has been underlined. The cluster data and the more discrete data lend strong support to the significance of peers as an influential reference group. These data are particularly pertinent because they portray a very discriminating adolescent. Yet the peer group maintained top rank in seven of ten issues. The data support the premise that the peer group is more than a haven, an escape from the changing mind, body, and views of society. The data lend support to a conceptualization of the peer group as an influential, active body to whom the immediately pertinent issues are selectively brought. Involvement with peers is not selected because of a paucity of other available sources for relationship but because it is seen as the arena into which to bring relevant concerns.

A Study of Interactons in Adolescent Discussion Groups

The findings of the reference group study can be viewed as lending additional support to the notion that the peer group is an affiliation of choice rather than of last resort or escape. The findings also support the notion that the adolescent peers occupy a strong position in one another's psychological field. Therefore within the context of the freshly documented relevant nature of the adolescent peer groups, we moved into the next phase of the study, which was designed to discover what actually happens when peer groups congregate.

The purposeful interactions dealt with by Leon Festinger in his theory of informal social communication (1950) and in its further development into a theory of social comparison (1954) seemed to speak directly to the uncertain, transitional state and status of the adolescent whose task it is to establish both identity and direction. Festinger's basic premise is that in a position where there is no objective standard or reality, the individual communicates in order to assess his own opinions and to establish some type of social framework. The same condition—the absence of objective standards—energizes the individual to engage in social comparison behavior designed to seek an evaluation of his own abilities. To elucidate further the basis for this position, Festinger presented evidence from his level-of-aspiration studies that showed the instability of one's evaluation of one's own abilities where opportunities for comparison with others do not exist. Festinger reasoned that a person's level of aspiration reflects what he considers a good performance to be. In the absence of both a physical and social comparison, subjective evaluations of abilities and opinions are continuously unstable. When the person has no opportunity to compare his performance with that of another, the level of aspiration fluctuates, as does the performance. Insecurity accompanies the instability. We cannot, however, compare meaningfully with just anyone. The object of the comparison is of great importance to the success of the comparison. In fact, Festinger specifies that the tendency to compare oneself with some other person decreases as the difference between one's own ability or opinion and that of the other increases. It follows, then, that if in the absence of objective standards it becomes necessary to compare in order for a subjective evaluation of opinions or abilities to be stable, the comparison must be with someone perceived as close to one's own opinions and abilities.

Adolescents, who are in the developmental stage of transition and change and are identified with neither child nor adult status, exist in a state of instability and uncertainty. The peer is perceived by the adolescent to be the most similar to him. Therefore it logically follows that it is with his peers that he will seek to establish a social reality, to evaluate abilities and opinions, and to remove the dissonance resulting from uncertainty and questioning. Furthermore in order to accomplish these goals, social comparison behavior would be engaged in. In a pioneer attempt, we elected to explore these processes in a group of male adolescents.

Interrelated hypotheses were structured from the blending of developmental and social psychological theory as a summary conceptualization of the nature and functions of adolescent social comparison. The first of the hypotheses was exploratory in nature. It was a prediction that comparison behavior would occur in the verbal interactions of adolescent peers. The second held that the comparison behavior functions in the service of individual evaluation of one's abilities and/or opinions. Eight specific types of comparison that would reflect the upward strivings associated with abilities and the need for self-validation that is associated with opinions and values were predicted. These predicted types of comparison were conceptualized as serving developmental concerns of this specific stage of growth. The third hypothesis held that the types of comparison engaged in would vary with the discussion topic; thus discussion content would act as determinant. The fourth hypothesis held that social comparison would stimulate dissonant as well as consonant nonverbal response (reflecting action of the affective components).

Types of Social Comparisons

Post-Festinger research delineated specific types of comparison into more discretely defined categories.[2] From this social comparison literature, five types emerged as relevant to the theoretical linkage with adolescent theory and were therefore seen as instrumental to the adolescent task of self-definition and self-direction (see Seltzer 1975).

1. Upward Comparison
    Conceptual definition: An individual (or group of individuals) who represents a superior condition, attribute, or achievement.
    Hypothesized function: Serves the evaluational and achievement orientation of the adolescent and thus is with a person who has already reached a higher plateau. It is differentiated from the positive instance by its implicit attainability.
2. Comparison with a Positive Instance
    Conceptual definition: An individual (or group of individuals) who represents the ultimate condition, achievement, or attribute and

who is characterized by a quality of unattainability [examples are the Superbowl star, the winner at Wimbledon, the Hollywood siren].

Hypothesized function: Offers an uppermost parameter to the quality or achievement strived for, reflecting the evaluational nature of a broadened exposure. It offers the opportunity to compare with the penultimate. (This type of comparison offers the shade of fantasy that is not possible with upward comparison.)

3. Downward Comparison

Conceptual definition: Another individual (or group of individuals) who represents an inferior condition, attribute, or performance.

Hypothesized function: Serves the evaluative nature of the adolescent and/or the defensive needs for ego enhancement.

4. Comparison with a Similar Other

Conceptual definition: Another individual (or group of individuals) who represents a parallel or like condition, attribute, performance, or point of view.

Hypothesized function: Serves to strengthen identification of aspects of self and the need for self-validation, which accompanies the identification of another who thinks, feels, and looks similar to himself. Particularly cogent for the adolescent who is unsure of himself and/or the value of his attributes.

5. Range Establishment[3]

Conceptual definition: A form of verbal seeking that takes the form of outlining parameters; search and discovery through citing a variety of instances, each implying a comparison of self with reference.

Hypothesized function: Establishing the boundaries of an interim framework

Three other comparisons seen as specific to adolescence were newly conceptualized:

1. Comparison with a Goal

Conceptual definition: Possessing the quality of going beyond daily parameters or time-limited status.

Hypothesized function: Serves to accomplish a positioning of self in relation to a goal, either immediate or long term.

Comparison with a goal taps the adolescent awareness of his own transition to adult responsibilities. It catches the adolescent need to go beyond comparison and relate the results of the comparison of a specific ability or opinion to where the peer compared with is in relation to a similar or a different goal relative to the distance he himself stands in relation to the same or different self goal.

2. Satiation

Conceptual definition: An internal resolution of alternatives manifested by an abatement of the need to compare. Reflected in a philosophical stance characterized by a reasoned argument on a given issue, tendency to attempt to influence, a willingness to stand by one's own position in spite of opposition.

Hypothesized function: Affords an opportunity for an experience of closure on an aspect of self or underscores a previous experience of closure. Heralds a transition to influencing and convincing.

Satiation taps the incremental transition into a status of greater certainty on specific issues, reflected in the lessening of the need to compare.

3. Comparison with a Nonsimilar Other

Conceptual definition: An individual (or group of individuals) who represents a condition, attribute, performance, or point of view unlike that of self.

Hypothesized function: Serves to strengthen identification of aspects of self through identification of characteristics in others that are not those of self.

Comparison with a nonsimilar other is the converse of comparison with a similar other and occurs as a consequence of sufficient comparison having already been engaged in so as to make a distinction between self and other. It is seen within this model as a forerunner of or integral to the process that leads to satiation of comparison. This type of comparison is indicative of an increasing ability to affirm that what one is through a consciousness of what one is not.

Miscellaneous comparisons that did not fall within these definitions were coded as "Other."

In sum, the types of comparison may be conceptualized in a unit. The adolescent, in transition between childhood and adulthood, perceives the similarity of peers and shrinks his world to a manageable one, the peer group. It is within this world that he now searches for self-knowledge in the service of self-prescription. His frame of reference is bounded by what he finds to be the range of the opinions and abilities of his peers. Within this range, he stablishes and/or assesses his own opinions and abilities, comparing with the positive instance for his criterion. He may engage in upward comparison (someone superior to him on the criterion) and/or downward comparison (someone inferior to himself on the criterion). In order to validate an aspect of himself, he may look for a similar other. By comparison with a nonsimilar other, he can distinguish himself against a foreign ground. He may be motivated or disillusioned by his own performance or the accomplishments of others with whom he wished to identify as he assesses his advance to the goal. He may move in the direction of closure, which heralds the satiation of comparison. Along the path, he may alternatively experience confidence or self-doubt and may react affectively with consonance and/or dissonance (discomfort). He may affect agreement or disagreement. Increased involvement or withdrawal may be manifest. Each of these concepts was operationalized so that the behavior could be observed for occurrence, and, if present, documented.

The Sample[4]

The design called for participation of young men in an age of transition who were pursuing their goals with continuity and regularity. The processes of social comparison were predicted to occur in relation to values and abilities. Hence the sample was composed of individuals to whom abilities were important, and therefore they were achieving students. The design called for verbal discussion. Since individuals who rank in the upper portion of their class are assumed to be more verbal than those drawn from a broader range of general scholastic ability, boys in the top one-third of the senior class were invited to participate in the study. The sample school drew from a city-wide population of a large eastern seaboard city rather than from a specific neighborhood. Accordingly the students represented a variety of socioeconomic backgrounds ranging from the professional and business class to the unskilled labor class.[5] Two fathers were retired, two were out of the home, one was deceased. Three racial groups (fifty-eight Caucasians, five blacks, three Orientals) and five major religions (Buddhist, Catholic, Greek Orthodox, Jewish, and Protestant) were represented. Ethnic backgrounds included first-generation Armenian, Italian, Ukrainian, and Russian, as well as second- and third-generation students of Anglo-Saxon and Middle European ancestry. Sixty-two of sixty-six families were intact, with both father and mother living at home. In order to ensure the presence in each group of figures who could represent upward, downward, and similar-other comparison figures, the design specified that each discussion group of six was to include representatives from each of these three perceived scholastic status positions. Two weeks prior to the study proper, all students participating were assembled in a group session and were asked to rank all other students listed to participate as to whether they were perceived as high, medium, or low in scholastic status. Discussion groups were assembled with two representatives from each of the three delineated status groups.

The Setting and Discussion Format

In order to simulate a friendship group as closely as possible, an informal conference room was arranged in a manner resembling a den or living room. Doughnuts and standardized casual topics of conversation served as warm-up. Eight minutes were accorded each of four topics that students were requested to discuss. The content of two topics was achievement related. "Pass-fail" related to a possible grading system to be considered; "peer rank" related to the possibility of introducing a student-administered ranking system. Two topics were value related. "Straight-A or all-around man" related to philosophies of life and "friendship" related to interpretations of friendship.

The Methodology

The order of topic presentation was rotated for the eleven groups of six boys. Each successive group began with the topic that was second for the preceding group. A minimum of one and a maximum of three short probe questions were allowed for facilitation of discussion in a retiring group. The experimenter's only participation was to present topics and probe questions from an unobtrusive position in the back of the room. Pretrained research assistants observed verbal who-to-whom and nonverbal behavior. The verbal observer recorded behaviors predefined into specific categories. Interrater reliability was established at 94 percent for verbal observers and 90 percent for nonverbal observers in pilot studies and from videotapes.

The sessions were taped so that records of the complete discussions would be available for the coding of social comparison content. Both the speaker and the person addressed were observed and documented by the verbal observer during the course of the discussion group. Therefore in the analysis of types of comparison behavior engaged in, the who-to-whom data were available for analysis, as well as the content of the discussions for determining the type of comparison engaged in. For example, if a perceived downward member said directly to a member of his group other than the other downward figure, "I would like to attack that problem like you do," the direction of the comparison would be identified as upward. If, however, the two individuals were speaking of a third individual not in the group, the content of the remark itself would be the determinant in analyzing the type of comparison, if any. For example, a remark like, "Tom was always worse at chess than anyone in our clique," would be a downward comparison, while "Tom was as good a man as any of us" would be comparison with a similar other. Interrater reliability on distinguishing types of comparisons was 92 percent; interrater reliability on distinguishing statements containing comparison from statements not containing comparison was 98 percent. In addition to the coding of comparisons within one of eight types of comparison, comparisons from the interaction observation were coded as *direct* if they were expressed by one member to another member in the discussion group proper; as *content* if they were not expressed directly to or about another member of the group; as *peer* if they referred to a member of any peer reference group; and as *other* if they referred to a member of any other reference group.

The Behavioral Measure

Following the discussion period, a bulletin board observation task afforded a behavioral counterpart to the verbal comparison. Subjects could choose to look at Scholastic Achievement Test (SAT) performance scores of students from other schools and/or performance scores from a group drawn from the general population. Scores of the various schools presented opportunities to compare scholastically upward (suburban school of high reputation), downward (inner city school), similar (city school of good reputation), and nonsimilar other (general population) status positions. Observers recorded the number of boards each subject consulted and the length of his stay in seconds at the particular board selected. Interrater reliability had been established in pilot studies at 86 percent.

Results

An analysis of variance was computed on each of the eight types of comparisons over the eleven groups of six. No significant differences were found between the groups; hence subsequent analyses utilized data of the entire group of sixty-six students.

Types and Frequency of Comparisons. Since the study was a pioneer investigation of comparison processes in adolescent peer groups, of primary import was whether comparison behavior actually occurred in the verbal interactions. Data revealed strong support for the prediction of the occurrence of comparison behavior in the verbal interactions of adolescent peers. Of the 2,913 verbal statements exchanged, 906 (31.1 percent) contained statements of comparison.[6]

A striking finding was that of the 1,226 comparisons made, only 9.7 percent (108) were comparisons with nonpeers. References to parents, siblings, older relatives, or commonly known public figures were virtually absent. A large 90.3 percent (1,118) of all the comparisons made were directed to adolescent peers.

A most intriguing corollary finding is that although the students compared almost exclusively with peers, they rarely compared directly with the other five individuals in their six-man group. Neither did they compare any members of their immediate group to one another. Only 1.8 percent (22) of the comparisons were made with peers in the immediate group; 98.2 percent (1,204) of the comparisons were with individuals not immediately present. The comparisons appeared in the content of the discussion and were to someone not present.

The two findings may appear contradictory. The former data reflect a dramatic comparison of almost complete exclusivity with peers; yet the subjects all but ignored their immediate peers. A closer look at the data enlarges our understanding. When we examine the two sets of discrete data together, the implications that seemed to point to a lack of interest by one peer in another now appear to be quite the opposite. It may have been that precisely because of the high degree of importance the immediate peers held for one another that they could not risk offending. The data suggest that by avoiding direct comparison with one another and through discussion of adolescent peers who were not in the group, the members were able to stay engaged and the opportunity for discussion and for comparison could continue. To have compared directly might have meant offending the peer addressed or omitted. What occurred was an exchange about other peers that afforded a dual blessing of freedom to concentrate on the relevant concern with a minimum risk of offending. Perhaps the data connote an unspoken, intuitive awareness of the delicate manner in which relationships of primary importance must be handled lest they be injured or lost.

The findings reported in table 7-6, which sets forth the total number of comparisons per individual topic, provide an interesting note to our interpretation of the data. Topics that explicitly involve peers (peer rank and friendship) show fewer total comparisons than the topics that do not as exclusively involve peers but allow a philosophical stance. The findings suggest the inference that the explicit demarkation of peer topics may automatically simulate a more cautious approach.

The second hypothesis predicted the types of comparison that would occur. Eight specific types were predicted, plus a general category of "other." The eight types fell within two axes, validational and evaluational.

Table 7-6
Number of Comparisons per Topic according to Reference Group Context

Topic	Peer	Other
Pass-fail	316	28
Straight A	326	54
Peer rank	240	15
Friendship	236	11
Total	1,118	108

Comparison with the positive instance, upward, downward, and comparison with a goal are comparisons that incorporate an evaluative component relative to a standard or an achievement. They were conceptualized to lie along a vertical axis. Range (finding and establishment), comparison with a similar other, and comparison with a nonsimilar other reflect a validational rather than an evaluational component. An orientation toward establishing current parameters, likeness, and/or foreignness characterizes these comparisons. They were conceived to lie along a horizontal axis. Satiation was seen as intrinsic to the resolution of a developmental issue and, accordingly, viewed as nondirectional in nature. All types of comparison that were predicted did, in fact, occur (table 7-7).

Of a total 1,226 occurrences of comparison behavior, the number of type-specific occurrences ranged from 37 to 281 (3 to 22.9 percent of the total comparisons). Comparison with a nonsimilar other occurred the least and downward comparison occurred most. The most frequently occurring comparisons fell along the vertical axis where the focus was evaluational in character. Upward comparisons ranked second in frequency (19.3 percent), comparison with a goal third (15.1 percent), comparison for range establishment fourth (12.4 percent), and comparison with the positive instance fifth (6.0 percent). If we consider the positive instance conceptually within the framework of a further extension of upward comparison (since it was conceptually defined as the penultimate), upward comparisons then account for 25.3 percent of the comparisons. Summing the two types of upward comparisons (25.3 percent) and then adding downward comparison (22.9 percent), we find that 48.2 percent of the comparisons had a directional quality. In other words, almost half of all the comparisons engaged

Table 7-7
Total, Mean, Standard Deviation, Rank, and Percentage of Comparison for Nine Categories

Category	Total	Mean	Standard Deviation	Rank	Percent
Range	152	2.38	2.45	4	12.4
Positive instance	74	1.18	1.55	7	6.0
Upward	236	3.69	3.57	2	19.3
Downward	281	4.39	4.04	1	22.9
Similar other	117	1.83	2.03	5	9.5
Nonsimilar other	37	.58	0.96	9	3.0
Satiation	63	.98	1.86	8	5.1
Goal	185	2.89	2.96	3	15.1
Other	81	1.27	1.63	6	6.6
Total	1,226				

in focused on whether the person compared with was in a superior or an inferior position to the individual making the comparison. The evaluational bent of adolescent peer interaction is thus underscored. Within the framework of this evaluational imperative, the data point to what may also be the presence of parallel and coextensive needs. While the amount of upward comparison reflected aspirational strivings of the participants, the high percentage of downward comparison underscores a search for some balance or perhaps the reduction of tension provided by a simultaneous cognizance of peers who represent the lower end of the achievement continuum. (Certainly for some, comparison with a downward figure may also serve ego-defensive needs.) The intriguing feature is that both upward and downward comparison occurred in considerable amount and in near proportion. Perhaps what is implied here is a dialectic of comparison, framed by the parameters of achievement, that allows a more comfortable structuring and then a restructuring of realistic potentially attainable goals.

The prominence of comparison with a goal, at 15.5 percent ranked just under upward and downward comparison, lends support to its introduction here as a type of comparison specific to and potent in adolescence. It is important to be aware that goal-related statements at this stage are conceived as incorporating more than an estimate of how far am I from the goal, implying that a goal is settled. More characteristic at this time is a measurement process of self in relation to one or a number of goals. Statements of comparison with a goal are conceptualized to reflect a continuous process of back-and-forth evaluation of self in relation to the feasibility, fit, and attainability of a specific goal or goals.

The second newly formulated category of comparison conceived as specific to adolescence, satiation, ranked eighth, occurring 5.1 percent of the time. Comparison with a nonsimilar other, its conceptual partner and also newly introduced in this study, ranked last and just below satiation. The development of these categories of comparison had been stimulated in some dimension by Gordon's conclusion in his 1966 study of influence and social comparison as motives for affiliation. He held that once an individual is satisfied as to the validity of his opinion (and thereby freed of the need for social comparison), a desire to demonstrate the ability to influence other people is activated. Gordon's notions seemed particularly pertinent to our theoretical conception of the adolescent developmental process so the new category of satiation of the need to compare had to be formulated on an inverse conceptual base, which assumed that this type of comparison, by nature of its conceptual definition (an internal resolution of alternatives manifested by an abatement of the need to compare), would be present in adolescent interactions to a very limited degree. Findings of this study lend initial support to this formulation. The data revealing that satiation of comparison comprised only 5.1 percent of the comparisons underscore the lack of readiness of this group of adolescents to discontinue comparison behavior or, conversely stated, the strength of the desire to continue comparing. The rank at the end of the scale of comparison with a nonsimilar other underscores the lack of interest in an individual who appears different. The thrust at this point in adolescent development appears still to be to compare on areas of self concern.

The data in table 7-7 reveal that comparison with a similar other (the cornerstone comparison of the Festinger theory) yielded but 9.5 percent of the comparisons. It is possible that this puzzling finding could be reflective of a perception of global similarity with immediate peers, which thereby reduced the need for an even further validation of self and the discussions could then more freely center on more discrete, evaluational comparisons. Another set of data, however, supply a different perspective. These data may be interpreted to mean that despite a sense of global similarity, the participants did engage the validational and anxiety-reducing functions of comparison; however, they appeared to take a more direct route than comparison with a similar other. They utilized verbal agreement, a conceptual cousin to comparison with a similar other. Findings of the agreement-disagreement observation disclose that of the 2,913 total communications, 842 contained statements with some type of agreement or disagreement. Of this number, 70 percent (590) contained agreement.

Conceptually it is important to recognize that agreement is temporally different from comparison with a similar other. Agreement is defined here as the end result of a process of comparisons that yield a conclusion of similarity. Implied in the term process and absent in the definition of comparison with a similar other is a period of cognitive deliberation. (Disagreement, the converse, is conceptually defined as the end result of a process of comparisons that yield a conclusion of nonsimilarity. It is a conceptual cousin of comparison with a nonsimilar other.) Hence, while the end function may be close to identical, the coding was kept separate.

Bearing the conceptual relatedness of agreement and comparison with a similar other in mind, we see that there was considerable comparison with a like other. The manner in which the disagreement, which serves to distance one from another, was carried out is interesting. The data reveal that of the 29.7 percent nonagreement, 18.5 percent was disagreement and 11.2 percent took the form of "yes, but." "Yes, but" is conceptualized within this formulation as a form of disagreement that is particularly relevant to adolescence. Its character is tenuous, its dimension bipolar. In this period of self-evaluation, the need to be like a similar other is represented in the "yes"; the impulse for individualization is present in the dissent, the "but." "Yes, but" seems to bridge the gap.

The freedom to express agreement directly in the discussion is not accidental. Peer relationships are handled with care. Statements of comparison that may be interpreted as divisive are accomplished indirectly in the content of the discussion. Agreement, which will for the most part be interpreted as confirmatory, will enhance the relationship and therefore is directly expressed. Absence of direct comparison and the presence of direct agreement may be seen as alternate forms of the impulse to maintain consonant relationships with peers.

Nonverbal Measure: The Bulletin Board Observation. The same sample participated in the bulletin board observation task immediately following the verbal discussion groups. The task, designed as a behavioral counterpart to the verbal comparison study, may be seen in the same dimension as other studies that followed Wheeler's original conception of motivation as a determinant of what Festinger called a "unidimensional drive upward" (1966). In a synthesis of the work that Wheeler inaugurated and that was further investigated by Thornton and Arrowood (1966) and later by Wheeler et al. (1969), the authors considered it likely that individuals strive to determine first the range of boundaries and then to determine which end they are nearest to. They found that nearness to those worst off seemed to cause the greatest concern.

All participants had completed their college entrance exams (SATs) and had received their scores. They were anticipating the receipt of notification of college acceptances. Students were offered the opportunity to consult no board at all or as many as four boards that contained SAT scores representing upward, downward, similar other, or comparison with the general population opportunities. Time spent at each board was conceptualized to be nonverbal comparison behavior. The voluntary nature of the task was conceived of as an index of the strength of the motivation to compare. Observers recorded the number of boards each subject consulted and the length of stay at each board, in seconds.

The findings of the behavioral measure generally supported the verbal measures (table 7-8). Time spent at the similar other board (46.5 percent)

Table 7-8
Time Spent at Each of Four Status Bulletin Boards

			School Status				General Population Status	
Upward			Downward		Similar			
Mean %	Standard Deviation	Mean %	Standard Deviation	Mean %	Standard Deviation	Mean %	Standard Deviation
11.10	14.29	13.4	16.35	46.5	29.80	24.2	22.75

Note: Percentages do not add up to 100 because some subjects spent zero amount of time at specifi boards.

strongly supports the agreement data and the original Festinger premise that individuals seek out others like themselves to compare with. The upward and the downward comparisons were in the same relative proportion in the nonverbal data as they had appeared in the verbal data. The verbal measure reported upward as 19.3 percent and downward as 22.9 percent; the nonverbal measure reported upward at 11.1 percent and downward at 13.4 percent. Thus data from two independently operating domains reflect the identical dynamic and lend strong support to the notion that there is indeed a pervasive need among adolescents to know the parameters of achievement. The implication that knowing the range then allows a review of own relative posture is present in the data of the study.

An unexpected finding was the 24.2 percent comparison with the nonsimilar other as represented in the general population board. This high proportion of comparison is not found in the verbal data. Three possible explanations may be considered. First, the student may have seen comparison with this group as an opportunity to compare with a population that represented a range of abilities. This explanation is congruent with the data reporting the number of boards consulted (table 7-9).

Of the sixty participants who voluntarily consulted the boards, fifty-one consulted more than one board. Two-thirds of the participants consulted at least three boards. The data reveal that students were interested in a range of scores. A second explanation for the popularity of the nonsimilar other board is in the nature of the sample. This city-wide sample drew from a variety of racial, religious, and ethnic backgrounds. The general population scores may therefore have been perceived by many as similar, not dissimilar. A third explanation, which seems to be more in concert with the data of the verbal measures, is that the general population may have been taken at face value and the students thereby saw an opportunity to compare with a group that represented adulthood and maturity. If so, these data would be congruent with the findings of table 7-7, which disclose the impulse to compare upward. Conceptually this type of comparison might more correctly be regarded not as upward comparison but as forward comparison, just short of comparison with a goal.

In sum, the data of tables 7-6 through 7-9 reveal the occurrence of nine types of social comparison behavior in adolescent peer-group interactions. The extent to which each type was engaged in appears consistent with the

Table 7-9
Number of Subjects Observing Zero to Four Bulletin Boards

Number of boards observed	0	1	2	3	4
Number of subjects observing	3	6	11	16	24

posture and tasks of adolescents as presented in the theoretical model. Seven types of comparison reflect the achievement- and goal-related orientation of the sample that operates in this period of uncertainty, in conjunction with a searching for an interim framework and for evidence supporting self-validation. The data also disclosed a minority of comparisons that are theoretically linked by this formulation to the resolution of uncertainties and the consequent behavioral translation into influence postures.

Effects of Discussion Topic on Comparison. The third prediction that discussion content (topic) will determine the categories of comparison behavior was confirmed. A repeated measure analysis of variance was computed on the eight types of comparison over four topics. Table 7-10 presents findings of significant differences in amounts of comparison between categories of comparison, between topics, and between categories according to topics. Highly significant main and interaction effects were attained.

Table 7-11 presents the types of comparison for each topic. We had conceived the "straight A" topic to be one of the two value topics. However, a review of the transcripts of the discussion on it confirmed that rather than focusing as anticipated on moral aspects such as philosophies of what makes a worthwhile life, the discussions related primarily to whether outside activities interfere with scholastic achievement. This value topic thus was handled by students as an achievement topic, eliciting achievement-related comparisons. This reorientation by the students again suggests their achievement- and goal-related priorities.

Contrasting the predominantly value-related topic of friendship with the other three predominantly achievement-related topics, we find that the latter stimulated more evaluational types of comparison (vertical axis: upward and downward comparisons); the value-related friendship topic stimulated more valuational comparisons (horizontal axis: similar other, range finding, and nonsimilar other). This is in line with theoretical expectations. The comparison with similar other, ranking fifth in overall frequency (see table 7-7), ranks first on the value topic of friendship and only sixth or

Table 7-10
Analysis of Variance between Nine Categories of Comparison, Four Topics, and Categories by Topics for Amount of Comparison

Source	Sum of Squares	Degrees of Freedom	Mean Square	F-Ratio	Significance
Category	216.030	8	27.010	30.835	.000
Topic	22.498	3	7.499	8.016	.000
Topic by category	145.531	24	6.606	8.860	.000

Table 7-11
Total, Mean, Rank, and Standard Deviation of Each Category of Comparison per Topic

Category	Pass-Fail[a]				Straight A[a]				Peer Rank[a]				Friendship[b]			
	Total	Mean	Rank	Standard Deviation	Total	Mean	Rank	Standard Deviation	Total	Mean	Rank	Standard Deviation	Total	Mean	Rank	Standard Deviation
Range	26	0.41	5	0.67	33	0.52	5	1.01	35	0.55	3	0.83	58	0.91	2	1.22
Positive instance	12	0.19	8	0.43	43	0.67	4	1.20	15	0.23	6	0.56	4	0.06	9	0.24
Upward	67	1.05	3	1.34	85	1.33	1	1.66	61	0.95	2	1.40	23	0.36	5	0.78
Downward	80	1.25	2	1.40	81	1.27	2	1.76	81	1.27	1	1.42	39	0.61	3	1.08
Similar other	24	0.38	6	0.72	20	0.31	7	0.71	11	0.17	7	0.46	62	0.97	1	1.25
Nonsimilar other	5	0.08	9	0.32	4	0.06	9	0.24	2	0.03	9	0.18	26	0.41	4	0.83
Satiation	19	0.30	7	0.77	26	0.41	6	7	5	0.07	8	0.41	13	0.20	6	0.62
Goal	81	1.27	1	1.51	72	1.13	3	1.49	24	0.38	4	0.77	8	0.13	8	0.38
Other	30	0.47	4	1.0	16	0.25	8	0.54	21	0.33	5	0.70	14	0.22	7	0.45

[a]Achievement-related topic.
[b]Value-related topic.

seventh, respectively, in the three achievement-related topics. Along the same lines, the nonsimilar other category, overall least employed in comparisons, remains lowest ranking in the achievement topics but ranks fourth in the discussion of friendship. Adding to the consistency of these differential patterns is the fact that the overall most frequent comparison category of downward comparison was in frequency among the two highest ranks in the achievement-related topics. While ranking third on the value-related topic of friendship choice, it occurred there with only half as much frequency as it did in any of the three achievement-related topics.

These trends lend some support to our hypotheses and underscore the highly achievement-oriented character of our sample. Indeed during the pilot work, which was concerned with selecting suitable discussion topics, interest and conversation about achievement-related topics was more readily elicited. The trends obtained with the four topics finally chosen indicate an impact of specific discussion content on social comparison evoked. The data suggest that study of a less highly achievement-oriented sample may indicate sharper and still more clear-cut differences between types of social comparisons elicited in discussions that are differentially meaningful and relevant to adolescents.[7]

Nonverbal Affective Responses to Comparison. This aspect of the social comparison study was designed to tap the affective response to verbal interactions in the discussion group. A basic assumption in our theoretical framework held that the peer group goes beyond being the haven described in the adolescent literature and is bipolar in character. This theoretical formulation holds that it is a place where important work is engaged in and that the nature and function of the peer assembly itself can yield affective responses of either consonance/ease or dissonance/discomfort. Festinger's initial formulation (1954) posits the presence of hostility as accompanying the cessation of comparison. Recent research (Mettee and Smith, 1977, Brickman and Bulman, 1977) has begun to question affective consequence of comparisons. Festinger had merely stated that derogation may be present to the extent that continued comparison implies unpleasant consequences. Since both positive and negative affect are considered within this theoretical formulation to be resultant of the comparison processes that were predicted to occur, a fourth prediction followed that both consonant and dissonant nonverbal behavior would occur during the course of the verbal discussions. Consonance was defined as an affective experience of joy, pleasure, satisfaction. Dissonance was defined as an affective experience of discontent, pain, anger. In order to differentiate a dissonant affective response from a cognitive disagreement, disagreement was defined as a cognitive experience of difference, incongruity, dissent, disapproval and was included in the design. Operational definitions for consonance and dissonance were framed. The operational definition for disagreement involved head shaking in a variety of forms, expressed individually or in mutual eye contact with a peer.

The data revealed an active nonverbal component accompanying the verbal behavior (table 7-12). In eleven six-man groups meeting for thirty minutes of discussion, 7,810 instances of nonverbal behavior were observed to occur with a mean per subject of 122.03 nonverbal responses. Fifty-nine percent of behavior was dissonant, 39.3 percent consonant, and 1.7 percent disagreement.

Not all nonverbal responses were handled similarly. Behavior was coded according to the dominant orientation: either individually or mutually communicated and received. Individually handled was coded where the subject responded individually and made no attempt to communicate or share his responses with another. Mutually communicated and received was coded where two or more subjects communicated or shared a response with one another. Unsuccessful one-way attempts were coded when one subject attempted to share a response but did not complete the communication to one or more subjects.

Table 7-13 shows that 5,002 responses (64 percent of the nonverbal behavior) were handled individually; 2,394 responses (30.6 percent) were expressed mutually; and 414 responses (5.4 percent of the behavior) were unsuccessful attempts at sharing responses. Even more striking, however, are the findings on the orientations selected for expressing the consonant or the dissonant response.

With regard to the dissonant responses (which accounted for 58.9 percent of the nonverbal behavior), 99.8 percent were not shared but were experienced on an individual basis. The data on consonance reveal a reverse phenomenon: of the total consonant behaviors (which constituted the remaining 39 percent of the nonverbal behaviors), only 11.8 percent was experienced privately; 75 percent of consonant behavior was experienced in mutual nonverbal exchange with another peer. These nonverbal data, taken together, indicate unambiguously that when adolescents experience unease or discomfort in the group, they handle it individually; by contrast, satisfying experiences are shared with peers even on the nonverbal level.

Table 7-12
Amount, Mean, and Percentage of Three Types of Nonverbal Behavior

Type	Total	Mean	%
Consonance	3,066	47.9	39.3
Dissonance	4,608	72.0	59.0
Disagreement	138	2.16	1.7
Total	7,810	122.03	

Table 7-13
Amount of Nonverbal Behavior according to Type and Orientation

Type	Orientation		
	Individual	Mutual	One Way
Consonance	362	2,325	379
Dissonance	4,599	3	6
Disagreement	41	66	29
Total	5,002	2,394	414

The nonverbal data complement the verbal findings. We have seen that social comparison was dealt with highly indirectly. Rarely was open comparison made between members of the six-man groups, just as nonverbal dissonance was almost always withheld from open view of other members. By contrast, verbal agreement was expressed directly and openly, as was nonverbal consonant behavior. The nonverbal data lend further support, from another perspective, to the position of high import that peers hold for one another and the care with which relationships are handled. Certainly the amount of dissonance and consonance documented begs a second look at the unilateral conceptions of the atmosphere of peer congregations. Both joy and pain appear to be experienced within the peer congregation, but only the former may be shared; the latter seems to be almost deliberately avoided.

Cognitive Awareness of Affective Responses to Comparison. For purposes of ascertaining a cognitive dimension to complement the observation of nonverbal consonant and dissonant behavioral response to peer-group interaction, a questionnaire was administered to participants immediately following each group discussion. The Likert type scale was designed to tap each subject's level of cognitive awareness of affective response. Response to specific questions pointed to the action of a global comparative stance operative during the discussion period. There was a 71.9 percent agreement to the question, "I was aware of whether I knew as much as the group as a whole"; 87.5 percent agreement to "When someone said something particularly pertinent, I was aware of whether or not I could have given that reply too"; and 86 percent agreement to "I was aware of my relative standing throughout the discussion." Cognitive awareness of the operation of a self-estimate seemed to be present when the response was seen as favorable. There was 98.5 percent agreement to the question, "It felt good when I seemed to know as much or more than the others." The affective consonant response to upward comparison, which is experienced as successful, is seen in the 60.9 percent agreement to the question, "I felt good when I knew as much as or more than the person who I felt knew the most." Interestingly the data also reveal that there is not so great a readiness to experience or to acknowledge an experience of negative-reflected appraisal. There was 61.9 percent disagreement to "I felt badly when the others did not receive my contribution well" and 82.9 percent disagreement to "I felt badly when I felt I knew less than the others." Along similar lines, either the subjects did not cognitively experience discomfort or they denied an awareness of it. There was 75.0 percent disagreement to "At various periods of this discussion, I had negative feelings about myself," and 96.9 percent disagreement to "This was an uncomfortable experience for me at times."

In sum, the pattern of response raises some question as to the selective nature of cognitive awareness of affective response to comparison and to comparing. The data reveal cognitive awareness of a good feeling when friends receive them well and when comparison reveals that they are on a par with or above their peers. However, subjects were either unaware of the more painful feelings, or, at least, they did not wish to acknowledge them publicly. These findings lead us to speculate that perhaps the high degree of nonverbal behavior, particularly the dissonant response, provides a primary means for the expression of the more painful responses to comparison cognitively denied but affectively experienced and expressed. These data enlarge our understanding of the nonverbal behavior where consonance was shared and dissonance was experienced privately. It may be that the painful response did not always register cognitively but that the nonverbal response carried the affect.

The data on nonverbal response to comparison support the notion of this formulation that the peer group is an arena where both consonant and dissonant reactions are experienced. For the most part, dissonant responses were experienced in private and consonance was primarily shared. Some of the discomfort observed is most likely characteristic of the chronological age, some individually idiosyncratic and habitual, and some due to the nature and content of the experimental condition itself. However, in view of the large amount of dissonance observed, a considerable amount is seen here as reactive to the comparisons experienced in the interactions.

Implications are present for a closer look at the laughing, jovial groups of adolescents. Membership in an adolescent peer group can be a very lonely experience. Perhaps in order to cope with affective response stimulated by the dynamics of the peer group and to comply with its prescriptions that consonance be experienced in order to retain group membership, displacements of painful affect become the adaptive mechanism. Perhaps parents, siblings, or even available community outlets are the recipients.

Conclusions

The findings revealed that the peer group is in fact not a haven at all but a place where potentially important, growth-producing work goes on. It seems to function as a sorting house characterized by a pulsating, evaluational tempo where participants use one another not so much to compete as to compare. Verbal and nonverbal social comparison are active. The peer group is the relevant arena. This congregation is not casual; it is functional. Consonance at being with those in a similar state is experienced, as is the dissonance of comparison with a peer who appears more intact, along a diverse number of possible dimensions. The care that peers take in their interactions, the eagerness with which they agree, and the manner in which they cloak their more negative or potentially negative affect sheds light on the importance they attach to peer group membership. No wonder. This study revealed that it is within the peer group that important growth-producing work is done. The positive instance of relevance for the developing adolescents is not someone of another reference group but a member of their own. Their business is with each other. Comparison, self-reflective assessment, and goal setting is the action. Peers serve as both mirrors and models—positive and negative—for one another.

Data from this study imply that the search for identity addresses not only the question of who am I but also, the complex question of which way I can be. So as to go beyond being told or advised, adolescents test and compare themselves against those who have followed the same paths for the same number of years. It is here that they display and they measure. Membership in the peer group may be looked upon as an essential opportunity for adolescents to take opinions and abilities out of the abstract into the concrete. The data disclosed that together adolescent peers engage in a sifting process of what is real. The study documented something of what they do.

Notes

1. Two separate analyses were computed on the basis of sibling position. Analysis III examined responses of students who were the oldest child, and analysis IV examined responses of the youngest. Each analysis was performed on a per-issue and on an overall basis. See Seltzer, 1975.

2. Discussion of these categories can be found in Latané 1966.

3. Range finding that was dealt with in the literature in relation to nonverbal behavior was expanded in this verbal comparison study to range establishment. Adjustment of range finding to range establishment fell into the configuration of the three other types of comparison, newly developed, that are considered to be specific to the adolescent condition.

4. This was the same sample as the sample of the reference group study. Knowledge of potency of peers as a reference group was necessary to an informed perspective on data of this study.

5. Twenty-six fathers fell into categories 1 and 2 of the Hollingshead (1957) occupational status scale, twenty-five into categories 3 and 4, and 8 into categories 5 and 6. The occupational scale from Hollingshead is:

1. Higher executives, proprietors of larger concerns, and major professionals.
2. Business managers, proprietors of medium-sized business, and lesser professionals.
3. Administrative personnel, small independent businesses, and minor professionals.
4. Clerical and sales workers, technicians, and owners of little businesses.
5. Skilled manual employees.
6. Machine operators and semiskilled employees.
7. Unskilled employees.

6. Documentation of the occurrence of verbal comparisons was complemented by findings from data of a prediscussion inventory (administered two weeks before the discussion group experience to the group of sixty-six in one sitting). It tapped the extent of awareness the subjects had of whether they engaged in comparison with others. Findings disclosed a high level of cognitive awareness of comparison. See Seltzer 1975.

7. Chapter 6 demonstrated that social comparison occurs almost exclusively in competitive achievement-related situations when compared with cooperative situations. It is interesting to note here further that that type of social comparison differs as well when achievement-oriented discussion content is compared with value-oriented discussion content.

8 Considerations of Scarcity Conditions: Second Graders' Reactions to Scarce Resources

In popular usage, the term *scarcity* is imprecise, denoting some kind of insufficiency of diverse matters including material objects, manpower, information, and so on, and ranging from a temporary nonavailability of luxury items to a severe and persistent shortage of the resources needed to maintain life.

Poverty is synonymous with scarcity, if the latter is defined as severe insufficiency of essential goods. Economists call their discipline the science of scarcity in the sense that their problems derive from and must solve questions of the distribution of economic goods. No society can produce as many economic goods as can satisfy all of its people, so scarcity is present in every society. Thus scarcity can be examined at the level of societal organization, as it has been by economists and anthropologists. It may also be examined at the individual level, but here it has been largely neglected in research. Of course the two levels are interrelated; societal norms pertaining to distribution are man-made and the resulting distribution practices in turn affect individual persons.

Our primary focus here is on the individual level. We delimit our area of concern further by considering only scarcity with regard to material goods. We looked at the psychological reactions of children when confronted with situations in which there are fewer needed resources than there are individuals who need these resources (our definition of scarcity for present purposes). The research reported here is based on a relatively small exploratory study; however, the concept of scarcity and a number of related issues pose such baffling and challenging theoretical problems that their examination would appear at least of equal importance as the empirical study of children's behavior in scarcity conditions. This chapter, then, is intended primarily to clarify some issues in an area that is an important preoccupation of the modern world. Our own interest in scarcity-related issues stems from several concerns. Very little needs to be said to justify interest in scarcity on practical grounds. Scarcity today certainly constitutes a real problem in most parts of the world, all too frequently an agonizing one when bare subsistence is involved. As nations are increasingly forced into greater political and economic interdependence, the crises of one affect us all. Leading analysts already refer to our time as the age of scarcity (Barnett 1978).

In the United States, the threat of scarcity so far has mostly affected certain segments of society, but the likelihood that it will become a grave national problem increases daily. We already have witnessed motorists willing to wait in line several hours to fill up their almost-full gasoline tanks. Reactions to announced current gasoline shortages or future oil shortages in themselves would bear study; they vary apparently from absolute denial of its existence to concern with self-protection in the form of severe measures, such as adding another gasoline tank to the standard equipment, buying up wood-burning stoves, and the like. We have seen shoppers descend on supermarkets like locusts and strip shelves of paper goods, coffee, sugar, or whatever item happens to be rumored as shortly becoming nonavailable. Even without explicit scarcity threat, the mere presence of others desirous of the same goods presumed to exist in limited quantity results on sales days in frenzied grabbing for garments piled on tables in department stores. No additional demonstration would seem to be needed of the social relevance of an inquiry into adult expectations of scarcity and their effects. Emphasis should be placed at least as much on children, who will have to deal with these problems in the future. Yet there are no systematic experimental investigations of social behaviors of either children or adults under conditions of various degrees of scarcity.

Understanding children's behavior when faced with scarcity of relevant objects is important in its own right. We have referred earlier to psychoanalytic emphases on the role of treasured objects. Children's attitudes toward inanimate objects are intricately interwoven into their relationships with human beings and into the establishment of their own self-concepts as well. Chapter 4 discussed the facilitating functions of toys in establishing peer contacts. It is likely that their divisive function is better known; parents are all too familiar with children's squabbles over possessions. Psychological research in this area is rare. A notable exception is Furby's (1978, 1979) present series of interview studies of the meaning of possessions in developmental and cross-cultural contexts. Laboratory research is almost wholly absent perhaps because conditions are not easily created in the laboratory that would result in public fights or quarrels which are normatively prohibited.

Yet our persistent questions about scarcity began to take shape in the laboratory, stimulated by our observations of children in competitive experimental conditions arguing over possession of blocks, snatching them away from each other, even hiding them under the work table. On the theoretical level, we questioned whether conditions of scarcity at bottom are not in fact simply identical with conditions of goal contriency and, if not, where the conceptual difference(s) lie. This question demanded prior consideration of the characteristics of scarcity conditions. It also appeared that, perhaps even more than individual determinants, normative factors play a large role in the perception and interpretation of, and consequent behaviors in, scarcity conditions.

The Nature of Scarcity

Desired States of Being Versus Desired Objects

Competition may be over goal objects and over desired end states of being. In the latter, persons wish to distinguish themselves from others in some personal characteristic(s): wanting to be the best pupil, the fastest runner, the fairest in the land, and so forth. In this sense, the concept of competition is more general than the concept of scarcity, which is generally restricted to desire for specific objects that are in short supply.

The distinction is easily blurred: competition may involve goal objects, and possessions of scarce resources may represent a desired end state of being as well. One does not only desire money to buy food but one also wants money so as not to be poor. In fact, one wants to be rich, not only for economic well-being, but for the social gains that accompany wealth as well. Any consideration of scarce material goods must therefore include their potential symbolic value as well. May and Doob (1937) say that "in all cultures, material objects and prestige are interrelated" (p. 96). They distinguish between natural objects (those that pertain to bare subsistence) and objects with prestige (those that become needs as the result of the impact of culture). Yet they argue also that "even an object which serves some basic biological drive like hunger or sex eventually can afford its possessor prestige" (p. 97). Cultural anthropology has since provided ample evidence to support this view.

The fact that desired material resources and desired prestigious or other states of being exist in complex interrelationships in society is no reason for not separating them conceptually. In fact, it is a strong argument for isolating the different elements in the laboratory, as we did here. Our definition of scarcity excludes conditions where goal exclusivity involves only human end states of being. The concept of scarcity is restricted to conditions where the goal exclusivity involves desired material goods whose prestige value is controlled or manipulated.

Nonuniqueness of Objects

A short supply of biologically essential objects would be devastating to humans were it not for one characteristic of nature: there seem to be exceedingly few essential objects that are so unique that they can be possessed only by one person. In the state of nature, most objects come in a form that can be shared by a large number of people.

In consideration of goal characteristics in competitive conditions, we have emphasized that goal exclusivity is a matter of degree, unless it is deliberately created by humans. Uniqueness seems to be invented by humans, who invent activities deliberately designed to allow entry into the goal region to one individual only, perhaps as a means of stimulating aspirations for excellence in all.[1] Rules about degree of exclusivity of states of being in the goal region may be changed at will; some teachers may rank order students, thus making achievement more exclusive than do other teachers who employ pass-fail evaluations. As far as exclusivity of goal objects is concerned, it is human intervention in nature for one's own purposes that attaches value to uniqueness, that attempts to retain elements of exclusivity by restricting production, raising prices of rare objects, and in other ways attempting to make the valued unique and the unique highly valued.

The relative absence of uniqueness of objects in a state of nature allows us to specify two other characteristics of objects that have important implications for scarcity: substitutability and divisibility.[2]

Substitutability of Objects

Objects might be ordered along a scale of substitutability, ranging from identical objects (wholly substitutable), through objects highly similar along one or more dimensions, to completely dissimilar (nonsubstitutable) objects. Substitutability allows the receipt of quantities wholly comparable to those of original objects and thus has the potential of providing objects that are equivalent to the original. This property may be considered an antidote to scarcity. What makes substitutability a highly potent variable is that both nature and humans are expert at providing substitutes. In nature, each species faithfully and abundantly duplicates its kind, thus offering, at least phenotypically, identical substitutes. A rose by any other name not only smells as sweet, but one rose smells as good as another, for most purposes. Rose fanciers may object, and indeed very fine discriminations are possible, although we would venture to say that within a given range even experts' senses will fail to make distinctions. Lest humans be bored with such identity, by ingenious design the genotype is made unique; this allows sufficient variability in the higher species on the phenotypical level, yet it provides the apparently also needed similarity. Poets may sing of the one true love, and indeed there are persons who refuse what they might dub as inferior or inadequate substitutes. But abundant empirical proof exists that our passions can be fairly quickly and wholly satisfied by another.

Furthermore humans can develop skills of substituting at will for objects even though they occur in a state of nature (vitamins instead of fruit and vegetables). Hothouses may be substituted for poor growing soil or climate, and cloud seeding for rain. Indeed, twentieth century man has, through the art of mass production, perfected object substitutability of his own creations: the rows of plaster *Davids* and gold framed *Primaveras* in Florentine shop windows attest to that.

Divisibility of Objects

Objects may also be ordered along a scale of potential divisibility ranging from potentially indivisible to potentially infinitely divisible. Divisibility seems to be a property of inanimate objects. Animate objects are increasingly indivisible; a plant can be split up and still continue to live and grow and so can a worm but not a squirrel.

Inanimate objects, such as a stone, can be almost infinitely subdivided. Objects made by man are combined in ways that may or may not make them divisible, depending on how they are bounded. A typewriter ceases to be a typewriter if divided, but a loaf of bread is made to be divided and a slice still remains bread. Obviously the more divisible an object, the less its scarcity potential, unless the smaller size fails increasingly to meet needs. Divisibility permits the sharing of objects; it permits distribution of objects to more people but generally diminishes the absolute quantity received per person. Substitutability does not entail such limitations and hence may be more crucial in preventing scarcity than the characteristic of divisibility.

The Nature of Objects and Scarcity

The relative lack of object uniqueness in nature and the possibility of substitutability and/or divisibility mitigates against goal exclusivity. This factor alone reduces competition. Additionally the development of large quantities of substitutes encourages collaborative solutions to scarcity. Since many more persons are needed to work together in the production process or distribution process of substitutes, individual self-sufficiency is decreased. This is true for people living in simple environments, be they primitive people, peasants in villages, or dwellers in small rural communities. For the twentieth-century urban dweller in industrial society, mass production and distribution magnifies these factors to the extent that scarcity may be controlled so that it may be made to increase or decrease almost at will, although on the collective level rather than on the individual level.

The objective degree of severity of scarcity may be defined by three criteria: availability of number of objects in relation to number of desirous people, the divisibility potential of desired objects, and the substitution potential of desired objects. Objective scarcity conditions may be said to be maximal (most severe) the greater the number of people desirous of one object that is indivisible and nonsubstitutable. Scarcity conditions may be said to be minimal (nonexistent) when there are more objects than people desirous of these objects, and/or when these objects can be infinitely subdivided to satisfy the needs of all, and/or when an infinite number of identical objects can be substituted.

A distinction may also be made between a present, established state of scarcity and an anticipated future state, referred to here as scarcity threat. Only empirical research can establish the extent to which present experience or future expectation of scarcity have different behavioral consequents. One might assume that scarcity threat represents a more uncertain and more unverifiable condition. If so, individuals subject to scarcity threat may be more open to social influences than they would once a definite degree of scarcity is actually established.

Scarcity and Goal Exclusivity

We can now reexamine the question posed originally: are scarcity conditions to be equated conceptually with competitive conditions? Following behavioral implications of the first criterion for the existence of a state of scarcity—availability of number of objects in relation to number of desirous people—we would have to say that if every person wanted some of the objects under consideration and some persons would have to go without, in that sense scarcity conditions may be said to represent conditions with various degrees of goal exclusivity. However, in the case of scarcity of objects, behaviors associated usually with contrient goal structures do not necessarily follow.

Scarcity conditions do not necessarily elicit self-maximizing behaviors because normative prescriptions of ways of dealing with such objects, and sanctions for their disregard, exist in most societies. This is so especially if the scarce objects play an important role in the society. Every culture has regulations pertaining to interactions not only with people but in regard to objects as well. Postindustrial societies are organized around large-scale markets that control the supply, demand, and distribution of objects. This large-scale economic structure makes it almost impossible to isolate normative codes with regard to scarce objects as they affect specific individuals personally. However, anthropological literature that deals with primitive or peasant societies can emphasize some concepts and enable us to formulate some generalizations about behavior under scarcity.

Behavior toward Scarce Objects

Normative Factors

If asked whether scarcity conditions are to be equated with competitive conditions, anthropologists answer with a resounding no. Margaret Mead (1936) was quite explicit on this point, arguing that the forms of dealing with scarcity, whether cooperative or competitive, are determined by many complexly interrelated factors making for a unique culture in each society. May and Doob (1937), attempting to generalize from the voluminous anthropological data, wrote that there is

> not a fixed connection between an economy of scarcity or an economy of abundance, on the one hand, and competition or cooperation on the other. . . . Scarcity is one of the requirements of competitive behavior, but at the same time such scarcity might lead people to realize that goals can be achieved only by working with one another, i.e. by cooperating. In like manner, abundance might promote cooperation since then the supply sought is not limited; but it can also be said to favor competition when social conditions in the population have produced rules which compel people to view one another as potential competitors anyhow. [P. 91]

May and Doob also provided capsule descriptions of the thirteen cultures that Mead and her colleagues studied. The following transmit the flavor of the complex relations between scarcity condition and the varied social behaviors with which they may be met in different cultures;

> The Bateiga of East Africa are always faced with a shortage of food supply . . . yet . . . there is practically no competition in the economic sphere. [P. 91].

The North American Ojibwa Indians, where the fear of starvation

> is almost always present . . . meet their problems of scarcity by strictly private ownership of hunting territory and communal ownership of fishing places (and yet each fisherman retains the catch for himself), they do not cooperate as do the Eskimos when one family is starving. [P. 92]

> The Iroquois have a plentiful supply of food at their disposal . . . but even though the women could tend the fields alone, they cooperate to secure the added pleasure of each other's company. [P. 99]

Finally there are the Kwakiutl Indians, who also have a plentiful food supply, but where

> after the requirements of bare subsistence are met, under prescribed cooperative rules, the surplus of food and shelter and ornaments are used in a terrific competitive battle for prestige and self-glory against certain specified individuals. [P. 92]

Distribution of food under scarcity appears to be one of the most widely researched anthropological areas, yet there seem to be as many different reported distribution solutions as there are societies examined. The manner of preserving and storing food is of interest to our inquiry particularly as it relates to hoarding. The term suggests accumulation of more goods than immediately needed by an individual or group; it implies also that this is accomplished by preventing others from obtaining their share. Hoarding thus might be expected to be one of the important behaviors that occur in conditions of scarcity. In ethnographic accounts, it is often difficult to distinguish between storage of food for future use and personal hoarding. Indeed in naturalistic observation this distinction may be untenable.

Scarcity and Hoarding

Research into physiological correlates of animal behaviors has demonstrated important relationships between early deprivation of nutritional elements such as food or water in infant animals of several species and their later hoarding behaviors (for example, Hunt 1941; Bindra 1948). No such corresponding biological relationships are known on the human level nor should they be expected. Once again the accounts of anthropologists emphasize the intricate articulation of peoples' attitudes toward food and other material objects with their total culture. Nor is the distinction easily made between storage or other means of preserving food for future use on the one hand and deliberate hoarding at the expense of depriving others.

Richard B. Lee's work (1968) is highly pertinent to our concerns. He suggests as one criterion of relative abundance or scarcity whether a population exhausts all of the food within an area. In his study of the Kung Bushmen of the Kalahari Desert, he describes their inhospitable environment, which provides relatively few resources. One of their chief staples is the Mongongo nut. He points out that "although tens of thousands of pounds [of these nuts] are harvested and eaten each year, thousands more rot on the ground for want of picking." Lee describes how the Bushmen hunt and gather each day together and, at the end of the day, pool whatever they have collected so that each person receives an "equitable share." He concludes that "because of the strong emphasis on sharing . . . surplus accumulation of storable plant food and dried meat is kept to a minimum. There is rarely more than two or three days' supply of food on hand."

Lee's account suggests that individual storing or otherwise accumulation of food would be disruptive of the close interpersonal relationships. Pertinent to this generalization is Michael Young's (1971) account of the Kalauna people, a Melanesian society. Here families diligently cultivate their gardens; but then they appear to let the crop rot in sight of others, while deliberately abstaining from eating. At harvest time, each household pretends that its crop is poor, but at night family members secretly carry their yams into the house. This individualistic way of preventing food shortage for one's family only could well be called hoarding. Perhaps to balance this potentially unequal distribution, the culture provides a distribution ritual in the form of a competitive food exchange, the Abutu, in which food is given aggressively to embarrass the receiver.

It would appear, then, that the storage of food by separate individuals or families is associated with hoarding and is disruptive of interpersonal relationships. Social scientists see ceremonial exchange rituals prevalent in many primitive societies as ways of ensuring a redistribution of wealth. This was also Mauss's (1965) conclusion in his account of normatively determined reciprocal exchanges of material goods in ancient societies. He too focuses on the giving of material objects as a means of maintaining interpersonal relationships, a conclusion that still receives support today (Tiffany 1975). This exploration into anthropological research indeed confirmed that hoarding as a systematic social pattern is tied to individualistic life-styles, constituting in simpler societies a major self-maximizing way of dealing with scarcity threat. Since American children's self-maximizing choices have been amply documented in the research literature, as do our own studies of suburban American children, hoarding became one of the major dependent behaviors examined in our exploration of children's reactions to scarcity.

The Perception and Interpretation of Scarcity

One last anthropological study may serve to introduce our move to the level of individual analysis. George Foster, another anthropologist, attempted a far-reaching conceptualization of a whole range of behaviors based on peasants' particular cognitive orientation toward life (1965). His generalizations presumably could extend to all simple societies that experience an unalterable fact of land shortage. According to Foster, in the peasant view, just as their land could be divided or subdivided but never increased, so were all other things in life deemed existing in finite, limited quantities. This concept is relevant to our analysis of what constitutes scarcity: land substitution and the artificial creation of new lands were not possible, and subdivision could only go up to a certain point when it became too small to satisfy individual family needs. Thus the Mexican peasants studied by Foster, the TzinTzunTzan, can be said to have experienced severe land scarcity. Foster documents the ensuing mutual distrust and the deceitful and competitive relationships smoldering beneath the surface, ready to explode when evoked by minor moves on the part of others interpreted as threatening to their own subsistence.

In Foster's later, more detailed description of this Mexican society, one finds also accounts of attempts at redistributing wealth and intricate collaboration among different social segments (Foster 1967). Here once more the normative culture steps in to curb behaviors that become destructive to the community as a whole. It is particularly interesting to note that Foster sees the negative social behaviors as a result of each individual's own experience with shortages rather than as socially induced cognitions.

Individual Estimation of Scarcity

The perception of scarcity or degree of scarcity threat is in part a function of object properties. Our definition prescribes an operation by which an objective state of scarcity may be determined: a nose count compared with an object count, or projected future count of availability of objects. This is a very satisfactory operation in the laboratory; however, in nature and in society these counting operations run into difficulties. In a complex society where material goods exist in distant places, their presence only inferred as contents within mammoth container trucks, a person is rarely in contact with consumer goods before they actually reach the store shelf. Even then it is difficult to evaluate a threatened shortage of coffee when the shelves are stacked with coffee cans and there is no way of estimating the likely weekly consumption of others.

Let us make it clear here that our considerations thus far are limited to a state where objects exist in abundance in the present and shortages are threatening in the future, the typical case of affluent America today and of the suburban children who served as our subjects. The millions of starving children around the globe experience no difficulty in identifying a state of scarcity.

It is difficult to give credence to rumors of crop failures in a different part of the country when the only sources are public news media and when, in fact, available evidence (such as fully stocked shelves) goes against the rumor and no other objective criteria are available to verify it. This dynamic became evident in the pilot studies when we found that the children paid very little heed to our inductions of scarcity threat when they saw a box filled to the brim with blocks. Reducing the number of blocks helped to reinforce our warning about a possible insufficiency of materials. Estimates of present scarcity are difficult to make; estimates of future shortage are almost impossible to make without a reliance on some outside authority.

The properties of divisibility and substitutability of objects increase the difficulty of estimating scarcity threat. Should we really worry about a potential gasoline shortage when gasohol may be substituted; worry about a scarcity of heating oil when new advances in heating technology are being promised? Divisibility of objects necessitates their distribution; modern distribution processes are for the most part given over to impersonal agents so that the bases of distribution and allotments to areas are unknown.

These factors combine to make modern adults' relationships to the procurement of goods—be they essential or merely a matter of luxury—very distant and uncertain. Even those who live closest to the earth, the farmers, are notoriously uncertain about the success of a given crop or its potential market. The conclusion is that man's relationship to economic goods even in the best of economic circumstances is objectively fraught with uncertainty about their availability. In the light of uncertainty, individuals will impose their own interpretations on unstructured situations or listen to those of others.

Scarcity and Relative Deprivation

An inability to determine the objective state of scarcity leads people to make estimates, which will differ considerably. In the face of rumored potential scarcity, Ms. Jones will conclude that severe scarcity exists, Mr. Jones will consider it mild, and Ms. Smith will take unlimited availability of goods for granted and, if the rumor persists, deny it altogether. The interpretation of the state of scarcity is relative to a person's state of need, previous experiences, and so forth. Indeed it appears that the quantity of objects tends to be judged relative to something else. Thus in spite of the fact that it is possible to define and to create different degrees of scarcity, the severity is evaluated against subjective standards. One's routine, well-paying job judged after a period of unemployment is one thing and appears quite different when evaluated against a prior job that was more lucrative and exciting. Our own apple crop gains meaning when it is sized up against the number and appearance of apples on our neighbor's trees.

We thus have the paradox that while measurement of scarcity seems simple, it is actually a very elusive psychological concept that is very much dependent on cohort factors, so much so that this may be the very reason why behavior toward scarce objects has not been studied per se; rather the research area dealing with the experience of scarcity is referred to as that of relative deprivation. Labeled as such, it is recognized as an important area of research (Adams 1965; Pettigrew 1967; Crosby 1976). When the concept was first introduced into behavioral science to explain resentments by soldiers of higher-ranking officers during World War II (Stouffer et al. 1949), it was directly linked to the concept of scarcity. That is, in overseas theaters of war, supplies of highly desired goods such as liquor, tasty meals, and entertainment were scarce; if they were available, they were given to officers. Relative to them, soldiers felt deprived.

In relation to the perception of scarcity of particular objects, in judgments of severity of such scarcity, as well as in behavior toward scarce objects, individual background variables must be taken into account. Adams (1965) isolated three different processes inherent in the concept of relative deprivation: (1) the concept of the justice of one's conditions, the latter being evaluated in terms of (2) expectations of what one is owed; in turn dependent on (3) comparison with either one's own prior status or that of relevant others. Since then, each of the three concepts has been pursued separately with an increasingly narrower focus.

The studies reported in this book have examined the role of social comparisons in children's coactions. Comparison with other children is likely also to play an important role in their attitude toward possession of objects. Does a child who observes her peer taking a fistful of cookies feel that she is entitled to the same treat? Do all children feel this way? Who feels more deserving of desired goods: an affluent child who has never experienced the impact of scarcity, or one for whom going to bed hungry is a familiar experience? And how is feeling entitled to possession of an object translated into action? Theories dealing with children's conception of justice have a direct bearing on answers to some of these questions.

Children's Behaviors in Situations of
Scarcity Threat

According to Piaget (1932), children's conceptions of justice move from the initial self-interest of the very young, to equality (parity), and toward equity based on considerations such as deservedness along with developing sociocentrism.

Lerner (1974; Lerner, Miller, and Holmes, 1976), concurring with Piaget, described children who were learning to forgo immediate gratifications and learning to invest their efforts instead into activities that will yield more desirable outcomes in the future. Through such investments, the child is said to gain a sense of what she in turn may anticipate from others or, put differently, what she is entitled to expect from others because of what she has sacrificed in the past. And so, children are said to develop a sense of their own deservingness.

Lerner and others (Leventhal and Anderson 1970) have demonstrated that children as young as 5 years old can use the principles of both equity and equality depending on situational demands. Older children who were making judgments in solving moral dilemmas were found to distribute rewards easily according to their inferences about the actors' relative deservedness. In all of these studies, however, the children were asked to judge hypothetical situations in which they themselves were not involved as participants. In other words, they were asked to solve an interpersonal relations problem on the cognitive level only.

Contrary to these studies, we wanted to explore children's actual behavior in scarcity situations. Such conditions can be said to constitute moral dilemmas also: whether to distribute scarce but needed materials along principles of equity (which would have presumably meant equality in our situation, and hence of necessity depriving oneself to some extent) or to engage in self-maximizing acts (which again necessarily would have meant depriving others). These are in fact the alternatives that we built into our design. In order to complete their task, each of the children needed the same materials as did the other children; however, there were not sufficient materials to satisfy the demands of each child. If they were motivated by equity considerations, their concerns may be assumed to be reflected behaviorally in various attempts to distribute scarce materials equally among the members. Concern with satisfying their own needs would be reflected in attempts at preventing others' access to needed objects and gaining them for their own use.

This first exploration could have been conducted in several different ways, depending on our particular theoretical emphasis. To permit inquiry into the emergence of perceptions of scarcity and accompanying behaviors, children would have had to be placed into fairly unstructured situations. Focus on the decision process of children when faced with limited supplies would have required a situation structured so that they were required to agree about a manner of distribution. Our final design incorporated some of each of these features in a controlled study. Two degrees of motivation were created on the assumption that a relatively weak need for scarce objects may favor other-oriented distribution factors, whereas a strong need may be expected to translate into self-maximizing actions. In the creation of strong need, we raised competitive motivations; we attempted to weaken these same forces toward competition in creating conditions of lower achievement-related involvement. Further we expected these relationships to be accentuated by the severity of scarcity. Hence two degrees of scarcity were created. In a low-scarcity condition, sufficient blocks were provided for each child to complete the task without needing substitutes. In a somewhat stronger-scarcity condition, a shortage of blocks was established but substitutes were provided.

In discussing American adults' reactions to scarcity, we emphasized the aura of uncertainty surrounding the objects presumed to be scarce. In order to represent such typical scarcity situations, no particular blocks were specifically identified to the children as scarce; rather we induced a general expectation of possible shortages, thus producing a generalized climate of scarcity threat. The actual degree of scarcity was allowed to emerge only during the children's experience in manipulating the blocks.

Theoretical analysis points to scarcity threat as one of the most interesting variables to be pursued with children from the developmental point of view. To act upon an expectation of future scarcity requires an ability to project into the future, to have the foresight to provide for a rainy day, perhaps even to forgo immediate gratification for future benefit. All of these anticipatory cognitions may be recognized as demanding a considerable degree of decentering. The young child, attending to the single aspect of here and now and lacking in foresight, will respond to materials as they appear in the present.

Because of these considerations, our pilot studies explored children of different ages. Second graders were selected since we had demonstrated to our satisfaction that they had the necessary abilities: skills for copying from a model, understanding properties of substitutability of objects, and, most importantly, understanding the meaning of potential future scarcity. Children in this age group also seemed to feel less need to inhibit the expression of anger or aggressivity in fighting for their share than did children in the upper elementary grades, a feature that was also desirable in this research.

The presence of foresight by itself does not necessarily determine distribution practice; awareness of scarcity threat may be used either to satisfy oneself or to share with others. According to Lerner, children in the primary grades have developed a sense of their own deservingness as well as a responsibility to others; their sense of justice or fairness, along with their motivational structure, should determine their decision to allow others to share scarce objects equally.

The interactions of interest involved behavior with regard to objects as well as toward other group members. Pilot studies confirmed that needs for the same objects that existed only in limited amounts necessitate increased interaction among children. The expected behaviors were clear-cut, either other-oriented acts aimed to do justice to each member and/or various counteractive behaviors were designed to further own interests over those of others. We expected that this group of suburban second graders would engage predominantly in the latter modes of behavior, judging by our earlier findings and those of other American researchers. We also expected that aggressive and counteractive interactions would be most likely to occur in the condition of greatest scarcity and highest competitive motivation.

The Scarcity Study

The Subjects

The sample was made up of 117 predominantly middle- and upper-middle-class white children from all second grades of one suburban school. Since the relevant literature as well as our own studies suggested the likelihood of sex differences in behavior, children were assigned randomly to like-sexed triads in each classroom. The school used no systematic method in assigning pupils to sections, and indeed no differences were apparent in their behavior as a function of classroom treatment, so we combined the data from all four classrooms in the analysis. Among the sample was a group of children who, because of their exceptionally high measured IQ and so-called creativity potential, had been assigned to a state-mandated enrichment program for exceptional children. Analyses revealed no significant differences in the performance and interpersonal behavior between these children and other subjects. This is not surprising, considering that the group as a whole was of above average intelligence (only 8 percent of the children scored below 105). Their average age was 8 years and 5 months. The final sample consisted of nineteen boys' groups and twenty girls' groups.

The Procedures

In all major respects, the experimental procedures were identical with the others using the Pep board methodology. Each triad was brought into the experimental room and assembled around the Pep board where the materials were demonstrated. Because this particular study demanded a full understanding of individual properties of the block pieces, especially with regard to substitution possibilities, special care was devoted to acquainting the children with the materials. Each child found on her third of the board a sample of the six types of geometric blocks. Children were encouraged to move the pieces about and explore in particular their properties of substitutability. (For some shapes—the square, the triangle, and one thin rhombus—there were no substitutes possible; other blocks could be combined to make up another shape.) Without exception, once children understood this principle, they were intrigued with its possibilities and explored freely, encouraged and helped by the experimenter when necessary. When the latter was satisfied that each child understood and was able to perform the substitute operations, each child was complimented on her skill. These procedures were intended to reduce individual differences in performance skill and induce equal confidence and expectations of success in the children.

In each of the four conditions to which different triads were assigned, the task was identical: to reproduce with the available blocks a design depicted on a model. The design was a circular starlike picture that utilized all six types of blocks in an intricate-appearing pattern. The design was shown to the children while the working procedures were discussed and removed before the start of work. When the model was first shown to the group of children, they invariably exclaimed over its difficulty. Then the experimenter helped by describing a facilitating procedure: starting with the innermost star, working outward, counting the number of necessary pieces, and so forth. In fact, what each child was asked to do was scaled down to be a fairly easy task for this age group. The instructions reduced initial differences in cognitive and motoric skills. The instructions also provided that each child proceeded in the same sequence and hence needed the same blocks at the same time, with relatively slight differences in performance speed, thus setting the stage for the scarcity conditions to make their impact.

Experimental Design: The Four Conditions

All triads were told that they could talk during work; they would have fifteen minutes to completion; and the task was to make the exact same picture as the demonstration model, using the exact blocks, but with substitutions if necessary. Two degrees of competitive motivation and two degrees of scarcity were created.

Competitive Motivations. Competitive motivation was varied independently of the goal contriency created by scarcity. In the Low Comp Condition (LoC), children were told, "We want to see how close you can come to making the exact same picture. This is not a test; we just want to see if teaching children different things about colors and shapes can help them remember more. So we hope to learn from you." Just before the children started to work, these instructions were essentially repeated, with encouragement to take one last look at the model.

In the High Comp Condition (HiC), children were told, "We want to see who can come the closest to making the exact same picture. The winner will be the one who comes closest to making the exact picture." Again instructions were repeated before children started to work, with encouragement to "take one last look if you want to be the winner."

Scarcity Conditions. The issue of sensitization to scarcity is interesting in and of itself; the amount of material shortage that must exist before a state of scarcity is perceived or acknowledged is likely to differ between individuals and cultures. Since in this study we wanted to determine children's reaction to shortage, we created an expectation of scarcity by the experimental instructions so that it would be perceived by each child. No specific type of block was designated to the children as scarce; rather a general scarcity threat was induced. We did not wish to create extreme scarcity such that none of the children could have completed their task; this appeared to create highly complex decision situations with which we did not wish to deal in this first exploration. Two degrees of scarcity threat were created, both relatively mild, differing only in degree to which there was a shortage in the blocks provided to make an exact replica of the model. Where such scarcity existed, substitutes were provided.

In the Low Scarcity Condition (LoSc), relevant blocks from two sets of pattern blocks were combined so that each child could obtain all of the necessary pieces, with many additional pieces left over. They were told that substitutes existed—an explanation designed to create a very mild degree of scarcity threat—and were assured that there would be more than enough needed blocks for each of them. Specifically the children were told, "There will be more than enough blocks you will need to make the picture. Should you not find a shape you need, you can substitute other shapes as you have learned, but there are more than enough blocks so everyone will have enough to make the exact picture."

In the High Scarcity Condition (HiSc), some blocks from the set were removed so that only one child could complete the pattern exactly as depicted. The other two children needed to substitute for completion, and there were enough substitutes. The children were told, "For some shapes there will not be enough blocks for what each of you will need to make the exact picture. Then you will have to substitute. You will have enough substitutes so that all three of you will be able to complete the picture, but the point is that there won't be enough for each of you to make the exact picture you saw."

The two factors of competitive motivation and scarcity were crossed to make the four experimental conditions. Like-sexed triads were composed at random within each classroom, and then an equal number of boys' and girls' groups from each classroom were assigned at random to one of the four conditions. The final design involved five boys' groups and five girls' groups assigned to each cell, except for the LoC-LoSc condition, which lacked one boys' group.

Behavior Observation Categories

The pilot stage preceding this study required almost half as many children from a different school. It was necessary to determine the optimal level of difficulty for second graders and the optimal number of blocks to evoke a scarcity threat while allowing all children to proceed long enough to make a reliable determination of interpersonal relations. While this methodology was being perfected, behavior observations were developed and refined, and observers were trained in their use. Behaviors were observed in their several subcategories.

One box containing all blocks was placed into the center of the Pep board. Two observers scored behavior in relation to the blocks and toward other members of the group.

Sensitization to Material Shortage. Included here were verbalizations during work about a shortage: "I don't think we'll have enough"; "She said there'd be enough blocks, but I can't find any more pieces"; "There are no more yellows." Additionally in a postwork interview carried out in private with each child, the child was asked to indicate on a six-point scale the degree to which she personally experienced shortage.

Hoarding of Materials. The behavior of simultaneous search was scored when a child inserted one or, often, both hands into the box while the other two members were also rummaging for pieces. Although this action appeared to be entirely justifiable and proper, it seemed to be used for different purposes than merely searching for pieces. The box was so small that three to six hands rummaging could not really find anything but other hands. The rummaging, however, enabled members to prevent others subtly from obtaining the desired blocks; and if they were successful, to amass the needed pieces for oneself and withdraw them casually from the pool without appearing grossly possessive. This behavior may be taken as indicative of competitive counteraction as well as being a first step in the chain of hoarding.

The category of amassing materials was scored each time a child removed three or more blocks at the same time from the common pool. Removing desired materials ahead of time was our major operational definition of hoarding. Some children took as many as twelve blocks at one time, the number needed to complete a whole row depicted in the model. In pilot studies we found that most children's hands were too small to take up twelve blocks at one time, even though they attempted to do so. Thus for this age group, we used the removal of three or more pieces as a measure of attempts at hoarding.

Concern with Justice in Distribution Practice. This category originally included verbal and nonverbal subcategories. The verbal category had been intended to classify children's enunciation of different principles of distribution—equity, equality, and other. The nonverbal category was reserved for eventualities such as one member's distributing needed pieces among all three members; giving to each member a needed block each time she takes one herself; taking substitutes for herself and giving scarce pieces to other or vice-versa; and any other nonverbal distributions that may reflect a concern with fairness. None of these behaviors occurred during the pilot studies. We still kept these categories but designed two additional ones for the type of concern with justice we did hear in the pilot work.

For attributions of hoarding, verbal comments were tallied that implied censure or overt criticism of others' unfairness. These ranged from an explicit, "You are taking all the blocks!" to a less explicit, "You can't do that" (while the other calmly removes all twelve pieces), to a thunderous "Margie-ie-ie-ie" (as the latter dips with lightning speed in and out of the block box).

The attribution of unfairness was determined by a question on the postwork interview that asked for a rating of the relative fairness of each of the members on a scale ranging from one to six.

Competitive Motivation. Several different types of measures were explored to tap competitive motivation. Counteractions were involved in two of them.

"Desire to win" was a self-rating on the postwork questionnaire in response to a question of how much a child had wanted to be first.

"Verbal besting" is the standard category employed in our studies of competition and consists of statements that indicate one child's wish, intention, or confidence in surpassing the other: 'I'm ahead"; "You are not, I am"; "I am going to beat you"; "Joan will win, darn it"; "My design is the best."

"Mild aggressivity" was shown by physically constraining another child from taking materials or grabbing from other (often accompanied by laughter or joke).

"Strong aggressivity" was defined as actual fighting over the blocks or physical attacks (deadly serious for the moment).

Helping. This category recorded instances where one child would hand another a block, help place a block correctly on another's design, instruct another verbally how to proceed, or otherwise impart information about materials or procedure that was helpful to another.

Reliability

The observers were kept unaware of the specific hypotheses being tested. In this coactive situation, there was not a great deal of verbal exchange, and only a limited type of nonverbal behaviors occurred that were easily observable and fitted into the categories designed specifically to catch them. Observers had no difficulty in reaching the criterion of 90 percent agreement for each category before the start of the experiment proper. Biweekly checks thereafter revealed not only that agreement did not deteriorate but that it was almost perfect except in the nonverbal competition categories where unitizing aggressive acts or determining the level of severity proved occasionally problematic.

Results

A 2 (sex) × 2 (motivation) × 2 (scarcity) ANOVA was performed on each of the dependent variables. Table 8-1 presents the means for behaviors

Table 8-1
Second Graders' Mean Behaviors in Different Conditions of Motivation and Scarcity Threat

| Dependent Behaviors | Sex | | | Experimental Conditions | | | | | | Significant Interaction Effects | F |
| | Boys | Girls | F | Competition | | | Scarcity | | | | |
				LoC	HiC	F	LoSc	HiSc	F		
Sensitization											
Verbalization during work	.54	.52	n.s.	.68	.38	n.s.	.18	.87	11.34***	Sx × Cx Sc	4.81*
Postwork ratings	2.33	2.05	n.s.	2.16	2.22	n.s.	1.96	2.40	5.52*		
Hoarding											
Simultaneous search	.84	1.30	3.18*	1.09	1.07	n.s.	.82	1.32	3.56*		
Amassing materials	1.32	1.28	n.s.	1.23	1.37	n.s.	1.04	1.55	4.44*		
Distributive Justice											
Equity concerns	0.00	0.00	n.s.	0.00	0.00	n.s.	0.00	0.00	n.s.		
Hoarding attributions	.37	.38	n.s.	.14	.60	7.56**	.11	.63	9.83**	Sc × C	5.59*
Unfairness attributions	19.18	13.52	25.39***	17.09	15.50	n.s.	12.93	19.45	33.27***		
Achievement-related acts											
Desire to win	2.65	2.63	n.s.	2.37	2.90	5.34*	2.23	3.03	11.72***	Sx × C	5.48***
Verbal besting	1.67	.62	5.33**	.51	1.72	8.02**	.19	2.02	21.15***	Sx × C / Sx × Sc / C × Sc / Sx × C × Sc	3.65* / 4.35* / 4.67*** / 9.65***
Mild aggressivity	.39	.12	4.88*	.25	.25	n.s.	.16	.33	n.s.		
Strong aggressivity	.79	.10	14.56***	.51	.37	n.s.	.05	.80	16.88***	Sx × Sc	9.58***
Helping	.46	.50	n.s.	.61	.35	n.s.	.21	.73	12.11***		

*p < .05.
**p < .01.
***p < .001.

and questionnaire responses for the three grouping factors. Levels of significance are indicated for main and interaction effects.

Sensitization to Material Shortage. We had intended to create two degrees of fairly mild scarcity threat. The data pertaining to sensitization indicate that we were successful; there was relatively little talk about shortage (on the average less than one comment), although significantly more of it in the HiSc conditions. The postwork interviews provide confirmation. In LoSc, the mean rating in answer to whether there had been sufficient materials was between 1 ("more than enough") and 2 ("enough"); in the HiSc condition it was between 2 and 3 ("somewhat short').

The level of verbalization during work decreased slightly in the HiC condition, though not significantly so. This trend is in line with the decrease in verbalization under competitive conditions demonstrated in earlier chapters. Although there were no main effects for sex, the significant triple interaction deserves some attention. Most talk about shortage occurred in the HiSc condition. When HiSc is combined with LoC (HiSc-LoC), girls in that condition had an average of 1.47. In the HiSc-HiC condition, girls averaged .20. This trend suggests that when girls experience scarcity and believe they are merely helping the experimenter (in HiSc-LoC), they are not threatened; they feel their abilities are not called into question, and their achievement motives and related fears of failure are not activated. Under those conditions, girls feel free to talk about not having enough materials to complete the task. When girls are asked to compete, they fall into silence when they experience scarcity. The trend for the boys was reversed: they almost doubled their talk about shortage in the HiSc-HiC conditions. This subtle but strong trend is indicative of additional sex differences in response to competition and scarcity.

Concern with Justice in Distribution Practice. It is evident that although the children acknowledged the scarcity threat, their responses to it were entirely individualistic. No group in any of the conditions, and not a single child in any of the groups, suggested by word or deed that there ought to be some sort of equitable distribution. This was so even when the scarcity threat was practically nonexistent and the children in the LoC-LoSc condition were told that they were only helping the experimenter. As shortage became apparent in the LoC-HiSc condition, still no one expressed care for the success of others in the group who might be deprived of the needed resources or substitutes.

Once the hypothesis has been rejected that these children were concerned with fairness to other members of the triad, all other data fall into place.

Hoarding and Besting Behaviors. In conditions of HiSc, as compared with LoSc conditions, children showed more simultaneous rummaging for blocks, taking more often more than three blocks at a time for themselves, and more often accusing each other of hoarding and unfairly taking blocks from the others. The increase in hoarding behaviors occurred only in the HiSc conditions and not in the HiC conditions, suggesting a difference between scarcity and competitive conditions. In the former, a relatively greater need for required objects seemed to be experienced. The significant interaction for the attribution of hoarding indicates that when high goal contriency is combined with scarcity threat (HiSc-HiC), children react to each other as competitors for scarce goods rather than looking for fair collaborative solutions.

The same trends were apparent when achievement-related behaviors were considered. Children in the HiC condition and the HiSc conditions expressed significantly stronger motivation to win than they did in corresponding Lo conditions. As expected, in both the HiSc and the HiSc conditions, there was significantly more besting. Strong motivation to win in the HiC condition did not elicit aggression, but strong aggression was found significantly more frequently in the HiSc condition. The children's attribution of the most unfair behaviors occurring in the HiSc condition in fact appears objectively so.

Sex Differences. Although girls hoarded as much as boys did, there was a strong trend for girls to engage in more simultaneous search than did the boys. These findings, along with the girls' strong motivation to win, suggest that the girls may be as achievement oriented as boys but respond in a more subtle, less aggressive way. Rummaging for blocks is a subdued but crafty and perhaps equally (or more) effective way of competing. Under the pretense of looking for blocks in the common box, the girls kept their hands in the box at the same time, held on to the needed pieces, and then quickly removed what they wanted, frequently preventing the other two from taking what they needed. This prolonged simultaneous search behavior was the only main effect for sex that showed a higher frequency for girls than for boys.

Boys were clearly more overt in their besting than were girls, they were more verbal in taunting their competitors, and they were physically more aggressive than the girls. The boys dispensed with polite pretense and expressed their wants physically and directly; they grabbed pieces from each other when they needed them (not with high frequency to be sure but significantly more often than did the girls), and consequently had open fights over (and sometimes with) the needed blocks. The various interaction effects both for verbal besting behaviors and nonverbal aggresion leave no doubt that when boys are highly motivated to win and needed supplies are scarce, they especially wish to maximize their own gain and actively fight to obtain it. In the HiSc-HiC conditions, boys had an average of 8.00 for verbal besting and 1.33 for strong aggressivity, as opposed to the girls' .53 and 0.00, respectively. Here, too, then, are objective reasons for boys to accuse each other of unfairness, for indeed they behaved in such a manner.

Helping Behaviors. We noted at the outset the absence of verbal concern for other groups members' performance outcomes. Different helping behaviors that might have aided the progress of coworkers—handing blocks to another child or suggesting procedures, for example—showed equally low averages in all conditions. Even so helping did occur with significantly higher frequency in the HiSc condition, a finding that contradicts our expectations. We had assumed that any helping or other-oriented behaviors would occur in the condition where materials were freely available and competition low. This trend must be viewed in relation to the significant triple interaction of sex × competition × scarcity. Girls in the HiSc-HiC condition averaged .33 for helping, as opposed to the significantly greater average for boys (.87). In all groups, children who had completed their task were asked to sit at another table and to wait for the others who were still working. A number of boys who had finished returned to the table and helped the losers to substitute blocks in order to complete the design. This behavior, of course, cannot be strictly regarded as helping since the boys demonstrated this behavior after they had finished. We could not determine whether the boys' return was prompted simply by boredom, by a need to assert their superiority once more, or by guilt and remorse over taking more than an equal share of scarce materials. The winning boys may have been the ones who were most highly motivated and, having battled their way by amassing the needed blocks quickly and by any means available, fair or not, they were first to finish. Once they were assured first place, they could afford to atone by being helpful to those whom they had caused to lose.

Concluding Considerations

The data on helping provide a fitting conclusion to consideration of children's behavior in response to scarcity threat, for they emphasize once more the limits of generalizability. It could be argued that children were asked to make an individual product, and hence, in seeking individualistic solutions, they were simply following experimental directions. In the light of comparable children's behaviors in competitive conditions, it is highly unlikely that the aggressiveness, besting, hoarding, and other self-oriented responses in this study could be attributable to experimental induction. We suspect that when this research is replicated with different samples in cross-cultural settings, more equitable distribution practices may be found.

It is also important to remember that in this particular study, the scarcity threat was mild and the actual scarcity level very low. Each child was able to complete the task, even though in the scarcity condition substitutes had to be used. The degree of scarcity in future studies should be extended to levels of severity such that none of the children has enough material to complete the task. Under these conditions, will the goal contriency intersect with severe scarcity so as to elicit the usual self-maximizing responses obtained in research with American suburban children? Or when individual efforts fail to bring about solutions to scarcity problems, will these children resort to collaborative solutions to scarcity as do the Bateiga of East Africa?

We had left the distribution of needed goods wholly up to the children, so that they would not feel constrained to act upon the experimenter's implied expectation to devise a just principle. Apparently we were successful, for no distribution principle was ever enunciated by children, much less obeyed in the group process. Accusations of hoarding and other attributions of unfairness implied reference to and understanding of an underlying equity norm such as was found in several other studies on moral development in children. However, in our situation, where individual actions were involved, this norm seemed to be brought into play only when others were in violation, particularly at the expense of the child who was the complainer. The norm, in other words, was evoked to control the behavior of others and was not applied to each child's own behavior.

The children did not appear helpless, confused, or lost. We had given them detailed instructions so as to minimize their individual differences in ability. The children knew what to do and proceeded to fend for themselves. The behavior of these children is similar to that of those children in the same suburban sample studied in competitive and cooperative conditions described in chapter 6. Is this not precisely the intended result of training for independence, individualism, and self-sufficiency?

Behaviors Related to Attaining Means versus End States. Our data disclosed a qualitative difference in children's behaviors in conditions of high competition as compared with high scarcity conditions. These findings were not anticipated; one might have expected both conditions of heightened motivation to result in the same type of behavior. Their consistency suggests that when children are motivated to obtain material resources that serve as means to success, physical counteractions occur around these objects. A focus on winning, rather than on the means that enable success is more abstract, more self-oriented and inhibits interaction as shown in chapter 6. When it is expressed verbally, children anticipate being in this state and variously fantasize out loud about being winners, excluding the other from reaching the same goal, taunt each other, and brag about their accomplishments. Future success may be imagined; the possession of needed objects is in the present and demands physical interaction.

On the Development of Children's Sense of Deservedness. Lerner (1974) postulates that children develop a sense of justice by learning to postpone their own gratifications for future rewards and coming to expect the same kind of behavior from others, presumably including age-related peers. He does not address questions of consequences of differential need-satisfying experiences. The theory can be extended to imply that children who are denied relatively little by their socializers and whose wishes and whims are met immediately, fully, and even beyond their asking, will come to expect such treatment. Unless faced with dissonant experiences, a child growing up surrounded in a world where much is given and little asked will come to believe that she is entitled to such treatment and will see a just world as one in which objects can be had for the asking or taking.[3] This state of affairs is extreme; nevertheless if it is assumed that the children in our sample have been denied relatively little and associate primarily with peers whose experiences are similar, one may understand our children's apparent sense of freedom to take what they need and their righteous indignation with others who frustrate their attempts to do so. We see one vital direction for developmental social research in the study of the effects of peers who constitute available social comparison figures during children's formative years.

On Sex Differences. Research on elementary school children's preferences for competitive or cooperative choices in many investigations, including our own studies involving children's competitive coaction, has disclosed no appreciable differences in boys' and girls' behaviors. This research is almost wholly devoid of requirements for active, prolonged social contact among children. Where such social encounters are essential aspects of competitive situations, boys are found to compete more vigorously and/or more aggressively. Further, boys prefer and are able to perform better in situations that are relatively unstructured and allow the exercise of their own initiative as opposed to experimenter inductions. Older boys are more willing to differentiate themselves from their peers than comparable girls (chapter 6).

Taken together, these results suggest that girls in middle childhood are equally strongly motivated to succeed as are their counterpart boys. However, in these studies girls appear more uncertain about ways to achieve their goals, hence rely more on, and are willing to accept more guidance from peers and adults. Boys, by contrast, reject or resent advice or inductions from experimenters (at least from female experimenters). Boys rise quickly to competitive challenges and overt combat to beat their opponents; such behavior is often more in the spirit of fun and good sportsmanship than serious battle. These generalizations are in accord with conclusions, albeit tentatively offered, by Maccoby and Jacklin (1974). They find more studies supporting generally higher activity level, dominance attempts, and aggression in boys' groups than in girls'. Of particular interest, and concurring with our observations, are suggestions that boys stimulate each other to increased activity and to mock fights in elementary classrooms. We have cited previously Ahlgren and Johnson's (1979) study, which found consistent and strong preference of girls at all grades for cooperative classroom structures, while boys were more inclined toward competition.

On the whole, these patterns conform to the sex role stereotypes prevalent in American society. We are left with the question whether today, after a decade of renewed questioning of role differentiation between the sexes, of enforcement of equal-rights legislation at home, in schools, and on jobs, these stereotypes will persist in the new generation of children.

The Escalation of Counteraction and Hoarding. One of the hypotheses that could not be tested in our study concerns the internal dynamics of groups. Earlier we had mentioned that sensitization toward a potential scarcity of desired objects is likely to create uncertainty and hence will leave a person open to social influences. In the presence of self-oriented others with similar needs, this may lead to an escalation of counteraction and increased hoarding. The dynamics appear to be as follows. A perception of others' attempts to obtain scarce goods and subsequent hoarding will not only serve as a stimulus to engage in similar behaviors but to an escalation of one's own needs and attempts at hoarding. This, in turn, will stimulate others to still greater heights of inventiveness of blocking, hoarding, and so forth. These spiraling effects thus may reach the level of well-known panic buying. In this chain, one person's hoarding seems to constitute a strong stimulus that challenges others to do likewise. The implication is that if hoarding is to be prevented, it needs to be done early in the chain before the behavior has a chance to spread and become uncontrollable.

Lippitt et al. (1952) have studied behavioral contagion effects in boys at summer camps, and Redl and Wineman (1951) in delinquent homes. It is quite possible that children, who are still unaware of many normative regulations and unsure about behavioral sanctions, may be generally susceptible to escalation effects. They may be particularly vulnerable in certain situations (for instance, where behavioral limits are not well defined) or at certain ages (when particularly open to peer influences). Boys, shown to engage more frequently in aggressive acts, may be especially prone to contribute to the escalation of aggression, and retaliation of aggression by aggression is well known to social psychologists. What would be novel and important is if the assumed openness to social influence under scarcity threat could be utilized to move adults and children alike toward a greater concern for collaboration or sharing with others who are also in need of the same scarce objects.

Notes

1. The original Greek Olympic Games are a classic example of such man-made conditions. There was only one winner; the rest of the contestants were all losers. Perhaps even the Greeks felt uneasy with such unique exclusive victories; at least this might be a partial explanation for the great number of contests in different fields of athletics, each of which allowed the emergence of a separate victor. The rewards for winning were most commonly nonmaterial, symbolized by a wreath to be worn by the victor. It was cut at Olympia from the sacred wild olive tree, from sweet laurel at the Pythian Games at Delphi, and from a wild cherry at the Istmian Games. At a few other games, material rewards were given. At the Panathenaea, the victor received olive oil in painted jars. These amphorae had a black picture of Athena painted on the surface, as well as pictures of athletes in active poses, and carried the inscription, "I am a prize from Athens." The countless pottery jars that have survived from the fifth century B.C. and now fill museums around the world are not only a testament to artistic and physical excellence but also to the inventiveness of the human spirit that could conceive of the highest exclusive standards yet make their attainment possible to many. Today, more prosaically, the concept of runner-up is another means of widening victory to more than one individual, as are any number and manner of other consolation prizes.

2. At least two eminent psychologists saw substitutabilty as a profoundly important aspect of human life. For Freud, this concept defined the essence of sublimation. Substitutability figures prominently in Lewinian conceptualizations; indeed some of the most famous early research on discharge of tension systems by substitution was carried out by Lewin's students (Lewin 1935, chap. 6).

3. The obverse should be equally true: children of poverty will accept their own state as just unless they are exposed to different comparison others. These hypotheses are being tested now.

Sex Role Mediation of Achievement Behaviors and Interpersonal Interactions in Sex-Integrated Team Games

Helen Harris Solomons

This chapter reports on an empirical study of the way in which two psychological factors, sex roles and achievement motivation, mediate behavior and interpersonal interactions in cooperative and competitive situations.

Sex Roles

Observations of young children have shown that there are very significant sex differences with respect to activity level and physical aggression: boys tend to be more active and more physically aggressive than girls (Brodzinsky et al. 1979; Tauber 1979; Frieze et al. 1978; Feshbach 1970). Most people tend to think of very active and physically aggressive behavior as boylike even when it is demonstrated by girls (the so-called tomboy) and passive quiet behavior as girllike even when it is demonstrated by boys (the so-called sissy). In other words, certain kinds of behavior have traditionally been considered appropriate to one sex and not to the other, even at a very early age.

Social norms that determine the way in which males and females are expected to behave group certain kinds of behaviors as male appropriate (masculine) and others as female appropriate (feminine). These groups of behaviors comprise what are referred to as sex roles.

Whether an individual belongs to the category male or the category female is determined biologically. (There is, of course, a small minority of transsexuals and other persons whose biological sex is not unambiguously male or female, but even these possess behaviors and personalities that tend to be associated with one or the other of the biological sexes). In contrast, although sex roles are related to biological sex, they are not biologically based. They are learned behaviors.

The learning of sex roles begins very early. An extensive review of research in this area (Maccoby and Jacklin 1974) shows that even at the developmental stage of infancy, it is difficult to distinguish between the inherent (biological) and the environmental (learned) causes of behavior. According to Maccoby and Jacklin, three major psychological theories describe how children learn the interests, attitudes, and behaviors associated with sex roles:

1. By imitation or modeling: They choose same-sex models according to which they pattern their own behavior.
2. Through reward and punishment: Boys are rewarded for masculine behaviors and discouraged from feminine behaviors, and vice-versa for girls.
3. Through socialization: A "child first develops a concept of what it is to be male or female . . . [and] attempts to fit his own behavior to his concept of what behavior is sex appropriate" (p. 1).

The research described in this chapter used a physical game as the setting to study the influence of these learned sex roles on achievement behavior. In such situations, it was believed, there would be marked attitudinal and behavioral differences between girls and boys.

Any of the three role-learning theories that Maccoby and Jacklin described can be used to support this hypothesis. For example, in American society children observe males engaging in sports and active physical behaviors significantly more often and more visibly than females do. There are relatively few female role models for these behaviors (President's Commission on Olympic Sport 1977; Michener 1976; Gerber et al. 1974; Gilbert and Williamson 1973). Second, children also observe that males are highly approved of and rewarded for such activities while females are less so, and they probably experience this differentiation personally too. According to the third theory, children uses these observations as a basis for deciding what is sex-appropriate behavior in sports and games. Thus each of these theories predicts that girls and boys develop significantly different skills in and attitudes toward sports.

Achievement Motivation

Throughout this book, cooperation and competition are treated as sets of circumstances that describe particular categories of social situation. People interact differently in a situation that is competitive from one that is not. In fact we expect differences in behavior. If Joan and Susan are playing on the same team, we expect them to help each other win the game. If they are on opposing teams, we expect each of them to hinder the other. These behaviors are considered to be appropriate; we expect them and generally do not wonder why they occur. Deliberately helping a member of the opposing team or hindering a member of one's own team is not expected, and we do wonder why it occurs. For example, when Joan helps Susan, who is on the opposing team, it may be that it is more important to her to please Susan, who is her friend, than it is for her to be on the winning team herself. Or it could be that she was placed on a team with people whom she did not like, so the success of the opposing team will please her more than the success of her own. Therefore, certain kinds of behavior in competitive or cooperative situations can be related to individual differences in terms of psychological needs. One such need—a very important one—that will influence behavior in either of these conditions is the need to achieve, to be successful at attaining one's goals.

The conceptual model of motivation developed by McClelland et al. (1953), "emphasize[d] the determinative role of expectation (or expectancy) of the consequences of action" (Atkinson 1964). What an individual believes about her chances of success or failure resulting from a given action is a powerful factor influencing her behavior. A person with a very strong need to achieve might be expected to put a lot of effort into reaching her goal. She might also be expected to have a very strong emotional response to failure. If the risk of failure following an action is very high, the resultant anxiety might influence her performance more than the strength of her need to succeed. Thus theories of achievement motivation have to include all of the complexities "how different factors *combine* at a particular time, to influence the direction, vigor, and persistence of an individual's behavior in a given situation" (Atkinson 1964).

In the United States there has been a great deal of research performed in the field of achievement motivation, for in this country individualism and personal achievement are highly valued. This emphasis on what McClelland et al. (1953) refer to as entrepreneurial personality characteristics is said to be directly related to the rapid evolution of this country from a frontier society to one of the most powerful, highly developed technological societies in the contemporary world, all within the period of only two hundred years

Since success has traditionally been highly valued in this society, it is not surprising that in social psychological research there has been a great deal of emphasis on attempts to discover and understand the personality characteristics of the successful man. My use of *man* is deliberate, for even though the body of research in this area has grown to considerable proportions since the classic studies by McClelland et al. on the psychological dynamics of high and low achievement in the early 1950s, until quite recently it has treated achievement as an almost exclusively male characteristic.

A serious limitation of achievement motivation theories such as that of McClelland et al. was their inability to explain on a consistent basis data collected on female subjects. Thus the data on male subjects collected by

McClelland and his colleagues yielded significant and readily replicable findings and fitted nicely into their theory, but in many cases the data on women were unused because they seemed not to make sense. This problem resulted from the fact that the theory had been developed from masculine models of achievement and success. Rather than modify the theory, however, McClelland and his coworkers chose to ignore these data on the grounds that the need for achievement did not appear to be as important as their affiliative and other needs in motivating female behavior.

Horner's Motive to Avoid Success

It was within the context of these basic inconsistencies with McClelland's theory that Horner attempted to resolve the confusion resulting from achievement research on female subjects. Believing that it was not sufficient to explain the results solely in terms of different perceptions of appropriate sex-role standards, she proposed an expectancy-value model and developed a measuring instrument designed to test her hypothesis (Horner 1968).

Horner's model went beyond expectancies concerning the consequences of an action with respect to success or failure to include the consequences of the outcome—that is, the consequences of success. She hypothesized that while men often experience extreme anxiety because of their fear of failure, some women experience anxiety because they fear success. For men the anxiety is related to the damage to their self-esteem in consequence of having failed; the women experience damage to their self-esteem in consequence of having succeeded.

Horner (1970) suggested that although a young woman attending the same high school or college as her male counterpart may appear to be provided with the same opportunity as he to achieve, there exists for her a psychological barrier to success. She referred to this barrier as the motive to avoid success: "This fear of success receives its impetus from the expectancy held by women that success in achievement situations will be followed by negative consequences, including social rejection and the sense of losing one's femininity." (p. 46).

Since Horner's original work, there has been a proliferation of studies and a concomitant proliferation of results (Condry and Dyer 1976; Tresemer 1974; Hoffman 1974; Alper 1971, 1974; Weston and Mednick 1970). Some of these support Horner, some do not. In fact some researchers question the generality and validity of the achievement motive. These criticisms have been based on studies of achievement in blacks. They ask whether a general motivation theory using choice of goals as a criterion can be applied when the differences between males and females, blacks and whites, and so forth may be not so much in choice of goals as in terms of the appropriateness of the goals, the expectations of attaining them, and the possible negative consequences of doing so. Thus the boy who achieves an A in his English class may not be rewarded with as high a level of status by his peers as the boy who gets a C in English but scores the most goals for his football team. For this boy, popularity with his peers might be much more rewarding than the approval of his teacher. Or the girl who is capable of getting the highest mark in her science class may have a strong need to achieve but may not perform well if she fears that as a result she might lose favor with her boyfriend. Pleasing her boyfriend might be a more important reward to the girl than achievement in her science class.

Problems of Measurement

These studies attempt to make predictions about people's expected behaviors in a variety of situations based on measurements of achievement need under specific laboratory conditions. In particular, the achievement situations for the majority of these studies have employed academic or intellectual tasks, and the methods have been indirect: written attitude tests (Broverman et al 1972; Alper 1971), projective techniques (Horner 1968, 1973; McClelland et al 1953), and expectancy/value scales (Mausner 1973). Even in a study that was concerned with the varieties of achievement motivation and included noncollege populations, basically the same methodology and intellectual tasks were used as before (Veroff, McClelland, and Ruhland 1975).

Although such methods may be legitimate and such tasks undoubtedly vital, it is reasonable to question whether these restrictions are either necessary or desirable. There is an important relationship between attitude and action (see, for example, Fiske 1979; Ross 1977; Jacoby 1975): what individuals say is often not nearly as enlightening as what they actually do. For example, the behavior of some politicians after they win an election is perhaps more indicative of their real motivations and attitudes than what they say during the campaign. Similarly there is reason to suggest that a man or woman responding to stories or pictures of other men or women in achievement-related situations may not always be providing the researcher with valid information concerning what he or she would actually do in a specific situation.

By the use of indirect methods, therefore, a direct relationship between a specific attitude and a specific achievement behavior may be difficult or even impossible to obtain. Nonbehavioral measures of attitudes—including the perceived value of success and the attribution of reasons believed to be the cause of successes and failures, and likes and dislikes—are needed in many situations and are an important part of social psychological research.

But it seems reasonable to postulate that whenever practicable, behavioral studies should be made by studying actual situation-relevant behaviors rather than by analyzing reported behaviors or inferring from instruments potentially heavily influenced by numerous confounding variables.

The Research Design

Researcher Bias

In a context such as the present one, research projects, particularly in the behavioral and social sciences, are subject to researcher bias. This factor can influence the design, execution, data analysis, or interpretation stages of a study or all of them. Research scientists are members of the society and as such are influenced by the dynamics of that part of the social environment under study. It is impossible to be competely objective about the topic being studied. It is possible, however, to be aware of one's biases and to take great care that they do not contaminate the design of the experiment or the analysis, interpretation, or reporting of the results.

The final section of this chapter provides a discussion of the implications of the results of the research, with suggestions and recommendations for their application. These are, quite legitimately, influenced by my personal value judgments. I took great care, however, to build into the research design as many precautions as possible to prevent my personal biases from influencing the study itself. Although I do not claim to have been absolutely objective when I began this study, my emphasis on the use of very distinct behavioral observations, on the use of a male as well as a female observer, and on the use of instrumental measures instead of subjective ones was a very serious and sincere attempt to collect data on what was really occurring, not what I thought was or ought to be.

Overview

The study was an attempt to obtain data on the influence of sex roles on achievement behaviors during the formative years of the relevant attitudes. The situation selected for this purpose was that of team ball games played in recently sex-integrated elementary level physical education classes.

Until a few years ago, a study of the extent reported here would have been difficult to carry out for lack of sufficient subject groups. In most schools only very young boys and girls played together, and their skills were too undeveloped for the kind of measurements required. New laws, however, such as the Title IX amendment to the Education Act of 1972 on the federal level and state regulations such as Pennsylvania Department of Education's Basic Education Curriculum 154 (1975) require that all elementary and secondary schools provide coeducational physical education classes.

   Although there had been much discussion by various advocates of and
opponents to the idea of sex-integrated sports regarding what might occur
in such group activities, hard data documenting the way in which boys and
girls behave in these activities did not exist. A study was designed,
therefore, to collect data in naturalistic and laboratory settings in which
ability behaviors could be measured objectively by instrumental means and
by direct observation. This was done by varying the situation so as to affect
those behaviors modified by the sex-role-mediated perceptions of the
children, selecting particularly behaviors relevant to achievement (scoring)
in these situations. These included not only measures of performance and
ability but also measures of levels of participation in the form of attempts to
score or prevent the opposing team from scoring.
   In addition to the observations and direct measurements, nonbehavioral
data on attitude, perception of own and others' ability, attribution of
causes of success and failure, interest and motivation, family background,
and sociometric patterns within classes were obtained from questionnaires
filled in by the children after each phase of the study.

The Games

Field and Laboratory Settings. There was a need for studies that could investigate direct relationships between relevant attitudes and achievement
behaviors in very specific situations, which should involve tasks, goals, and
circumstances that are the same as or similar to those that occur normally in
the experience of the population being studied. The naturalistic setting used
in experiment 1 of the study is such a situation. It employs observations of
games played in regular sex-integrated physical education classes in a
number of different schools.
   Field studies of this sort, however, are often limited in that behaviors of
interest may not always occur sufficiently frequently or consistently to be
studied properly. They often need to be followed up by laboratory studies
that permit the control of significant variables. The special team game
created for part of our study (experiment 3) allowed the necessary isolation
and control of variables, and it also can be said to represent a naturalistic
situation. The game was played in the school gymnasium; it involved tasks
and goals very close to those observed in the field study; and the laboratory
manipulations were built into the situation as rules of the game and were
therefore undetectable by the players.

Cooperation and Competition. In order for a behavior to be studied, it is
necessary to have or to create a situation that will elicit that behavior.
Cooperation and competition are inherent to team sports and games, so
there is no need to create them artificially. Thus these games involve ex-

treme examples of goal contriency whereby the attainment of the goal (winning) by one team precludes goal attainment by the other team. Intrateam competition can also occur when individual players try to outperform other members on their own team. Competitive conditions can be observed in overt form during team games; a player can be seen to block an opponent's attempts to reach her goal, for example. In other words, team sports provide optimal conditions for observing competitive counteractions.

Team games also provide within-team cooperation because team members share the goal of achieving a better score than the opposing team. Cooperative conditions are also created by the task requirement of games, as can be readily observed in the form of passes between teammates or by a player's acting as a buffer between a same-team member and an opponent. Cooperative interactions of this kind are a special feature of team games. They are highly instrumental, and they can involve skills that are as much admired as competitive ones. The way in which team members work together is as much a part of a team's ability to win a game as the superior ability of an individual team member to outperform an individual member of the opposing team.

Sex Roles. Team games played by sex-integrated classes are especially useful for sex role-mediated achievement studies because interactions between same-team members and opposing team members of like and unlike sex may be observed. If, as postulated, girls and boys have different sex role conditioning, the differences between them in interests and attitudes should result in an important dynamic with respect to interpersonal interactions in this situation.

Some interesting questions arise when two different sex groups are combined into one team playing against another team also composed of both girls and boys. Will each team emerge as a new psychologically integrated group with a single set of standards? Or will there be subgroups within a team with, for example, girls behaving according to one psychological reference group and boys to another?

Behavioral Observations. One of the attractions of team games and the reason why people will pay to become spectators of such events is that intense drives toward the goal are demonstrated in the form of highly visible and often very dramatic physical actions. It is true that there is no way of knowing what players are thinking—whether they are really desirous of reaching the goal because of a high need for achievement of success or simply because they wish the game to end in order to go home. But there is a very clear distinction between the behavior of a person who merely stands still when the ball approaches and one who acts.

Further goal-directed counteractions such as attempts to score (for example, throwing the ball across a volleyball net) and the consequences of attempts to score (the catching or dropping of the ball, hitting the net, or going outside the court) can be clearly seen and recorded. Intrateam interactions (passing to others, encouraging their scoring attempts, and similar cooperative acts) can also be clearly seen.

These are the kinds of behaviors we wanted to observe. Several criteria were used in selecting measures of these behaviors:

1. The behavior should be distinguishable. It must be operationally definable in such a fashion that two or more observers can agree as to whether it has occurred. For example, observers can generally agree that a player is or is not holding a ball.
2. For useful data to be obtained, the behaviors studied must be observable. That is, the behavior must be large enough to be clearly apparent to the observer. Catching a ball is one such behavior; holding the thumb next to or away from the other fingers while catching is probably not.
3. The behavior should preferably be discrete. It should be finite and of short duration so that it can be recorded in the form of frequency of occurrence (counts). Ball games contain large numbers of discrete behaviors: throws or catches of a ball, jumps, runs, passes and falls, to name only a few.

The Experimental Design

Theoretical Model

This model was based upon a pilot study carried out in 1974 (Solomons 1976) and involves a cycle that can progress in either of two directions. That shown in figure 9-1 is for the high-ability case and refers to people perceived as performing successfully in games. A similar cycle (not shown) operating in the reverse direction applies to people perceived as poor at games.

The cycle shown in figure 9-1 is intended to describe effects on and consequences of subjective judgments about levels of ability and how these judgments are related to certain sequences of interpersonal interactions. Each element in the sequence interacts with the next and is, in turn, acted upon by the one preceding it. That is, judgments about a player's ability (perceived ability) influence his performance, while the way in which a player is seen to perform influences other players' judgments about his ability, and so on.

Since each part of the model is interrelated in this way, it seems at first that no single part of it can be studied except by studying the whole. This is

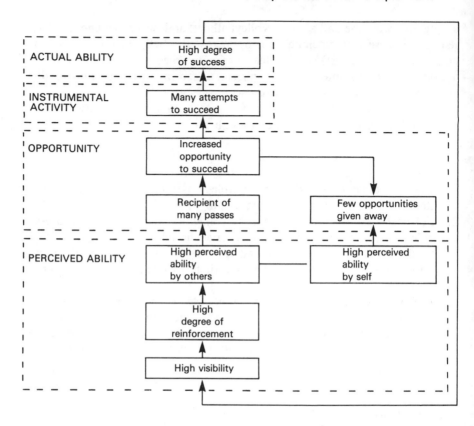

Note: Being cyclic, the sequence can be entered at any point.

Figure 9-1. Schematic Model for Actual and Perceived Ability. Shown here is a case in which high actual ability is partly a function of high perceived ability.

not so, however; the different mechanisms operating at different points in the cycle can be isolated and studied independently.

Because the model describes a cycle it can be entered at any point in the sequence. As shown in figure 9-1, the model can be seen to consist of the following sequences:

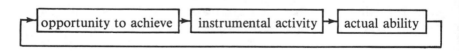

with perception of self and perception of others affecting the extent to which opportunities are proffered or used. Thus the model shows how the perception of ability and the development of actual ability are related to opportunities. Without an opportunity to participate, a player cannot be reinforced for successes or practice skills or be seen and so perceived as a high-ability player. Some of these opportunities arise from self-initiated activities leading to additional ball contacts (such as running and jumping). Others arise from being the recipient of passes through being perceived as a high-ability player by others, whereas passing the ball to others corresponds to giving opportunities away.

If we enter the cycle at the top—actually ability—it can be seen that actual ability is related to high visibility at the bottom of the chart. Thus players with a high level of ability would be expected to be successful in their attempts to score or prevent the opposing team from scoring. These attempts and successes would be seen by teammates, whose responses would presumably be positive and hence reinforce these continued high levels of activity. Success, visibility, and reinforcement would all contribute to these players' being perceived as high-ability players both by themselves and by others.

The next part of the chart shows how perceived ability relates to opportunity. Players who believe themselves to be high in ability will tend to try to create as many opportunities as possible to help their teams succeed and will probably be provided with additional opportunities by teammates who also believe them capable of scoring for the team. Thus in a ball game that involves the passing of the ball from one player to another on the same team, high-ability players might be expected to retain the ball and attempt to score themselves rather than pass to another player. Less-able players might be expected to pass the ball to another team member who, they believe, is more able to score successfully.

Similarly high-ability players might also be expected to be very active in initiating contacts with the ball because they believe that their chances of success are very high and because successful scoring leads to rewards (such as cheering from teammates and praise from the teacher). An increase in the level of participation is therefore expected to occur, together with a higher frequency of opportunities to score and opportunities to practice skills and improve performance and, hence an eventual increase in the level of actual ability.

The cycle demonstrated in figure 9-1 thus illustrates a self-fulfilling prophecy or Rosenthal effect (Rosenthal and Jacobson 1968), but it formulates it in such a manner as to make it possible to test the different parts of the mechanism that is operating the cycle.

The Subjects

The subjects were fifth-grade students in a large suburban school district. Experiment 1 of the study involved 8 physical education teachers (all male) and 426 children (228 boys and 198 girls) in eighteen classes from eight different schools; 332 of these children were included in experiment 2 (177 boys and 155 girls), and 112 were selected for experiment 3 (56 boys and 56 girls).

The use of all of the schools in the district permitted the inclusion of children from all socioeconomic levels. Black children were underrepresented in the sample relative to their numbers in the general population, as is usually the case for major city suburban districts. Since almost the entire fifth-grade population of the district was involved, however, they were properly represented for that district.

Fifth-grade children were selected for the study for three reasons. First, these were the first classes that had to comply with legal regulations on the provision of coeducation classes. Second, at this level the children have had little or no history of sex-segregated-class conditioning effects. These children had always had sex-integrated physical education and had therefore always shared exactly the same program and opportunity to learn the same skills. Had it not been for the new laws referring to the fifth-grade level in this particular school district, however, these children would have been separated at this age. In previous years, fifth-grade girls and boys had participated in separate programs, with the central activity for the boys emphasizing team sports and that for the girls emphasizing gymnastics. Third, and perhaps most important, is that fifth-grade girls tend to be, on the average, about two years in advance of boys in physical maturation (Torg and Torg 1974; Ausubel and Sullivan 1970; Maccoby 1963), with a mean height and weight equal to or greater than the mean height and weight for males of the same age.

In the civil rights case by the National Organization for Women (NOW) against Little League, Inc. New Jersey (August 1972), this aspect of childrens' physical development was a central issue. Expert witnesses gave testimony that girls had physical advantages over boys in the 8- to 12-year-old age group in terms of height, weight, and bone maturation. The case was decided in favor of NOW on the grounds that there was no physiological evidence for any difference between girls and boys under the age of 13 if they were similarly treated in terms of activity programs.

In the context of our desire to relate performance to psychological factors (such as the need to achieve and the strength of the psychological drive to reach the goal) and to separate these from the ability to achieve at a particular task, this last point is extremely important. Superior height and weight are closely related to success in physical achievement (Wyrick 1974). On the average, therefore, fifth-grade boys might be expected to be at a slight physical disadvantage compared with their female agemates. Any superiority of boys over girls in games of physical skills at this age would therefore be more readily ascribable to environmental conditioning than to physiological superiority.

Procedures

Experiment 1: The Field Study

The first phase of the study was concerned with the need to check whether the cycle shown in the theoretical model was indeed operating in a naturalistic setting. It involved observations carried out in ordinary physical education class games. These enabled us to isolate specific behaviors for more intensive study that could be objectively and unambiguously measured.

The children were observed according to a behavioral observation schedule intended to test each part of the model as they played a regular class game of newcomb. A schematic diagram of the theoretical model for this game is shown in figure 9-2. Observations made included measures of active participation, opportunities for practice and reinforcement, and skills such as throwing and catching the ball.

The Game. Newcomb is a team ball game played in elementary schools as a preparation for the similar but more highly skilled game of volleyball. The game begins with each of the two teams arranged in three rows on its side of the net on a marked volleyball court. The player in the back right corner (facing the net) serves the ball by throwing it over the net. The players on the opposite side of the net must try to catch the ball before it hits the floor inside their court. If they are not successful, the serving team scores a point.

Catching the ball successfully in this competitive situation is the way by which a player prevents the opposing team member from scoring (and thus moving toward the goal of winning the game. If the ball is caught, the catcher may throw the ball back over the net to try to score a point for his team. A point is scored by throwing the ball in such a way as to have it clear the net, not be caught by one of the opposing team members, and land inside the marked court. Alternatively the catcher may pass the ball to a teammate who may either try to score or pass the ball again.

After each point is scored, the rows rotate so that each team member has a turn to serve. The rotations mean that every child in the class holds the ball at least once (when it is his turn to serve). In addition, each child moves from position to position on the court and is at some times at the very back of the court (needing a hard throw to clear the net) and at other times in the front row, very close to the net.

In order to identify each child clearly, so that no matter where he moved on the court the observers could record an individual child's behavior, each player was provided with a painter's hat with a large fluorescent number painted on it. This hat and the provision of written instructions to the teacher concerning the specific rules of the game to be used, together with a request to divide the class into two teams with as equal proportions of boys

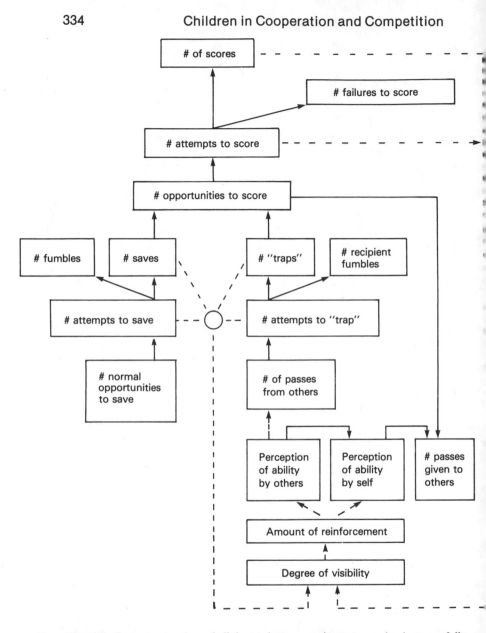

Note: "Save" indicates a case when a ball thrown by an opposite team member is successfully caught, and thus the opposing team is prevented from scoring a point. "Trap" indicates a case when a ball is passed to a member of the same team who successfully catches it.

Figure 9-2. Scheme for Newcomb Game. This relates to the high-ability case of figure 9-1.

and girls on each as possible, were the only differences between these games and ordinary class games. One could suggest that the presence of the observers created a significantly different situation, but except for initial curiosity, the players became completely involved in the competition once the games began. Apart from a few requests from some children as to who was winning once it was discovered the the observers always knew the score, the children ignored the observers.

Behaviors listed in the observation schedule were tape-recorded by observers as they occurred, in the form of a running commentary. Modified microphones were used to prevent the noise of the game from being picked up or the observers from being overheard by the teacher or players. To minimize observer bias and improve reliability, two observers (one male and one female) were used to record overlapping information at all times and the same information on spot-check occasions. A high degree of agreement was obtained: in a typical medium-length game (approximately four hundred plays) only two minor discrepancies were found. The recordings were transcribed and coded immediately after the game for computer analysis.[1]

Field Study Results and Relationships to the Model. The cycle shown in the model postulates a relationship between opportunity (being the recipient of passes), instrumental activity (attempts to succeed), and performance (number of successful catches) and therefore predicts positive correlations between these measures.

Pearson product-moment correlations carried out to test the relationships between the participation level variables strongly support this part of the model. Those girls and boys who had the highest counts of instrumental activity behaviors—such as running toward the ball, jumping when the ball was high, or bending when the ball was low—also received the largest number of passes from others. Conversely those who were the least active received the fewest number of passes.

Significant positive correlations were found between activity levels and attempts to catch, activity levels and number of successful catches (preventing the opposing team from scoring), and successful catches with number of attempts. These relationships were significant at the 0.001 level and held for both girls and boys. Thus active players tended to exhibit a wider variety of instrumental behaviors than less active players, and those who made most attempts tended to have the largest number of successes.

Sex Differences. Boys had significantly higher participation levels than did the girls in the class games (table 9-1). Boys received more passes than girls

Table 9-1
Summary of Experiment 1 Behaviors, by Sex

Measure	Boys' Mean (n = 228)	Girls' Mean (n = 198)
Attempts to catch throws and serves	7.17	4.27
Total passes from others	2.93	1.37
Attempts to catch, including passes	10.10	5.64
Successful catches of serves and throws	4.88	3.28
Actual holdings of ball, including passes	8.44	4.08
Sum of instrumental activities	7.10	2.55
Leaps	2.55	1.11
Runs	2.98	1.21
Collisions	0.09	0.03
Falls	1.48	0.21

from teammates and more frequently initiated actions that increased their chances of making contact with the ball either to score or to block a scoring attempt by the opposing team.

During these eighteen games we found that, on the average,

Boys made over twice as many attempts to catch the ball as girls did.

Boys made almost twice as many successful catches as girls did (preventing the opposing team from scoring).

Boys had more than twice as many contacts with the ball as girls did (opportunities to attempt to score or prevent scoring).

Boys received about three times as many passes as girls did.

Boys leaped, ran, fell, and collided almost three times as frequently as girls did.

With respect to quality of performance, one measure of skill in these games is the proportion of all throws that are accurate (good throws). Looked at another way, what proportion of throws are bad (throws that hit the net or go out of the court) and thereby earn penalty points for the opposing team?

Table 9-2 shows that boys threw both more good and more bad balls than did girls ($p < 0.000$, $p < 0.01$, respectively), but if we consider the proportion of throws that were bad, there is very little difference: bad throws/total throws = 0.33/5.5 (60 percent) for the boys and 0.16/2.7 (59 percent) for the girls. Similarly small skill differences with respect to catching the ball were also found: 55 percent success for boys and 49 percent for girls.

Table 9-2
Experiment 1 Mean Throwing Skill Scores, by Sex

Measure	Boys	Girls	t-value
Total throws	5.49	2.65	6.43**
Good throws	5.17	2.49	6.44**
Bad throws	0.33	0.16	2.62*

*$p < .01$.
**$p < .001$.

Perceived versus Actual Ability. Responses on questionnaires given to the players after the game showed that both boys and girls said they very much wanted their teams to win. The girls' interest in being on the winning team was also made very clear by their behavior: they cheered, jumped up and down with excitement (most of the jumping counted during the game for girls was this kind of nontask-oriented activity), and got into as many arguments with the teacher as did the boys regarding penalty points awarded to the opposing team. Yet in spite of motivation, the girls tended to remain still and wait for the ball to come to them. In extreme cases, a girl might make no visible effort whatsoever to catch the ball even when it was landing at her feet.

This low activity level was, as predicted by the model, related to the finding that girls were perceived as low-ability players relative to boys. (Girls received only about one-third the number of passes that boys did.) The accuracy of this perception can be determined by observing that in terms of quality of performance, boys did not demonstrate a much greater level of ability than did girls. The evidence provided by their actual performances did not support their beliefs.

Data on the relationships among performance, actual ability, and perception of ability for the girls were obtained only for the very small sample of girls who participated actively in the experiment 1 games. Because the relationships could not be tested adequately without corresponding information concerning the majority of the girls and some of the less active boys, experiment 2 was designed to obtain this information and thus strengthen the evidence concerning this part of the model.

Experiment 2: A Study of Individual Skills

In experiment 2 we studied that part of the cycle involving actual ability. The experiment was designed to serve two functions. The first was to obtain data on actual ability under conditions in which performance was not influenced by the presence of other children or by variations in the extent of opportunity to be in contact with the ball. These data on ability could then be compared with performance levels from experiment 1. The second was to obtain data for use in designing experiment 3.

The Alone Game. Two pieces of apparatus were especially designed to measure the ability skills identified from the field study.[2] One was an eight-foot-high target board electronically wired so that it measured and recorded the force and accuracy of each throw of a volleyball. The second was a ball-throwing device that ejected a ball with constant force and trajectory to test catching skills.

The children were called out of class one at a time and taken to the place where the apparatus was set up. Male and female observers alternated in giving directions and operating the ball-projection device. The children were not informed that the force and trajectory of the ball was mechanically controlled, all they saw was a man or woman pulling a string that released the ball so the effects of the sex of the thrower and perceived difficulty of the throw could be investigaed without any actual differences in the throws to influence results.

The child stood at a mark on the floor while the person throwing the ball placed it in the projector and fired it. The child was located thirty feet from the throwing apparatus and from the target board, since this is the average throwing distance on newcomb and volleyball courts.

First each player received a practice throw from the machine and a trial throw at the target board, which they were told would not count, and were given instructions to try their best. Each player was then told that she would receive one point for each ball caught and points for accuracy (how close she came to the bull's eye) and force of impact (how high the pointer on the force scale registered). Each child then had ten catching and ten throwing attempts, which were recorded as data.

Records were kept of the number of catches and drops, of the force of impact and accuracy scores from the electronic meters, and of the manner in which the child threw the ball at the target. A composite throwing score was computed for each child by combining the separate accuracy and force of impact scores using a method of weighting that strongly emphasized accuracy.[3] The children were not informed of their scores.

Results. To examine the validity of using the composite score, the relationship between the different instrumental measures of impact force and accuracy was examined by correlation analysis. The relationship between throwing and catching skills was also tested. All correlations were at the 0.001 level of significance, and the values were approximately the same for boys and girls. Thus those children whose throws registered in the higher ranges on force of throw also tended to score most points for accuracy and to be good at catching the ball. Conversely a player who was poor at catching also tended to be toward the lower end of the ability measures of throwing skills.

We also conducted an analysis concerning the sex and size of the experimenter because of our belief that some children might perceive throws when the ball-throwing device was operated by the male researcher to be more difficult than those when the (much smaller) female operator was operating the mechanism. This factor might affect performance on throwing as well as catching attempts. An analysis of variance, however, showed no influence of the experimenter on the number of unsuccessful catches or the scores for any of the throwing measures for either boys or girls.

Actual Ability

Catching Skills. It had been thought that because boys were expected to have had more practice in ball-catching games outside school, their catching skills would be more highly developed than those of girls. This was not supported by the data. There was only a very small difference, with boys generally being only slightly better at catching than girls; 95 percent of attempts to catch were successful for boys, 89 percent for girls. Since the mean proportion of unsuccessful catches taken over all of the more than three hundred students participating was only 7.5 percent, this failure to obtain a significant sex difference in catching skills may have resulted from the need to launch the ball for a fairly easy catch due to space limitations. It may be that with more difficult throws to catch, sex differences would have showed up.

Accuracy, Force, and Composite Scores. Girls missed the target board, thereby scoring zero for both accuracy and force, significantly more frequently than was the case for the boys. Proportionately nearly seven times as many girls as boys missed the target for all ten of their tries (48 of 155 girls compared with 8 of 177 boys). In order to be able to compare the quality of those throws that actually hit for as many of the girls and boys as possible, mean scores of accuracy, force, and the weighted composite score were also computed over the number of actual hits as well as over the total of ten throwing tries. That is, these scores were adjusted to eliminate the influence of misses.

On all forms of the throwing measures, however, boys scored significantly higher in this experiment than did girls. For example, the boys had a mean accuracy score over ten throws that was slightly more than double the mean score of the girls. The difference between the sexes for mean accuracy over actual hits was less, but boys on the average scored close to 50 percent more than girls, so the difference was significant.

With respect to force, the sex difference was so great that even when these misses were taken into account, the difference remained high. The boys' mean score over all ten throws was more than three times greater than that of the girls, and their mean score over actual hits was more than double. These results can be expressed in the form of distribution patterns. Table 9-3 illustrates this for the case of composite force-accuracy scores. Even though accuracy was weighted more heavily than force in computing these composite scores, the two sexes had similar, heavily skewed distributions; the boys were predominantly skilled and the girls predominantly unskilled.

Throwing Skills. The decision to measure throwing skills by accuracy and force was based upon our observations during experiment 1 class games where these skills were seen to be directly related to ability to achieve. Another behavior selected for measurement during experiment 2 was the way in which players threw the ball, for some of the least successful children in experiment 1 seemed to be unaware of the most effective way to throw a ball.

The majority of zero scores (misses of the target board) by girls resulted from throws that were too gentle and thus failed to cover the thirty-foot distance between the thrower's line and the target board. Failure to score was caused by a ball that was not launched with sufficient force so that the ball fell short. A miss by a boy, on the other hand, was most often the result of a very forceful but inaccurate throw, which passed the target to strike the wall behind the board. This is comparable to the finding in the experiment 1 class games that bad balls thrown by boys were out significantly more than was the case for girls; when girls threw bad balls, they tended to be throws that could not clear the net. The sex difference on the force score was much larger than on the accuracy score. We therefore looked to see if there was a relationship between the number of improper throws (any throw other than the baseball pitch) and the number of times the target board was missed.

Only 53 percent of the girls but over 94 percent of the boys threw the

Table 9-3
Distribution of Composite Accuracy-Force Scores

Rank in Class	Boys	Girls
Top quartile	75 (42%)	8 (5%)
Second quartile	54 (31%)	29 (19%)
Third quartile	32 (18%)	51 (33%)
Bottom quartile	16 (9%)	67 (43%)

ball properly for all of their ten throws. A total of 597 improper throws were counted; 558 of these (93.5 percent) were thrown by girls. Of the ten boys who threw some incorrect balls, three of them missed all ten of their shots (scoring zero), one each missed eight or nine of the ten, two missed five or six, and the last missed four of the ten shots.

Almost all of the children, even those who threw correctly, missed the target for some of their throws. Only 1.3 percent of the girls and 2.8 percent of the boys did not miss the target with any of their ten throws. The sex difference in number of misses, however, corresponds to the sex difference with respect to the number of improper throws: 68 percent of the boys hit five or more times, while only 24 percent of the girls did so.

When we computed correlations between the number of throws and the number of misses for those girls who threw improperly one or more times, there was a clear and highly significant positive relationship. Only 10 boys (out of 177) fell into this category, and there was no such relationship.

These force-of-impact results suggest that the boys in our study were stronger than the girls. This finding is supported by Ausubel and Sullivan's observation (1970) that because boys in American society tend to be more physically active than girls, even those in the prepubescent age groups very often have more highly developed muscles. Physiological effects such as this result from the different ways in which the two sexes use their bodies and can therefore be related to sex role stereotyped child-rearing practices and attitudes.

It seems that in consequence, the thirty-foot throw required to hit the target board may have been within the throwing ability of most of the boys but only some of the girls. Since most of the boys used the proper throw and could throw thirty feet without much difficulty, their infrequent improper throws and target misses were not related. But if the girls were throwing near the limits of their capacity, throwing incorrectly (using an improper throw) could have meant that they did not make full use of the strength and eye-hand coordination they had and may have led to missing the target completely.

Validity and Reliability of Scores. The superior scores of the boys relative to the girls suggest that the slight physical advantage posessed by the girls in this age group in terms of height and weight was outweighed by the social psychological and relevant skills practice advantages of the boys. Evidence from the literature of social learning and the fact that there is a close relationship between actual practice and physical skill development indicate that on the whole boys perform closer to their potential actual ability level than girls do. Because the majority of boys are expected and encouraged to be physically active throughout their childhood, even those with average or below average potential develop physical skills that may be greater than girls who have more potential ability but little or no practice in team ball game skills.

Comparisons between athletically trained and untrained women demonstrate that there are much larger differences between these two groups on physical ability measures than between trained and untrained men (Wyrick 1974). Thus the average untrained man tends to be more physically active than the average untrained woman. We would therefore expect the difference in scores between the highest scoring girls and the average girls to be greater than the difference between the highest scoring boys and the average boys, most of whom would have had more practice at ball throwing and catching than the majority of the girls. This expectation was supported by the data.

Another relevant sex difference relating to these results concerns the ball-throwing task itself. The instructions given to the children in experiment 2 tests were to throw the ball as accurately and as hard as possible: "Try your hardest." To follow these instructions with respect to the ball-throwing task involved physical aggressiveness (striking an object with as much power as one can generate). Previous studies report a clear sex difference from very early ages with respect to aggressiveness, with boys observed as exhibiting more aggressiveness than girls as early as 2 or 3 years of age (Maccoby and Jacklin 1974; Ausubel and Sullivan 1970; Feshbach 1970; Bandura and Walters 1963b). Thus boys may have been generally more comfortable than the girls with both the task and the instructions and therefore were better able to obtain scores that were congruent with their potential ability to perform at this task.

Whatever the reason for the sex differences found in scores on the ability test, any advantages that the boys may have had over the girls in performing on the experiment 2 measures of actual ability would be the same as those that they had in the mixed-sex physical education class of experiment 1. The scores obtained in experiment 2 can therefore be considered reasonably reliable and valid measures of actual ability at ball throwing and catching in an ordinary game.

Relating the Findings from Experiment 2 to Experiment 1. It was found in experiment 1 that the passing patterns of the players indicated that girls were judged as having less ability than boys. At that point we did not have sufficient data to check the accuracy of this belief. The results reported here for the experiment 2 ability tests, however, support the assumption that the children's perception of the girls' relative lack of ability was accurate.

The analyses showing the sex difference on the ability tests, however, were based on pooled data: the average of scores for all of the boys and all of the girls who participated. In contrast, the games described in experiment 1 were played by individual classes.

Even though the boys overall demonstrated superior levels of skill on the measures of actual ability compared with the girls, when the scores were printed out in rank order for each of the classes separately, they showed that almost all of the classes had a few girls who scored higher than at least a few boys. (There was only one class in which all of the boys were at the top of the ability distribution and all of the girls were at the bottom, with no overlap at all.)

An examination of the number of passes received in the experiment 1 class games by the high-ability girls identified in experiment 2 showed that they had received fewer than high-ability boys, significantly fewer in the majority of classes than boys who had scored very much lower than they on the ability tests.

The very low participation level of girls in the experiment 1 games, however, meant that the data for them on any of the behavioral measures were very sparse. Thus, for example, while comparisons between ability measures from experiment 2 and number of passes to others in experiment 1 showed that high-ability boys passed less frequently than boys of lower ability, many of the girls, even those of high and moderately high ability, did not pass at all. The reason was that many of the girls had no contacts with the ball other than serving and thus never had an opportunity to pass. The decision as to whether to pass or to try to score never arose for them.

Experiment III

Planning. The purpose of the third part of the study was to investigate the perceived-ability sequence of the model by testing whether within-team cooperation was based on sex or actual ability. Was the relationship between perceived and actual ability as described in the model, and was it the same for both boys and girls when they were matched on the ability measure?

The ability scores of the children from experiment 2 were listed in rank order for each class and divided into quartiles to obtain a high, medium-high, medium-low, and low-ability group for each class. Our objective was to make up as many four-player teams as possible for the experiment 3 laboratory games by uniting high-ability girls with low-ability boys, and vice-versa, within classes. We could then make direct comparisons between girls and boys of similar and different ability levels on measures of actual performance and perceived ability.

Making up these teams proved to be one of the most difficult parts of the project. The difference in scores for boys and girls was so large that many classes could not be used at all. For example, 42 percent of the boys but only 5 percent of the girls were in the high-ability group, and 43 percent of the girls but only 9 percent of the boys were in the low-ability group. Overall 73 percent (nearly three-fourths) of the boys scored above the median score in their class, and 76 percent (three-fourths) of the girls scored below the median score in their classes. Because of the resulting scarcity of boys of lower ability than their female classmates and, conversely, the even smaller group of girls of higher ability than their male classmates, only 112 children (56 boys and 56 girls) from thirteen classes who had been in the first two parts of the study could be selected to participate in this final phase.

Controlled Team Play. This part of the study involved a team game very similar to the "alone game" played in experiment 2. The skills required for achievement were the same, but each child now had three other persons on the same team and four other persons on the opposite team with whom to interact. Thus interactions in this "laboratory" situation were similar to those of the "natural" situation of experiment 1. For this experiment, two teams competed in a game using the same apparatus as in experiment 2 and the throwing and catching skills required in games of newcomb, under scoring rules that guided the players into passing to teammates perceived as high in ability.

Each child started off with exactly the same number of opportunities to try to score. The difference was that in experiment 2, each child had to attempt ten throws, but in experiment 3 players could choose not to throw but to pass and could thus give away as many of their opportunities as they wished. This meant that players believing themselves to be very low in ability but wanting very much to be on the winning team could give all of their opportunities to the person believed to be best. Such players could potentially—without contributing any effort themselves toward scoring—end up as members of the winning team.

The Game. Groups of eight children, comprising two teams each containing two boys and two girls, were selected from the same class for each game. Selections were based on ability scores and class ranks from the experiment 2 skills tests. of the twenty-eight teams that participated, fourteen had a girl as the player who ranked the highest on ability in the team and thirteen had a boy who ranked lowest on ability.

The children were called from the classroom eight at a time (two teams) and taken to the playing area, where they were instructed how to play the target board game. The members of each team (identified as "Red" and "Blue") were called out by name to receive numbered hats and told which team to join. The assignment to teams was explained as being the result of random selection by the computer. (The children accepted this without argument, even though the experimenter had the impression that some of them did not want to be on the same team as others they perceived as poor players.)

The game was played on a marked court (see figure 9-3) with a thrower's mark fifteen feet from the target board. This distance had been

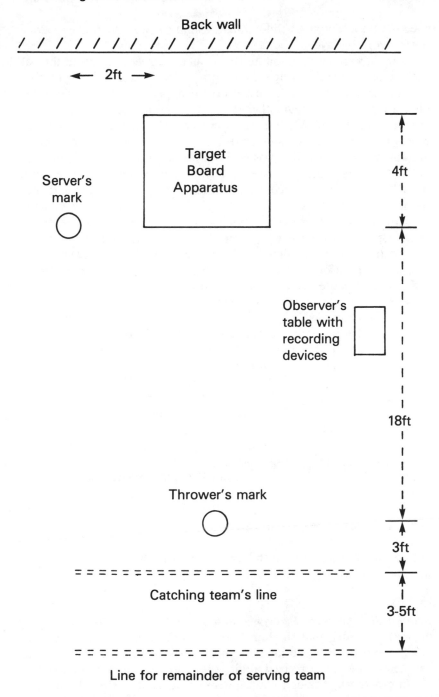

Figure 9-3. Game Court Layout for Experiment 3

tried out on a sample of children and found to be in the range of even the lowest-scoring players.

The first server stood on a mark near the target and served the ball to each player on the throwing team in turn. Only the player whose turn it was could catch the ball. Having caught (or dropped) the ball served to her or him, a player could then either throw the ball at the target or pass it to another member of the same team considered better able to score more points for the team. An unlimited number of passes was permitted, thus allowing the recipient of a pass who did not want to use the opportunity to give it away. As in the class newcomb games, no player was allowed to hold the ball longer than five seconds without incurring a penalty, to add urgency to the need for a decision.

After each member of the serving team had taken a turn at serving four balls, the teams were rotated; the team at the throwing line moved to the serving line, and player number one on the original serving team moved to the thrower position. Games consisted of four such sets of sixteen serves by each team. Because the games took a long time, however, some had to be curtailed at the two-set point to meet the needs of the school.

The data recorded by the observers included measures of performance such as number of catches, accuracy and force of impact scores, number of misses, kind of throw, and each pass from or to a player.

In order to increase motivation and involvement, the inherently competitive situation was reinforced by telling the children that the experimenters were visiting all of the schools in the district trying out a new team game and that the winning team of each game would have a chance to become the championship team for the whole school district; the team with the most points would win. In all cases the word *championship* had a very strong effect on many of the children; there were loud cries of excitement, much jumping up and down, and immediate planning of strategy with other players on their team.

Game points for each catch and throw were computed on a continuous basis by one of the experimenters. As in the experiment 2 skills tests, accuracy was rated more valuable than strength (force of impact) or catching. Points were reported to the children after each set, and the winning team was announced at the end of the game.

Results

Relationship between Perceived and Actual Ability. According to the theoretical model, participation level and skill level are related to opportunity and then to perception of ability by self and others. The relationship between actual and perceived ability therefore is an important one.

In experiment 3 poorer players were encouraged by the rules to increase the score of their team by passing the ball to better players. The first question we asked was whether the children did in fact tend to pass to the highest-ability players on their teams. If so, then the highest-ability player on a team should have received more passes than the second highest-ability player, while the lowest-ability player should have given away more passes than the second from the bottom and so on. This proved to be exactly what happened. Table 9-4 shows how players of different levels of ability (according to their experiment 2 performance) behaved with respect to their passing behaviors. Passing patterns were in the predicted order. There was a positive correlation between ability and frequency of receiving passes and an inverse relationship between ability and giving passes away.

Perceived and Actual Ability and Sex. If we take sex as well as ability into consideration, the pattern changes. It can be seen from table 9-5 that girls who were the highest-ability players on their teams gave away twice as many passes as boys who were the highest-ability players on their teams. The high-ability girls acted as though they believed themselves to be lower in ability than lower-ability boy members of their teams, and high-ability boys acted as though they believed themselves to be the best and able to score more for their teams than other players. These same highest-ability boys received twice as many passes from other children as the high-ability girls did. Other children seemed to recognize the high-ability boys as being the most likely to be able to score for their teams, but they failed to recognize the high-ability girls. Girls who were the second highest-ability players on their teams received fewer passes than boys who were the lowest. In this case, the very lowest-ability boys were seen by other players as higher in ability than girls who were considerably more able than they were. These same girls, however, gave away fewer of their throws than the lowest-ability boys. The girls themselves apparently thought they were better than the lowest-ability boys even though they were not treated that way.

Of nearly 450 opportunities to throw and to score, over one in five of their throwing turns were given away by the girls; over 80 percent of these were passes to boys and just under 20 percent were passes to other girls. Girls

Table 9-4
Relationship between Rank Order of Ability and Passing Behavior

Rank Order of Ability in Team	Total Passes Given Away	Total Passes Received
1	8	75
2	24	38
3	32	12
4	66	5

Table 9-5
Relationship between Rank Order of Ability and Passing Behavior, by Sex

Rank Order of Ability in Team	Mean Passes Given Away			Mean Passes Received		
	By Boys	By Girls	Ratio of Boys to Girls	By Boys	By Girls	Ratio Boys Girls
1	0.2	0.4	0.5	3.4	1.9	1.8
2	0.4	1.8	0.2	1.8	0.3	6
3	0.0	1.8	0.1	1.0	0.1	10
4	2.1	2.6	0.8	0.4	0.0	4

tended to regard boys as being better able to score points for the team than other girls, regardless of their actual ability. The boys, on the other hand, tended to keep their turns for themselves, passing only once in twelve times, and then twice as often to boys as to girls. Only 20 percent of the boys passed, but 50 percent of the girls did. Boys tended to believe that they could do as well as or better than any other member of their team.

There was nevertheless a strong positive correlation between perception of ability by others and actual ability for both boys and girls at either extreme of the distribution of actual ability scores. It was for the middle range of actual ability scores that perception was most clearly mediated by sex role stereotypes. Thus it can be seen from table 9-5 that with respect to the frequency of receiving passes from other players, there was a larger ratio difference between the top-ranking girl on a team and other girls than is the case for top-ranking boys and other boys. There is also a larger difference between boys in the top three ranks and those in the lowest-ability group than is the case for the lowest-ability group of girls and the other girls. When perception of ability differs from actual ability, it tends to be moved upward for boys in the medium range of ability but downward for girls in the same medium range of ability groups, in accordance with the theoretical model.

Performance. We wondered whether the tendency in experiment 3 to treat high-ability girls differently from high-ability boys was related to the way in which the girls were actually performing during the games. If these girls were not playing as well as they really could when other children were around, the other children could not know their true capabilities and so would not pass to them.

Because of the passing patterns, there was a sex difference in the number of throws actually made. To take this into consideration, the average scores per actual throw were computed for all of the girls and all of the boys separately. Girls scored slightly more for accuracy per actual throw than did boys, but boys scored higher than girls on mean force of impact (table 9-6).

These findings support our observations during the game that the actual successes and failures of boys and girls were being perceived differently. For example, some of the boys who got many additional throwing opportunities from other children continued to get them even after they had missed the target board completely and had failed to score any points at all, several times in succession. On the other hand, a few girls who scored many points by hitting the bull's eye did not thereafter receive any passes from other children. The children appeared to be prejudging; failing a few times did not seem to damage a boy's reputation, but succeeding a few times did not seem to improve that of a girl.

Group Pressure. We have seen how boys retained more of their throwing opportunities than did girls of comparable ability and have suggested that this was related to the different ways in which the children of each sex tended to make subjective judgments about their own ability to achieve in this team game situation. These differences are believed to be related to an individual player's expectations concerning success or failure on the ball-throwing task.

Another element in the decision to throw or pass was, we believe, related to the intrinsic satisfaction of throwing the ball against the target. It is possible that at times, individual players retained their throwing turns not because they believed they could score more for their team than other team members but simply because they wanted to have a turn at this new game, because it was fun.

In many instances, however, girls were persuaded by their team to sacrifice their turn at throwing the ball at the target for the benefit of the team while boys were not. Unfortunately it was not a formal part of the research to study how group pressure was exerted on boys and girls with

Table 9-6
Mean Number of Points Scored in Experiment 3 Games, by Sex

Basis for Comparison	Mean Score (Electronic Apparatus)	
	Boys (n = 56)	Girls (n = 56)
Composite Score	7.76	8.84
Force	237	228
Accuracy	2.34	3.85

respect to such decisions. Some incidents observed during the games provide an idea of the qualitative differences that occurred. These examples of within-team interactions may provide some understanding of the reasons why 80 percent of the boys did not pass at all whereas only 50 percent of the girls did not.

During one game, a girl in the second highest-ability group had the ball. Her teammates hissed at her to, "Pass to Bobby"; Bobby, meanwhile, was jumping up and down at her elbow chanting, "Pass it to me. Come on, pass it to me." The girl was obviously very uncomfortable: what if she threw and did not do well? What would her teammates say then? Maybe Bobby could do better than she, even though he had not done as well as she so far in the game. But maybe that was just luck; how could she be sure that she could do it again? This was not the kind of situation in which she could relax and be free to concentrate on doing her best. Very red in the face, she gritted her teeth and threw the ball, to a chorous of complaints from her teammates. It was not a perfect shot, but it was well above average, and the children did not make any further comments. When it was this girl's turn to throw once more, the other children again shouted at her to pass. This time she shrugged and with a gesture of obvious disgust passed the ball to Bobby, who had missed the target completely his previous two shots. The other children were very pleased; the other girl on the team even patted her on the arm as if to assure her she had done the right thing.

One of the interactions between two boys contrasts starkly. During one game, the lowest-ability player on the team (a boy) passed the ball to the second highest-ability player (a boy), saying that he believed the other could do better. The better player returned the ball with the comment, "No, you ought to try it yourself. You need the practice." The low-ability boy passed the ball back, saying he was not very good. The higher-ability boy returned it again, with an encouraging, "Go on, Jimmy, you can do it. Just do your best." Meanwhile standing beside them were the two girl members of the team, one the highest-ability player and the other the third highest. Both passed several times to the better of the two boys; he never returned it to them the way he had to the other boy, nor did any one suggest that he ought to.

Perceived Ability. The perception of ability was measured by subjective responses on the questionnaires, as well as in the form of passing behaviors. These questionnaire responses differed from the objective measures of per-throw skills; there were many more citations of boys than of girls as the highest scorer on both force and accuracy, especially by the boys. Thus a boy was cited as having scored the highest on force by forty-seven boys (84 percent) and thirty-five girls (63 percent), compared with citations of a girl by only nine (16 percent) boys and twenty-one (37 percent) girls. For the accuracy measure, on which, in fact, girls had on the average scored slightly higher than boys, a boy was cited as the highest scorer by thirty-seven (66 percent) of the boys, while a girl was cited as being the highest scorer by only nineteen (34 percent) of the boys. The girls seemed closer to the actual scores since twenty-seven (48 percent) of them cited a boy as highest scorer, while twenty-nine (52 percent) cited a girl as having scored the most.

A further analysis was made to determine how accurate the children were in naming the player who scored the most points in a game against the objective measures of each player's performance as recorded by the meters. We found that the girls and boys were approximately equal in their ability to identify correctly those who had actually scored the highest number of points, were the most accurate, or hit the target hardest, whether this was a boy or a girl. However, when making incorrect identifications, boys tended to name other boys as highest scorer, and girls named other girls. In other words, when players were clearly superior, the children could identify them with ease. When they were less outstanding, they were identified in terms of same-sex bias. These findings are in striking agreement with other studies of social judgment. In these a clearly structured stimulus pattern was less subject to social influence than an ambiguous one (see Asch 1956).

Comparison of Questionnaire Responses and Behavioral Measures. People's behavior is often not congruent with what they claim they would do in certain circumstances. This is borne out by the discrepancy between the subjective (questionnaire) measures of perception of ability and the behavioral measures of these perceptions.

The results from the behavioral observations showed a bias according to sex role stereotypes, with boys being preferred over girls. These sex role stereotypes were carried over into actual play, with boys getting more opportunities (receiving more passes) and giving away fewer opportunities (passing away to others) than girls. In contrast, on the subjective measure of ability from the questionnaire responses, a same-sex bias was found.

The different situations in which the two kinds of data were collected permitted these discrepancies to be demonstrated between those who were said to be best and those who were treated as best during the games. The behavioral data were collected under conditions in which there was the possibility of peer pressure, overt or imagined, regarding whether to pass and to whom to pass. Further the game condition involved a public revelation of whom the child perceived as better (to whom the child passed), and when the child thought herself or himself to be better (retaining the ball). This must be contrasted with the privacy of the questionnaire condition. Privacy permits the expression of praise for self and personal preference for friends without public censure, a well-known psychological phenomenon that could be operating here (Deutsch and Gerard 1955).

The Model and the Games

Experiment 1 showed how those who made the largest numbers of attempts to succeed also had the largest number of successes. Those players whose active behaviors demonstrated the strongest motive to achieve also tended to be those for whom reinforcement to continue in their efforts would be most likely to occur.

A number of experiments have demonstrated that if individuals are led to believe that a task requires abilities that they think they possess, they will work harder at it (Vroom 1964). Thus the boys in the class games would be expected to try harder than the girls if they believed that they possessed abilities, by virtue of their sex, that would enable them to do well on the ball-throwing and catching task. On the other hand, if many of the girls believed that, again by virtue of their sex, they did not possess these abilities to the same extent as boys, they would be expected to reduce their efforts.

Motivation to continue in an activity is also affected by success or failure (see Heckhausen 1967). Research has shown a sex difference with respect to the response to failure, with girls reducing their aspirations following a single incidence of failure significantly more than boys (Parsons 1974).

Success and failure, however, are subjective as well as objective evaluations. Being told one has failed can operate as effectively as a real failure in terms of motivation to try again. The girls received numerous verbal and nonverbal cues from their peers regarding their likelihood of failure. The small number of passes made to them constituted a form of nonverbal cue. Boys were expected to succeed more often than was the case for girls so, according to this assumption, they generated opportunities to try to score (by moving around actively) and were given opportunities to try to score by receiving passes. Girls, on the other hand, were often expected to fail, which served to depress their efforts to create opportunities to score and to increase the likelihood that they would give away opportunities to boys by passing the ball and not be the recipient of opportunities in the form of passes from others.

For some of the girls, a high level of involvement in the game (a strong need to be on the winning team) might have been the reason why their very minimal levels of participation were being reinforced. These players may have believed that the chances for their teams to score were improved by passing the ball to a boy player so that he could assume responsibility for making a scoring attempt. They may have been motivated by what Zander (1971) describes as a group- rather than an individual-oriented achievement need. These girls may have believed that they were able to contribute the most to their team's efforts by keeping away from the ball as much as possible because of a high risk of failure due to their perceived inadequate level of skill compared to that of most boys. In doing so, however, not only were these girls giving away opportunities both to practice skills and to be seen as high-ability performers by other players, they were also receiving reinforcement for their passing behaviors. For example, if one girl player passed the ball to another boy who threw the ball and successfully scored, the behaviors of passer and thrower were reinforced simultaneously. This pattern of reinforcement would tend to reduce the girls' already infrequent participation behaviors.

Over a period of time, this mechanism could lead to a reduction in the ability levels of the girls below that of the originally relatively lower-ability boys on measures of both actual and perceived ability. Unless there is intervention to change the dynamics at some point in the cycle described in the model, the very significant sex differences obtained in these experiments would be expected to continue, and perhaps increase.

The Low-Ability Boys

In these experiments it was found that most boys in the lowest quartile of ability in the experiment 2 skills tests tended to be more active in the class games and to receive more throwing opportunities in the experiment 3 games than girls in the second and third quartiles. There was, however, a very small minority of boys in the lowest-ability group for whom the sex role-mediated expectations for achievement operated in a downward cycle similar to that which applied to the majority of the girls. For these boys, who were unable to perform at the standard expected of boys, there was an additional dynamic involved.

Ability at sports-related tasks and social popularity and status among peers of both sexes has been found to be positively related for boys (see Coleman 1961) though not for girls. Even though high-ability girls tended to be perceived and treated as though they were like the majority of the other girls—low in ability—low-ability girls were generally not blamed for being inept. They were pressured to pass to others, shouted at in the class games to keep out of the way and not attempt to catch or throw the ball, and suffered occasional rather mild negative remarks from boys or high-ability girls. The sociometric data for the classes, however, showed that some of the lowest-ability girls were very popular and were in some cases close friends with high-ability girls or boys.

Very low-ability boys, however, tended to be social isolates. The consequences of falling too far beneath the minimal standard for boys can be very damaging. The attacks by other children against such boys during the experiment 3 laboratory games were occasionally extremely vicious, with girls often being much more unkind than were boys.[4] Thus the use of defense mechanisms by many of the boys such as saying that and acting as though they had done well in the experiment 2 tests when they had not can be understood, for the consequences of failure with respect to peer approval and self-image were far more immediate and dramatic for the boys than was the case for the girls.

Implications of the Study

Sex-Segregated versus Sex-Integrated
Physical Education Classes

Data obtained during the course of the research demonstrated significant differences between the sexes with respect to their levels of performance and opportunities for achievement in class games. The majority of boys enter these classes with an already more highly developed level of relevant experience and practice in physical perceptual and motor skills than is the case for the majority of the girls. Yet the coeducational classes observed during this study were conducted in such a way that those who began with these advantages obtained opportunities for reinforcement and further development of skills and interest, while those who lacked this advantage receive little reinforcement and tended to lack opportunities for participation and improvement. We believe that this is likely to lead to many girls' dropping out from all physical education and sports programs in the school as soon as this is permissible.

This situation exists even more dramatically (and is more punishing) in the case of the minority of boys who enter classes with low levels of basic motor skills and team ball game practice than in the case of girls. However, many of the physical education teachers with whom we spoke during the study provided extra practice and coaching for such boys, though they did not provide these opportunities to the many girls who were in this situation and did not acknowledge a need to do so.

We believe that it is necessary and desirable to develop intervention techniques to help girls obtain equal educational opportunities in these coeducational physical education classes and that these would also be necessary for low-ability boys. This leads to an important question concerning these classes: Should the children be separated according to ability rather than according to sex? Put another way, should all of the children who have not attained a basic level of motor skills be put into special enrichment classes? Because of past practices this option would probably lead to a situation in which there would be de facto sex segregation, with the special classes being made up of a majority of girls and a very few boys.

If our study can be taken as indicative of a more general state of affairs in public schools, then one might conclude that the newly sex-integrated physical education classes are not achieving their goal of providing equal educational opportunity to boys and girls. Only those who already are skilled seem to benefit, and most girls tend not to be skilled. It is therefore reasonable to ask whether mixed-sex classes should be abolished in favor of single-sex classes, or whether sex-integrated classes should be continued and teaching techniques be developed to help change the existing cycle.

The Courts

The new laws and regulations concerning coeducational physical education came into being because of the high value placed by this democratic society upon equal educational opportunity regardless of sex or race. In an open, individualistic society, people should have equal opportunity to compete according to their ability and interests, not according to their sex or race. Sex segregation and differentiation with respect to physical education programs do not preclude the possibility of equal opportunity, but the historic Supreme Court ruling regarding black civil rights that separate can never be equal suggests that a similar situation in terms of educational opportunity exists for the sexes. This is in agreement with the observation made by Holter (1975) that while division of tasks between men and women and the accompanying differences in personality formation of the two genders may be universal, discrimination of women usually follows from most known gender differentiations. Support for this statement is to be found in the form that sex segregation of physical education and sports programs has taken in most of our educational institutions (NOW Survey 1979; Womensports 1974). Thus the historical record indicates that the desired goal of equal educational opportunity cannot be obtained in single-sex situations.

The Development of Teaching Techniques

The data collected during this study have implications not only in terms of contributing to the knowledge on achievement motivation and behavior but also for teachers of physical education. There is no reason why low-ability children could not receive added instruction within sex-integrated classes. In the early grades especially, girls tend to be more advanced in the development of language skills than boys yet boys are taught to read and write in the same classes as girls.[5] No one suggests that boys might be holding back the more advanced girls, and no one has ever proposed sex-segregated reading classes. Since low-ability readers can be taught successfully in the same classroom as high-ability readers, the same principles can be applied to physical education classes. Peer teaching, for example, has shown splendid results. Nothing would seem easier than pairing more accomplished athletes with those who need to learn some basic skills. For some it could be an exchange of skills situation: the good reader who helps a slower reader in one class might be able to receive help from that person in the physical education class, with each child in turn enjoying the status of tutor.

The behavioral observation method used in the class games and the computer program that produced a printout of every observed behavior for each individual player during a game could be adapted for a variety of different games and used as a diagnostic tool by teachers. Which children were not participating, and events in the game that related to this lack of participation, could thus be identified and lead to the development of appropriate intervention methods.

The apparatus used in the experiment 2 ability tests could also be used as a means of improving and shaping skills through the immediate feedback provided by the meters. At the same time, these objective measures could provide accurate information on an individual's performance in order to bring perception of ability closer to actual ability. For the child with poorly developed skills, reading an objective measure of even very small improvements might lead to increased motivation to try harder, and thus lead to continued effort and attempts to participate and practice.

Use of the apparatus in group games might also help to change existing attitudes that mediate perception of one's own and others' ability and influence opportunities for participation and reinforcement. For example, if a high-ability girl player consistently registers a high number of points on the meters, would her male and female peers accept her as a high-ability player and treat her as one?

In-Service Teacher Training Workshops

In order to develop appropriate teaching techniques for the mixed-sex physical education classes required by title IX, more research is needed to augment the data on achievement motivation currently available. These data are very limited in scope, but existing teaching techniques are heavily dependent upon them. As a beginning, teachers might learn how some of their behaviors may affect their students and serve to maintain and reinforce the sex differences reported in this study.

Basic Skills. Children entering the school program bring with them a variety of experiences, interest, and aptitudes. In particular, girls often enter the physical education program with a different set of attitudes and related skills practice than is the case for most of the boys. For example, both the kind of toys played with by boys and the games they play tend to develop and build on the kind of intergroup competition and intragroup cooperation central to the kind of team games discussed in our study (Blakemore, LaRue, and Olejnik 1979; Connor and Serbin 1977; Hoffman 1977; Smith and Connolly 1972). Studies have shown that boys' toys tend to be more complex and encourage more active and social play than girls' toys. The latter generally promote more solitary, passive, and simple play whereas many so-called boys' toys involve the development of eye-hand coordination and team skills (Goodman and Lever 1975). This relatively new but now extensive body of research on the sex typing of childrens' toys and games also demonstrates that children, especially boys, learn to prefer sex-appropriate toys and activities from a very early age (Maccoby and Jacklin 1974).

Physical education teachers need to acknowledge this socially conditioned sex difference. At the elementary level and even beyond, many girls need extra help in the development of basic motor skills. Many of the girls in the classes observed in our study, for example, needed to learn how to throw and catch a ball, run, jump, and fall.

Throwing. In experiment 2 a large number of the 10-year-old girls did not know how to throw a ball in the most effective way (54 percent of the 198 girls compared with only 5 percent of the 228 boys).

Many teachers we observed did not appear to be concerned about this lack of knowledge when it was demonstrated by a girl. In fact, in a few cases the use of underhand throws by the girls in the newcomb class games was encouraged. When we asked one teacher why he did this if the correct throw was overarm, he asserted that many of the girls were used to throwing this way and so could do better than when they threw in a style to which they were not accustomed. Since the most effective throw was overarm, however, the teacher should have been showing these girls how to do it and encouraging them to practice it, not permitting them to continue to throw incorrectly simply because they were girls. There is nothing about the structure of a girl's arm that can justify one style of throw for her and another for boys. It is the function of the game that dictates the throw, not the sex of the player.

Falling and Body Image. One of the reasons why physical achievement was considered a useful means of studying sex-role-mediated achievement behaviors was the belief, expressed in the theoretical model used, that any psychologically inhibiting factor would have an effect on performance and thus could be observed through overt behaviors. Children who possess feelings of mastery over their environment or believe in their own competency should therefore be observed to participate in a game to the highest level possible by making the fullest use of all opportunities and would take every possible action to increase their number.

Indicators of a child's sense of her or his own level of competence could also be related to feelings about her or his own body in this physical task. Some children ran toward a ball as fast as possible but withdrew when approached by another child who was also competing for the ball, through fearing possible physical contact with the competitor. Such a child could not be said to be free to participate as fully as the child who persisted in competing for the ball until the outcome of the play was final and one or the other had the ball in hand, even if this involved a collision.

It is believed that the effects of sex role socialization practices influence the body image (and, of course, the self-image) of boys and girls. Thus even high-ability girls tended to be more like other girls than high-ability boys in terms of instrumental activity behaviors, while low-ability boys tended to be more like other boys than like low-ability girls.

Observations made during the games indicated that the collisions that did occur for the girls may have been qualitatively different from those that occurred for the boys. The majority of the collisions by boys seemed to be the result of competing for the ball—running toward the ball into the path of another child also striving for it. Collisions for these players were part of self-initiated instrumental activity; avoiding the risk of a collision meant moving away from the path of the ball and permitting the other child to get it. This behavior meant withdrawing from the competition. Collisions involving girls were less than one-third as frequent as for boys and were, in contrast, often accidents; a more active child racing for the ball would bump into her before she had a chance to move away, or she might be impatiently pushed out of the way by someone (usually a boy) attempting to reach the ball.

The willingness to risk collisions on the part of high-ability, high-activity players is related to their strong motivation to achieve by getting to the ball. It also seems to be related to body image in that boys also fell seven times more frequently than girls did. This first became apparent during pilot study observations of soccer games (Solomons 1976), in which boys were seen to run full tilt toward the ball, often tripping and falling to the ground, whereas even the highest-ability girls seemed to avoid falling in the direct unfearful way most boys did.

The casual way in which boys appeared to experience contact with the ground compared to girls and the different ways in which these incidents were viewed by others (including the teacher) are suggested by various observations. Boys often fell or rolled over on the ground together for the fun of it while waiting for play to begin. They would also throw themselves onto the ball for a dramatic catch or go down on their knees to catch a ball even when this was unnecessary (this was most apparent in experiment 2 when the mechanism kept the throws constant and consistently high). Such behavior is related to high visibility; a ball caught in this way looks more difficult to catch than others even when it is not. Only high-ability girls did this, and then very infrequently.

When a boy fell, the teacher and other children made no comment unless, as in one case, the child was badly bruised, obviously in pain and requiring a visit to the nurse. When a girl fell, however, the game was stopped and more attention was paid: perhaps because it was so infrequent, perhaps because of the teacher's fear of parents' responses to a daughter's bruises compared with those of a son's; perhaps because of the socially conditioned fragile image of the (physically strong) 10-year-old girl; perhaps because she made a fuss about it (all of these things are related). In one case, after stopping the game the teacher held the girl and comforted her even though she was not hurt at all, merely frightened. Nevertheless she sat on the side for the remainder of the game keeping score. (Perhaps she was frightened because the teacher's attention indicated to her that there was something to be frightened about.)

The observations suggest that teachers should be alerted to the possibility that many girls need to learn how to fall in order to achieve a sense of confidence that their bodies will not fail them and that they can take the moderate physical risks involved in carefully supervised class team games as freely as do their more confident male and female peers. Such training and new awareness on the part of teachers could also be helpful to the boys in terms of their ability to perceive and so treat a girl according to her ability rather than to her sex.

Standards and Expectations. Many teachers appeared to have different standards for judging good and bad plays and performance for the boys and girls in their coeducational classes. One teacher had a special serving rule for all girls: they could choose to do so from the middle row rather than the back regardless of ability. The teacher explained that girls simply could not throw hard enough to clear the net from the back row so that it was not fair to expect them to. Like the teacher who permitted girls (but not boys) to throw underarm, he was genuinely well meaning. But our observations showed that some of the girls in his class could serve properly from the back row (others too, if they had been taught how to throw properly), while some of the boys could not. Several of the boys in this class complained that the rule was unfair and they they ought to be able to serve from the middle row if they wanted to. The rule should have been according to ability, not sex.

Teacher expectations were also expressed in less overt ways; for example, girls were congratulated for doing something not nearly as well as a boy was expected to do. Even more important, when a girl performed badly this was often ignored, patronized ("That was a really nice try, Caroline"), or even encouraged (such as the underarm throw), whereas similar errors by boys were criticized and corrected.[6]

This kind of differential response to the performance of boys and girls implies an attitude that the teacher does not expect Caroline to do any better, but he does expect Billy to; he thinks Billy, but not Caroline, can do it if he works at it. Billy must try harder to get a reward; Caroline need not try at all. This also leads to boys' resenting girls because they are favored by the teacher. Because Billy's errors are consistently responded to, whereas sometimes Caroline's successes and failures are noticed and sometimes not, Billy can learn exactly whether he is doing something right or wrong, while she cannot. Billy knows what to do in order to improve, but Caroline does not even if she thought she could or wanted to.

Sex Integration of Sex-Integrated Classes. Some of the teachers we observed complied with the new equal opportunity laws in letter but not in spirit. For example, some alternated girl- and boy-type activities for the classes or had boys involved in one kind of activity and girls in another during the same class. Some chose to cope with the newly sex integrated classes by using one kind of activity for them and another for sex-segregated extracurricular activities after school or during lunch time.

All of the teachers demonstrated some, and often many, attitudes that conveyed the message that they thought of boys as one group and girls as another. For example, children would often be lined up by sex to be given instructions or critiques of games rather than as teams or as individuals. One teacher repeatedly called out, "Hey, you fellows, give the girls a chance, too" regardless of the individual boys who were not doing well and the individual girls who were.

These examples show that rather than attempting to change attitudes concerning girls' lack of ability and interest in sports compared with boys, many of the teachers were inadvertently reinforcing them.

Role Models. Throughout the school district we studied, there was not one female physical education teacher for first through sixth graders. The small number of female students electing to specialize in elementary physical education compared with the number of men who are doing so suggests that this situation may not be unusual.

Female role models in the schools may well be an important factor for the girls in developing interest and motivation in the school physical education programs. This is especially important since there are fewer and less visible female role models in the media and outside school for girls than is the case for boys.

We suggest that in schools where the physical education teachers are all or predominantly males, female teaching assistants, visits by sportswomen, visits by the children to athletic events involving women, and films should be used to provide role models for the girls. Simultaneously, boys might thus be given the opportunity to learn that females can succeed in sports.

Long-term Implications of the Study

The Relationship of Physical Education to Other Kinds of Achievement

Ever since the time of the ancient Greeks (and probably even before that), training through sports has been accepted as a means of developing the personality characteristics and skills that are need for many other kinds of achievement: at school, at work, and, of course, at war. Corporations recognize this when they recruit executives from the ranks of varsity athletes. As Korda points out in his book on success, "Nothing is more universally respected than sports achievement, which is assumed to indicate strength of character and the will to win" (Korda 1977).

Strength of character and the will to win are positive human traits that can be applied in many different kinds of situations and directed toward many different kinds of goals: working to improve the quality of education in our schools, or to promote (or impede) the passage of laws such as the equal rights amendment, for example, as well as helping an ambitious individual climb to the top of the corporate ladder. The traits and personal skills that are associated with athletics involve goal-oriented instrumental behaviors that are crucial to success at just about any activity.

One line of research by Sutton-Smith and his coworkers suggests that the games children play are related to adult achievement. These researchers found a relationship between child-rearing practices, the games children play, and the degree of achievement as adults, in a number of different cultures (Sutton-Smith, Roberts, and Kozelka 1963); Sutton-Smith, Rosenberg, and Morgan 1963). In many countries, including the United States, games of physical skill were associated with men and higher status, and games of chance with women and lower status. They also found evidence that practice in games of physical skill was practice for a particular achievement style later on in life. In games of physical skill, success depends upon a display of power, motor skill, or courage, which the player can do something about. Playing games of chance, on the other hand, means practicing a style in which success depends upon luck, and this is, of course, outside the player's control. Persistent practice at a particular type of game involves rehearsing the success style associated with that kind of play. When they participate in games, children (and, to a lesser degree, adults) learn intellectually and socially as well as physically, and this learning eventually contributes "to the participant's ability to survive in the full scale success system of the larger culture'' (Sutton-Smith, Roberts, and Kozelka 1963; Roberts and Sutton-Smith 1962).

Those qualities that differentiate the woman athlete from her less active sisters, such as "independence, initiative and assertiveness," are those that according to Maccoby (1970), are highly related to the development of the ability to think analytically. Longitudinal studies by workers at the Fels Institute on the antecedents to the development of high-achieving females suggest the importance of a high degree of physical activity in childhood. In this project large groups of high- and low-achieving women were studied in depth over many years. The investigation found a recurring theme for all high-achieving women that differentiated them from low achievers and led to the comment that "the simplest way to put it is that she must be a tomboy at some point in her childhood" (pg. 22). The high-achieving women in another study (Birnbaum 1975) agreed with the Fels Institute comment. They described themselves as having been "cheerful, independent, 'tomboy,' active, competitive, sometimes even aggressive" as children, in contrast to low-achievers who remembered themselves as "friendly, good, docile, or compliant."

It would seem that the behaviors practiced by the very active girl (the so-called tomboy) help her to achieve at school and at work even though she may cease all athletic or sports-related activities when she enters young womanhood.

Physical Education and Changing Roles of Women

It could be suggested that the physical activity, competitiveness, and aggressiveness described by high-achieving women as part of their childhood experience indicates that they were successful in a man's world because they learned to play the games intended to prepare boys for that world.[7] These women could be departing from their stereotypical sex roles. While the achievement motive may be as strong in women as in men, for most women achievement is confined to areas that are culturally defined as feminine (Stein and Bailey 1973).

The high achievers in Birnbaum's studies cannot be termed deviant, however, in view of their numbers and the kinds of changes in adult roles that have taken place for the majority of women in the United States since the early 1960s. In this light, the dependency demonstrated by those girls in our study who tended to rely on others, particularly boys, to score for them and the passivity associated with very low participation levels in the games seem to indicate a withdrawal from active competition. This may not be important in fulfilling the traditional domestic roles of women but may very well prove to be very important with respect to the actual future adult roles of most of these fifth-grade girls.

The kind of role expectations that once formed the basis of the different physical education programs for the sexes and that were a real part of the experience of many of the teachers, parents, and other significant adults in the lives of these children may no longer be valid. It cannot be assumed that only the unusual woman works outside the home, for example, when 90 percent of all women do so at some time during their lives.

The historical evidence shows that changes in the adult female world are qualitatively and quantitatively much greater than those for the male. If we accept Sutton-Smith's findings that adult achievement styles are developed through the game styles of childhood, lack of participation in the safe achievement environment of elementary school team games can assume important dimensions. For example, while women still tend to be crowded into low-status, low-paying service jobs, opportunities for employment in upper-level careers are increasing quite rapidly. The kind of achievement skills developed by appropriate children's games might assist many girls to take advantage of the opportunities that will one day be open to them. Early experiences in sex-integrated competitive team games might also help prepare males to accept them when they do.

More research is needed on the effects of sex-integrated classes on the students participating in them and on ways of developing the most effective teaching techniques for them. If the creation of sex-integrated physical education classes was intended to promote the goal of equal educational opportunity for the sexes and if this goal is to be attained, putting boys and girls into the same classes together is only a beginning.

Notes

1. The several computer programs used in reducing the running commentaries and other measurement data to a form that could be used as input data for statistical analysis programs were designed and written by Dr. Cyril Solomons.

2. I wish to acknowledge the assistance of Dr. Cyril Solomons who designed and constructed the apparatus described in this chapter in accordance with my directions and tiny budget.

3. The scoring was such that the accuracy score was inversely proportional to the probability of hitting the given ring of the target by chance once the ball was within the total area covered by the target and therefore provided a measure of compensation for random effects of luck. Thus, for hitting ring five having an area of fifty square inches, twice as many accuracy points were awarded as for hitting ring one (outmost) having an area of one hundred square inches.

4. In one instance, the attacks against one unskilled boy were so horrifying—the ball was hurled directly at the boy's face though he wore glasses,

accompanied by cries from team members on both sides of "tear his head off" and "kill him"—the experimenters had to intervene and stop the game.

5. From a review of the research on this topic, Maccoby and Jacklin (1974) concluded that there was no consistent evidence supporting a significant superiority of girls over boys in verbal skills until around age 10 or 11. Instead, they suggested, although boys tend to have reading problems more frequently than girls in the elementary grades, it is not until high school and college that females outperform males in tests of verbal skills. Nevertheless the belief that girls are more advanced than boys in the development of language skills from a very early age is still widely held by educators, so the analogy to the physical skills situation is valid.

6. The class in which the smallest sex differences in participation, performance, and ability levels were found was taught by a teacher who directed critical comments to girls as frequently as he did to boys. He expected more from them, and he appeared to get it.

7. For an interesting presentation of this view see B.L. Harragan's *Games Mother Never Taught You: Corporate Gamesmanship for Women* (New York: Rawson Associates, 1977).

10 Effects of Preaching, Practice, and Helpful Evaluations on Third Graders' Collaborative Work

Nina B. Korsh

The recent popular innovative trend in American primary schools toward open education reflects more a shared philosophy about children and their learning than a single, unified approach to education. Central to this philosophy is the assumption that classroom activities derived largely from spontaneous and natural interests of children are more likely to lead to positive attitudes toward school, learning, peers, and teachers than are prespecified classroom activities (Katz 1972).

Although ostensibly influenced by the British approach to primary education, the open classroom movement has its roots in John Dewey's philosophy of education. In *Experience and Education*, Dewey (1952) contrasted traditional and progressive education and in so doing capsulized the essence of his philosophy. In traditional education, there is an accepted body of knowledge, including standards of conduct, developed in the past and handed down to docile, receptive students, who obediently acquire this static knowledge. Progressive education stresses learning through experience and acquiring knowledge as a means of attaining ends. Dewey believed that traditional education produces "learning in isolation" (p. 8), which does not last because it does not serve a current need. Rather it is a kind of serving up for the benefit of adults of what has been taught by adults. In contrast, Dewey (1900) pointed to the importance of firsthand experience with materials and processes of manipulation: "No number of object-lessons, got up *as* object-lessons for the sake of giving information, can afford even the shadow of a substitute for acquaintance with the plants and animals of the farm and garden acquired through actual living among them and caring for them" (p. 8). These same educational objectives are also reflected in the literature on open education: "Open educators are more concerned about the kinds of experiences students should have in school than about the cognitive, conative, and affective outcomes students should be expected to display as a result of having attended school" (Traub et al. 1972, p. 71).

In addition to the obvious influence of John Dewey on open education, Piaget's stage theory of cognitive development is important to educational practices. According to Piaget, concept formation in children proceeds in an inalterable sequence of stages but at varying rates. Since young children, age 7 and under, are strongly tied to the concrete and those between 7 and 11 very closely tied to the concrete, it is considered more important for teachers to encourage children to learn through manipulation and to provide the time and freedom to learn through exploration of the various concrete aspects of each concept than to teach by abstract explanation in the traditional way (Ginsburg and Opper 1969).

Throughout the literature on open education, there appears the basic assumption that children learn best through firsthand experience with materials and processes of manipulation, when they are pursuing interests they are developmentally ready to handle at their individual rates of learning. The implication is that children should work independently from each other. But there is the assumption that children will learn from peers as well as from materials (Barth 1972) and that such learning will result from children working in interdependent settings. Indeed, a major expected outcome of open education is collaboration in group problem solving.

The emphasis on cooperation as opposed to the traditional educational emphasis on competition is basic to open education (Marshall 1972).[1] In a study of the relative effectiveness of praise and group competition as motivating incentives for task persistence in young children, Senior and Brophy (1973) concluded that competition is not a desirable incentive because of possible negative side effects. Praise is simpler and equally effective.

The objective of cooperation in open education seems to stem from the assumption that free-flowing interaction among students will be more prevalent in open than in traditional programs. As students pursue their individual interests, they will encounter other students doing the same. The hoped-for outcome is cooperation: "Conflicts inevitably occur as do situations in which the interests of several individuals can be met most satisfactorily only if they cooperate with one another" (Traub et al. 1972, p. 72). However, it is important to recognize that an alternative outcome of such conflict is competition for resources and materials, as well as for teacher attention.

It is known that competition can arouse anxiety (Senior and Brophy 1973) and can lead to hostile group climates (Sherif 1964). It is also known that one way to increase collaboration is to create conditions of intergroup competition (Bronfenbrenner 1970; Sherif 1964). Because of harmful side effects, this is clearly not a desirable method of achieving cooperation in schools. Senior and Brophy (1973) found competition significantly more effective as a motivator than praise only on boring tasks. The open classroom, since its goals include challenging children intellectually by teaching concepts that grow out of individual needs and interests, has no need of using competition to make dull tasks more interesting.

This area, however, has not been fully thought out or explored in the literature on open education. The whole concept of individualization, of students following their own interests at their own rates, employing methods and materials provided for them by the teacher, necessitates their working alone or in small groups utilizing other students as resources. The aim of individualized learning may at times be in direct opposition to the aim of collaborative learning. Certainly it would help for teachers to be clear about what they require from students in different situations in order to arrange classroom conditions to meet these requirements best.

In order to facilitate children's interaction with the various levels and kinds of materials and with their peers, teachers usually organize the classroom into learning centers or activity areas, following the British model (Silberman 1971). These areas are characteristically occupied by small groups of children. There is indeed evidence that children in open classrooms spend more time in small groups and interact more with and feel closer to their classmates than do children in traditional classrooms (Brandt 1972; Stallings, Steinmetz, and Wilcox 1973; Brody and Zimmerman 1975).

Throughout the literature on open education, there runs the following duality: individualize learning but divide the classroom space logistically so that students work together in small groups; each individual will work on activities of her own choosing according to her unique way of learning and will use her peers as resources.

The question of what actually happens when children are in these small groups is very important; it is also one that has not been sufficiently investigated. Some relevant data stem from Torrance's (1970) study of the differential effects on the small group behavior among 5-year-old children of three alternative approaches to educational stimulation. The children were divided into groups of four and were instructed to work on their tasks as teams, each team at a separate table. In the first approach, the traditional kindergarten, children were characterized as "alert, cooperative, enthusiastic, organized, and friendly." The second, utilizing a creative-aesthetic approach, aimed to develop intellectual skills, abilities, and attitudes through creative and aesthetic experiences. In this condition, children were said to be "bickering, fighting, absorbed, and enthusiastic." The cognitive-structured approach, emphasizing cognitive development through highly structured activities, was characterized as "somewhat apathetic, inattentive, low in friendliness, and lacking in organization" (p. 79). Torrance concluded that "the results suggest that the new preschool programs of educational stimulation may be neglecting some of the socialization goals emphasized in the traditional preschool approaches" (p. 81).

Torrance's study is suggestive in its application to open education, but it is certainly not conclusive since it deals with preprimary youngsters involved in an educational approach with goals and atmosphere that are similar to those of the open classroom. In addition, it is unclear what transpired in the creative-aesthetic experiences that resulted in the bickering and fighting Torrance reported. The general literature on small groups in the open classroom is disappointing because it is largely theoretical and is written by convinced proponents of open education. There is a widespread conviction that when the traditional restrictions against peer interaction are removed and children are encouraged to work together and share their learning experiences, the result will be increased resourcefulness and cooperation (Barth 1972; Ridgway and Lawton 1969). Despite the centrality of this assumption to open education, there has been no systematic effort to research the question of what happens when open classroom children are together in small groups. Do they work together? How do they get along with each other? Do they work on the tasks at hand? What does the product look like?

Children are members of many small groups within the larger classroom. They interact with each other differently under different conditions. Other children in the class are not simply resources but are feeling, thinking, acting human beings with different abilities and different needs to be satisfied. The combination of these qualities varies with changes within the classroom situation. In order to examine how elementary school children interact in various types of small group settings, we must extrapolate from the literature on group dynamics as well as from the literature on education.

The accepted definition of a group requires that the individuals who comprise it be interdependent in some significant way (Cartwright and Zander 1968). It is often assumed that children in the presence of other children form a group, but this is not necessarily the case. Since learning in the open classroom is highly individualized, there is likely to be a substantial choice of activities at each activity area, and children may be working independently at different tasks while they are physically together for a given period of time. There is some tentative evidence that the presence of other children where there is not task interdependence distracts children from working on the tasks at hand (Farran 1973; Korsh 1973). If each child is working individually on a different task, it is difficult, if not impossible, for children to work together. When there is interaction, it tends to be of a social nature or related to common tasks or interests. In a sense, then, the presence of other children can directly conflict with task completion. In fact, Pepitone and Hannah in chapter 4 showed that working on identical tasks can produce competition.

A further complication is that the teacher is often absent from the group in open classrooms where students are expected to work independently. When this happens, the presence of peers decreases the probability that the children will be working on task (Collins and Guetzkow 1964; Korsh 1973).

In addition to the possible distracting influence of the presence of peers at a learning center, there remains the fact that within the ordinary classroom environment, the traditional measure for success has always been based on competition. A change in educational philosophy in the classroom does not immediately ensure a commensurate change in student behavior. Pepitone (1973), exploring the behavior of small groups of fourth graders under coactive conditions, noted that on the average these youngsters did not take advantage of opportunities given them to work together. Indeed when they tried to collaborate, they found it difficult to do so.

This poses a problem for open education: working on different, individualized tasks while in the presence of a group of peers may result in less task-oriented interaction and less on-task behavior, while working on identical tasks may result in increased competitive motivation. Work conditions and task requirements are very important and need to be specified if desired goals are to be achieved.

This theoretical analysis suggests that children in the open classroom will not automatically work together cooperatively or help each other with classroom tasks. Steps must be taken to ensure that children will work together when it is desirable for them to do so. The first requirement toward achieving this end is the creation of task interdependence for those tasks on which collaboration is necessary or desirable.

Dewey (1952) recognized the need for interdependence and placed the responsibility on the teacher to "arrange conditions that are conducive to *community* activity and to organization which exercises control over individual impulses by the mere fact that all are engaged in communal projects" (p. 64). Early on he stressed that the activity to be pursued require "natural divisions of labor, selection of leaders and followers, mutual cooperation and emulation" (1900, p. 12). While his colleague at Columbia University, William Kilpatrick, worked out some of these educational principles in the project method (1918), this practice was never systematically assessed. In fact, very little research on children's collaboration is available. The evidence presented by Pepitone in chapter 5 does support Dewey's stated principles. In her study of patterns of interdependence in cooperative work of elementary school children, Pepitone (1977) found that although goal interdependence did induce some positive social behaviors that are characteristic of collaborating groups, it did not maximize the occurrence of these behaviors. Her results showed that prosocial behavior and task performance were significantly greater where task requirements, task roles, and group roles were present together.

Cooperative group process, or positive social interaction in classroom groups, falls under the domain of affective education. Within recent years, much attention has been focused on promoting affective awareness and facilitating positive interaction among children.

According to Khan and Weiss (1973), it is often assumed that students will acquire relevant affective behaviors as a result of cognitive learning:

The belief that a student will develop positive attitudes toward subject matter, school, education, the teacher, and others, just by coming to school and interacting with curriculum materials, other students, and the teacher is an untenable assumption. . . . If desirable affective goals are to be realized as a result of the educational process, relevant formal learning situations have to be developed and the effects of such learning experiences will have to be systematically appraised. [p. 760]

Many formal programs have been developed in the field of affective education. They have been especially popular in open classroom settings because the goals of affective education are an integral part of the goals of open education. The values clarification approach developed by Raths, Harmin, and Simon (1966) and extended by Simon, Howe, and Kirschenbaum (1972) emphasizes the process by which values can be acquired. The authors suggest a large variety of strategies for classroom teachers to use with individual students and with groups. Several studies have been made to test Raths's assumption that the strategies have an effect on affective responses of a general nature, as well as on affective responses toward specific subject matter covered by special lessons, such as, literature and social studies. However, all of these studies, reported by J. Raths (1962) and Raths, Harmin, and Simon (1966), had major methodological shortcomings, such as lack of control groups, and were thus inconclusive.

Since the values clarification approach has not been adequately researched (Khan and Weiss 1973) and is basically not concerned with group process but with individual decision making. It has not been adapted as a formal program of affective education with the objective of improving cooperative social interaction in elementary classroom groups.

Two different studies that deal with values are especially relevant here. Both aimed not to clarify but to change values. The first (Hancock 1961) determined that desirable modifications in social values held by sixth-grade students could be brought about through a listening and discussion approach with selected textbook materials in social studies. The second (Lewis 1967) had more specific goals and was more extensive than the first. Its purpose was to examine the impact of selected literature on aggressiveness, selfishness, and nurturance. The sample consisted of 216 sixth-grade students who were tested before and after treatment by a semiprojective test of values in story form that the experimenter had constructed. The subjects were divided into four groups. Over a period of six weeks, group I read eleven short stories portraying the desirability of nurturance and the undesirability of aggressiveness. Following reading, they discussed the stories and the values presented. Group II read the same stories but did not discuss them. Group III discussed the values without reading the stories. Group IV read no stories and had no discussion. The results showed that reading without discussion produced significant change through an increase in aggressive feeling, a decrease in selfish feeling, and a decrease in feelings of nurturance; the discussion of values without reading produced no significant changes; reading followed by discussion produced significant change through decrease in aggressiveness, with a trend toward increase in nurturance; and group IV had no change in any values. Lewis believes that the children who read stories dealing with values developed an increased awareness of the values and negative feelings about them through concretizing the issues involved and emotional identification with characters. Free discussion allowed for the release of these feelings and for group interaction during which the students could achieve consensus by taking a stand on the issues and adopting group values or norms.

A second formally developed program that falls under the rubric of affective education and in which classroom groups play a major part, is described in Glasser (1969).[2] The author provides a model for a total approach to education, including affective education, and divides it into two categories. The first concerns the responsibility of teachers and students. It stresses the importance of emotional involvement between teachers and students and the use of reality therapy techniques. The second, the responsibility of the school, stresses that schools teach a relevant curriculum and teach the child to understand its relevance and that they establish daily classroom meetings either to attempt to solve social or educational problems or to discuss any thought-provoking questions related to students' lives.

The relationship between Glasser's approach and open education is very close. Both stress the need for schools to develop areas of learning out of the child's experiences and in response to the child's needs. It would be quite feasible to include Glasser's approach in an open school. Indeed this has been done, and research has been reported on its success as compared with a traditional school program (Singh 1972). After one year, students in the open classroom (Glasser program) had better self-concepts, liked school better, and had better attitudes toward creative writing than those students in the nonprogram classroom.

Engle, Keepes, and Thorne (1973) evaluated a school modeled on Glasser's approach during its first three years of operation. The study involved a pretest-posttest design, with a control school as a comparison. The control school was in the same district as the experimental one with the most equivalent student body available. They found that self-concept was slightly higher in the experimental school than in the control school in the first year of operation, but there was no difference in the second year. The student sense of responsibiilty and control was significantly higher in the experimental than in the control school after the second year; thus length of time in the experimental school had a significant positive effect on this variable. And from behavior observations made on all classrooms during the last two years of the evaluation, it was found that children at the experimental school were more likely to talk to each other about school-related matters than were those at the control school. While more recent literature on Glasser's program has focused more on descriptions of his method of classroom discussions (Kelly 1974), it is clear that Glasser's approach is related to improved student self-concept and attitude toward school, as theorized, and may have some important contributions to make to an effective experimental model for use in affective education.

One of the major attempts to use the entire classroom group to facilitate affective education has been through the human development program which uses a developmental model to promote social and emotional growth in children (Palomares and Rubini 1973). In the elementary school, the students meet with their teacher for approximately twenty minutes daily, in a "magic circle . . . the process by which the teacher and students explore their thoughts, feelings, and behaviors on a daily basis" (p. 654). The teacher is trained to act as group facilitator to ensure that each child is included in the group's activities. The teacher's main role is to introduce the tasks suggested and model active listening and positive behavior patterns. With time, the group takes over leadership so that students are given practice in these positive behavior patterns. The emphasis is on communication skills to promote awareness of self, mastery, and better social interaction (awareness of and valuing of others):

> In general, the Human Development Program helps children learn to be better listeners. They become more involved with each other and their teacher. Group cohesiveness is strengthened. . . . They learn to verbalize their thoughts and feelings and to understand their behaviors. They learn the dynamics of interpersonal relationships. [P. 656]

The human development program thus recognizes the importance of the group and devotes its efforts largely to training the teacher to act as group facilitator, to ensure that each child participates and is included in group activities. But there is not much research on the effects of using the program methods.

The most serious omission in all of these methods or programs when applied to improving collaborative group interaction is the lack of attention paid to the first principle of group dynamics: the members of the group must be interdependent in order to qualify as a group. Students physically together are not necessarily interdependent; indeed it is likely that they see themselves not only as independent but as competitive as well. Aronson (1978), recognizing the importance of group interdependence, has developed a different approach to human relations. His aim was to improve racial relations in newly integrated schools. His method was to involve students in activities where their interdependence was visible and their individual success in school depended on their success as a group. Deciding not to isolate affective education from other areas of learning in school, he combined academic and affective learning.

Aronson first analyzed traditional elementary schools, where the teacher is at the head of the class and students learn that their success in school comes from pleasing the teacher. This is basically a competitive process and guarantees that students will not learn to like or understand one another. Desegregation, with its concomitant racial tensions added to this situation, serves to intensify the competition. Aronson divided a fifth- and sixth-grade class into small learning groups of five or six students each. He used the jigsaw puzzle method with students replacing the teacher as the major resource so that competitiveness would be incompatible with success. Each child was given a piece of information pertaining to a subject to be learned; thus all of the group members had to put the information together. Each child had to master his piece and teach it to the others. It took several days before students could break their old competitive habits and listen to each other. Half of the class was experimental and the other half traditional, with appropriate controls for attention from experimenters.

There were no significant differences between the experimental and control groups in learning the material, but the experimental children increased their liking for team members after the treatment. Aronson replicated and extended his study, concluding that interdependence was of vital importance to the change in group climate.

Aronson did not teach the value of peer understanding, nor did he use group processes in isolation, as might happen in a group meeting, where for half an hour daily students explore feelings and then go on with being involved in all of the activities of the classroom. Generally they return to their predominantly individual-oriented, competitively motivated ways.

One ought not assume that students learn about the effects of their behavior on others by being allowed to express their feelings in group meetings, nor ought one to assume that increased self-awareness will lead to an increased awareness of others and to better group relations and more collaboration in the classroom. Furthermore there is evidence contrary to the assumption that children naturally become better able to work together as they grow older. Research reported in chapter 6 speaks to this point; Cook and Stingle (1974) state that although collaborative behavior in American children increases with age, so does competitive motivation. Indeed they found that 7- to 9-year-old American children behave in a more "irrationally competitive" (p. 921) manner than 4 to 6 year olds (irrational because the behavior does not allow any of the subjects to reach a goal). One source of this nonadaptive behavior appears to be rivalry (behavior intended to lower the achievement of a peer), which emerges as a significant, sometimes dominant, response set in children aged 8 to 10.

Because most of the activities in classrooms are characterized by goals that are attainable by individuals working alone and many of these activities may stimulate besting responses, it becomes increasingly important to find ways of fostering the development of collaboration in school children. Students do indeed need to learn the effects of their behavior on others. Learning about oneself and one's effect on others is exactly that; it is a form of learning and must be thought of in this way. Dewey (1900) has exhorted us not to set school apart from practical living as a place to "learn lessons" (p. 11). The same principle applies to affective education. It ought not to be set apart from other studies. Understanding oneself and one's effect on others is a very important part of one's total being. Children must learn about themselves through "directed living" instead of through school lessons with "an abstract and remote reference to some possible living to be done in the future" (p. 15).

Similarly Piaget has applied his principles of active and concrete learning to the affective area of learning:

> When I say "active", I mean it in two senses. One is acting on material things. But the other means doing things in social collaboration, in a group effort. This leads to a critical frame of mind, where children must communicate with each other. This is an essential factor in intellectual development. Cooperation is indeed Co-operation. [Duckworth 1964, p. 173]

How, then, do young children learn about their effect on others and learn to communicate more effectively? In order for 7- or 8-year-old children (in Piaget's concrete operations stage) to become less egocentric in their relations with others, it would appear necessary for them to learn this concretely and not simply through participating in a general group discussion. The children may learn the positive behavior patterns expected of them—for example, in the magic circle—by modeling their teacher during these class meetings. The question is whether they will apply these patterns or communication skills at other times, such as, when working on tasks in small groups in the classroom.

Children of this age do not readily apply what they have learned in one situation to a different situation. They must have practice in generalizing, and their practice must be reinforced (Chittenden 1972). An effective way to achieve this generalization of learning is through specification of the goal of the task, the instrumental means of achieving the goal, and feedback as to the attainment of the goal (Greenfield 1971). Also important is relating the task goal to its larger end in the environment. Greenfield wrote that "what are learned best, that is, in the most generalized form, are those verbal concepts that function as means to many desired ends. These are concepts that have 'relevance' to larger enterprises; the child thus has a 'reason' or motive to learn about them" (p. 256).

Applying Greenfield's and Aronson's results to the classroom would lead one to hypothesize, for example, that the magic circle technique would be more effective in improving group functioning in the open classroom if it were applied to specific small task group interaction. That is, when small groups of children are working on interdependent tasks, part of the goal should be cooperative group interaction and application of the group process communication skills. In addition, the group members should receive feedback from the teacher and from each other about how well they collaborated and about the quality of the product. If this were done regularly in classroom groups, one would expect quite an improvement in cooperative social interaction.

In our society with its historical emphasis on individualism and individual success, schools have been traditionally geared more to competition than to cooperation. In traditional classrooms throughout the United States, children are exhorted to work individually, to guard their work from others' eyes, and generally to ignore the other children in the class (Holt 1969; Silberman 1971). In fact, however, children spend a good bit of time comparing their work to that of others, and this comparison behavior appears to fulfill a need for them to gauge their performance against that of their peers and determine the appropriateness of their work (Festinger 1954). When restraints against comparing, communicating, and helping each other are experimentally removed, children still do not naturally begin working well together. These restraints are theoretically removed in the open classroom, but being provided a classroom climate conducive to cooperative interaction is not a sufficient requirement for collaboration. Elementary school children must be taught the social skills needed to be cooperative members of groups, and they must be taught to apply these skills to specific task groups.

Although the open classroom approach to education recognizes and provides materials to satisfy the child's need for concrete manipulation when learning new academic concepts, similar needs for concreteness have been neither recognized nor provided for in the affective domain. The approach to affective education, which includes improving group interaction, has been dealt with mainly on an abstract level through various types of group meetings.

The purpose of this study was to create a sequence of conditions that would work toward optimizing the development of collaborative social interaction around small group task performances. Just as the first step in any teaching is a clear presentation of the material to be learned at a level that can be understood by the learners, students must first meet in groups and be presented with age-appropriate material clearly stressing the group skills that are valued and will be expected of them. Then the students must be involved in group discussion of the material. Were we to stop here, we would make the same mistake previously attributed to the isolated use (perhaps misuse) of many of the existent affective education programs. The learning that has taken place thus far would remain abstract, with no concrete application to working in groups. Just as with any academic lesson, then, the next step is to break up into smaller groups and work on the material presented so that the students and the teacher can see whether the material has been understood. Thus, in addition to the discussions, it is necessary that the students work together in small groups on tasks. When they do so, the group members must be interdependent by working on a task with a common goal. Work in these task groups must also be linked to prior discussion of group skills. Students must be reminded of previously discussed group skills and instructed to apply these skills to their task performance. They must be made aware of the behaviors expected of them and of the goals of the task.

In addition to these clear instructions, feedback is necessary. One way of doing it is as we did it. Following task performance, the group members were asked to evaluate their own group functioning in terms of the specific group skills stressed; in addition, group members received experimenter feedback about their group functioning. Another way of providing feedback is through teacher criticism, although as Torop (1973) showed, without helpful explanation, it confuses and upsets the children.

This series of events composed the experimental model presented here: group discussion of particular group skills stressed in large group settings; task performance in small, interdependent groups with group members instructed to apply these group skills to their task performance; evaluation by group members of their own group functioning in these small task groups; and feedback by the experimenter about how well the group members actually applied group skills to their task performance. It was hypothesized that the application of this experimental treatment would increase group-oriented behavior on the task performance of small groups of interdependent children when compared with another experimental treatment and a control condition.

Design and Procedures

Following the administration of a pretest, children met together in large groups twice weekly and collaborated in triads once weekly for a period of three weeks, under three different conditions. A posttest, exactly the same as the pretest, followed, and behavioral change was measured from pretest to posttest.

The Subjects

The subjects were ninety-three third-grade students in open classrooms in two suburban elementary schools of similar socioeconomic distribution.

The great majority of subjects in this study had been in open classrooms since beginning school and therefore were unfamiliar with the traditional classroom's mode of operation.

Individual students within each classroom were rated by their teachers as being of high, average, or low overall academic ability. Children were assigned to like-sexed triads, one child from each of the three ability categories, so that each group was made as heterogeneous as possible with respect to ability.

The Experimenters

Two female experimenters were employed—myself and a volunteer who was unfamiliar with the overall research design and hypotheses.

The Observers

Three observers, all unfamiliar with the research design and hypotheses, were rotated for all task sessions; one was present at a session. Each observer covered triads in all conditions, classes, and schools and worked with both experimenters. Reliability checks were run periodically for all observers. Interobserver reliability averaged 84 percent per behavior category.

The Pretest

A pretest was administered to each triad, composed of performance on a construction task, which consisted of using cuisenaire rods to build a mutually agreed-upon construction.[3] Each student was asked to write down something she would like to build with the rods. Then all choices were read aloud by the experimenter, and the group members were instructed to decide together upon one of the objects and to build it together, all within a ten-minute time limit.

Behavioral Ratings of Group Process

During the administration of the pretest, the observer obtained measures of the group's performance by tallying all verbal statements into three categories.[4] The first measured group-oriented behavior:[5]

1. Structuring the group. Included assigning roles, dividing labor, planning a strategy, concern with procedure or progress.

2. Responsiveness. Included statements implying an awareness of and responsiveness to others' inferred feeling states or attitudes.
3. Helping with the task. Included all cooperative task-oriented behaviors, such as offering help, offering to share, and giving or asking for information.

The self-oriented behavior categories had two measures:

1. Competition-related verbal behavior. Included giving orders in a negative manner (tone of voice "bossy"), besting, expressing hostility, refusing to help.
2. Egocentric expression of own needs and opinions. Included statements reflecting that the child viewed the task in relation to herself rather than as a group project.

The third category, neutral, included nonwork-related talk that was neutral in tone. But since so few comments over the task performance sessions fell in this category, it was dropped from the analysis.

Tallies were also made for the nonverbal behaviors of physical aggression and knocking down the group product or another person's product without permission.

Ratings of Group Products

Ratings were also made of the group's product. An instant-camera snapshot was taken of each triad's construction. These photographs were rated on the dimension "goodness of creation" as poor, average, or good by two raters unknown to each other and unfamiliar with the students or with the research design. The average agreement between raters was 90 percent.

Treatment

Following the administration of the pretest, triads were placed into one of three treatment conditions. The treatment took place over a period of three weeks and consisted of listening to stories in large groups (the content of the stories being determined by the particular treatment condition) twice a week, and performing a practice construction task in triads, once a week. Materials for this task were the Pep board and 245 Pattern Blocks. First, the children were familiarized with the materials. Then they were instructed to write down what each would like to make with the materials. They were asked to "make a picture of something from the gym, art, or music room here in school." The procedure for selecting one idea on which the group could work together was the same as in the pretest. The task practice session always took place after the two story sessions, and each of the three sessions was on a different day of the week.

The task practice sessions served a control function. Communication within a group develops with the ongoing life of the group. Since communication was a focal point of this study, task practice sessions provided that all triads in both experimental and control conditions have equal opportunity to meet together and become familiar with the group members' characteristic modes of interaction in a group setting. Providing for the ongoing, continuous work experience within each triad over the three-week period also increased the rigor of this study. In most open classrooms, the same students generally do not work together on the same tasks for a period of weeks. Meeting the latter condition in the present study meant that the variability that would have occurred due to interaction of different members with each other was reduced.

Treatment Conditions

Condition 1, the control, consisted of passive listening to stories unrelated to group functioning and task practice.[6] It is well known that simply participating in an experimental program can raise the productivity of a group (the so-called Hawthorne effect). This condition controlled for this effect by providing that the subjects meet with the experimenter for the same amount of time each week (listening to stories and performing tasks) as experimental subjects. However, the content of their interaction with the experimenter was quite different from that of the experimental subjects. In no way were the students in the control condition involved in considerations of their own group functioning. Thus this condition controlled also for the effects of story content and for the effects of group discussion.

Condition 2, the experimental group, consisted of passive listening to verbal stress on good group functioning and task practice. During their story sessions, condition 2 subjects heard taped stories designed to develop specific group process skills in children.[7] These stories were selected from a kit put out by the American Guidance Service, entitled *DUSO (Developing Understanding of Self and Others*, Dinkmeyer 1970). There were no discussions of any of the story material, nor did the experimenter ever verbally link the group skills stressed in the stories to the skills needed to perform the tasks presented in the task-practice sessions. In this respect, condition 2 subjects were experiencing a program similar to those affective education programs that remain at the level of the abstract, large-group presentation.

Condition 3 was the experimental group with active participation in discussion of good group functioning, task practice, application-set, evaluation, and feedback. The stories in condition 3 were the same as in condition 2; but there were three major differences between conditions 2 and 3. First, condition 3 children engaged in group discussions led by the experimenter (using a script), following each story. Second, in condition 3, prior to each task practice session, the experimenter briefly reviewed all group process skills stressed in previous story sessions, and instructed the triad members to apply these particular skills to their task performances. These instructions are referred to as application-set. Third, following all condition 3 task practice sessions, evaluation and feedback by group and experimenter took place. The feedback was tied to the specific group process skills covered in the story sessions and also followed a script.

Posttest

Following the three-week treatment period, a posttest, an exact repeat of the pretest, was administered to each triad in each of the three conditions. Instructions for all triads were the same across all conditions, and process and product were measured just as in the pretest.

Hypothesis

It was hypothesized that treatment condition 3 would increase group-oriented behavior and improve group products more than conditions 1 or 2 would.

Statistical Procedures of Analysis

A preliminary analysis revealed no significant differences between schools on any of the process or product ratings. Therefore data from both schools were combined for the analysis of treatment effects.

A similar analysis showed that there were no initial differenes between sexes on any of the process or product ratings. Results of a classic two-way analysis of variance showed that there were no significant effects of sex and no significant interaction between sex and treatment on any of the measures. Therefore male and female triads in each condition were combined for the main analysis of treatment effects.

The focal interest of this study was the change that took place in the behavior of triads within the three conditions from pretest to posttest. Thus multivariate analyses were performed (in addition to analysis of variance) to determine the effects of treatments.[8]

Multivariate analyses of covariance were run for all of the response indexes of change (that is, for changes measured in group product ratings and in all rating categories of group process, verbal and nonverbal).[9] Fortran programs were used for each of these analyses, comparing treatment conditions 1 with 2, 1 with 3, and 2 with 3, to determine whether there were significant differences between these treatments.[10] In addition to examining all the change measures of group process and product, a Statistical Program for the Social Sciences (SPSS program) was used to perform discriminant analyses for the change measures, to locate those response indexes of change that most discriminated between treatment conditions 1 and 3. Following the discriminant analyses, further multivariate analyses were run comparing treatment conditions to determine whether there were significant differences between two treatments for just those response indexes that most discriminated between treatment conditions 1 and 3 because this comparison was of primary interest.

The Results

The response variables predicted to be most affected by treatment were product ratings, structuring behavior, responsiveness, helping behavior, egocentric behavior, and competition-related behavior. Of these, only product rating and competition-related behavior were not selected as most discriminating between conditions 1 and 3.

The results of the multivariate analyses for all response indices of change, as well as for the most discriminating change indexes, are presented in table 10-1. These data represent overall effects and show a significant difference between experimental condition 3 and control condition 1 when

Table 10-1
Multivariate Analysis of Difference between Treatments

| | p Values (Significance Levels) of Comparisons | | |
	Treatments 1 versus 2	Treatments 1 versus 3	Treatments 2 versus 3
All change measures of group process and product	.2589	.0468[a]	.2273
Most discriminating change measures of group process and product	.3383	.0008[c]	.0670

[a]Indicates $p < .05$.
[b]Indicates $p < .01$.
[c]Indicates $p < .001$.

all change measures are considered and that this difference becomes even more significant ($p < .001$) when only the most discriminating change measures are considered. The data also show that experimental condition 2 does not differ significantly from control condition 1 in either case. Overall, treatments 2 and 3 do not differ significantly; however, there is a strong trend toward a significant difference between them ($p = .67$) when only the most discriminating measures are considered.

Table 10-2 allows us to examine the treatment effects in more detail by showing which behaviors in each condition were affected, as well as the direction of the change.[11] Table 10-3 presents comparisons between pairs of treatments by showing the differences between the means of each set of compared treatments and the significance of these differences.

With the single exception of egocentric behavior, all changes in condition 3 (as compared with condition 1) were toward increased group-oriented behavior, as predicted. In addition to the significant changes in increased structuring of the group and in decreased amount of physical aggression, there were strong trends in the predicted direction in both helping behavior and competition-related behavior. However, the prediction that triads in condition 3 would produce significantly more improved products than triads in condition 1 was not confirmed.

The comparison of condition 2 with condition 1 produced an entirely different picture. With the notable exception of an increase in structuring behavior, condition 2 triads in many respects became more self-oriented.

Table 10-2
Relative Means of Treatment Conditions 1, 2, and 3 for Each Response Index of Change

Change Response Index	Condition 1	Condition 2	Condition 3
Product measures			
Product rating	.00	− 1.54	.447
Process measures			
Structuring	.00	13.34	15.41
Responsiveness	.00	.36	.75
Helping	.00	− 7.91	15.82
Competition-related behavior	.00	− 1.85	− 9.35
Egocentric behavior[a]	.00	10.19	8.36
Physical aggression[b]	.00	.42	− .96
Knocking product[b]	.00	.09	− .23

[a]Denotes self-oriented behaviors predicted to decrease (change in negative direction).
[b]Denotes quite negative behaviors that should ideally decrease (change in negative direction).
[c]Means of control group adjusted to zero, for ease of comparison.

Table 10-3
Differences between Means of Treatment Conditions for All Response Indexes of Change

Response Index of Change	Treatments 1 versus 2	Treatments 1 versus 3	Treatments 2 versus 3
Product measures			
Product rating	-1.55^a	.446	1.99^b
Process measures			
Group oriented			
Structuring	13.34	15.41	2.07
Responsiveness	.36	.75	.39
Helping	-7.91	15.82	23.73^b
Self-oriented			
Competition-related behavior	-1.85	-9.35	-7.50
Egocentric behavior	10.19	8.36	-1.83
Physical aggression	.42	$-.96^a$	-1.38^a
Knocking product	.09	$-.23$	$-.32$

Note: Comparisons between treatments, 1 versus 2 and 1 versus 3, were made using a univariate F-ratio with 1 and 18 degrees of freedom, while comparisons between 2 versus 3 involved i and 20 degrees of freedom.
[a] $p < .05$.
[b] $p < .01$.

The average quality of the product worsened significantly and helping behavior diminished, while egocentric behavior and physical aggression toward other children and toward the group's product increased.

As a result of these changes in condition 2 triads (toward more self-oriented behavior) and those in condition 3 triads (toward more group-oriented behavior), the differences between 2 and 3 are quite large on several of the rating categories and reach significance in the cases of quality of product, helping behavior, and physical aggression.

In sum, it may be concluded that triads in condition 3 changed more from pretest to posttest in the direction of having significantly more of their behavior falling in the group-oriented categories than did triads in conditions 1 or 2. Indeed the only verbal behavior coded that did not move in the expected direction for triads exposed to condition 3 was egocentric behavior, which increased. However, it did not increase as much as competition-related behavior decreased, so the net result was an overall reduction in the amount of behavior falling in the self-oriented categories.

Third-grade children are still rather egocentric in their cognitive and affective development. The egocentric behavior category included statements reflecting that the child viewed the task in relation to himself rather than as a group project; the child's own needs surfaced, but the group's progress was not necessarily harmed thereby. This is in contrast to the competition-related category, which included hostile, negative statements that were definitely not helpful to task completion. It may be unjustified and perhaps unnecessary to expect that students of this age will become less egocentric in performing a group task when their egocentric behavior in fact has no ill effect on the product. Egocentric behavior in this case may be in part simply a reflection of personal involvement.

It may also be the case that egocentric behavior serves to elicit responsiveness on the part of the other group members. If a child either directly or indirectly calls attention to her contribution to the group product and another child recognizes and responds positively to that need for attention, the latter response would be coded in the responsiveness category. Initially there were very few remarks that fell into this category. Triads in condition 3 did increase their responsiveness more than those in the other treatment conditions, although this category remained a sparsely populated one.

Since the data do not show the sequence of communications (which type of verbal response follows which type of statement), it is not possible to determine whether the increase in egocentric behavior did indeed elicit greater responsiveness for triads in condition 3. Nonetheless it is clear that condition 3 triads, who experienced the full experimental sequence of events, increased their collaborative behavior and positive social interaction. An interesting aspect of this improvement is that the two behaviors that changed to a statistically significant degree are also of great practical significance to group functioning. Physical aggression, which decreased significantly, is a behavior that one would not expect to occur to any great extent in a small group within a suburban elementary school. However, when it does occur, it is extremely destructive, not only to the small group in which it occurs but to the class as a whole. The fact that these behaviors decreased significantly in condition 3 is an important finding; the implication is that even the extremely negative behaviors of children may be greatly improved by this method of teaching group skills.

The other significant change in behavior within triads in condition 3 was the increase in structuring. Structuring the group is a higher level of behavior than is helping because structuring involves making decisions as to how the group will go about a task; the children must plan a strategy, divide the labor, assign roles, and express concern with group procedure and/or progress. These are organizational skills important to group functioning on any level and on most tasks. If a group can decide on a procedure for approaching a problem and evaluate this procedure and the group's progress along the way, this is the core of problem solving, what Steiner (1972) refers to as the capacity of group members to "evaluate and reorganize their collective behaviors" (p. 185). The behavior included under structuring may be considered as expressions of group process roles. In chapter 2, these kinds of behavior were contemplated as constituting required group process roles. Thus the increase in structuring contributed significantly and meaningfully to the overall increase in cooperative behavior among triads in condition 3.

In contrast to this increase, an unexpected result of this study was the deterioration of group process and product in the performance of triads in condition 2. One of the important contributing factors to the poorer product rating was the number of products each triad made. The instructions were to select one object to build together. If the group members could not agree and each built a separate object, the product(s) received the lowest rating. Treatment 2 triads tended to agree less and to work on separate products more than did triads in the other treatment conditions.

As for the group process in condition 2, the balance of change clearly was in the direction of greater self-oriented behavior. Particularly telling are the increases in knocking down others' products and in physical aggression, behaviors that ought to be fairly well suppressed in third graders in a school setting, especially when three children are performing a task in a room with two relatively unfamiliar adults observing. The fact that these behaviors actually increased, to the point that the difference between triads in conditions 2 and 3 in physically aggressive behavior was significant is worthy of notice.

How is one to interpret these findings? Why should triads exposed to condition 2 change in the direction of poorer performance and increased physical aggression? A possible explanation is found in Lewis (1967), who obtained similar results while studying the impact of specially selected readings and/or discussion on feelings of aggressiveness. The study reported that reading without discussion produced a significant increase in aggressive feeling. Lewis speculated that reading stories dealing with values about aggressive behavior increased an awareness of the values as well as negative feelings about them through emotional identification with the values, while not permitting the release of these feelings through discussion.

It might be helpful to look at condition 2 as a case of children being preached to without their being given the opportunity to express themselves. It may be assumed that this situation is anxiety arousing. Since the DUSO story content focused attention on the child's behavior toward others, the child's anxiety may be aroused if his behavior falls short of the standard being held up. Where group discussion of this standard is permitted, the anxiety may be released as children share feelings with each other. Also there may occur a group consensus in which group members agree that the values presented are indeed valuable to them and should be adopted as the norm within their group. Where discussion is not permitted, the anxiety remains.

In addition, feelings of frustration may be built up because the children are not given a chance to voice an opinion. The theory that this combination of feelings of anxiety and frustration leads to increased aggression is based clinically in Freud's work and experimentally in the work of Dollard et al. (1939).

Another possible contributing factor to the deterioration evidenced in condition 2 is that the stories may lead each child to expect that the other group members will change their behavior toward him. When this change is not forthcoming, the child's own behavior may become less cooperative and more aggressive. The evidence for this interpretation comes from the discussion records of condition 3 subjects. Immediately following the DUSO stories, virtually all of the children verbally identified with the underdog. Then the children proceeded to a more general discussion of the desirability of being aware of others and considerate of their feelings in a group situation. This entire process could not take place in condition 2.

It is not possible to separate out which experimental variable(s) in this study might account for the large differences in effects of conditions 2 and 3. The experimental variables applied in condition 3 were seen by the experimenter as a necessary sequence of events. Further studies are required to test any of them individually or in other combinations. Such studies would also shed more light on the results obtained for condition 2 triads. If it is indeed the case that lack of group discussion is an important factor, this information should prove quite valuable to teachers attempting to change affective behavior in classrooms.

Implications

This study represented a rather stringent test of whether one can improve collaborative interaction in small groups by combining traditional lessons with instruction-group functioning. All children in the three conditions met and interacted personally with the experimenter both in the large and small group settings. Virtually all of these contacts were pleasant and intimate. The students certainly were open and uninhibited with the experimenter. There was ample opportunity over the three-week period within this rather accepting personal environment for triads in all conditions to develop positively in their social interaction with each other. Normally it is not the case that these small, intimate groups establish this kind of ongoing relationship in classes with twenty to thirty children in a room. Rather group discussions usually take place with the entire class present, with only occasional follow-up in smaller groups. Thus the changes that took place in condition 3 (but not in the other two conditions) are strongly indicative that the sequence of experimental variables applied actually was instrumental in effecting these changes.

Furthermore the actual treatment period involved each student for only forty-five minutes each week (spread over three different days) for a total of three weeks. When one considers all of the events that occur in the course of the school day—the academic material presented and worked on and the many different kinds of school activities and outside events woven into life in the classroom (such as fair day, olympic games, trips, snowstorms, and special assemblies)—all of which this study had to contend with and make room for and work around (just as all classroom teachers do), it is truly remarkable that any changes at all were effected. Nonetheless positive behavioral change (as well as negative behavioral change) was effected; the students in condition 3 did improve their group interaction and collaborate better. The implication is clear; how much more effective it would be if the teacher were to incorporate this procedure into the daily life of the classroom.

Teaching children how to get along with their peers in groups is an important classroom function, and, as teaching, it is very much the domain of classroom educators. It need not and should not be set apart from other areas of teaching. Rather if the goal is to increase cooperative group functioning in the classroom, then cooperative group functioning needs to be clearly included as a goal within the context of many classroom tasks. Group discussion certainly appears to be vital to this process, so that this goal is accepted by the students. Students then should be given feedback as to whether they attained the goal. This process must be repeated again and again so that learning takes place.

If this were to occur within the context of the open classroom where materials of interest to the children abound, where freedom to interact with peers exists, and where most academic skills are taught in just this way, the results might prove startling. The "rivalrous" response described by Cook and Stingle, which is "irrationally competitive" (1974, p. 922), but dominant in many American youngsters, might give way under these circumstances to a dominant cooperative response. The needs of our society could be beneficially served by such a change.

Notes

1. Educators and researchers generally do not distinguish between cooperation and collaboration. Therefore, for the purpose of consistency with the literature discussed here, *cooperation* and *competition* will be used interchangeably with *collaboration* and *besting*, respectively.

2. This widely read volume also contributed at the time more generally to humanizing education.

3. A verbal task was also employed; results are found in Korsh (1975).

4. For fuller explanation of behavior categories, see Korsh (1975).

5. These categorical distinctions are based on Pepitone (1977).

6. The stories for condition 1 groups were: *Caps for Sale* by Esphyr Slobodkina, *Alexander and the Car with a Missing Headlight* by Lynn Ward, *Charley, Charlotte and the Golden Canary* by Charles Keeping, *Little Toot* by Hardie Gramatky, and *Gilberto and the Wind* by Marie Hall Ets. All are on sound filmstrips tape cassettes by Weston Woods.

7. The content of DUSO story session 1, for example, was "The Underwater Problem Solvers." It dealt with rules for group discussion. Duso the Dolphin is introduced in this session and talks about group discussion. This story is about the methods he and his underwater friends use to solve their problems. Each of Duso's friends has a characteristic that points up a particular discussion rule. For example, Lefty is an octopus. His rule is to "raise your hand." Soupy Turtle tends to go inside his shell when he is not talking. His rule is to "listen carefully." Clarissa Clam has to be encouraged to present her thoughts. Her rule is, "Don't clam up." And Spike the Swordfish reminds everyone to "stick to the point." When Duso and his friends use those rules and remember to think together because five heads are better than one, they are able to help each other solve problems.

8. In all analyses, adjustments were made by stepwise forward multiple linear regression for differences in relevant demographic variables (including average within-triad teacher rating of individual ability, average age, and other information from sociogram ratings) among the treatment conditions, in order to account for the effects of such demographics on treatment effects. Multivariate analyses take into account dependence among the variables and thus yield a more clear-cut interpretation of the results. In this case, results of the analysis of variance were consistent with results of the multivariate analyses. Therefore to avoid duplication, only multivariate analysis results were presented.

9. Response index of change: the change in the value of response variable $\times$, from week 1 (pretest) to week 5 (posttest) equals the observed value of the difference in response variable $\times$ from week 1 to week 5, minus the expected value of the difference in response variable $\times$ from week 1 to week 5 based on demographic predictors obtained by multiple regression (Korsh 1975, p. 117).

10. Programs were written by Gaston Mendoza, Department of Statistics, Temple University, Philadelphia, Pennsylvania.

11. The relative means for each possible behavioral change in response are presented for all treatment conditions, with means of condition 1 adjusted to zero for ease of comparison.

Social Roles and Family Interaction in Collaborative Work

Judith Milner Coché

Despite current thinking on the demise of traditional family structure in the world (Mead 1973), the importance of the family in the development of the child and in the satisfaction of human needs has long been realized. Much has been written about family. Hill and Hanson (1960), pioneers in this area, discussed a number of conceptual frameworks within which the family has been studied in the related fields of sociology, anthropology, psychology, and social work. Straus (1965), Turner (1970), Bott (1971), Rapoport and Rapoport (1971), and Bryson and Bryson (1978) have recently written on sex role within the family. However, Framo (1965), and Riskin and Faunce (1972) discuss the paucity of controlled, systematic research on the interactional process within the family.

It is with this area of normative research on the social psychological processes in the normal family that the present study was concerned. The study proposed to reduce the existing distance between family clinicians and academicians by operationalizing and testing basic family role concepts as developed by Talcott Parsons. It also proposed to increase clinical understandings of the normal family as an interacting unit, based on reliable, experimental observations of the total family.

Both Framo (1965) and Riskin and Faunce (1972) discuss the need for social psychologically based research with normal families. Framo holds that it is better to observe people directly in interaction than to rely on interviews and attitude surveys and favors using videotapes to study both verbal and nonverbal patterns of families who are in family therapy. Riskin and Faunce, on the other hand, are more experimental in their approach. They give high priority to improving and developing methods of studying the family but hold that the family task, such as that developed by Straus (1965), provides an ideal method by which to study family interaction patterns. They maintain that ideally one should be studying such variables as support, control strategies, who-to-whom speaking patterns, and decision-making patterns. They call for the need for replication of such studies and of relating this research to other indications of family functioning. They also speak to the need for communication among fields. Very few people have been trained in both research and in clinical work with families, and it is precisely from this type of person that the most promising increase in knowledge can come.

A Theoretical View of Family Roles

The major theoretical view of roles within the family has been presented by Talcott Parsons, who began a formal conceptualization of family processes in the 1950s. Parsons's is a theory of systems within systems within systems. The individual is a system composed of an organized personality, a life-style, and habitual patterns. Society is composed of social systems within social systems, formulated in what Parsons thinks of as concentric circles. Parsons assumes that every social system, regardless of level, faces the same problems and operates under the same laws. Thus all social systems are dynamically analogous, and the analysis of all social systems then receives a structural functional emphasis. One must consider all of the ways a role or institution meets some problem of the social system by discovering what functions it performs. Using five pattern variables (affectivity versus affective neutrality, specificity versus diffuse relationship, quality versus performance, self-orientation versus collectivity orientation, universalism versus particularism), Parsons traces the way the particular combinations of these pattern variables are functionally useful for maintaining that specific type of social relationship or system (Parsons and Shils, 1953).

According to Parsons (1955), "The main outlines of the structure of the nuclear family can be treated as a consequence of differentiation on two axes, that of hierarchy or power, and that of instrumental versus expressive function" (p. 45). His distinction between these axes is difficult to follow; it appears that power is "simply the quantitative degree of influence on others by a family" (p. 45) while the instrumental or expressive axis is concerned with "the distinction of function in terms of external or internal functions of the system" (p. 47). Studies of role in the family can then be differentiated along two dimensions, the instrumental role and the expressive role.

Baldwin (1967) considers social role to be Parsons's primary unit of analysis in the description of a social system. Role is defined as the actual behavior of the person filling a status position (while status is culturally defined as the job that is filled by a large number of different people). For example, father and mother are positions, and the people who fill them are exhibiting role behaviors. One analyzes a social system such as the family by examining the roles and positions in the system and by showing how each is functional and relates to the functions attached to the other positions (see Parsons 1955; Slater 1961; Rodman 1965). It now becomes useful to examine these role-related concepts related to the nuclear family since the family is the primary unit of socialization.

Parsons makes specific hypotheses about the frequency and nature of the parental roles that are easily testable through research once one defines his terms operationally. He maintains that the analysis and understanding of roles in the family is highly complex because individual members in it can perform different roles for one member than for other members. For example, although the marriage partners in contemporary Western society are bonded by affectional ties and hence perform primarily expressive roles for one another, the husband tends to take the more instrumental role even in his relationship to his wife in that he is primarily the money earner. Despite his awareness of more recent changes within the family compared, for example, with the colonial family, Parsons still maintains that the husband has the primary adaptive responsibilities relative to the outside situation (Parsons 1955). Internally in the family, the father is primarily the giver of care and only secondarily the giver of love.

Parsons posits that the child's relationship with his father is highly achievement oriented. The father demands achievement and recalls or gives approval dependent on whether it is deserved. Further although more numbers of women have recently entered the labor force, Parsons believes that the wife still has a more expressive role in the family as a whole, both in relationship to the husband and her children. In relation to her husband, she is more the child while he is more the mother: she is more the giver of love while he is more the giver of care. By care Parsons refers to the activities involved in taking care of, being in charge of, performing those duties to ensure the economic well-being of the children. However, in relation to her children, particularly when they are young, the wife must take over disciplinary functions while the father is away and must take a primarily instrumental role in relation to her children. With younger children, for example, the mother makes the primary task-oriented decisions.

Both Bales and Zelditch (in Parsons and Bales 1955) offer approximations of behavioral definitions of these roles. The task leader in a group is an example of instrumentality, and instrumental leadership is defined by statements like "leader of the hunt, boss manager, control over the children" in the Zelditch study. Expressive function "concerns the internal affairs of the system, the maintenance of integrity relations between members, and regulation of the patterns and tension levels of its component units" (p. 47). Again using both Bales and Zelditch for operationalizing these definitions, the social emotional leader in the group is concerned more with the expression of feeling as an index of expressiveness. Expressive leadership in the Zelditch study is characterized as "the role of mediator, family conciliator, affectionate, warm, emotional to the children, relatively indulgent, and relatively unpunishing."

What develops is a highly differentiated and complex set of hypotheses concerning the role of each member in relation to all the other members at any given time. In general, the husband has a more highly developed instrumental complex of motivational components and the wife a more highly developed expressive complex of motivational components; however, each must be balanced by the development of the other motive as well. For instance, each parent must assume both roles at some time or another, both in relation to the children and in relation to each other. Thus the marriage roles must be integrated with the roles as a parent. The entire system is complex. Parsons is also quick to say that this is a typical and ideal theoretical framework that has relevance in theory but may not be exactly operative in a given family. Nevertheless he presents a model or differentiation of role in the typical family consisting of father, mother, son, and daughter (figure 11-1).

Baldwin (1967) credits Parsons with first recognizing the place that the child has had, not only in being affected by the family but in affecting it. He states:

It is impossible to isolate the development of the child from family variables. Such families . . . must be investigated as units; the investigations must not assume that the changes in the child are developmental processes in the child alone. . . . If the natural unit for the description of child development is the family, and not the child, this has great implications for theory.[P. 573]

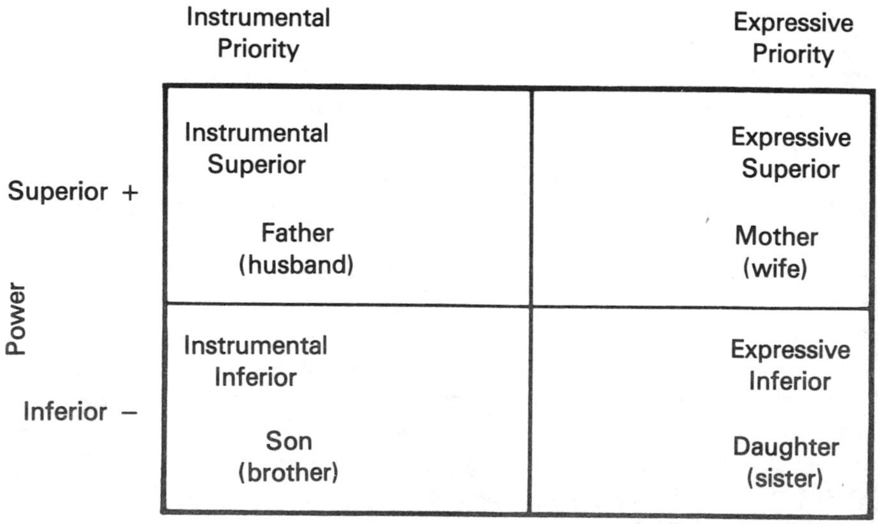

	Instrumental Priority	Expressive Priority
Superior +	Instrumental Superior Father (husband)	Expressive Superior Mother (wife)
Inferior −	Instrumental Inferior Son (brother)	Expressive Inferior Daughter (sister)

Power

From T. Parsons, "Family Structure and the Socialization of the Child," in T. Parsons and R.F. Bales, eds., *Family Socialization and Interaction Process.* Glencoe, Ill.: Free Press, 1955, p. 46.

Figure 11-1. Basic Role Structure of the Nuclear Family

Theoretical Framework of the Present Research

The definition of role I favor is similar to those advanced by Slater: problems in social role are valuable for research only if conceived of in interpersonal terms, as being related to the position or status of one or more members within a given family, relative to the position or status of other members. Moreover I agree with Slater that Parsons's use of the term lacks specificity; for him *role* most often sounds synonymous with *power*, the amount of a given behavior by a member unrelated to other members, although at other times role is clearly conceived of as a relationship statement. For this study I assumed the former definition of role as Parsonian, in agreement with Bergen (in Slater 1961) and Jackson (1965).

Jackson also conceived of the family as a system. He emphasized the natural development of the individual as a product of the system and change agent within it; however, he saw individual family members to a greater extent independent of biological determinism. Jackson posited that categories of difference, such as sex-role stereotypes, diminished the importance of the husband-wife relationship as the basis for successful marriage and child rearing. The individual differences that are unquestionably present among family members are the results of actively working out relationships. Jackson posited that as long as an equable working relationship is maintained, the marriage will remain successful. This organized patterning of behavior according to stated or unstated relationship agreements between family members he called family rules. These rules can be but are not necessarily in keeping with sex role stereotypes. Jackson held that family rules, not roles, organize members' interaction into a reasonably stable system. Family rules are a series of unstated relationship agreements among all members within the family that prescribe and limit each individual's behaviors over a wide range of content areas.

The Study

This study explored three hypotheses that developed from our set of assumptions concerning the importance of modifying considerably Parsonian theory and of adopting an alternate set of understandings. Hypothesis 1 stated that following Talcott Parsons's definition of family role, members of a family will carry out role behaviors that follow traditional sex-linked patterns: fathers will have a significantly higher amount of instrumental behaviors than other family members and mothers will have a significantly higher amount of expressive behaviors than other family members.

Hypothesis 2 considered the alternate model, proposed by Jackson, Slater, and others, which contains more varied patterns of role enactment than in the Parsonian approach. Accordingly a total of at least five patterns of role enactment were thought to exist in different families: traditional sex-role patterns, role duplication, role exchange, parentification of the child, and low role fulfillment.

Hypothesis 3 stated that the optimal level of family functioning is reflected in the way the family works together. We predicted that when a family was assigned a family task under experimental conditions, those who worked better together would be more active and would receive better product ratings and more adaptive clinical ratings than families who worked less well together.

Experimental Procedures and Design

Basic procedures were similar to those described in other chapters. The Pep board was adapted for use by families through pilot investigation done in 1973. In addition, clinical and product ratings enriched the experimental behavior observation of families along role dimensions. The overall design attempted to satisfy criteria discussed by Framo (1965) and by Riskin and Faunce (1972).

The Subjects. Subjects were part of the population for the Delaware Family Study, a longitudinal study of adopted children and their families. Funds were supplied by grants to Bryn Mawr College, Department of Education and Child Development, under the guidance of Janet Hoopes. Funds originated from the Children's Bureau, Wilmington, Delaware.

Letters were sent to the original 276 families, and a series of introductory meetings was planned between May and July 1974. The sample for this study was drawn from the larger population. All families with two children and having no serious, known mental health problems were listed. An attempt was made to include families with both working and unemployed mothers. "Working" was operationally defined as twenty or more hours weekly of paid employment. Haley's negative criterion (Haley 1972) was used to classify families as within the normal range of adjustment. In only nine of the families was any mental health testing or treatment reported, and in none was hospitalization considered for any family member. All families were Caucasian, but the sample was selected to represent a range of socioeconomic and educational levels. There were three types of families, and attempts were made to get representation from each: those with two parent-born children, those with two adopted children, and those with one parent-born and one adopted child.

From this population, letters were sent and telephone calls made to seventy-five Caucasian families with two children ages 6 to 15, living in

Delaware, Pennsylvania, New Jersey, or Maryland. All were intact and were one of the three types of families. Nine had two children born of the parents, thirty-two had two adopted children, and eight had mixed birth status. Of these, forty-nine two-children families were available as subjects during the summer and fall. One proved unusable due to severe mental health problems and the father's absence.

The Experimental Session. Families met in an institutional loungelike setting either at the Children's Bureau or Bryn Mawr College. After a brief interview, which functioned to put the family somewhat at ease as well as to gather information, the family was introduced to the family task. Members were introduced to the observers and received standardized verbal instructions once gathered around the Pep board.

One function of this study was to adapt the Pep board for family use. The board lends itself easily to working with families and meets criteria for family tasks discussed by Coche (1978a) and Haley (1972). It is something that everyone can do regardless of age and is fast moving, sufficiently ambiguous, challenging, and engrossing so that participants' absorption diminishes the impact of the observation technique. The board also has a projective component when choice of subject matter and execution is left to the family's imagination and fantasy. Once gathered around the board, the family was told:

> Come closer and you can feel the board. It is fuzzy; it is made of industrial felt. There are blocks of different shapes, sizes and colors which have Velcro on the back, so that they stick to the board. You can put them together in different ways so that they make different things. We would like you all to make a person or persons doing something. That is essentially it, but before you begin we would like you to sit down over here in the chairs and plan what you are going to make. We would like you to be as specific in your planning as possible: think about the age of the person or persons you are going to make, the sex, what he/she or they are doing, and if you make more than one person how the people know each other. The instructions that I'm giving you are repeated here on the planning sheet. We would like you to write down what you plan on this sheet of paper before you begin to work. After you are done planning, come over to the board. We encourage you to take your time and to enjoy yourself as much as possible. That is it. There is no time limit.

After the instructions were given, the observations began. The observers attempted to be natural, yet neutral, throughout the experiment. When questions were directed toward them, they simply restated the original instructions or made a neutral comment such as, "Do what you like." The amount of time spent in this condition varied, ranging from five to forty-one minutes and averaging seventeen minutes.

Posttask Activities. After the family had indicated that it had finished working, one observer asked the family to stand the board up so that the other observers could see it. The family was asked, "Describe what you've made. I know we were all here when you made it, but it was difficult to see what you were doing." As the family responded, they were asked, "Is there any special reason you have chosen this theme?" "Does it have any special meaning for you as a family?" Their answers and description of the product were recorded. After these questions, the families were told that the observers would like to take two photographs, one to be taken home as a souvenir and the other to be kept for the research. The family was then given cookies and juice and an opportunity to ask any questions about the nature of the project.

The Observation of Behavior. Three clinically trained observers watched the families. These observers had been trained over a period of one month until reliability was adequate on the dimensions of instrumentality and expressivity.

An objective, microscopic observation system focusing on instrumentality and expressivity was developed, based heavily on the SIMFAM system (Straus and Tallman 1971).[a] In addition, a more global clinical description of the family in operation was included. The two types of observation systems, devised to complement each other, resulted from our cognizance of the controversy between hard researchers and more clinically oriented therapists (Framo 1972). There is general agreement in the field that family interaction research is too young to have developed adequate methods of capturing through categories the global and multilevel complexity of family interaction. Therefore it seemed advisable to complement the more objective system with an overall global description and clinical ratings.

SIMFAM. SIMFAM (simulated family activity measurement) is a technique for studying families that consists of a family game and an interaction observation system. Only the observation system was used in this study. The choice was made over Bales's interaction process analysis, the only other system that uses Parsonian theory as a foundation and measures instrumentality and expressivity. Straus (1965) and Riskin and Faunce (1972) consider SIMFAM an offshoot of Bales's work, designed for use with normal families.

Scoring Instrumentality. Instrumentality definitions were modified from the variable *power* in the SIMFAM system where it was defined as "any direction, instruction, suggestion or request intended to control, initiate

[a]Professor Straus's personal communication with regard to some issues of definition is gratefully acknowledged.

change, or modify the behavior of another member of the family" (Straus and Tallman 1970, p. 14). In SIMFAM, power can be accepted, ignored, or rejected and can be used to measure instrumental leadership, as described in the Parsonian mode. This system was considered too gross to tap the subtle influence process in families. Minor modifications were needed to bring the system closer to the theoretical definitions provided by Parsons. In this study, therefore, instrumentality was broken down into three parts. An instrumental influence attempt was defined as any task-oriented action, instruction, suggestion, gesture, request, statement, or question intended to further the task toward the stated goal by eliciting, controlling, modifying, or directing the behavior of another member of the family. The attempt could be successful or unsuccessful. A successful instrumental influence attempt was defined as any attempt that did in fact elicit or control the behavior of another member of the family or the whole family in the desired direction. Such an attempt usually had an observable effect on the family product. An unsuccessful instrumental influence attempt was defined as any attempt that was either ignored or in some fashion countermanded. Additionally a category of other-instrumental behavior was created. It was defined as any task-oriented action, instruction, suggestion, gesture, request, statement, or question intended to further the task toward the stated goal but with no observable or ascertainable intent to control, modify, or direct the behavior of another member of the family.

Scoring Expressivity. Expressivity was derived from the dimension *support* in the SIMFAM system, where it was defined as "a verbal or non-verbal interaction which is assumed to have a positive or negative contribution to group solidarity or integration" (Straus and Tallman 1970, p. 6). In SIM-FAM, it is broken into S+ and S− and can be used to measure expressive leadership in the Parsonian model. Minor modifications were needed to bring it closer to the Parsonian model. In our system, expressivity was scored along three broad categories. Positive expressivity was defined as any affect-laden remark, question, term of endearment, or nonverbal expression intended to increase the solidarity of the group or the self-esteem of individual members, including oneself. Negative expressivity was defined as any affect-laden remark, question, direction, or nonverbal expression intended to decrease the solidarity of the group or the self-esteem of individual members, including oneself. A category for mixed expressivity was included because it occurred so frequently in families. Mixed expressivity was defined as any verbal or nonverbal affect-laden expression containing both positive and negative components and directed toward another individual or the group as a whole.

Global Observation. The observer was instructed to "paint a picture of this family as it interacts around the task it has been asked to do. What unique gestalt does it present that distinguishes it from other families? Concentrate especially on patterns of influence and support, expressivity, and instrumentality. What roles do family members play which seem typical of their behavior in other family situations?'' The global observer concentrated on whatever stood out in the families' interaction, on clinically oriented impressions of how the roles were carried out, how the family communicated, the presence of dyads and subgroupings, and noticeable favoritism, isolation, or scapegoating. From this record, a typewritten summary of one or two paragraphs was gathered for each family, describing globally its interaction around the board.

Posttask, Clinical, and Product Ratings. In addition to the formal observation of interaction along role dimensions, clinical and product ratings were obtained for each family.

Posttask Ratings. After the family left and while the observation was still fresh, the observers completed a posttask information sheet, discussed the family process, and made their ratings. Consensus was reached on the primary and secondary spokesperson in the posttask interview, whether someone contradicted the spokesperson, and who recorded the planning on the planning sheet. Also time used in planning and in working were computed in minutes, and the number of pieces used in the product were counted and recorded.

Clinical Ratings. Each observer was asked to rate the family on different aspects of the family interaction. First was family structure, specifically the existence of dyads, triads, or isolates in the family. The second concerned the dimensions of the product itself: contents, interrelatedness of theme, existence of a special meaning for the family, activities of figures, and similarity between finished product and the planning sheet. The third category related to the patterns of family interaction: the family's naturalness, its anxiousness to impress the observers, overall family type based on global impression, presence of interrelatedness within the family, and parent versus child domination.

Results

Hypothesis 1. Three types of reliability were computed: interrater reliability for formal scoring dimensions ($r = .63-.91$), for product ratings ($r = .45$), and for clinical ratings (67.95 percent agreement). All reliability figures were adequate.

Specific to hypothesis 1, table 11-1 indicates that fathers were significantly higher on mean amounts of successful instrumentality and total instrumental behaviors and had the highest share of influence in the family. Mothers led in the amount of positive total expressivity.

Parsons expected that fathers and sons will be most instrumental, while mothers and daughters will be most expressive. By ranking the mean for all forty-nine fathers, mothers, and older and younger children (table 11-1), along with expressive behavior, instrumental behavior, and ratios of these to total behaviors, respectively, it was possible to arrive at a diagram profiling the mean, or typical, father, mother, and older and younger child for this sample. Figure 11-2 shows that the average father was high on successfully and unsuccessfully influencing others and low in criticizing others. The average mother was likely to be high on expression of feeling, especially support and sarcasm, but low on working independently. The older child led in critical comments but was last on support and sarcasm and influence attempts. The younger child led on working alone, presumably behaving in ways that he thought were expected of him. In sum, the results based on the total mean behaviors for forty-nine fathers, mothers, and children across all families indicate that parents are more active on both role dimensions than children, as stated in hypothesis 1. However, data also reveal no sex differences in family role behaviors for children, a contradiction to Parsonian theory. Parsonian theory is useful in understanding roles assumed by the average or modal father and mother in the average or modal family. To understand how well Parsonian theory is supported by forty-nine functioning, living families, it becomes necessary to examine these parental behaviors in relation to their own families.

Hypothesis 2. To explore the meaning of role behaviors for the families in question, each family within a given category was reviewed by examining clinical ratings, global observation, and product. Sketches for the individual families were compared and communalities noted within each category to discover what noticeable similarities existed in families who structure role behaviors in the same way and whether the patterning seemed related to their ability to work together, as demonstrated by their product's rating. The major nosological categories are summarized in table 11-2. They may be characterized as follows.

1. Parent-dominated families. Seen by clinical raters as containing a thread of interconnectedness between family members, these families left the observer with a sense of the family as a unified group. Moreover these families tended to be precise, making the product exactly or nearly as they had planned. A chi-square comparing the frequencies of adult- versus child-dominated families with frequencies of families making the product as planned versus somewhat or very different yielded a chi-square value of

Table 11-1
Mean Amounts, Ranks, and Ratios of Role Behaviors for Family Members[a]

Dimension	Role[b]	Positive Expressivity		Negative Expressivity		Mixed Expressivity		Total Expressivity	
		Rank	Amount	Rank	Amount	Rank	Amount	Rank	Amount
Mean	F	2	.23	4	.06	2	.17	2	.46
Espressive	M	1	.35	3	.12	1	.21	1	.68
behaviors	O	4	.09	1	.19	3	.15	3	.43
	Y	3	.19	2	.18	4	.12	4	.42

Dimension	Role[b]	Successful Influence		Unsuccessful Influence		Work Behavior		Successful Instrumentality		All Influence	
		Rank	Amount	Rank	Amount	Rank	Amount	Rank	Amount	Rank	Amount
Mean	F	1	.35	1	.39	3	.56	1	.91	1	.74
Instrumental	M	2	.27	2	.31	4	.51	4	.77	2	.57
behaviors	O	4	.20	4	.25	2	.57	3	.77	4	.44
	Y	3	.24	3	.25	1	.61	2	.85	3	.49

Dimension	Role[b]	Expressive[c]		Supportive[c]		Influential[c]		Supportive[d]		Critical[d]	
		Rank	Amount	Rank	Amount	Rank	Amount	Rank	Amount	Rank	Amount
Ratios or	F	3	.26	2	.11	1	.35	2	.29	4	.14
shares	M	1	.38	1	.19	2	.24	1	.45	3	.23
	O	4	.26	4	.04	4	.20	4	.11	2	.29
	Y	2	.27	3	.07	3	.21	3	.15	1	.32

[a]Controlled for time.
[b]F = father; M = mother; O = older child; Y = younger child.
[c]Ratio of this behavior to total individual behavior.
[d]Share of member in family.
[e]Ties were broken according to the third number behind the decimal point.

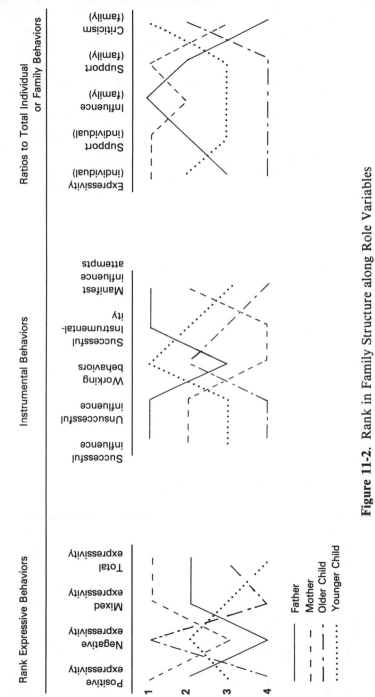

Figure 11-2. Rank in Family Structure along Role Variables

Table 11-2
Family Role Configurations Observed

Subconfiguration	Subtype	Definition	Characteristics
Shared parental	Classic Parsonian role structure, or variation in sibling structure (N = 2)	Father leads on instrumental behaviors, mother on expressive: boy second on instrumental, girl second on expressive behaviors	Families insecure, concerned with precision and struggling; father's leadership seemed out of a need to structure the situation; families somewhat constricted and frightened
	Role exchange in parents (N = 2)	Mother leads on instrumental, father on expressive behaviors	Parents self-assured and at ease with roles, as though in keeping with natural tendencies; mutual respect between parents, not anxious to impress observers
One parent dominated	Father-dominated role structure (N = 4)	Father leads on both expressive and instrumental behaviors	Conflict seemed clear but subtle, covered by joking or reserve; sex-linked dyads in three families; poor products
	Mother-dominated role structure (N = 7)	Mother leads on both expressive and instrumental behaviors	Families anxious to impress observers; forced, dynamic quality; mother-daughter dyad in three families; mother as a strong personality, sometimes with passive father
Shared leadership	Shared leadership: child instrumental, parent expressive (N = 12)	One child leads on instrumental, one parent leads on expressive behaviors	Two types, in both family struggling: (1) older, adolescent child replaces passive parent (2) both parents incapable of leadership, and children wildly needing structure and limits
	Shared leadership: parent instrumental, child expressive (N = 10)	One parent leads on instrumental, one child leads on expressive behaviors	Absence of passive parent more apparent to observers than child's leadership; in seven families, child led while mother

Child dominated	Same child-dominated role structure (N = 3)	One child leads on both instrumental and expressive behaviors	Child leader in dyad with mother in all families; leader older child in two families; warmth apparent in all cases
	Both-children-dominated role structure (N = 4)	One child leads on instrumental, second leads on expressive behaviors	Parents passive and overwhelmed by children in each case; children floundering and respond by sulking, clinging, or acting out; parents angry at selves or others; poor products; rated as struggling or isolated, and needy of mental health help
Role duplication	Role duplication (N = 5)	One or both roles taken by more than one family member	Seems less a type than a chance circumstance

10.96 ($df = 3$), $P = .01$. Members worked well independently and had a proportionately high ratio of success when attempting to influence others. Within the larger categorization, a subtle difference occurred between families in which the father led on instrumental dimensions (classic and father-dominated patterns) and those led instrumentally by mother (role exchange and mother dominated). In the former, fathers needed to structure the situation rigidly to allay discomfort or conflict that was noticeable to three observers, whereas spontaneity and expressivity were more common where the mother led instrumentally. Especially in the mother-dominated families, there was a spirit of warmth and products were scored high. In summary, there was less apparent struggle in the adult-dominated families, especially where the mother was active instrumentally.

2. Shared leadership families. In twenty-one families, leadership was split between one parent and one child. With the exception of a subgroup of highly expressive child-centered families, these families seemed to be struggling to maintain harmony and open communication channels. Abnegation of one role was often present where one parent seemed passive to the observers. In a number of cases, the father successfully provided instrumental leadership, while the mother passively gave the family blocks or stood back and the children were lively and expressive. In a few, similar to child-dominated families, parents were passive and the absence of leadership was replaced by acting out from the children. This group seemed highly varied, functioning adequately according to clinical and product ratings and self-report about mental health help.

3. Role duplication families. The category was defined operationally by the scores by two or more members on role dimensions. It occurred in five families, but no trends were visible. The category seemed more a chance occurrence than a natural grouping.

4. Child-dominated families. In seven families, children or one child scored high on both dimensions. The families, categorized as child dominated, seem to break naturally into two differing subgroups. In the three families where one child functioned as leader, this was always the older child who formed a dyadic relationship with the mother. In the four families where both children took over, families seemed chaotic and members struggling unsuccessfully to avoid an isolation that was apparent between members. Products were lowest of all subgroups, and observers felt that each family needed mental health care. The parents were overwhelmed by their children and expressed anger in each case at themselves, their children, or the adoption agency. These seven families as a whole were less self-assured and less able to channel their energies constructively in setting needed limits for their children, or working on a joint product.

Hypothesis 3. Hypothesis 3 concerned the relationship between family role configuration and the family's ability to work together, as measured by independent product ratings. Quality of product was related to family thread, a clinical rating that bears great conceptual similarity to the small group variable of cohesiveness and other variables that are indicators of working well together (see Coché 1976).

As families began to participate in this study, we became aware that a subtle yet powerful factor was operating within some of them. As some families left, the observers found themselves relaxed, smiling, and feeling comfortable about being with the family. Another group of families had a mixed impact, and a third group left the observers feeling sad, anxious for the well-being of the family members, and uncomfortable about the family interaction they had just observed. The research team agreed that something was operating, but were not sure how to operationalize and score the phenomenon. They felt that there seemed to be a natural flow of inter-relatedness present to different degrees within different families. This feeling aspect seemed akin to the small group concept of cohesiveness (Cartwright and Zander 1968).

A typology was developed that proved more difficult to define than to recognize since categorization was based on sensed, nonverbal, global impressions that are difficult for clinicians to label. Overall interrater reliability for the degree of interrelatedness was established ($r = .80$), but agreement between the two most experienced clinicians was even closer ($r = .92$). The central ingredient involved the amount of presence or absence of this quality, labeled "thread of interrelatedness," among families. Families were then loosely grouped into three categories:

1. Integrative families. Getting along successfully, without much effort. Energies within the family flowed easily and spontaneously. Despite conflict in the family, there was a lack of struggle for relatedness. Communication channels for the expression of feelings were relatively open. In many families, it seemed as if the observers were merely dropping in on them while they were doing something together. Despite some desire to make a good impression, there seemed to be relative satisfaction with their image as a family.

2. Struggling families. Getting along, but struggling. The family seemed to be straining and stretching its energies and capacities to keep open communication channels that would otherwise close off. Effort at togetherness was apparent to the observer although perhaps not to the family itself. There was a forced quality to the interaction, often combined with a lack of comfort with themselves or the observers. The family was trying but lacked the interpersonal and personal ease needed to diminish the struggle.

3. Isolating families. Struggling, but not succeeding. There was an observable failure in present or past attempts to bind the family unit. Communication lines were closed off within the system as a whole and between individual members. Physical or psychological separateness and isolation or scapegoating of one or more members was apparent.

Correlations were computed, significantly relating the variables "thread" and "family type" to overall goodness of product creation, independent product rating, and to influential and expressive behavior in the family. Moreover this global product rating was correlated with mixed emotion (sarcasm) and successful and unsuccessful influence.

With these technical definitions and statistical procedures in mind, it is valuable to examine the data. Families who work well together (make good products) interact in certain ways with one another. On the assumption that family type may be considered continuous, ranging from integrative to isolating, a correlation to the product rating was computed and proved positive. This means that there was a natural flow of interrelatedness in families who made good products. Further this thread within the family had typical components. When the family expressed feelings to one another, communications were direct rather than mixed or sarcastic. Moreover members in families who made the best products attempted to influence each other significantly less frequently. They did not tell each other what to do as frequently as did members of other families. Rather they acted as a cohesive unit and used time and work material effectively in achieving the stated goal. They planned for longer periods of time, typically dividing labor and reaching their goal through mutual consensus rather than from an order from one member. This ensured members more energy to get involved in the task, demonstrated by longer working times and more complex products than in less successful families. The overall picture was of a cohesive group who, because communications were fluid, could plan and work as an integrated unit. Each member was assured of his or her ability to contribute to and enrich the group effort.

This situation was in marked contrast to the tightly constricted, authoritarian structure suggested by families who made poor products. Here group cohesiveness seemed low and attempts to tell each other what to do were high. The atmosphere was one of pressure and was not conducive to a relaxed, creative, cooperative effort.

An analysis of variance of thread with the clinical rating, parent or child domination in the family, was significant at the .001 level. In a child-dominated family, parents appeared incapable of fulfilling the parental role; they did not set limits or make necessary plans or decisions. In a parent-dominated family, the parents provided support and structure. They might be lively and easygoing, but it was clear to the children and observers who the parents in the family were. The analysis shows that the cohesive families consisted of parents who fulfilled the parental functions of structure and support.

Implication for Theory and Social Change

The findings of our study led us to a deeper understanding of family functioning and hence to a recasting of the original theoretical formulations.

One can look at the three hypotheses that have guided this research as representing three different ways of conceptualizing the nature of relationships among family members. In each of the models, the concept of role relationships figures predominantly. Although the Parsonian sex-linked model was formed to give an accurate account of the average instrumental and expressive families, it was inadequate for the description of each separate family. When the focus was on each unique family system, the four different patterns of role relationships that we plotted proved useful, particularly in relation to family communication and the ability to work well together. Still we found this conceptualization inadequate to deal with the aspect of interdependence and feelings that appeared basic to family functioning and related to differences among families. Thus using Jackson's concept of roles as relationships, our own conception of possible relationships evolved (figure 11-3).

The value of the social psychological concept of roles leads one to wonder which other social psychological variables are conducive to natural interrelationships and mutual trust within the family. We would posit, based on the writings of others (Satir 1967; Bowen 1966) and on clinical expertise, that key factors include an open communication of feelings within the family and acceptance of the position of other members. The family rules that Jackson referred to need to be that the norm for family interaction is that messages of trust and honesty about feelings and about self are highly valued behaviors within the family and become transmitted to the children as roles vis-à-vis one another. Appreciation of age is important in determining roles or positions vis-à-vis one another. Children need the awareness that the parents can and will model expressivity, consistency, and limit setting, as ways members relate to one another.

Which parents seem best able to model open relationship as role modelling activities? We know of no research in this area but venture that adults who have developed fairness, honesty, consistency, and caring in relation to themselves are best able to model these behaviors quite naturally within their roles as parents (Coché 1978).

Clinical Applications. To illustrate these points, we have included two global family reports of interaction around the Pep board. The two were selected because the reports are illustrative of the verbal and nonverbal communications along the dimensions of task-oriented and feeling-oriented communications. The first family is in trouble, although it is not desirous of clinical intervention. The second family shows the thread of interrelatedness, or cohesiveness, which seems crucial to optimal family functioning.

Family A consists of a father, mother, adopted son, age 11, and adopted daughter, age 8. The family product was described in this way: "Boy, age 11, and girl, age 8, are building sidewalks leading to house.

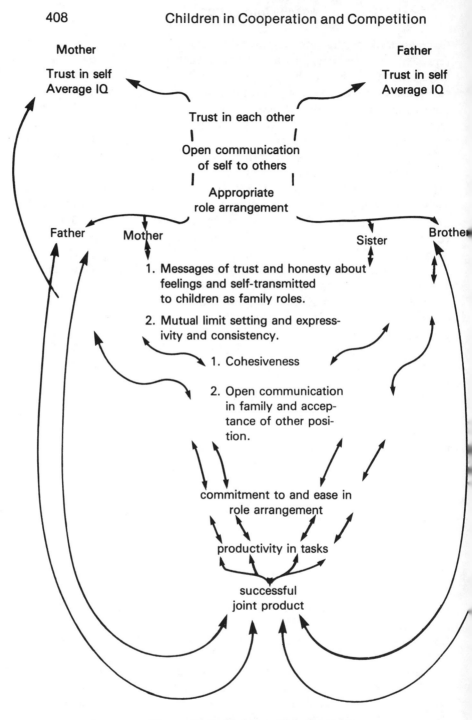

Figure 11-3. Roles as Relationships

House is long, one-story house. They were smoothing the concrete. Boy and girl are friends. They put up a sign saying, 'wet cement.' It is expected that the boy and girl will grow up, get married, live happily, die, and be buried.''

After family A left, the observers were quiet and pensive, finally verbalizing the feeling that they had seen a family in which the parents did not parent. Although the parents were older, so are many other parents. However, in this family, what leadership there was was literally handed to the son and daughter by the father. The father began by giving the boy the board, and the boy responded somewhat angrily, "Are you going to let me write this?" The task was finished by the father's giving the board back to the son and asking him to check to see whether the family had done the task well. At the same time, the father kept praising, stroking, and making the younger daughter the center of attention. He would refer to her as "our favorite storyteller" over and over, saying that this was her role in their family. The observers were impressed by the differential treatment that the son and daughter received. The father seemed most concerned with the daughter and seemed to favor her.

The mother made very few comments and inputs into the family's interaction. She said, "I need help in building this," and this seemed representative of her role within the family. Because the father was also hesitant about assuming an instrumental or an expressive role, there was a vagueness and confusion in the air while the family was working. The father attempted to counteract this by drawing out in great detail the very simple product that the family made. He could not leave the story alone, and the older son was particularly bored by the father's continuation. He finally turned to his sister and said in baby talk, "Who coo-coo." In the writing of the task, it seems very symbolic that the father had to ask the son how to spell the simple word *bury*.

There was a sadness about the children, who seemed pensive and withdrawn. The daughter said very little during the task; the mother seemed to have a nervous cough that she could not control; the father had a nervous laugh. All of this seemed reflective of the confusion and lack of role clarity within the family.

Family B consisted of a father, mother, daughter, age 15, and daughter, age 11. Their family product was "the 'B's' family orchestra. Mother is playing the piano, dad is on the flute, older daughter plays the marimba with mallets, while younger daughter plays the drums. The family dog is listening.'' The product represented a favorite family pasttime, since family members played two or more instruments.

There was a quiet, creative flow running among the members of this family. It was not ostentatious but rather a thread of interrelatedness that seemed to mark some of the families with some of the best products. Both roles, expressive and instrumental, were filled by the father who was a dynamic, energetic force within the family. He gave a lot of support and joked in a gentle teasing way with his wife, "Are you thirty-nine already?"The family decided not to make members individually but to work together on one part of the product at a time. They seemed quite relaxed in this situation, which allowed them to get really involved and let ideas flow. The observers remarked how this thread of interrelatedness is helpful in producing creativity. For example, in making the piano keys they searched for black mosaics but found that there were none. Someone thought of turning the mosaics over on its back to expose the black Velcro underneath. In this way, they made optimal use of materials with limited possibilities.

Much of the joking was between father and older daughter, who both wielded a lot of influence and assertiveness within the family. She stood with her hands on her hip, in a close-fitting blouse, and had a repartee with the father of a teasing nature. For example, she criticized the father's dog by saying, "It looks like a duck," in a gentle manner. The younger daughter seemed more dependent on the father for support and looked to him a number of times. She was less the center of attention than her sister and had to make sure that she fixed her own figure since no one was about to do it for her.

Further Directions. The concept of roles in families as static, normative lists of who should exhibit which behaviors in order for family health to prevail has outlived its usefulness for the professional who seeks to understand, to predict, and to treat relationships among members of a family. Talcott Parsons's ideas had importance in focusing the attention of social scientists on the relationship between social psychological functioning and mental health among members of a nuclear family. The study described in this chapter points to the incompleteness of the theory for our current understanding of families and suggests that behaviors inherent in traditional social roles can more heuristically be considered as a means to an end than as valuable goals. Families consist of individuals in an interlocking system of relationships with one another. As long as these relationships allow for mutual respect, support, and consistency within and across generations, the patterning of the role behaviors can take many forms. The set of family role habits is a convenient means for getting family needs taken care of. It is not a genetically predetermined hierarchy of unfolding sex-linked behaviors.

This examination of family roles can aid our understanding and treatment of recent developments in family patterning. Single-parent families and families involving dual-career marriages are two examples of patterns that are increasingly becoming part of our daily existence in Western civilization.

Forty percent of all women's marriages beginning in 1978 will end in divorce (Bohannan 1971). The family in which divorce has occurred must shift from earlier role patterns. Clinical experience and my position as advisory board member to Parents Without Partners has sensitized me to this group of parents' initial shame and discomfort at not providing their children with the usual family role model and their questions about how to parent effectively, given their insecurity around being an unusual kind of family. In these families with one custodial parent in residence, the contribution of the absent parent and the contribution of developmental age level to role functioning are two areas that need to be explored through research and to be dealt with clinically.

Recent attention to the dual-career marriage and the continually increasing percentage of child-bearing women in the work force points to another contemporary family constellation that needs clinical and research consideration. Specific factors worthy of attention here include the contribution of the day-care center or child nurse as role model for children of these marriages and the effect of two working parents on social role assignments within the family and the household.

Dual-career marriages and single-parent families are but two of a kaleidoscope of role variations in today's families. The ideal Parsonian family has never existed in great numbers. Instead of continuing our attention in this direction, let us study in depth the cooperative, collaborative relationships within the family, in an effort to gain greater understanding of which ingredients in family members' relationships with one another combine to create a growth-producing social climate for the individuals within the system. How valuable for us all to discover that in our relationships with one another, with our parents, our siblings, and our children, the secret to effective and satisfying role enactment probably lies.

References

Abelson, R.P., and Rosenberg, M.J. Symbolic psycho-logic: A model of attitudinal cognition. *Behavioral Science*, 1958, *3*, 1-13.

Adams, J.S. Inequity in social exchange. In L. Berkowitz, ed., *Advances in experimental social psychology*, 3:267-299. New York: Academic Press, 1965.

Ahlgren, A., and Johnson, D.W. Sex differences in cooperative and competitive attitudes from the 2nd through the 12th grades. *Developmental Psychology*, 1979, *15*, 1, 45-49.

Allport, F.H. *Social psychology*. Boston: Houghton Mifflin, 1924.

Allport, G.W. The historical background of modern social psychology. In G. Lindzey, ed., *Handbook of social psychology*, *1*, Cambridge, Ma.: Addison-Wesley, 1954.

_____ . *The nature of prejudice*. Reading, Mass.: Addison-Wesley, 1954.

Alper, T.G. Achievement motivation in college women: A now-you-see-it-now-you-don't phenomenon. *American Psychologist*, 1974, *29*, 194-203.

Ames, C., and Ames, R. Thrill of victory and agony of defeat: Children's self and interpersonal evaluations in competitive and noncompetitive learning environments. *Journal of Research and Development in Education*, 1978, *12*, 79-87.

Anthony, E. The reactions of adults to adolescents and their behavior. In A. Esman, ed., *The psychology of adolescence; essential readings*. New York: International Universities Press, 1975.

Aronson, E. *The jigsaw classroom*. Beverly Hills, Calif.: Sage Publications, 1978.

Aronson, E.; Blaney, N.; Sikes, J.; Stephan, G.; and Snapp, M. The jigsaw route to learning and liking. *Psychology Today*, 1975, 43-50.

Aronson, E.; Bridgeman, D.C.; and Geffner, R. The effects of a cooperative classroom structure on student behavior and attitudes. In D. Bar-Tal and L. Saxe, eds., *Social Psychology of Education: Theory and Research*. Washington: Hemisphere Publishing Corp., Halsted Press, Wiley, 1978.

Arrowood, A., and Friend, R. Other factors determining the choice of a comparison other. *Journal of Experimental Social Psychology*, 1969, *5*, 233-239.

Asch, S.E. Studies of independence and conformity: A minority of one against a unanimous majority. *Psychological Monograph*, 1956, *70*(9), 177-190.

Ashton, N.L., and Severy, L.J. Arousal and costs in bystander intervention. *Personality and Social Psychological Bulletin*, 1976, *2*, 268-272.

413

Atkinson, J.W. *An introduction to motivation.* Princeton: Van Nostrand, 1964.

Ausubel, D. *Theory and problems of adolescent development.* New York: Grune and Stratton, 1954.

Ausubel, D., and Sullivan, E. *Theory and problems of child development.* 2d ed., New York: Grune & Stratton, 1970.

Baldwin, A.L. *The theory of Jean Piaget. Theories of child development.* New York: Wiley, 1967.

Bales, R.F. *Interaction process analysis.* Cambridge, Ma.: Addison-Wesley, 1950.

———. Task roles and social roles in problem solving groups. In E.E. Maccoby, T.M. Newcomb, and E.L. Hartley, eds., *Readings in social psychology*, 3d ed., 437-447. New York: Holt, Rinehart & Winston, 1958.

Bales, R.F., and Slater, P.E. Role differentiation in small decision-making groups. In T. Parsons and R.F. Bales, eds., *Family, socialization and interaction process*, 259-306. New York: Free Press, 1955.

Bandura, A., and Walters, R. Aggression. In H.W. Stevenson, ed., *Sixty-second yearbook*, National Society for the Study of Education, Part 1: Child psychology. Chicago: University of Chicago Press, 1963a.

———. *Social learning and personality development.* New York: Holt, Rinehart & Winston, 1963b.

Barker, R.; Dembo, T.; and Lewin, K. Frustration and regression. *University of Iowa Studies in Child Welfare*, 1941, *18*, 1.

Barnett, R.J. No room in the lifeboats. *New York Times Magazine*, April 16, 1978.

Bar-Tal, D. Attribution theory and achievement. *Review of Educational Research*, 1978, *48*, 259-271.

Barth, R.S. *Open education and the American school.* New York: Agathon Press, 1972.

Benedict, R. Continuities in cultural conditioning. *Psychiatry*, 1938, *1*, 161-167.

Benne, K., and Sheats, P. Functional roles of group members. *Journal of Social Issues*, 1948, *4*, 41-49.

Berenda, R.W. *The influence of the group on judgments of children.* New York: Kings Press, 1950.

Bestor, A.E. *Educational waste lands; the retreat from learning in our public schools.* Urbana: University of Illinois Press, 1953.

Bindra, D. The nature of motivation for hoarding food. *Journal of Comparative and Physiological Psychology*, 1948, *41*, 211-218.

Birnbaum, J.A. Life patterns and self-esteem in gifted family-oriented and career-oriented women. In M.T.S. Mednick, S.S. Tangri, and L.W. Hoffman, eds., *Women and achievement.* New York: Wiley, 1975.

Blakemore, J.E.D.; LaRue, A.A.; and Olejnik, A.B. Sex appropriate toy preference and the ability to conceptualize toys as sex-role related. *Developmental Psychology*, 1979, *15*(3), 339-340.

Blanchard, F.A.; Adelman, L.; and Cook, S.W. Effect of group success and failure upon interpersonal attraction in cooperating interracial groups. *Journal of Personality and Social Psychology*, 1975, *31*(6), 1020-1030.

Blanchard, F.A., and Cook, S.W. Effects of helping a less competent member of a cooperating interracial group on the development of interpersonal attraction. *Journal of Personality and Social Psychology*, 1976, *34*(6), 1245-1255.

Blanchard, F.A.; Weigel, R.H.; and Cook, S.W. The effect of relative competence of group members upon interpersonal attraction in cooperating interracial groups. *Journal of Personality and Social Psychology*, 1975, *32*(3), 519-530.

Blaney, N.T.; Stephan, S.; Rosenfield, D.; Aronson, E.; and Sikes, J. Interdependence in the classroom: A field study. *Journal of Educational Psychology*, 1977, *69*, 121-128.

Blos, P. *On adolescence: A psycholanalytic interpretation*. New York: Free Press, 1962.

Bohannan, P., ed. *Divorce and after*. New York: Anchor Books, 1971.

Borke, H. Interpersonal perceptions of young children: Egocentrism or empathy? *Developmental Psychology*, 1971, *5*, 263-269.

Boszormenyi-Nagy, I., and Spark, G.M. *Invisible loyalties: Reciprocity in intergenerational family therapy*. Hagerstown, Md.: Harper & Row, 1973.

Bott, E. *Family and social network*. New York: Free Press, 1971.

Bowen, M. The use of family theory in clinical practice. *Comprehensive Psychiatry*, 1966, *7*, 345-374.

Brandt, R.M. Three weeks in British infant schools. In D. Hearn, J. Burdin, and L. Katz, eds., *Current research and perspectives in open education*. Washington, D.C.: American Association of Elementary-Kindergarten-Nursery Educators, 1972.

Brehm, J.W. *A theory of psychological reactance*. New York: Academic Press, 1966.

Brickman, P. and Bulman, R.J. Pleasure and pain in social comparison. In J.M. Suls and R.L. Miller, eds., *Social comparison processes: Theoretical and empirical perspectives*. Washington, D.C.: Hemisphere Publishing Corp., Halsted Press, Wiley, 1977.

Brody, G.H., and Zimmerman, B.J. The effects of modeling and classroom organization on the personal space of third and fourth grade children. *American Educational Research Journal*, 1975, *12*(2), 157-168.

Brodzinsky, D.M.; Messer, S.B.; and Tew, J.D. Sex differences in childrens' expression and control of fantasy and overt aggression. *Child Development*, 1979, *50*(2), 372-379.

Bronfenbrenner, U. Socialization and social class through time and space. In E.E. Maccoby, T.M. Newcomb, and E.L. Hartley, eds., *Readings in social psychology*, 400-425. New York: Holt, Rinehart & Winston, 1958.

———. *Two worlds of childhood*. New York: Russell Sage Foundation, 1970.

Brotsky, S.J., and Thomas, K. Cooperative behavior in preschool children. *Psychonomic Science*, 1967, *9*, 337-338.

Broverman, I.K.; Vogel, S.R.; Broverman, D.M.; Clarkson, F.E.; and Rosenkrantz, P.S. Sex-role stereotypes: A current appraisal. *Journal of Social Issues*, 1972, *28*, 59-78.

Bryan, J.H. Children's cooperation and helping behavior. In E.M. Hetherington, ed., *Review of child development research. 5*. Chicago: University of Chicago Press, 1975.

Bryan, J., and Walbeck, N. Preaching and practicing generosity: Children's actions and reactions. *Child Development*, 1970, *41*, 329-353.

Bryson, J., and R. Bryson, eds. *Dual career couples*. New York: Human Sciences Press, 1978.

Buhler, C. *The first year of life*. New York: Day, 1930.

Burlingame, W. An investigation of the correlates of adherence to the adolescent peer culture. Ph.D. dissertation, University of Washington, 1967.

Cartwright, D., ed. *Field theory in social science, selected theoretical papers by Kurt Lewin*. New York: Harper & Brothers, 1951.

Cartwright, D., and Zander, A., eds. *Group dynamics: Research and theory*. 3d ed. New York: Harper & Row, 1968.

————, eds. 1953, 1960. *Group dynamics: Research and theory*. White Plains, New York: Dow, Peterson and Co., 1953; 2d ed. 1960.

Castore, C.H., and DeNinno, J.A. Investigations in the social comparison of attitudes. In J.M. Suls and R.L. Miller, eds., *Social comparison processes: Theoretical and empirical perspectives*, 125-148. Washington, D.C.: Hemisphere Publishing Corp., Halsted Press, Wiley, 1977.

Catalogue, 1977. Palo Alto, Calif.: Creative Publications, 1977.

Chittenden, E. Research and assessment strategy. In D. Hearn, J. Burdin, and L. Katz, eds., *Current research and perspectives in open education*. Washington, D.C.: American Association of Elementary-Kindergarten-Nursery Educators, 1972.

Chittenden, G. Experiences in which young children may learn to share. *Yearbook of the National Society for the Study of Education*. Chicago: University of Chicago Press, 1947.

Clifford, M.M. Effects of competition as a motivational technique in the classroom. *American Educational Research Journal*, 1972, *9*, 123-137.

Coché, J. Patterns of role behaviors in families: An experimental study. *Dissertation abstracts international*, 1976a, *36*. University Microfilms No. 76-6007, 268.

————. A tentative nosology of family functioning relating to openness of communicative patterns. In R.W. Manderscheid and F.E. Mandersheid, eds., *Systems Science and the future of health*, 23-28. Washington, D.C.: Groome Center, 1976b.

_____ . The application of family role research to family therapy practice. Paper presented at the XIXth International Congress of Applied Psychology, Munich, July 1978a.

_____ . The uniqueness of family therapy outcome research: Critical research issues. Paper presented at the ninth annual meeting of the Society for Psychotherapy Research. Toronto, 1978b.

Cockrell, D.L. A study of the play of children of pre-school age by an unobserved observer. *Genetic Psychology Monographs*, 1935, *17*, 377-469.

Coleman, J.S. *The adolescent society: The social life of the teenager and its impact on education*. New York: Free Press, 1961.

Coles, R. *Children of crisis*. Boston: Little, Brown, 1977. *1-5*.

Collins, B., and Guetzkow, H. *A social psychology of group processes for decision making*. New York: John Wiley, 1964.

Condry, J., and Dyer, S. Fear of success: Attribution of cause to the victim. In D.N. Ruble, I.H. Frieze, and J.E. Parsons, eds., Sex-roles: Persistence and change. *Journal of Social Issues*, 1976, *32*(3), 63-83.

Connor, J.M., and Serbin, L.A. Behaviorally based masculine and feminine activity-reference scales for pre-schoolers: Correlates with other classroom behaviors and cognitive tests. *Child Development*, 1977, *48*, 1411-1416.

Cook, H., and Stingle, S. Cooperative behavior in children. *Psychological Bulletin*, 1974, *81*(12), 918-933.

Cook, S.W. Motives in a conceptual analysis of attitude-related behavior. In W.T. Arnold and D. Levine, eds., *Nebraska Symposium on Motivation, 17*. Lincoln: University of Nebraska Press, 1969.

_____ . Interpersonal and attitudinal outcomes in cooperating interracial groups. *Journal of Research and Development in Education*, 1978, *12*, 1, 97-113.

Cottrell, N.B. Social facilitation. In C.B. McClintock, ed., *Experimental social psychology*. New York: Holt, Rinehart and Winston, 1972.

Crandall, V.C. Sex differences in expectancy of intellectual and academic reinforcement. In C.P. Smith, ed., *Achievement-related motives in children*. New York: Russell Sage Foundation, 1969.

Crawford, J. Comparison behavior in the classroom: The role of informational and evaluational processes. Master's thesis, Bryn Mawr College, 1970.

Cremin, L.A.: *The transformation of the school: Progressivism in American Education: 1876-1957*. New York: Vintage Books, 1961.

_____ . *American education: Some notes toward a new history*. Bloomington, Ind.: Phi Delta Kappa International, 1969.

_____ . *American education. The colonial experience: 1607-1783*. New York: Harper & Row, 1970.

Crombag, H.F. Cooperation and competition in means-interdependent triads. *Journal of Personality and Social Psychology*, 1966, *4*, 692-695.

Crosby, F. A model of egoistical relative deprivation. *Psychological Review*, 1976, *83*, 2, 85-113.

Darley, J., and Aronson, E. Self evaluation vs. direct anxiety reduction as determinants of the fear-affiliation relationship. *Journal of Experimental Social Psychology*, 1966, Supplement, 66-79.

Dashiell, J.F. Experimental studies of the influence of social situations on the behavior of individual human adults. In C. Murchison, ed., *A handbook of social psychology*. Worcester, Ma.: Clark University Press, 1935.

Deci, E.L. *Intrinsic motivation*. New York: Plenum Publishing Corp., 1975.

Deutsch, F. Female preschoolers' perceptions of affective responses and interpersonal behavior in videotaped episodes. *Developmental Psychology*, 1974, *10*, 733-740.

Deutsch, M. A theory of competition and cooperation. *Human Relations*, 1949a, *2*, 129-151.

————. An experimental study of the effect of cooperation and competition upon group process. *Human Relations*, 1949b, *2*, 199-231.

————. Social relations in the classroom and grading procedures. *Journal of Educational Research*, 1951, *45*, 145-152.

————. *Conditions affecting cooperation: I. Factors related to the initiation of cooperation. II. Trust and cooperation.* Final technical report for the Office of Naval Research, 1957.

————. Trust and suspicion. *Journal of Conflict Resolution*, 1958, *2*, 265-279.

————. Cooperation and trust: Some theoretical notes. In M.R. Jones, ed., *Nebraska Symposium on motivation*. Lincoln: University of Nebraska Press, 1962.

————. Socially relevant science: Reflection on some studies of interpersonal conflict. *Journal of Abnormal and Social Psychology*, 1969, *24*, 1076-1092.

————. Education and distributive justice: Some reflections on grading systems. *American Psychologist*, 1979, *34*, 391-401.

Deutsch, M., and Collins, M.E. *Interracial housing: A psychological evaluation of a social experiment*. Minneapolis: University of Minnesota Press, 1951.

Deutsch, M., and Gerard, H.G. A study of normative and informational social influence upon individual judgment. *Journal of Abnormal and Social Psychology*, 1955, *51*, 629-636.

Deutsch, M., and Krauss, R.M. The effect of threat on interpersonal bargainings. *Journal of Abnormal and Social Psychology*, 1960, *61*, 181-189.

Deutsch, M., and Lewicki, R.J. "Locking-in" effects during a game of chicken. *Journal of Conflict Resolution*, 1970, *14*, 367-378.

DeVries, D.L., and Slavin, R.E. Teams-Games-Tournaments (TGT): Review of ten classroom experiments. *Journal of Research and Development in Education*, 1978, *12*, 1, 28-38.

Dewey, J. *Experience and education.* New York: Macmillan, 1952.

––––––. *The school and society.* 8th Phoenix edition. Chicago: University of Chicago Press, 1966.

Dinkmeyer, D. *Developing understanding of self and others.* Circle Pines, Minn.: American Guidance Service, 1970.

Doland, D.J. Personal communication to Vanderbilt, March 31, 1970.

Doland, D.J., and Adelberg, K. The learning of sharing behavior. *Child Development*, 1967, *38*, 695-700.

Dollard, J.; Doob, L.W.; Miller, N.E.; Mowrer, O.H.; and Sears, R.R. *Frustration and aggression.* New Haven: Yale University Press, 1939.

Duckworth, E. Piaget rediscovered. *Journal of Research in Science Teaching*, 1964, *2*, 172-175.

Eckerman, C.; Whatley, J.; and Kutz, S. Growth of social play with peers during the second year of life. *Developmental Psychology*, 1975, *11*, 42-49.

Elkin, D.G. *The influence of the group on the process of recall.* Detsky Collectivi Rebenok, 1926, 221-226.

Elliot, R., and Vasta, R. The modeling of sharing: Effects associated with vicarious reinforcement, symbolization, age, and generalization. *Journal of Experimental Child Psychology*, 1970, *10*, 8-15.

Engle, P.; Keepes, B.; and Thorne, L. Glasser's school without failure: A three-year evaluation. Paper presented at the meeting of the American Education Research Association, New Orleans, 1973.

Erikson, E. *Childhood and society.* New York: W.W. Norton, 1950.

––––––. *Identity and the life cycle.* New York: International Universities Press, 1959.

––––––. *Identity: Youth and crisis.* New York: W.W. Norton, 1968.

Exline, R.V. Explorations in the process of person perception: Visual interaction in relation to competition, sex, and need for affiliation. *Journal of Personality*, 1963, *31*, 1-20.

Farran, D.C. Exploratory study of productivity in academic groups in two open classrooms. Unpublished manuscript, Bryn Mawr College, 1973.

Feldman, K.A., and Newcomb, T.M. *The impact of college on students.* San Francisco: Jossey Bass, 1969.

Feldman, N.S., and Ruble, D.N. Awareness of social comparison interest and motivation: A developmental study. *Journal of Educational Psychology*, 1977, *69*, 579-585.

Feldman, S., ed. *Cognitive consistency: Motivational antecedents and behavioral consequents.* New York: Academic Press, 1966.

Feshbach, S. Aggression. In P.H. Mussen, ed., *Carmichael's manual of child psychology*, 3d ed., *2*:159-261. New York: Wiley, 1970.

Festinger, L. Informal social communication. *Psychological Review*, 1950, *57*, 271-282.

_____ . A theory of social comparison processes. *Human Relations*, 1954, *7*, 117-140.

_____ . *A theory of cognitive dissonance*. Evanston, Ill.: Row, Peterson, 1957.

Fisher, W.F. Sharing in preschool children as a function of amount and type of reinforcement. *Genetic Psychological Monographs*, 1963, *68*, 215-245.

Fiske, D.W. Two worlds of psychological phenomena. *American Psychologist*, 1979, *34*(9), 733-739.

Flavell, J.H. *The developmental psychology of Jean Piaget*. Princeton, N.J.: Van Nostrand, 1963.

_____ . *The development of role-taking and communication skills in children*. New York: Wiley, 1968.

_____ . *Cognitive development*. Englewood Cliffs, N.J.: Prentice-Hall, 1977.

Foster, G. Peasant society and the image of the limited good. *American Anthropologist*, 1965, *67*, 293-315.

_____ . *Tzin Tzun Tzan. Mexican peasants in a changing world*. Boston: Little, Brown, 1967.

Framo, J.L. Systematic research on family dynamics. In I. Boszormenyi-Nagy and J.L. Framo, eds., *Intensive Family Therapy*. Hagerstown, Md.: Harper & Row, 1965.

_____ , ed. *Family interaction: A dialogue between family researchers and family therapists*. New York: Springer Publishing Company, 1972.

Freedman, J.J.; Sears, D.O.; and Carlsmith, J.M. *Social Psychology*. 3d. ed. Englewood Cliffs, N.J.: Prentice-Hall, 1978.

French, D.C.; Brownell, C.A.; Graziano, W.G.; and Hartup, W.W. Effects of cooperative, competitive and individualistic sets on performance in children's groups. *Journal of Experimental Child Psychology*, 1977, *24*, 1-10.

French, J.R.P., Jr. Organized and unorganized groups under fear and frustration. *University of Iowa Studies in Child Welfare*, 1944, *20*, 229-308.

Freud, A. *The ego and the mechanism of defense*. New York: International Universities Press, 1948.

_____ . *Adolescence: Psychoanalytic study of the child. 13*. New York: International Universities Press, 1958.

Freud, S. *An outline of psychoanalysis*. New York: Norton, 1949. (Originally published 1938.)

Friedenberg, E. *The vanishing adolescent*. Boston: Beacon Press, 1959.

———. *Coming of age in America: Growth and acquiescence*. New York: Random House, 1963a.

———. *Society's children*. New York: Random House, 1963b.

Frieze, I.H.; Parsons, J.E.; Johnson, P.B.; Ruble, D.N.; and Zellman, G.L. *Women and sex roles: A social psychological perspective*. New York: W.W. Norton, 1978.

Furby, L. Possession in humans: An exploratory study of its meaning and motivation. *Social Behavior and Personality*, 1978, *5*, 49-65.

———. Inequalities in personal possessions: Explanations for and judgments about unequal distribution. *Human Development*, 1979, *22*, 180-202.

Gardner, J. *Excellence: Can we be equal and excellent too?* New York: Harper & Row, 1961.

Gerber, E.W.; Felshin, J.; Berlin, P.; and Wyrick, W. *The American woman in sport*. Reading, Mass.: Addison-Wesley, 1974.

Gergen, K.J. *The psychology of behavior exchange*. Reading, Mass.: Addison-Wesley, 1969.

Gilbert, B., and Williamson, N. Women in sports. *Sports Illustrated*, May 28, 1973.

Ginsburg, J., and Opper, S. *Piaget's theory of intellectual development*. Englewood Cliffs, N.J.: Prentice-Hall, 1969.

Glasser, W. *Schools without failure*. New York: Harper & Row, 1969.

Glidwell, J.C.; Kantor, M.B.; Smith, L.M.; and Stringer, L.A. Socialization and social structure in the classroom. In L.W. Hoffman and M.L. Hoffman, eds., *Review of Child Development Research*, 2:221-256. New York: Russell Sage Foundation, 1966.

Glucksberg, S.; Krauss, R.M.; and Higgins, T. The development of communication skills in children. In F. Horowitz, ed., *Review of child development research*, *4*. Chicago: University of Chicago Press, 1975.

Goethals, G.R., and Darley, J.M. Social comparison theory: An attributional approach. In J.M. Suls and R.L. Miller, eds., *Social comparison processes: Theoretical and empirical perspectives*. Washington, D.C.: Hemisphere Publishing Corp., Halsted Press, Wiley, 1977.

Goldberg, M.H., and Maccoby, E.E. Children's acquisition of skill in performing a group task under two conditions of group formation. *Journal of Personality and Social Psychology*, 1965, *2*, 6, 898-902.

Goodenough, F.L. *Measurement of intelligence by drawings*. New York: Harcourt, Brace & World, 1926.

———. Studies in the psychology of children's drawings. *Psychological Bulletin*, 1928, *25*, 272-283.

Goodman, N., and Lever, L. In M.K. Martin and B. Voorhies, eds., *Female of the species*. New York: Columbia University Press, 1975.

Goodman, P. *Growing up absurd*. New York: Random House, 1956.

Gordon, B. Influence and social comparison as motives of affiliation. *Journal of Experimental Social Psychology*, 1966, Supplement 1, 55-65.

Gottheil, E. Changes in social perception contingent upon cooperating or competing. *Sociometry*, 1955, *18*, 132-137.

Graves, N.B. *Egocentrism and cultural deprivation: Empirical evidence for the ethnocentric bias of Piagetian theory. 12.* Auckland, New Zealand: South Pacific Research Institute, 1976.

Graves, N.B., and Graves, Th.D. *The impact of modernization on Polynesian society; or how to make an up-tight, rivalrous Westerner out of an easy-going, generous Pacific Islander. 7.* Auckland, New Zealand: South Pacific Research Institute, 1975.

Graves, Th.D., and Graves, N.B. Demographic changes in the Cook Islands: Perception and reality; Or, where have all the Mapu gone? In *Journal of the Polynesian Society*, 1976, *85*, 4, 447-461.

_____ . *Altruism in Aitutaki: Development of rivalry in a cooperative society. 15.* Auckland, New Zealand: South Pacific Research Institute, 1977.

Greenberg, P.J. Competition in children: An experimental study. *American Journal of Psychology*, 1932, *44*, 221-248.

Greenfield, P.M. Goal as environmental variable in the development of intelligence. In R. Cancro, ed., *Intelligence, Genetic and Environmental Influences*. New York: Grune & Stratton, 1971.

Grossack, M. Some effects of cooperation and competition on small group behavior. *Journal of Abnormal and Social Psychology*, 1954, *49*, 341-348.

Hackman, J.R. Effects of task chracteristics on group products. *Journal of Experimental Social Psychology*, 1968, *4*, 162-187.

Hackman, J.R., and Morris, C.G. Group tasks, group interaction process and group performance effectiveness: A review and proposed integration. In L. Berkowitz, ed., *Advances in Experimental social psychology. 8.* New York: Academic Press, 1975.

Hakmiller, K. Need for self-evaluation, perceived similarity, and comparison choice. *Journal of Experimental Social Psychology*, 1966a, Supplement 1, 49-55.

_____ . Threat as a determinant of downward comparison. *Journal of Experimental Social Psychology*, 1966b, Supplement 1, 32-39.

Haley, J. A critical overview of the present status of family interaction research. In J. Framo, ed., *Family interaction*, 13-44. New York: Springer, 1972.

Halisch, F., and Heckhausen, H. Search for feedback information and effort regulation during task performance. *Journal of Personality*, 1977, *55*, 117, 724-733.

Hall, G. *Adolescence*. New York: Appleton, 1916. 2 vols.

Hammond, L.K., and Goldman, M. Competition and non-competition and its relationship to individual and group productivity. *Sociometry*, 1961, *24*, 46-70.

Hancock, J.H.T. The effect of listening and discussion on the social values held by sixth grade children. Ph.D. dissertation, University of Colorado, 1960. *Dissertation abstracts*, 1961, *21*, 3377.

Handlon, B.J., and Gross, P. The development of sharing behavior. *Journal of Abnormal and Social Psychology*, 1959, *59*, 425-428.

Hannah, B.H. Cooperation and competition in the classroom: Effects of the degree of similarity of the task on the behavior in children's groups. Ph.D. dissertation, Bryn Mawr College, 1970.

Hare, A.P. Small group development in the relay assembly testroom. *Sociological Inquiry*, 1967, *2*, 169-182.

———. *Handbook of small group research*. 2d ed. New York: Free Press, 1976.

Harragan, B.L. *Games mother never taught you: Corporate gamesmanship for women*. New York: Rawson Associates, 1977.

Harris, D.B. *Children's drawings as measures of intellectual maturity*. New York: Harcourt, Brace & World, 1963.

Hartley, E. *Fundamentals of social psychology*. New York: Alfred A. Knopf, 1952.

Hartup, W.W., and Coates, B. The role of imitation in childhood socialization. In R.A. Hoppe, G.A. Milton and E.C. Simmel, eds., *Early experiences and the process of socialization*, 109-192. New York: Academic Press, 1970.

Heckhausen, H. *Anatomy of achievement motivation*. Translated by K.F. Butler, R.C. Birney, and D.C. McClelland. New York: Academic Press, 1967.

Heider, F. Social perception and phenomenal causality. *Psychological Review*, 1944, *51*, 358-374.

———. *The psychology of interpersonal relations*. New York: Wiley, 1958.

Hill, R., and Hansen, D.A. The identification of conceptual frameworks utilized in family study. *Marriage and Family Living*, 1960, *22*, 299-311.

Hoffman, L.W. Early childhood experiences and women's achievement motives. *Journal of Social Issues*, 1972, *28*, 2, 129-156.

_____ . Fear of success in males and females: 1965 and 1971. *Journal of Consulting and Clinical Psychology*, 1974, *42*(3), 353-358.

_____ . Changes in family roles, socialization, and sex differences. *American Psychologist*, 1977, *32*, 644-657.

Hoffman, P.J.; Festinger, L., and Lawrence, D.H. Tendencies toward group comparability in competitive bargaining. *Human Relations*, 1954, *7*, 141-159.

Hollingshead, A. *Two-factor index of social position*. New Haven: Yale University Press, 1957.

Holt, J. *The Underachieving school*. New York: Pitman, 1969.

Holter, H. Sex roles and social change. In M.T.S. Mednick, S.S. Tangri, and L.W. Hoffman, eds., *Women and achievement*. New York: Wiley, 1975.

Horner, M.S. Sex differences in achievement motivation and performance in competitive and non-competitive situations. Ph.D. dissertation, University of Michigan, 1968.

_____ . Femininity and successful achievement: A basic inconsistency. In *Feminine personality and conflict*. California: Wadsworth, 1970.

Horner, M.S.; Tresemer, D.W.; Berens, A.E.; and Watson, R.I. Scoring manual for an empirically derived scoring system for motive to avoid success. August 31, 1973. Unpublished.

Hunt, J.McV. The effect of infant feeding-frustration upon adult hoarding in the albino rat. *Journal of Abnormal and Social Psychology*, 1941, *36*, 338-360.

Hutchins, R.M. *The conflict in education in a democratic society*. New York: Harper, 1953.

Hyman, H. The psychology of status. *Archives of Psychology*, 1942, 269, 5-38, 80-86.

Inhelder, B., and Piaget, J. *The early growth of logic in the child*. New York: Basic Books, 1958.

_____ . *The growth of logical thinking from childhood to adolescence*. New York: Basic Books, 1958.

Jackson, D. The study of family. *Family Process*, 1965, *4*(1), 1-20.

_____ . *Human communication*. Palo Alto, Calif.: Science and Behavior Books, 1968. 2 vols.

Jacobs, Ph. *Changing values in college*. New York: Harper & Row, 1957.

Jacoby, J. Consumer psychology as a social psychological sphere of action. *American Psychologist*, 1975, *30*(10), 977-987.

Jensen, R.E., and Moore, Sh.G. The effect of attribute statements on cooperativeness and competitiveness in school-age boys. *Child Development*, 1977, *48*, 305-307.

Johnson, D.W. Cooperativeness and social perspective taking. *Journal of Personality and Social Psychology*, 1975, *31*, 241-244.

Johnson, D.W., and Johnson, R.T. Instructional goal structure: Cooperative, competitive or individualistic. *Review of Educational Research*, 1974, *4*, 2, 213-240.

———. *Learning together and alone: Cooperation, competition and individualization*. Englewood Cliffs, N.J.: Prentice-Hall, 1975.

———. Conflict in the classroom: Controversy and learning. *Review of Educational Research*, 1979, *49*, 51-70.

Jones, E.E. *Ingratiation*. New York: Appleton-Century-Crofts, 1964.

Jones, E.J., and Gerard, H.B. *Foundations of social psychology*. New York: Wiley, 1967.

Jones, S., and Regan, D. Ability evaluation through social comparison. *Journal of Experimental Social Psychology*, 1974, *10*, 133-146.

Jones, S.C., and Vroom, V.H. Divisions of labor and performance under cooperative and competitive conditions. *Journal of Abnormal and Social Psychology*, 1964, *68*, 313-320.

Josselyn, I. *Adolescent and his world*. New York: Family Service Association of America, 1952.

Kagan, S. Social motives and behaviors of Mexican-American and Anglo-American children. In J.L. Martinez, ed., *Chicano Psychology*. New York: Academic Press, 1977.

———. Cooperation in the classroom: Cultural and situational sources of variance. Paper presented at the International Convention on Cooperation in Education, Hertzlia, Israel, July 1979.

Kagan, S., and Knight, G.P. Cooperation-Competition and self-esteem: A case of cultural relativism. *Journal of Cross-Cultural Psychology*, 1980 (in press).

Kagan, S., and Madsen, M.C. Cooperation and competition of Mexican, Mexican-American and Anglo-American children of two ages under four instructional sets. *Developmental Psychology*, 1971, *5*, 32-39.

———. Experimental analyses of cooperation and competition of Anglo-American children and Mexican children. *Developmental Psychology*, 1972a, *6*, 49-59.

———. Rivalry in Anglo-American and Mexican children of two ages. *Journal of Personality and Social Psychology*, 1972b, *24*, 214-220.

Kaplan, L.J. *Oneness and separateness*. New York: Simon & Schuster, 1978.

Karier, C.J. *Shaping the American educational state: 1900 to the present*. New York: Free Press, 1975.

Katz, L. Research on open education: Problems and issues. In D.D. Hearn, J. Burdin, and L. Katz, eds., *Current research and perspectives in open education*. Washington, D.C.: American Association of Elementary-Kindergarten-Nursery Educators, 1972.

Katz, M.B. *Class, bureaucracy, and schools: The illusion of educational change in America*. 2d ed. New York: Praeger Publishers, 1975.

Kelley, H.H. Two functions of reference groups. In G. Swanson, T. Newcomb, and E. Hartley, eds., *Readings in social psychology*. Rev. ed. New York: Holt, Rinehart, & Winston, 1952.

_____ . Attribution theory in social psychology. In D. Levine, 2 ed., *Nebraska Symposium on Motivation*. Lincoln: University of Nebraska Press, 1967.

_____ . *Personal relationships: Their structures and processes*. New York: Wiley, 1979.

Kelley, H.H., and Thibaut, J.W. *Interpersonal relations: A theory of interdependence*. New York: Wiley, 1978.

Kelly, E.W., Jr. Classroom discussions for personal growth and democratic problem-solving. *Elementary School Journal*, 1974, *75*(1), 11-15.

Keniston, K. *The uncommitted*. Harcourt, Brace & World, 1965.

Keniston, K., and Carnegie Council on Children, eds. *All our children: The American family under pressure*. New York: Harcourt Brace Jovanovich, 1977.

Khan, S.B., and Weiss, J. The teaching of affective responses. In R.M.W. Travers, ed., *Second handbook of research on teaching*. Chicago: Rand McNally, 1973.

Kilpatrick, W.H. *The project method*. Teachers College Record, *19*, 1918.

_____ . *Foundations of method*. New York: Columbia University Press, 1925.

Knight, G.P., and Kagan, S. Development of prosocial and competitive behaviors in Anglo-American and Mexican-American children. *Child Development*, 1977, *48*, 1385-1394.

Kohn, M.L. Social class and parent-child relationships: An interpretation. *American Journal of Sociology*, 1963, 68, *4*, 471-480.

_____ . *Class and conformity—A study of values*. Homewood, Ill.: Dorsey Press, 1969.

Koppitz, E. *Psychological evaluation of human figure drawings*. New York: Grune & Stratton, 1968.

Korda, M. *Success*. New York: Random House, 1977.

Korsh, N.B. An exploratory study of the relationship between structure in the open classroom and students' activity patterns. Unpublished manuscript, Bryn Mawr College, 1973.

_____ . Effects of interventions designed to improve cooperative social interaction and performance in small groups of third-grade students in the open classroom. Ph.D. dissertation, Bryn Mawr College, 1975.

Latané, B., ed. Studies in social comparison. *Journal of Experimental Social Psychology*, 1966a, Supplement 1.

_____ . Introduction and overview in studies in social comparison. *Journal of Experimental Social Psychology*, 1966b, Supplement 1, 1-5.

Latané, B., and Darley, J.M. Group inhibition of bystander intervention. *Journal of Personality and Social Psychology*, 1968, *10*, 215-221.

———. *The unresponsive bystander: Why doesn't he help?* New York: Appleton-Crofts, 1970.

Latané, B., and Rodin, J. A lady in distress: Inhibiting effects of friends and strangers on bystander intervention. *Journal of Experimental Social Psychology*, 1969, *5*, 189-202.

Lee, R.B. What hunters do for a living, or: How to make out on scarce resources. In R.B. Lee and DeVore, I. eds., *Man the hunter*. Chicago: Aldine, 1968.

Leichter, H.J., ed. *Families and communities as educators*. New York: Teachers College Press, 1979.

Lerner, M.J. The justice motive: "Equity" and "parity" among children. *Journal of Personality and Social Psychology*, 1974, *29*, 539-550.

Lerner, M.J.; Miller, D.T.; and Holmes, J.G. Deserving and the emergence of forms of justice. In L. Berkowitz and E. Walster, eds., *Advances in experimental social psychology. Equity theory: Toward a general theory of social interaction. 9*:133-162. New York: Academic Press, 1976.

Leuba, C.J. An experimental study of rivalry in young children. *Journal of Comparative Psychology*, 1933, *16*, 367-378.

Leventhal, G.S., and Anderson, D. Self-interest and the maintenance of equity. *Journal of Personality and Social Psychology*, 1970, *15*, 57-62.

Lewin, K. *Dynamic theory of personality*. New York: McGraw-Hill, 1935.

———. *Principles of topological psychology*. New York: McGraw-Hill, 1936.

———. Defining the field at a given time. *Psychological Review*, 1943, *50*, 292-310.

———. Frontiers in group dynamics. *Human Relations*, 1947, *1*, 5-42.

Lewin, K.; Dembo, T.; Festinger, L.; and Sears, R. Level of aspiration. In J. McV. Hunt, ed., *Handbook of Personality and the behavior disorders*. New York: Ronald Press, 1944.

Lewin, K.; Lippitt, R.; and White, R. Patterns of aggressive behavior in experimentally created "social climates." *Journal of Social Psychology*, 1939, *10*, 271-299.

Lewis, I.R. Some effects of the reading and discussion of stories on certain values of sixth-grade pupils. Ph.D. dissertation, University of California, Berkeley, 1967. *Dissertation Abstracts*, 1968, *28*(A), 4513-14.

Lippitt, R. An experimental study of the effect of democratic and authoritarian group atmosphere. *University of Iowa Studies in Child Welfare*, 1940, 16, *3*, 45-195.

Lippitt, R.; Polansky, N.; Redl, F.; and Rosen, S. The dynamics of power. *Human Relations*, 1952, *5*, 37-64.

Lippitt, R., and White, R. *Autocracy and democracy: An experimental inquiry*. New York: Harper & Row, 1960.

Lloyd, F.H. An exploratory study of social influences in parallel play. Master's thesis, Bryn Mawr College, 1970.

Loeb, H.W. Social interactions and performance under competitive and cooperative working conditions: A developmental study of elementary school children. Ph.D. dissertation, Bryn Mawr College, 1975.

_____ . An exploration of transfer effects on performance between cooperative and competitive working conditions. Paper presented at the International Conference on Cooperation in Education, Hertzlia, Israel, July 1979.

Lucker, G.W.; Rosenfield, D.; Sikes, J.; and Aronson, E. Performance in the interdependent classroom: A field study. *American Educational Research Journal*, 1977, *13*, 2, 115-123.

Lynd, A. *Quackery in the public schools*. Boston: Little, Brown, 1953.

Maccoby, E.E. Woman's intellect. In S.N. Farber and R.H.L. Wilson, eds., *The potential of women*. New York: McGraw-Hill, 1963.

_____ . Feminine intellect and the demands of science. *Impact of science in society*, Jan.-Mar., 1970, *20*, 13-28.

Maccoby, E.E., and Jacklin, C.N. *The psychology of sex differences*. Stanford: Stanford University Press, 1974.

Madsen, M.C. Cooperative and competitive motivations of children in three Mexican subcultures. *Psychological Reports*. 1967, *20*, 1307-1320.

_____ . Developmental and cross-cultural differences in the cooperative and competitive behavior of young children. *Journal of Cross-Cultural Psychology*, 1971, *2*, 365-371.

Madsen, M.C., and Shapira, A. Cooperative and competitive behavior of urban Afro-American, Anglo-American, Mexican American and Mexican Village Children. *Developmental Psychology*, 1970, *3*, 16-20.

Madsen, M.C., and Yi, S. Cooperation and competition of urban and rural children in the Republic of South Korea. *International Journal of Psychology*, 1975, *10*, 269-274.

Mahler, M.; Pine, F.; and Bergman, A. *The psychological birth of the human infant*. New York: Basic Books, 1967.

Marrow, A.J. *The practical theorist: The life and work of Kurt Lewin*. New York: Basic Books, 1969.

Marshall, H.H. Criteria for an open classroom. *Young Children*, 1972, *28*(1), 13-19.

Masterson, J. The psychiatric significance of adolescent turmoil. *American Journal of Psychiatry*, 1968, 124, 11, 1549-1554.

Mausner, B. Subjective expected utility model for the relation of attitude and behavior. Research proposal submitted to National Science Foundation, March 14, 1973.

Mauss, M. *The gift: Forms and functions of exchange in archaic societies.* New York: W.W. Norton, 1965.

May, M., and Doob, L. *Competition and cooperation.* New York: Social Science Research Council, 1937.

Mayer, A. Über Einzel-und Gesamtleistung des Schulkindes. *Archiv für die Gesamte Psychologie,* 1903, *1,* 276-416.

McClelland, D.C.; Atkinson, J.M.; Clark, R.A.; and Lowell, E.L. *The achievement motive.* New York: Appleton-Century, 1953.

McClintock, Ch.G. Preferences among alternative test outcomes: A classroom measure of social motives. *Journal of Experimental Education,* 1978, *26,* 2, 21-27.

————— . Development of social motives in Anglo-American and Mexican-American children. *Journal of Personality and Social Psychology,* 1974, *29,* 348-354.

McClintock, C.G., and McNeel, C.P. Cross-cultural comparisons of interpersonal motives. *Sociometry,* 1966, *29,* 406-427.

McClintock, C.G., and Moskowitz, J.M. Children's preferences for individualistic cooperative and competitive outcomes. *Journal of Personality and Social Psychology,* 1976, *34*(4), 543-555.

McClintock, C.G.; Moskowitz, J.M.; and McClintock, E. Variations in preferences for individualistic, competitive and cooperative outcomes as a function of age, game class and task in nursery school children. *Child Development,* 1977, *48,* 1080-1085.

McClintock, C.G., and Nuttin, J. Development of competitive game behavior in children across two cultures. *Journal of Experimental Social Psychology,* 1969, *5,* 203-218.

McDougall, Wm. *Introduction to social psychology.* London: Methuen, 1908.

McNeal, C.P.; McClintock, C.G.; and Nuttin, J.M., Jr. Effects of sex-role in a two-person mixed motive game. *Journal of Personality and Social Psychology,* 1972, *24,* 372-378.

Mead, M. Anthropological insights into depression. Paper presented at the first annual Clinical Conference, November 1973, Friends Hospital, Philadelphia, Pa.

Mead, M., ed. *Cooperation and competition among primitive peoples.* New York: McGraw-Hill, 1936.

Merton, R., and Rossi, A. Contributions to the theory of reference group behavior. In R. Merton, ed., *Social theory and social structure,* 225-275. New York: Free Press, 1957.

Mettee, D.R., and Riskind, J. Size of defeat and liking for superior and similar ability competitors. *Journal of Experimental Social Psychology,* 1974, *10,* 333-351.

Mettee, D.R., and Smith, G. Social comparison and interpersonal attraction: The case for dissimilarity. In J.M. Suls and R.L. Miller, eds.,

Social comparison processes: Theoretical and empirical perspectives. Washington, D.C.: Hemisphere Publishing Corp, Halsted Press, Wiley, 1977.

Michaels, J.W. Classroom reward structures and academic performance. *Review of Educational Research*, 1977, *47*, 87-98.

Michener, J. *Sports in America.* New York: Random House, 1976.

Midlarsky, E., and Bryan, J.H. Training charity in children. *Journal of Personality and Social Psychology*, 1967, *5*, 408-415.

Miller, L.K., and Hamblin, R.L. Interdependence, differential rewarding and productivity. *American Sociological Review*, 1963, *28*, 768-778.

Mintz, A. Nonadaptive group behavior. *Journal of Abnormal and Social Psychology*, 1951, *46*, 150-159.

Minuchin, S. *Families and family therapy.* Cambridge: Harvard University Press, 1974.

Moede, W. Der Wetteifer, Seine Struktur und sein Aussmass. *Zeitschrift für Pedagogische Psychologie*, 1914, *15*, 353-368.

_____ . Einzel-und Gruppenarbeit. *Praktische Psychologie*, 1920, 21, 2, 71-81, 108-115.

Morris, C.G. Task effects on group interaction. *Journal of Personality and Social Psychology*, 1966, *5*, 545-554.

_____ . Changes in group interaction during problem-solving. *Journal of Social Psychology*, 1970, *81*, 157-165.

Mueller, E., and Brenner, J. The origins of social skills and interaction among play group toddlers. *Child Development*, 1977, *48*, 854-861.

Mueller, E., and Rich, A. Clustering and socially-directed behaviors in a toddler's playgroup. *Journal of Child Psychology and Psychiatry*, 1976, *17*, 315-322.

Murdoch, E.M. A developmental study of social behaviors which are related to performance under competitive and cooperative working conditions. Ph.D. dissertation, Bryn Mawr College, 1974.

Neill, A.S. *Summerhill: A radical approach to child rearing.* New York: Hart Publishing Company, 1960.

Nelson, L.L. The development of cooperation and competition in children from ages five to ten year old: Effects of sex, situational determinants, and prior experiences. Ph.D. dissertation, University of California, 1970.

Nelson, L.L., and Madsen, M.C. Cooperation and competition in four-year-olds as a function of reward contingency and subculture. *Developmental Psychology*, 1969, *1*, 340-344.

Newcomb, T.M. *Personality and social change.* New York: Holt, Rinehart & Winston, 1943.

Offer, D. *The psychological world of the teenager.* New York: Basic Books, 1969.

Osgood, C.E., and Tannenbaum, P.H. The principle of congruity in the prediction of attitude change. *Psychological Review*, 1955, *62*, 42-55.

Palomares, U.H., and Rubini, T. Human development in the classroom. *Personnel and Guidance Journal*, 1973, *51*, 653-57.

Parsons, J. The development of achievement expectancies in girls and boys. Paper presented at Eastern Psychological Association Conference, Philadelphia, 1974.

Parsons, J.E., and Ruble, D.N. The development of achievement-related expectancies. *Child Development*, 1977, *48*, 1075-1079.

Parsons, T. Family structure and the socialization of the child. In T. Parsons and R.F. Bales, eds., *Family socialization and interaction process*. Glencoe, Ill.: Free Press, 1955.

_____ . The normal American family. In S.M. Farber et al., eds., *Man and civilization: The family's search for survival*. New York: McGraw-Hill, 1965.

Parsons, T., and Shils, E.A., eds. *Toward a general theory of action*. Glencoe, Ill.: Free Press, 1953.

Parten, M. Social participation among preschool children. *Journal of Abnormal Social Psychology*, 1933, *27*, 243-269.

Parten, M., and Newhall, S.M. Social behavior of preschool children. In R.J. Barker, J.S. Kounin, and H.F. Wright, eds., *Child behavior and development*. New York: McGraw-Hill, 1943.

Pasternack, M., and Silvey, L. *Pattern block activities*. Palo Alto: Creative Publications, 1975.

Pepitone, A. Toward a normative and comparative biocultural social psychology. *Journal of Personality and Social Psychology*, 1976, *34*, 4, 641-653.

Pepitone, E.A. Responsibility to the group and its effects on the performance of members. Ph.D. dissertation, University of Michigan, 1952.

_____ . The effects of instructional practices on student learning, emotional growth and interpersonal relations. II. The teaching and learning of helping. Proposal for research submitted to the U.S. Commissioner of Education, 1971.

_____ . Comparison behavior in elementary school children. *American Educational Research Journal*, 1972, *9*, 1, 45-63.

_____ . Facilitation of cooperative behavior in elementary school children. Paper read at American Educational Research Association, Annual Meeting, New Orleans, La., March 1973a.

_____ . *Final report: The teaching and learning of helping*. Washington, D.C.: U.S. Department of Health, Education and Welfare, 1973b.

_____ . Patterns of interdependence in cooperative work of elementary children. *Contemporary Educational Psychology*, 1977, *2*, 10-24.

Pepitone, E.A.; Loeb, H.W.; and Murdoch, E.M. Social comparison and similarity of children's performance in competitive situations. Paper presented at meetings of the American Psychological Association, San Francisco, 1977.

Pettigrew, T. Social evaluation theory: Convergences and applications. In D. Levine, ed., *Nebraska symposium on motivation*, 241-311. Lincoln: University of Nebraska Press, 1967.

Phillips, B., and D'Amico, L. Effects of cooperation and competition on the cohesiveness of small face-to-face groups. *Journal of Educational Psychology*, 1956, *47*, 65-70.

Piaget, J. *The language and thought of the child*. New York: Harcourt & Brace, 1926.

———. *The moral judgment of the child*. London: Kegan Paul, 1932.

———. *The psychology of intelligence*. New York: Harcourt & Brace, 1950.

———. *The origins of intelligence in children*. Translated by M. Cook. New York: W.W. Norton, 1952.

———. *Play, dreams and imitation in childhood*. New York: W.W. Norton & Co., 1962.

———. *The child's conception of number*. New York: W.W. Norton & Co., 1965.

Piliavin, J.A., and Piliavin, I.M. Effect of blood on reactions to a victim. *Journal of Personality and Social Psychology*, *23*, 353-362.

President's Commission on Olympic Sport, 1975-1977. *Final Report*. Jan. 1977, U.S. Government Printing Office, 0-226-538. (Womens' sports, 109-115).

Radloff, R. Opinion evaluation and affiliation. *Journal of Abnormal and Social Psychology*, 1961, *62*, 578-585.

———. Social comparison and ability evaluation. *Journal of Experimental and Social Psychology*, 1966, Supplement 1, 6-26.

Rapoport, R., and Rapoport, R. *Dual-career families*. Baltimore: Penguin Books, 1971.

Raths, J. Clarifying children's values. *National Elementary Principal*, 1962, *42*(2), 35-39.

Raths, L.E.; Harmin, M.; and Simon, S.B. *Values and teaching: Working with values in the classroom*. Columbus, Ohio: Charles E. Merrill, 1966.

Raven, B.H., and Eachus, H.T. Cooperation and competition in means-interdependent triads. *Journal of Abnormal and Social Psychology*, 1963, *67*, 307-316.

Reckman, R.F., and Goethals, G. Deviancy and group-orientation as determinants of group composition preferences. *Sociometry*, 1973, *36*, 419-423.

Redl, F., and Wineman, D. *Children who hate; The disorganization and breakdown of behavior controls*. Glencoe, Ill.: Free Press, 1951.

Rheingold, H.L.; Hay, D.F.; and West, M.J. Sharing in the second year of life. *Child Development*, 1976, *47*, 1148-1158.

Rickover, H.M. *Education and freedom*. New York: Dutton, 1959.

Ridgway, L., and Lawton, I. *Family grouping in the primary school*. New York: Agathon Press, 1969.

Rippa, S.A. The textbook controversy and the free enterprise campaign, 1940-1941. *History of Education Journal*, 1958, *9*, 3, 49-57.

_____. Dissemination of the free-enterprise creed in American schools. *School Review*, 1959, 409-421.

_____. Retrenchment in a period of defensive opposition to the New Deal: The business community and the public schools, 1932-1934. *History of Education Quarterly*, 1962, *2*, 2, 76-82.

_____. The business community and the public schools on the eve of the great depression. *History of Education Quarterly*, 1964, *4*, 1, 33-43.

_____. *Education in a free society*. 3d ed. New York: McKay, 1976.

Riskin, J., and Faunce, E. An evaluative review of family interaction research. *Family Process*, 1972, *11*(4), 365-463.

Roberts, J.M., and Sutton-Smith, B. Child training and game involvement. *Ethnology*, 1962, *1*, 166-185.

Rodman, H. Talcott Parson's view of the changing American family. Merill-Palmer Quarterly, 1965, *11*, 209-227.

Rosen, B., and D'Andrade, R. The psychological origins of achievement motivation. *Sociometry*, 1959, *22*, 185-218.

Rosenthal, R., and Jacobson, L.R. Teacher expectations of the disadvantaged. *Scientific American*, 1968, 218, 19-23.

Ross, E.A. *Social psychology*. New York: Macmillan, 1908.

Ross, L. The intuitive psychologist and his shortcomings: Distortions in the attribution process. In L. Berkowitz, ed., *Advances in experimental social psychology*, *10*. New York: Academic Press, 1977.

Ruble, D.N.; Feldman, N.S.; and Boggiano, A.K. Social comparison between young children in achievement situations. *Developmental Psychology*, 1976, *12*, 192-197.

Ruble, D.N., and Nakamura, C.Y. Outerdirectedness as a problem solving approach in relation to developmental level and selected task variables. *Child Development*, 1973, *44*, 519-528.

Rushton, J.P. Generosity in children: Immediate and long-term effect of modeling, preaching and moral judgment. *Journal of Personality and Social Psychology*, 1975, *31*, 459-466.

_____. Socialization and the altruistic behavior of children. *Psychological Bulletin*, 1976, *83*, 898-913.

Rutherford, E., and Mussen, P. Generosity in nursery school boys. *Child Development*, 1968, *39*, 755-765.

Satir, V. *Conjoint family therapy*. Palo Alto, Calif.: Science and Behavior Books, 1967.

Scandura, J.M. *Problem solving: A structural/process approach.* New York: Academic Press, 1977.

Schachter, S. *The psychology of affiliation.* Stanford: Stanford University Press, 1959.

Selman, R.L. Taking another's perspective: Role-taking development in early childhood. *Child Development,* 1971, *42,* 1721-1734.

_____ . Social-cognitive understanding: A guide to educational and clinical practice. In T. Lickona, ed., *Moral development and behavior.* New York: Holt, Rinehart & Winston, 1976.

Selman, R.L., and Byrne, D.F. A structural-developmental analysis of levels of role-taking in middle childhood. *Child Development,* 1974, *45,* 803-806.

Seltzer, V.C. An exploratory study of the adolescent reference field and of the processes of social comparison with specific regard to their function in development. Ph.D. dissertation, Bryn Mawr College, 1975.

Senior, K., and Brophy, J. Praise and group competition as motivating incentives for children. *Psychological Reports,* 1973, *32,* 951-958.

Senn, M.J. Insight on the child development movement in the United States. *Monographs of the Society for Research in Child Development,* 1975, *40*(3-4), 161.

Shantz, C.V. The development of social cognition. In E.M. Hetherington, ed., *Review of Child Development Research. 5.* Chicago: University of Chicago Press, 1975.

Shapira, A., and Madsen, M.C. Cooperative and competitive behavior of kibbutz and urban children in Israel. *Child Development,* 1969, *40,* 609-617.

_____ . Between and within group cooperation and competition among kibbutz and non-kibbutz children. *Developmental Psychology,* 1974, *10,* 140-145.

Shapira, A., and Lomranz, J. Cooperative and competitive behavior of rural Arab children in Israel. *Journal of Cross-cultural Psychology,* 1972, *3,* 353-359.

Shaw, M.E. *Group dynamics: The psychology of small group behavior.* 2d ed. New York: McGraw-Hill, 1976.

Sherif, M. *The psychology of social norms.* New York: Harper & Row, 1936.

_____ . *An outline of social psychology.* New York: Harper, 1948.

_____ . Experiments on group conflict and cooperation. In W.W. Charters, Jr., and N.L. Gage, eds., *Readings in the social psychology of education.* Boston: Allyn & Bacon, 1964.

Sherif, M.; Harvey, O.J.; White, B.J.; Hood, W.R.; and Sherif, C.W. *Intergroup conflict and cooperation: The robber's cave experiment.* Norman: University of Oklahoma, Institute of Group Relations, 1961.

Shirley, M.M. *The first two years*, 2. Minneapolis, Minn.: University of Minnesota Press, 1933.

Silberman, C.E. *Crisis in the classroom*. New York: Vintage Books, 1971.

Simon, S.B.; Howe, L.W.; and Kirschenbaum, H. *Values clarification*. New York: Hart Publishing Co., 1972.

Singh, J.M. Reporting on an open classroom. *Pennsylvania School Journal*, 1972, *120*(5), 166-168.

Slater, P. Parental role differentiation. *American Journal of Sociology*, 1961, 67, 296-308.

Slavin, R.E. Classroom reward structure: An analytical and practical review. *Review of Educational Research*, 1977, *47*, 633-650.

_____ . *Cooperative learning*. Baltimore: John Hopkins University Center for Social Organization of Schools, December 1978, *267*.

_____ . Student teams and comparison among equals: Effects on academic performance and student attitudes. *Journal of Educational Psychology*, 1978, *70*, 4, 532-538.

_____ . Effects of biracial learning teams on cross-racial friendships. Journal of Educational Psychology, 1979, *71*, 3, 381-387.

Smith, C.P., ed. *Achievement-related motives in children*. New York: Russell Sage Foundation, 1969.

Smith, M. *The diminished mind: A study of planned mediocrity in our public school*. Greenwood Press, 1954.

Smith, P.K., and Connolly, K. Patterns of play and social interaction in preschool children. In N.B. Jones, ed., *Ethnological studies of child behavior*. London: Cambridge University Press, 1972.

Solomons, H.H. Interpersonal dynamics of sex-integrated physical education classes. In *Bruder-Immaculata Papers: Women in Sports*. Immaculata College, 1976.

Spring, J. *American education: An introduction to social and political aspects*. New York: Longman, 1978.

Stallings, J., Steinmetz, G.; and Wilcox, M. Observational findings for differences in follow through and non-follow through classrooms. Symposium presented at the meeting of the Society for Research in Child Development, Philadelphia, 1973.

Staub, E. A child in distress: The effects of focusing responsibility on children in their attempts to help. *Developmental Psychology*, 1970a, *2*, 152-154.

_____ . A child in distress: The influence of age and number of witnesses on children's attempts to help. *Journal of Personality and Social Psychology*, 1970b, *14*, 130-140.

_____ . A child in distress: The influence of modeling and nurturance on children's attempts to help. *Developmental Psychology*, 1971a, *5*, 124-133.

_____ . The use of role-playing and induction in children's learning of helping and sharing behaviors. *Child Development*, 1971b, *42*, 805-817.

_____ . *Positive social behavior and morality. Social and personal influences. 1.* New York: Academic Press, 1978.

_____ . *Positive social behavior and morality. Socialization and morality. 2.* New York: Academic Press, 1979.

Staub, E., and Baer, R.S., Jr. Stimulus characteristics of a sufferer and difficulty of escape as determinants of helping. *Journal of Personality and Social Psychology*, 1974, *30*, 279-285.

Staub, E., and Sherk, L. Need for approval, children's sharing behavior, and reciprocity in sharing. *Child Development*, 1970, *41*, 243-253.

Stein, A.H., and Bailey, M.M. The socialization of achievement orientation in females. *Psychological Bulletin*, 1973, *80*, 345-366.

Steiner, I.D. *Group process and productivity.* New York: Academic Press, 1972.

Stendler, C.; Damrin, D.; and Haines, A.C. Studies in cooperation and competition. I. The effect of working for group and individual rewards on the social climate of children's groups. *Journal of Genetic Psychology*, 1951, 79, 173-197.

Stone, L.J., and Church, J. *Childhood and adolescence: A psychology of the growing person.* 3d ed. New York: Random House, 1973.

Stouffer, S.A.; Suchman, E.A.; DeVinney, L.C.; Star, S.A.; and Williams, R.M. *The American soldier; Adjustment during army life.* Princeton: Princeton University Press, 1949, *1.*

Straus, M.A. Methodology of a laboratory experimental study of families in three societies. Paper presented at the Ninth International Seminar on family research, Tokyo, September 1965.

Straus, M.A., and Tallman, I. SIMFAM: A technique for observational measurement and experimental study of families. Unpublished manuscript, 1970. Enlarged in J. Aldous, ed., *Family problem solving*, 380-438. Hinsdale, Ill.: Dryden Press, 1971.

Suls, J.M., and Miller, R.L., eds. *Social comparison processes: Theoretical and empirical perspectives.* Washington, D.C.: Hemisphere Publishing Corp., Halsted Press, Wiley, 1977.

Sutton-Smith, B. Toys for object and role mastery. In K. Hewett and L. Roomet, eds. *Educational toys in America: 1800 to the present.* Burlington, Vt.: Robert Hull Fleming Museum, University of Vermont, 1979.

Sutton-Smith, B.; Roberts, J.M.; and Kozelka, R.M. Game involvement in adults. *Journal of Social Psychology*, 1963, *60*, 15-30.

Sutton-Smith, B.; Rosenberg, B.G.; and Morgan, E.F. Jr. Development of sex differences in play choices during preadolescence. *Child Development*, 1963, *34*, 119-126.

Tauber, M.A. Parental socialization techniques and sex differences in children's play. *Child Development*, 1979, *50*(1), 225-234.

Thibaut, J.W., and Kelley, H.H. *The social psychology of groups*. New York: Wiley, 1959.

Thomas, J. Effects of facilitative role interdependence on group functioning. *Human Relations*, 1957, *10*, 347-366.

Thornton, D., and Arrowood, A. Self-evaluation, self-enhancement, and the locus of social comparison. *Journal of Experimental Social Psychology*, 1966, Supplement 1, 40-48.

Tiffany, S.W. Giving and receiving; Participating in chiefly redistribution activities in Samoa. *Ethnology*, 1975, *14*, 3, 267-286.

Toda, M., Shinotsuka; H., McClintock, C.G.; and Stech, F.J. Development of competitive behavior as a function of culture, age and social comparison. *Journal of Personality and Social Psychology*, 1978, *36*, 8 825-839.

Torg, B.G., and Torg, J.S. Sex and the little league. *Physician and Sports Medicine*, May 1974, 45-50.

Torop, N.R. The effects of adult evaluation on elementary school children's work and social interaction: An experimental study of affective tone and helpfulness. Ph.D. dissertation, Bryn Mawr College, 1973.

Torrance, E.P. Small group behavior of five-year-old children under three kinds of educational stimulation. *Journal of Experimental Education*, 1970, *38*, 79-82.

Traub, R.E.; Weiss, J.E.; Fisher, C.W.; and Musella, D. Closure on openness: Describing and quantifying open education. *Interchange*, 1972, *3*(2-3), 69-84.

Travis, L.E. The influence of the group upon the stutterer's speed in free association. *Journal of Abnormal and Social Psychology*, 1925, *20*, 142-146.

Tresemer, D. Fear of success: Popular but unproven. *Psychology Today*, March, 1974

Triplett, N. The dynamogenic factors in pacemaking and competition. *American Journal of Psychology*, 1897, *9*, 507-533.

Turner, C.E. Test room studies in employee effectiveness. *American Journal of Public Health*, 1933, *23*, 577-584.

Turner, R. *Family interaction*. New York: Wiley, 1970.

Ugurel-Semin, R. Moral behavior and moral judgment of children. *Journal of Abnormal and Social Psychology*, 1952, *47*, 463-474.

U.S. Office of Strategic Services Assessment Staff. *Assessment of Men*. New York: Rinehart & Co., 1948.

Vanderbilt, C.E. Sharing in kindergarten children as a function of the perception of others' need, own surplus and self-related variables. Ph.D. dissertation, Bryn Mawr College, 1971.

Veroff, J.; McClelland, L.; and Ruhland, D. Varieties of achievement motivation. In M.T.S. Mednick, S.S. Tangri, and L.W. Hoffman, eds., *Women and achievement*. New York: Wiley, 1975.

Vinacke, W.E. Variables in experimental games: Toward a field theory. *Psychological Bulletin*, 1969, *71*, 293-318.

Violas, P.C. *The training of the urban class: A history of twentieth century American education*. Chicago: Rand McNally, 1978.

Vroom, V.H. *Work and motivation*. New York: Wiley, 1964.

Walster, E., Walster, G.W., and E. Berscheid. *Equity: Theory and Research*. Boston: Allyn and Bacon, 1978.

Watson, J.B. *Psychology from the standpoint of a behaviorist*. New York: Lippincott, 1919.

Weigel, R.H., and Cook, S.W. Participation in decision-making: A determinant of interpersonal attraction in cooperating interracial groups. *International Journal of Group Tensions*, 1975, *5*, 4, 179-195.

Weigel, R.H., Wiser, P.L.; Cook, S.W. The impact of cooperative learning experiences on cross ethnic relations and attitudes. *Journal of Social Issues*, 1975, *31*, 1, 219-244.

Weiner, B. *Achievement motivation and attribution theory*. Morristown, N.J.: General Learning Press, 1974.

Weiner, B., and Kukla, A. An attributional analysis of achievement motivation. *Journal of Personality and Social Psychology*, 1970, *15*, 1-20.

Weston, P.J., and Mednick, M.T.S. Race, social class, and the motive to avoid success in women. *Journal of Cross-cultural Psychology*, 1970, *1*(3), 283-291.

Wheeler, L. Motivation as a determinant of comparison upward. *Journal of Experimental Social Psychology*, 1966, Supplement 1, 27-32.

Wheeler, L., and Zucherman, M. Commentary. In J.M. Suls and R.L. Miller, eds., *Social comparison processes: Theoretical and empirical perspectives*, 335-367. Washington, D.C.: Hemisphere Publishing Corp., Halsted Press, Wiley, 1977.

Wheeler, L.; Shaver, K.G.; Jones, R.A.; Goethals, G.R.; Cooper, J.; Robinson, J.E.; Gruder, C.L. and Butzline, K.W. Factors determining choice of a comparison other. *Journal of Experimental Social Psychology*, 1969, *5*, 219-232.

Whiting, B.M., and Whiting, J.W. *Children of six cultures: A psychocultural analysis*. Cambridge: Harvard University Press, 1975.

Winterbottom, M.R. The relation of childhood training in independence to achievement motivation. In D.C. McClelland, J.W. Atkinson, R.A. Clark, and E.L. Lowell, eds., *The achievement motive*. New York: Appleton Century, 1953.

Wohlwill, J.F. *The study of behavioral development*. New York: Academic Press, 1973.

WomenSports. *Revolution in women's sports*. Special Supplement published by *WomenSports*, September 1974, 35-56.

Wrightsman, L.S., O'Connor, J.; and Baker, N.J. *Cooperation and competition: Readings in mixed motive games*. Belmont, Calif.: Wadsworth, 1972.

Wyrick, W. Biophysical perspectives. In E.W. Gerber, J. Felshin, P. Berlin, and W. Wyrick, eds. *The American woman in sport*. Reading, Mass.: Addison-Wesley, 1974.

Yando, R.; Seitz, V.; and Zigler, E. *Imitation: A developmental perspective*. New York: Wiley, 1978.

Young, M.W. *Fighting with food*. London: Cambridge University Press, 1971.

Zajonc, R.B. Social facilitation. *Science*, 1965, *149*, 269-274.

Zajonc, R.B., and Sales, S.M. Social facilitation of dominant and subordinate responses. *Journal of Experimental Social Psychology*, 1966, *2*, 160-168.

Zander, A. *Motives and goals in groups*. New York: Academic Press, 1971.

Zanna, M.P; Goethals, G.R.; and Hill, J.F. Evaluating a sex related ability: Social comparison with similar others and standard setters. *Journal of Experimental Social Psychology*, 1975, *11*, 86-93.

Zelditch, M. Role differentiation in the nuclear family: A cooperative study. In T. Parsons and R.F. Bales, eds., *Family socialization and interaction process*, 301-352. Glencoe, Ill.: Free Press, 1955.

Zigler, E., and Yando, R. Outerdirectedness and imitative behavior of institionalized younger and older children. *Child Development*, 1972, *43*, 413-425.

Index

About the Author

Emmy A. Pepitone is a social psychologist with a background in social-learning theory, at Yale, and field theory, as a project director at the Research Center for Group Dynamics of the University of Michigan. Her major research focus is on interpersonal relations in group settings, but her professional interests extend to other behavioral sciences, particularly anthropology, sociology, philosophy, and education. She began her teaching career at Vassar College, and is now associate professor in the Department of Education and Child Development at Bryn Mawr College. This association has enabled her to integrate her varied interests within the context of human development. In addition to seminars in the social psychology of education, Dr. Pepitone also teaches undergraduate and graduate courses in social foundations of education, urban sociology of education, history and philosophy of education, as well as family theory.

About the Contributors

Judith Milner Coché received the M.A. in psychology from Temple University in Philadelphia and the Ph.D. in child development and counseling from Bryn Mawr College. She is currently clinical assistant professor at the Hahnemann Medical College and Hospital, where she supervises doctoral students in clinical psychology. A member of the Family Institute of Philadelphia and president-elect of the Philadelphia Society of Clinical Psychologists, she also engages in independent practice in Philadelphia.

Beth H. Hannah received the M.S. in education from the University of Pennsylvania and the Ph.D. from Bryn Mawr College. Since 1970 she has taught at Connecticut College, where she is currently an associate professor of education and coordinator of student teaching. Her interest in the creativity of children led her to design and teach a seminar class for gifted children in Monterey, California. Her educational publications include *Creativity and Learning* (1974), a booklet of ideas for teachers, and *The Unschool Box of Things to Do and Undo* (1975), activity cards for elementary school children.

Nina Brind Korsh graduated from the University of Pennsylvania and received the Ph.D. in child development and counseling from Bryn Mawr College. She is a certified counselor and licensed psychologist, currently working as a psychologist for the PASS program, a federally funded agency that serves nonpublic schools in Philadelphia. Her work includes counseling of children and parents and psychoeducational consultation with school personnel.

Florence H. Lloyd graduated from Vassar College and received the M.A. in social psychology of the school and child development from Bryn Mawr College. She is currently working toward the Ph.D. at Bryn Mawr College.

Helen Ward Loeb received the Ph.D. in social psychology and sociology of the school and in child development from Bryn Mawr College. She is currently a professor at Eastern College, St. Davids, Pennsylvania, where she heads the Department of Education and is in charge of the undergraduate teacher-training program for elementary and secondary schools. Among her long-standing interests in education are those issues connected with minorities. She is currently codirector of the Norris Square Neighborhood Project, an urban bilingual education project in Philadelphia.

Vivian Center Seltzer received the B.A. from the University of Minnesota, the M.S.W. from the University of Pennsylvania, and the Ph.D. from Bryn Mawr College. She is currently assistant professor in the Graduate School of Social Work and Social Research at the University of Pennsylvania. Her major teaching areas are psychological growth and development and research methodology. Her special interest is adolescent development. Dr. Seltzer is also a consulting clinical and school psychologist, specializing in the field of family functioning with specific emphasis on child-related issues of learning and adaptive functioning. She is currently a University of Pennsylvania exchange professor at the University of Edinburgh.

Helen H. Solomons received the Ph.D. in the counseling psychology program at Bryn Mawr College for research on sex roles and achievement motivation. Her interest in human-resource development and management training developed at the Office of Career Planning and Placement, Bryn Mawr College, where she was directing the women and work program at Jewish Employment and Vocational Services, and while she was associate director of higher education resource services, mid-Atlantic, at the University of Pennsylvania. She became an independent consultant in human resource and organizational development in 1976. At present she is director of human resources at Kulicke and Soffa Industries, Inc.

Christa Vanderbilt received the B.A. from Swarthmore College and the M.A. and Ph.D. from Bryn Mawr College. She is currently a psychologist at the Terry Children's Psychiatric Center, Delaware, and is in private practice.